The Story of Scotland

Uniform with this book

THE STORY OF ENGLAND

THE STORY OF WALES

THE STORY OF IRELAND

THE STORY OF NEW ZEALAND

THE STORY OF CANADA

THE STORY OF AUSTRALIA

THE STORY OF SOUTH AFRICA

THE STORY OF THE RHODESIAS AND NYASALAND

The Five Sisters of Kintail, seen from Mam Rattigan.

The Story of Scotland

by

JANET R. GLOVER

FABER AND FABER

24 Russell Square

London

*First published in mcmlx
by Faber and Faber Limited
24 Russell Square London W. C.1
Second Impression mcmlxi
Printed in Great Britain by
R. MacLehose and Company Limited
The University Press Glasgow
All rights reserved*

© Janet Reaveley Glover 1960

In memory of
ALICE AND REAVELEY GLOVER

Contents

PART I. EARLY AND MEDIEVAL SCOTLAND

PART II. THE REFORMATION AND THE COVENANT

PART III. THE EIGHTEENTH AND NINETEENTH CENTURIES

Contents

Illustrations

11

Maps

12

Foreword and Acknowledgements

There is much more interest nowadays than formerly in the traditions of the past, perhaps because they are becoming so rapidly overlaid, and there is also more speculation as to why Scottish people think and react as they do in the contemporary situation. At the same time, people are able to enjoy the Scottish countryside more readily than their parents and grandparents could, and this enjoyment is enhanced by some knowledge of what went on there in earlier times. While therefore the publications of specialists who have pursued close research are of the greatest value, there remains still a real need for general histories of a more popular nature. This book has been written specially for the general reader in an effort to meet that need.

I am grateful for the advice so generously given me on certain points by the Rev. Stewart Mechie, M.A., B.D., of Glasgow: and by Professor G. O. Sayles, M.A., D.Litt., M.R.I.A., Mr. W. R. Humphries, M.A. and Mr. J. M. Henderson, T.D., M.A., of Aberdeen University.

Mrs. Arnold Gomme has devoted her scholarship and skill to the construction of the maps which make the relevant narrative much easier to follow.

My friends Mrs. M. O. Clarke and Miss R. I. M. Murdoch, Mr. and Mrs. A. D. Cuthbert and Mr. John Rannie have all encouraged me by patiently reading a number of the chapters and discussing them with me. My sisters, Mary and Elizabeth Glover, have gone through the whole book in manuscript; indeed without their help I would have had the utmost difficulty in completing it.

Mrs. Winifred Shaw has shown great consideration in typing and retyping almost every chapter, often completing sections at short notice.

I owe much to all these people and of course to many more. In particular, I must refer to the members of Laurel Bank School, Glasgow, who have given me such courteous attention in Scottish History classes, but who have never let me off without vigorous and critical scrutiny of the conclusions we have arrived at together.

JANET R. GLOVER

GLASGOW
December, 1958

PART ONE

Early and Medieval
Scotland

CHAPTER 1

Pioneers

Not far from Oban, there stand cliffs which thousands of years ago were battered by powerful seas. The breakers hollowed out caves in these sea-walls and gradually smooth beaches were formed in front of them; later on the seas retreated and the line of cliffs now stands far back from the shore. The caves became the homes of the earliest inhabitants of Scotland about whom we have any knowledge.

These people came from Europe. They crossed to Britain from the Baltic shores, and they settled in the Oban caves and in some of the Hebridean islands, especially Tiree. This was probably some 3,000 years before the birth of Christ. They were followed by other immigrants from Europe, who worked their way to Scotland by sea from Mediterranean regions. Some of their sites have been detected near Stirling, which was at the head of a huge estuary sweeping right inland: there is evidence that whales were stranded by ebbing tides on mudflats in parts of the Forth valley now far from the coast. Stone Age culture has also been traced in Galloway, Argyll, the Hebrides, Caithness, Sutherland and the Orkneys.

While there are naturally no written records of these early immigrants, the land is rich in remains of prehistoric building sites, often unfortunately concealed by later dwellings super-imposed upon them. Primitive people left garbage lying around in such quantity that archaeologists can sort out the contents of their middens or rubbish dumps and form some impression of how they lived. Geologists can tell us something about their agriculture by analysing soil, and air photography reveals evidence of ancient tillage.

These people brought seed-corn and domesticated animals with them. They hacked at the soil with clumsy bone and stone implements, choosing places where virgin forest was not too dense, and they produced patches of bere, a primitive form of barley. For lack of winter fodder, they slaughtered many animals young. They made stone bobbins and whorls and wore rough textiles, fixing their garments with bone pins and brooches. Their women liked beads and painted their faces with home-made beauty preparations. They all ate quantities of shell-fish. Professor Piggott has described in *Scotland Before History* the constant need these people had for durable flint axe heads: he suggests that Stone Age men in Scotland imported them from the English Lake District and from Antrim. For all their primitive ways, Stone Age people could organize barter from far afield and they travelled great distances for the purpose. One advantage they enjoyed was kinder weather than we now know in Scotland. The prevailing winds were easterly, harsh storms less frequent, hours of sunshine longer. The mainland and some of the islands were clothed by splendid pine forests, which farmers found very difficult to clear, but as yet the peat blanket had not yet appeared and so the soil was easier to till.

In the Bay of Skaill, on the West Mainland of Orkney, there lies a settlement now known as Skara Brae, constructed probably rather later than 2,000 B.C. Its inhabitants made their way to that windswept site across the Pentland Firth, bringing with them sheep, goats and cattle. Even in those days, Orkney yielded no timber suitable for building, so most ingenious use had to be made of the local flagstone. How long they lived there we do not know, but they abandoned Skara Brae suddenly and in panic, because of a dreadful storm. The village was completely engulfed in sand, which preserved the fabric for many centuries, and in the 1930s it was excavated under the direction of Professor Childe. Today it is roofless, but you can walk through its passages, stand in tiny houses, and handle the shelves, the neat little stone dressers, the hearths, the box-bed frames, and the stone limpet boxes where the shell-fish were stored in seawater. The Skara Brae people knew nothing of sanitation and lived in appalling filth, munching their mutton bones in bed and pitching remains of their meals and other refuse onto rubbish dumps over the wall. They had neither textiles nor grain, unlike their contemporaries in Scotland and the Hebrides; in fact, they maintained a way of life characteristic of a much earlier age. The designs they scratched on their stones were derived from a Mediterranean culture and their pottery was of a type used in southern England.

Some of the Stone Age settlers in Scotland were of the culture known as Megalithic. This name is derived from two Greek words meaning 'big stones' and it was their ability to handle enormous blocks of stone which caused this distinctive title to be given them. They erected burial vaults for their dead, some quite small and some imposingly large. Most of these vaults are approached by narrow passages tunnelled through the earth, many are now covered by conical mounds of grass-grown turf, but some were entirely underground. Some have several compartments or stalls, some only a single chamber. Their erection implies a large labour force, considerable engineering skill and strong views about the after-life, derived from a Mediterranean civilization. Even if you are unaccustomed to archaeological study and unattracted to prehistory, you cannot fail to be awed by the magnificent examples of Megalithic work, nearly 4,000 years old, still standing in the Orkneys. Maes Howe in Stenness is the best known. Its mound is 24 feet high and it is 115 feet in basic diameter. In it are slabs of dressed stone 8 to 10 feet in length. How stones of such weight were transported, tooled, erected, nobody exactly knows.

Some time between 1800 and 1500 B.C., there came a fresh incursion into Scotland by people known as Beaker Men. Some archaeologists suggest that they had originally lived on lands now drowned by the North Sea. Others say that they came from the North European plain. They settled at points along the east coast of Scotland and gradually moved inland. They merged well enough with the Megalithic settlers and their sites are identified by remains of their more refined pottery. They buried their dead in individual, not in communal, graves, and beside the corpses they put personal possessions, such as flint knives, flint-tipped arrows and sometimes bows. These people used bronze for some of their implements, and they were the first in Scotland who did so.

Later on other bronze-users came to Scotland from Europe, some time after 1500 B.C. These were the people who set up the huge circles of carefully spaced upright blocks of stone, which

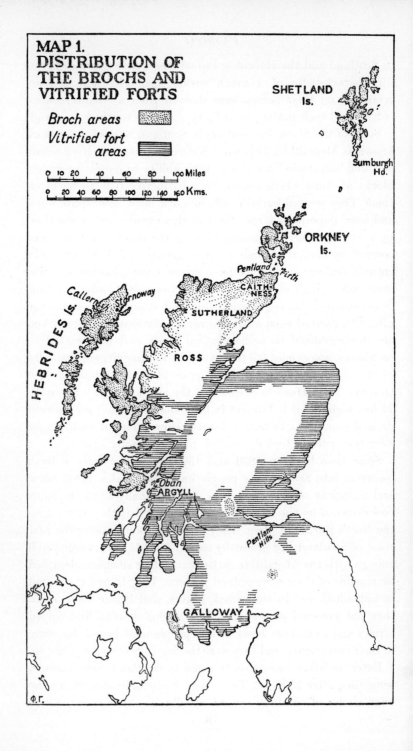

MAP 1.
DISTRIBUTION OF
THE BROCHS AND
VITRIFIED FORTS

Broch areas

Vitrified fort
  areas

0 10 20   40   60   80   100 Miles
0 20 40 60 80 100 120 140 160 Kms.

SHETLAND
Is.

Sumburgh
Hd.

ORKNEY
Is.

Pentland Firth

HEBRIDES Is.

Callern.

Stornoway

CAITH-
NESS

SUTHERLAND

ROSS

Oban
ARGYLL

Pentland Hills

GALLOWAY

Ф.Г.

still survive in considerable numbers, often much damaged, sometimes almost obliterated. You can see such circles in many parts
of Scotland, but especially in the outer Hebrides. One of the
finest stands a hundred feet above the seashore near Callernish,
approached by a splendid avenue of monoliths, and embracing in
its midst a chambered cairn. At Stenness in Orkney, there is an
even larger and more magnificent circle called the Ring of
Brodgar, as solitary and imposing as any man-made monument
could be. We do not know the philosophy which inspired the
builders, but these structures had religious significance, probably
connected with worship of the sun. The Avebury Circles in
Wiltshire are of the same era.

Bronze Age men liked gold, which they got from Ireland, and
which they made into personal ornaments. They seem to have
been tireless seamen, undertaking journeys to Ireland, the Outer
Hebrides, Scandinavia and Europe. They took to cremating their
dead, and they left little in the way of refuse dumps—two serious
disadvantages for the archaeologist.

It was not until about the 10th century B.C. that people of
Celtic stock, speaking a Celtic language, appeared in Scotland.
They too were bronze-users and their ancestral home lay somewhere between the head waters of the Danube and the Rhine.
They are known to historians as Goidelic Celts and they made
their first settlements in Western Scotland and Ireland. Their
very ancient Indo-European language influenced many parts of
Europe and formed the basis of Irish, Manx and Gaelic. Much
later, about the 4th century B.C., they were joined by another
influx of people originating from the same stock, known as
Brythonic Celts, from whose language Breton, Welsh and Cornish
derived.

One branch of the Brythonic Celts was formed by the Picts.
They are perhaps the most elusive of the peoples whose journeys
brought them to Scotland in prehistoric times. They probably
settled first in Ireland and thence crossed to the West of Scotland,
though when they did so is uncertain. They established a hold on
almost the whole area north of the Forth, and traces of their hill
forts have been found from the Pentland Hills to the Pentland
Firth—indeed the name Pentland is believed to derive from an

early form of the name Pict. They made settlements in Orkney and Galloway too. While they preferred hill-tops, they sometimes drove stakes into bogs or marshes and erected platforms on them to form buildings now known as crannogs. Although they apparently had a written literature, it has not survived and little is known about their language, but they were skilled and fearless seamen and like other Celtic invaders they could handle iron with artistry and dexterity.

Perhaps the strangest relics of the century before Christ, in our country, are the stone towers known as brochs. These are believed to have been built by the Picts, or by one branch of them. Several hundred were built in the north and west of Scotland, in the Shetlands, Orkneys and Hebrides, but very few elsewhere. The towers were all planned to type, probably within a short period of time. They are almost all placed so as to command a wide view of some estuary or sea inlet, though by no means always near a good harbour. The sea entries they overlooked in the Orkneys were of such significance that in the Second World War the British had defensive posts near most of them.

Whoever designed the master plan was an architect of genius. The broch is a circular tower, with a slight inward slope like a lighthouse. The walls of the tower are double, with a space between the outer and the inner face, spanned by stone landings and by a winding staircase. As you climb this staircase, you can see into the circular court within the tower, because there are windows cut in the inner wall. No lime or mortar was used in making the brochs, each one of which required about 4,500 tons of stone. There was only one entry into each of the towers, defended by a great inner door and by guardrooms cut in the thickness of the wall. Outside the entrance were clusters of huts and hovels, whose owners could retreat for safety into the tower when necessary. The people who lived there were fishermen and farmers, they wore woven textiles, kept domestic animals, and used iron tools, though not many such tools and no weapons of war have been unearthed on the sites.

Who designed the brochs and why? Who could command the labour force required? We do not know. No other country has similar buildings. The brochs must have been almost impregnable shelters when they were built, but useless as bases for aggressive warfare. As you pick your way through the huddled ruins round the broch of Gurness, or look out from the summit of the almost perfect broch of Mousa, you sense the unanswerable problems of a forgotten people. The problems are made more complex because, well into medieval times, families squatted in these lonely and insanitary strongholds, so that enormous middens of broken and squalid refuse collected around them.

It is no easier to discover the truth about the other architectural triumph of this period, the vitrified forts, so called because their stone walls have been fused by heat. These castles were probably built earlier than the brochs, not by northern people but by invaders from Gaul. These Gallic builders often chose hill-top sites for their castles, which are comparable to a type common in western Europe. Some were oblong, some rounded, but all had double walls of solid masonry, with wooden tiebeams built across the intervening space. By means and for reasons not fully understood, these beams were burnt out in almost all the Scottish forts of this type, and the fierce heat fused the stones in the walls.

The vitrified forts were built by people who made their way up the east coast and crossed to the west by the Great Glen. Remains are found in Argyllshire, along the estuaries of the Forth and the Clyde and in Galloway, and often they were placed with obvious regard to the strategy of coastal defence. It appears that the forts fell into disuse some time in the 2nd century B.C., though descendants of the original Gallic inhabitants lived on in southern Scotland until Roman times.

Little as we know about Scotland in the decades preceding the Christian era, historians agree that the people north of the Border hills developed a political organization, with a central authority capable of exacting obedience, that they were skilled in metallurgy and that more travelling was done by sea and by land than one might suppose. It is clear, too, that there was a strong sense of the presence of supernatural powers, an expectation of life after death and an urge to make provision for it.

That all the various groups of settlers owed much to Europe is obvious, for it was from Spain, France, the Low Countries,

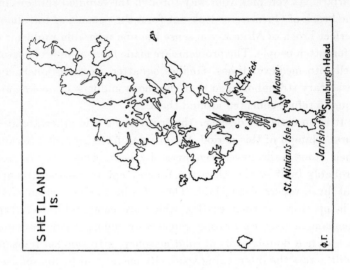

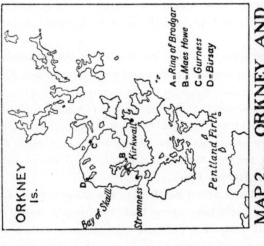

ORKNEY
IS.

A = Ring of Brodgar
B = Maes Howe
C = Gurness
D = Birsay

Bay of Skaill
Stromness
Kirkwall
Pentland Firth

0   5   10   15   20   25   30   35   40 Miles

MAP 2. ORKNEY AND
SHETLAND ISLANDS

SHETLAND
IS.

Lerwick
Mousa
St. Ninian's Isle
Jarlshof Sumburgh Head

Φ.Γ.

Germany and the Baltic regions that they came. No race settled
north of the Border which did not also settle south of it. The
centuries before the Christian era will become better known to
us as the evidence of hidden hut-foundations, burial places,
ploughed sites and middens is interpreted, if only the work
involved can be carried through before our own contemporary
building projects have destroyed too many ancient monuments.
Such study will reveal much that is common to the origins of
both Scotland and England.

CHAPTER 2

Legions

The earliest written records of Scotland were the work of a foreigner and they make sad reading. In the 1st century, A.D., the historian Tacitus married the daughter of Agricola, a Roman general who invaded Scotland. Most areas reached by the legions suffered the miseries of Roman invasion without enjoying the benefits of Roman civilization. In three and a half centuries the Romans succeeded in imposing military control here and there in Scotland, but only in the south-east did they establish law and order. Tacitus makes this clear in his record of Agricola's work and no subsequent commander was able to alter the picture.

In 81 A.D., Agricola advanced to the Forth-Clyde line, which he planned to hold by a chain of forts. During the next fourteen months he established a headquarters at Stirling, already recognized as a point of supreme strategic advantage, and he intended to push north, camping beside navigable rivers, building forts as he went, and always keeping in touch with his fleet.

In the late summer of 83, the northern Pictish tribes, described by Tacitus as Caledonians, made a massed resistance, and there took place the first in the agelong series of battles in which Highland dwellers pitted ferocious courage and outdated weapons against metal armour and disciplined experience. The Picts were led by the first military chieftain whose name has been recorded in Scottish history, Calgacus. They suffered a crushing defeat at the hands of Agricola's 9th Legion at Mons Graupius, a battle-site not yet exactly identified, though it is known to have been near the Roman fort called Raedykes, not far from Stonehaven. After the battle, Agricola fell back to winter-quarters at Inchtuthill, but he ordered his fleet to survey the coast as far north as possible. Inchtuthill is ten miles north of Perth on the north bank of the Tay. The camp covered fifty-five acres of ground and had accommodation for seven to ten thousand officers and men, a hospital, an administrative block and well-surfaced roads for transport.

Agricola was disgusted early in 84 to receive orders recalling him from the north, and his departure meant the end of the Roman advance in strength towards the Moray Firth. Thus the Picts discovered, as other people in Scotland were to do, that defeat in pitched battle need not spell political subjection. What happened to the 9th Legion is unknown, but disaster obliterated it early in the 2nd century. It disappeared, as the legions of Varus had done in the German forests about a century earlier.

Hadrian, a most dynamic Roman, made a tremendous effort to stabilize the frontier against the Caledonians in 121 A.D. He built the wall which bears his name and which can still be seen at certain points in Northumberland. It stretched for 73 miles from South Shields to Carlisle and was flanked by defensive posts on the Cumberland coast. Some 14,000 men were employed in the building, which must have absorbed two million cubic yards of material. The eastern sections of the rampart were faced with dressed stone and measured eight to ten feet wide at the base, six feet at the top: towards the west, turf and clay were substituted for stone.

In 140 A.D., Lollius Urbicus became Governor of Britain. He pushed north again to the Forth-Clyde isthmus to build the wall named after the Emperor Antonine. This was 37 miles in length, and defended by 19 forts. It was more economically constructed than Hadrian's because it was made of turf on the western stretches, clay on the eastern, without stone, and the barracks for the men were cheaply assembled wooden hutments. Lollius Urbicus used some sites originally developed by Agricola and he advanced north as far as Inchtuthill, while the garrisons on Hadrian's Wall were still maintained. It looks as if the Romans meant to establish control over the areas between the walls and even to extend their rule into Perthshire.

The legions employed in these enormous undertakings included men from Germany, Gaul, Spain, Egypt and the Middle East, and the medley of camp-followers and merchants which followed them was also drawn from many countries. Rome believed in transporting subject tribes almost wholesale, and while continentals were serving on the Borders, British conscripts were at work in the Württemberg forests. The foreign legionaries in Scotland married local girls and founded families, whom they nurtured in the faith of their childhood. Altars to Mithras, Mars, Isis and other gods have been found on the walls.

There had been Christians in the Roman army since the days when St. Paul converted the guards to whom he was chained. Christian legionaries brought their faith to Britain and tiny communities began to practise the new rites and to attract other worshippers as well. As early as 208, Tertullian wrote that 'places among the Britons unpenetrated by the Romans have come under the rule of Christ'. Christian worship was practised among some of the soldiers on the walls and it was carried thence into regions more remote than Tertullian guessed.

Little is known of how ordinary people lived at this time. The Picts were the dominant race in Scotland, with thriving communities in the valleys of the Tay and the Earn, and a centre of considerable importance at Dunkeld. Their buildings varied from district to district, but one type has recently become better known to archaeologists. This is the 'wheelhouse', a roughly circular building, about 35 feet across, divided into ten or twelve separate dwellings by stone piers, set in radial fashion from the outer walls to the middle of the enclosure. In 1957, excavation for a rocket site on South Uist laid bare several wheelhouses, and others have been discovered on the mainland.

The Picts exploited their natural advantages against the Romans. The mountain barrier of the Grampians and the thick forest enabled them to wage guerrilla warfare, and the legions found their task most unpalatable. By the end of the 2nd century and the beginning of the 3rd, it was clear that the ambitions of Lollius Urbicus could not be realized, especially in view of the troubles south of the Border. Severus made a naval base at Cramond on the Forth in 208, but soon afterwards Antonine's Wall was abandoned and the northerly stations evacuated.

In the middle of the 3rd century however the Picts were faced with new dangers from another quarter. Now began the pressure of those Scots, who later bestowed their name upon the country they invaded, but who at this time came from Ireland. Like the Picts, they were of Celtic origin, though their speech had developed differently and they were to all intents and purposes foreigners. They settled between Oban and Lochgilphead, pushed into Kintyre, Arran, Islay and other western islands, also along the shores of Loch Fyne and Loch Long and elsewhere on the western coast. Their territory became known as Dalriada, after their Irish homeland.

The Scots from Ireland were in constant conflict with the Picts, but in the middle of the 4th century the two hostile peoples joined together in a violent attack upon the Romans, with a third and ominous ally—the Saxons, now beginning to penetrate the eastern approaches to the heart of Scotland. This onslaught was stimulated partly by hatred of the common enemy, partly by the weather. During the 4th century, a period of heart-breaking rains began, which made agriculture more difficult than ever before. Driven by a land-hunger which affected all western Europe too, and by savage dislike of the Romans, the Picts attacked Hadrian's Wall. From 367 onwards, they battered it, overwhelmed its garrisons, then stormed across the Border hills, while the Scots and the Saxons came in by sea from the west and the east. There followed a barbarous adventure across Britain, in which many villas were destroyed, though some of the towns survived, because of their stalwart defences.

From this disaster Roman authority in Britain would certainly have recovered, but for the multiplication of troubles within the Empire, in the face of which all armed manpower had to be recalled from the fringes and frontiers. By the end of the 4th century the Roman stations in Scotland had been stripped of soldiers.

What did Roman influence in Scotland amount to? The Ordnance Survey Map of Roman Britain, published in 1956, shows that military roads ran further north and Roman sites were more numerous than earlier maps suggested. In the Lowlands, in Perthshire and up the east coast, Pictish tribesmen must have become all too familiar with Roman military authority. As far away as Shetland, Roman coins have been unearthed on

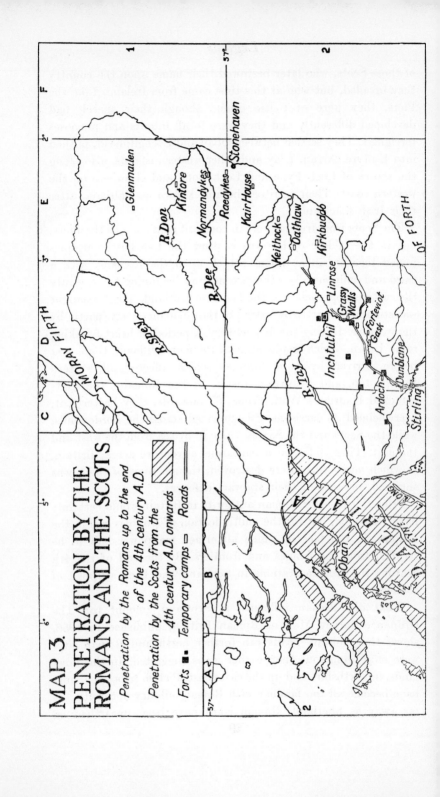

MAP 3.
PENETRATION BY THE
ROMANS AND THE SCOTS

Penetration by the Romans up to the end
of the 4th. century A.D.

Penetration by the Scots from the
4th century A.D. onwards

Forts ▓ Temporary camps ▭ Roads ═══

Glenmailen

R.Don
Kintore
Normandykes
Raedykes
Stonehaven
Kair House
Keithock
Oathlaw
Kirkbuddo
Linrose
Grassy Walls
Inchtuthil
Forteviot
Gask
Ardoch
Dunblane
Stirling
Oban

R.Dee
R.Spey
MORAY FIRTH
R.Tay
OF FORTH

D A L R I A D A

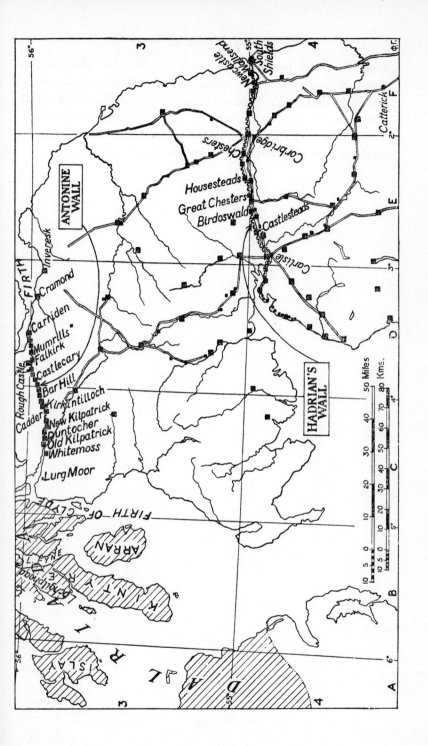

ANTONINE WALL

HADRIAN'S WALL

Newcastle
Wallsend
South Shields

Chesters
Corbridge
Housesteads
Great Chesters
Birdoswald
Castlesteads
Carlisle
Catterick

Inveresk
Cramond
Carriden
Mumrills
Falkirk
Castlecary
Bar Hill
Rough Castle
Kirkintilloch
Cadder
New Kilpatrick
Duntocher
Old Kilpatrick
Whitemoss
Lurg Moor

FIRTH

FIRTH OF CLYDE

ARRAN

KINTYRE

Lochindaal

ISLAY

DAL

RIADA

50 Miles
80 Kms.

55°
56°
2°
3°
4°
5°
6°

broch sites. But Scotland was never absorbed into the Empire. Town life, ordered civic prosperity, easy transport by well-metalled trunk roads, regular commerce and business and social life—none of these great benefits was established in Scotland, where Rome was known only as an alien power seeking to establish military occupation by ruthless force of arms.

CHAPTER 3

Evangelists

At the end of the 4th century, the Picts were supreme from Caithness to the Forth. Their internal communications were somewhat impeded by the bony shoulders of the Grampians, whose diagonal slant across Perthshire was known to early historians as the Mounth, but there were well-known passes over these great hills, and the Picts made ample use of their fleet along the east coast. Because they were skilled seamen, they kept in reasonably close touch with their outposts in the Orkneys, despite the dangers of the Pentland Firth. Here and there they penetrated by the Great Glen towards the Hebrides and they had settlements on Skye, Raasay, Bute and the Mull of Kintyre.

The long mountain barrier from Loch Lomond to Cape Wrath formed a more difficult obstacle than the Mounth, and it defied travellers except at a few crossing places such as Glengarry. It was known as Drumalban and west of it lay Dalriada, the area colonized by Scots from Ireland in the late 4th century and greatly developed by them afterwards. Around the southern shores of the Clyde estuary lived the Britons, people who had come from Cumbria during the Roman conquest, while across on the east, the Angles were beginning to make settlements in Lothian. The country as a whole was known to early chroniclers as Alban, a name coined perhaps because of the snow-capped mountains.

Between the 4th and the 7th centuries, Picts, Scots, Britons and Angles were all converted to Christianity. The Christian missionaries who did this tremendous work faced not only traditions of paganism but also political divisions and barriers of language and geography. The missionary movement of these centuries produced many strong characters who deeply impressed

MAP 4.

DRUMALBAN AND
THE MOUNTH

Land of 1000 feet and over
Boundary of Dalriada

0 10 20 40 60 80 Miles

CAITHNESS

SUTHERLAND

MORAY FIRTH

ROSS

MORAY

Deer
New Old

Raasay

Applecross

R. Spey

Skye

Glenshiel

NORTHERN PICTS

R. Don

INVERNESS

R. Dee

Arisaig

The Great Glen

Tiree

Ionar

Morvern

Lorne

THE SOUTHERN PICTS

Dunnichen

THE MOUNTH

Dunkeld

R. Tay

Dunsinane

FIRTH OF TAY

Forteviol

St. Andrews

Dunadd

Tarbet

R. Forth

Dunfermline

FIRTH OF FORTH

Tarbert

Bute

Queensferry

ANGLES Edinburgh

Glasgow

R. Clyde

Holy
L

Kintyre

BRITONS

R. Tweed

Carham

Alnwick

DALRIADA

Dumfries

Whithorn

Φ.Γ.

their contemporaries, but among them all there were four of special distinction. These were St. Ninian, St. Columba, St. Moluag and St. Maelrubha.

How St. Ninian first learned his faith is unknown, but it seems that his parents were Christian, influenced perhaps by Roman legionaries or camp-followers. During his youth Ninian went to Rome. What he thought about the corruption flourishing there, even among religious leaders, we do not know. On his way back to Scotland, Ninian stayed at Tours, the monastic centre of St. Martin, an experience which was for him a spiritual climax. There he found men dedicated to poverty, living in solitude, devoted to meditation and worship.

When he returned to Strathclyde in 397 or 398, Ninian founded a monastery, known as Candida Casa, at Whithorn near the Solway. A little west of it, he established a group of cells on a lonely promontory, the Isle of Whithorn. At an even less accessible spot, for uninterrupted meditation, he selected a cave in the cliffs. In this way he gave Scotland its first monastic institution, following the example of St. Martin. It is difficult for us to realize what an immense instrument for good the monastic system was in its early days. It gave dedicated men time for regular prayer and recollection, it showed secular people the love and humility of Christ in action, and it gave the early missionaries the support of an organized spiritual community.

Candida Casa became a centre for training missionary monks and a starting-place for evangelists. The men whom Ninian trained learned from him the liturgy of St. Ambrose, the order of service used in Rome when Ninian made his pilgrimage there. For lack of stately buildings and trained choirs, they could not have followed it exactly, but the beautiful Latin prayers, responses and hymns gave them a matchless vehicle for worship, which sustained them wherever they went. Through this order of service Christians living in pagan surroundings emphasized the heavenly realities so easily missed by people untrained in the discipline of worship.

Variations of ceremony and custom were inevitable in a country so remote from the rest of Christendom. The churches founded by Ninian and his successors adopted the calendar and the date of

Easter approved by the Council of Arles in 314. Twice in the 5th
and once in the 6th century, Rome altered this calendar, and the
final dating of the Christian year was different from that observed
in Scotland. The Celtic monks also adopted a different style of
tonsure. These and other ritual matters were to cause controversy
later on.

St. Ninian began his work in his own Strathclyde amongst the
Britons, then went to eastern and central Scotland among the
Picts, who would have no difficulty in understanding him. His
mission extended through the passes in the Mounth, towards
Sutherland and Caithness, and down the Great Glen. The men
who made these journeys had to endure wild weather and unsatis-
fied hunger, to make steep climbs and to pass cold nights in the
open. The traveller in Scotland's forests and hills might encounter
bears and wolves, boars and wild cats. He could have a shot at
red deer and, in northern parts, probably reindeer too—and what
he did not use for his own meal the eagles would finish for him.
The earliest missionaries must have been men of strong physique
and nerve. The spiritual vitality of Ninian and his colleagues is
revealed in the fact that remote communities of Picts were indeed
converted and did learn to worship in tiny churches which were
established all along these routes. It seems that it was the
humbler people who were influenced, as in New Testament times,
and that the royal house continued in its pagan beliefs.

Ninian's monks went as far as the Orkneys and Shetlands,
where churches were established on some of the smaller islands
and on lonely promontories rather like Whithorn itself. It seems
that the Scots of Dalriada had little share in this mission, partly
because of their strange language, partly because of Drumalban's
barrier.

But Christians and others suffered from the marauding habits
of the men in Irish Dalriada. One Irish king, Niall of the Nine
Hostages, has various claims to notoriety. Tradition has it that
in his last raid on Strathclyde he captured a Christian boy called
Patrick. For six years Patrick slaved in Ireland as a swineherd,
until he escaped to France, where he nearly died of exposure.
When at last he returned to his home in Strathclyde, this extraordinary saint found himself compelled by spiritual guidance to

return to Ireland, the land of his misery, as an evangelist, drawn in part no doubt by recollection of the close communion with God which he had experienced there in his lonely boyhood. He went back about 432, the year when St. Ninian is believed to have died. St. Patrick was successful in this venture, in spite of opposition, and he attracted a number of followers from Candida Casa, whose influence was thus strengthened among the Irish Picts.

The Scots of Ireland, meantime, had been consolidating their gains in Scotland. Fergus MacErc with his two brothers, Angus and Loarn, led a fresh invasion in 498. Parts of Argyllshire were occupied by Loarn, whose name survives in Lorne, and his head-quarters were at Dunnolly Castle, near Oban. Fergus founded a royal line, whose capital was fixed at Dunadd, near Crinan, where a large castle became the residence of the kings of Dalriada. They were still to some extent controlled from Ireland and they were obliged to pay taxes to the rulers there.

The Scots of Ireland developed a Christian Church of their own, and they sent missionaries to their colonists in Dalriada. One of these was St. Oran, who established holy places in Iona, Mull and Tiree, though it seems unlikely that he touched the mainland. He died of plague in 548. That Dalriada was beginning to experience Christian influences made the growing menace of its strength no more pleasing to the Picts, who deeply resented their unwelcome neighbours. In 560, the Pictish King Brude MacMailchon inflicted a crushing defeat on the Scots, in which their king was killed. His successor Conall was deprived by Brude of the right to call himself king. This reverse greatly dispirited the men of Dalriada, whose future now seemed much less assured.

In these circumstances, Columba's arrival in Dalriada in 563 was an event of major importance, politically, as well as in religious matters.

Columba's was a strange and complex character. His royal descent from Niall of the Nine Hostages may account for his ambition, his pride, and his explosive spirit. He had unlimited energy of mind and tireless physique, so that he was able to give full rein to his numerous gifts—seamanship, statecraft, evangelism, administration. The other side of his character is shown in his feeling for poetry, his delight in the subtle loveliness of the Hebridean islands, his joy in the changing colours of sky and sea and mountain, in the delicacy of wild flowers, in the flight and song of birds. As he grew older, he became gentler and more loving towards the plain folk around him, over whom he came to exercise an influence at once magnetic and charitable. Throughout his eventful life, Columba was possessed by a passion for worship, which gripped him no less when he was involved in one of his bitter quarrels or deep-laid political schemes than when he was lost in mystic contemplation of God's goodness, in the exquisite solitude of Iona.

Columba was renowned in Ireland as a founder of many churches—Derry, Durrow and Kells for example—and he was probably well known to Oran's successors in the Hebrides. He embarked for Iona because of a tragedy, so familiar that it is easy to overlook the extraordinary way in which he lived it down. Always an ardent collector and copyist of manuscripts, he had secretly transcribed a rare Gospel belonging to one of his teachers at Moville in Ireland, a man named Finbar, who had originally come from Candida Casa. The document may have been brought from Rome or Tours by Ninian himself. When Finbar discovered that Columba had copied it, he claimed the new manuscript as his own. Columba appealed against the decision in hot anger, and lost the appeal. The case became a public scandal and furious partisanship on each side led to civil war. Columba was excommunicated, and though the excommunication was later annulled, he was advised to leave Ireland.

Columba departed in a mood of intolerable grief, caused more by nostalgia for the land of his birth than regret for the outrage. His penance gave him new purpose in life however. He intended to build up the church in Dalriada and to re-establish the broken political fortunes of his countrymen there.

In fulfilment of his first aim, Columba set up his headquarters in 563 on Iona, which became a centre for many journeys among the islands and on the mainland, the inspiration of the second main stream of Celtic evangelism, one which influenced the Scots as profoundly as St. Ninian's had affected the Britons and the Picts. He has been described as a 'golden-mouthed preacher of

Christ'. He and his companions worked ceaselessly among the
Scots west of Drumalban and established many churches along
the estuaries and in the glens. Columba visited Skye, an outpost
of Pictish territory, and in old age he went to the mainland and
met Kentigern, the much-revered saint whose centre was Glasgow.
These however were incidental journeys, as his special sphere
was always Dalriada. Perhaps his most famous departure from it
was when he paid a state call on King Brude at Inverness, along
with the two Irish Picts named Kenneth and Comgall, who
probably carried through the negotiations for Columba, because
he was never fluent in the Pictish language. Their business was
to secure Brude's sanction for a mission to the Orkneys, and the
extent of his authority is revealed in the chroniclers' assurance
that Cormac, the leader of the Orkney venture, was saved from
martyrdom by Brude's safe-conduct.

Columba was determined to redress the political disasters of
560 and to re-establish the monarchy. He persuaded the Scots to
pass over the rightful successor of the demoted king and to
appoint instead a man named Aidan. This king earned an
uncomfortable title—Aidan the False—but he turned the tide
of misfortunes for the Scots, who once again began to outrival
the Picts in strength and influence. Columba also negotiated a
relief from tax payments by Dalriada to Ireland.

Columba's biography was written within a century of his death
by Adamnan, an abbot of Iona. Like many medieval works, it is
full of highly exaggerated stories designed to magnify the piety
of its subject, but it gives interesting information. We learn of
Columba sharing in the field-work, of corn being ground in the
mill, of a horse drawing a wheeled cart—so there was a well-
organized system of agriculture, and people could make roads
with reliable surfaces. There is an irresistible ring of truth in an
anecdote about a monk called Baithene. So holy was he, that
while carrying a sheaf of corn in one arm, he extended the other
in grateful prayer, and 'in his devotion did not even remove the
midges which settled on his face'. When the monks needed to
repair their buildings, timber was in such short supply that they
went to Glenshiel for logs, lashed them on behind their coracles,
and towed them all the way back to Iona, grousing, as sailors

will, when they had to wait for a suitable following wind. So many
sea journeys in all weathers are recorded that one is lost in
admiration of the men who built and navigated those tough little
coracles.

One reads too of much hospitality, of friendship offered to
undistinguished sufferers, of affectionate personal relationships
between Columba and his companions, of passionate and deeply
sincere prayer. From Adamnan one can catch something of
Columba's spirit, for the snatches of conversation recorded show
his awareness of beauty, his poet's flair for descriptive phrase,
also a certain astringency which reveals the saint's sterner side.
Adamnan wrote most beautifully about Columba's death and
then addressed himself to future copyists: 'I beseech all those
that may wish to copy these books, nay rather I conjure them
through Christ, the judge of the ages, after carefully copying
them to compare them with the exemplar from which they have
written and also to append this conjuration in this place.'

Iona, like Whithorn, became a training centre for missionaries,
the inspiration of St. Cuthbert, who worked in Lothian, St. Aidan
of Northumbria and very many more, whose names are recorded
and whose foundations are known. But it was not the only focus
of Christian work. There is no space here to give a full account of
the different missionary influences at work in the land, but two
especially interesting saints, both trained at Bangor in Ireland,
must be mentioned. St. Moluag was an Irish Pict who came to
Scotland in 562 and made Lismore his centre. This island lies
in the mouth of the Great Glen, a point from which one can travel
to the islands or journey across the great rift of Scotland to the
east coast. From Lismore, Moluag developed a mission among the
Picts. He went to the Moray Firth and worked in the Spey
Valley, on the Aberdeenshire coast, on Skye and Raasay and for
awhile on the Campsie Hills near Glasgow. He seems to have been
a gentler person than St. Columba, but he won the title 'Moluag
of the Hundred Monasteries.'

The other missionary giant of the period lived later and his
foundation was the most remote of all. He was called Maelrubha
and like Columba he was descended from the royal Niall. He
trained at Bangor and became Abbot there, but in 671 he

resigned his post and set off for Scotland. He worked in Kintyre, on Loch Fyneside, at Arisaig and afterwards in Skye, which he came to know well. He founded his monastery at Applecross in 671. It is a delectable spot, readily reached by boat from Skye, but blocked off from neighbouring glens by miles of gaunt, rock-strewn mountain, still a handicap to travellers by road, impass-able during winter months. None the less, Maelrubha travelled even further than Columba or Moluag, to and fro in Dalriada and right into the heart of Pictish territory.

The attraction of island and peninsula sites for these early missionaries is very noticeable. You see this at Birsay on the north-west edge of the Mainland of Orkney, where a tiny church was built in the late 7th century, a place you can approach only at low tide over a ridgeway of stones. A similar site is the one on St. Ninian's Isle in Shetland, where excavations in July 1958 led to the discovery of a 12th century church, superimposed on the much earlier one: a hoard of beautiful metal ornaments made with Celtic designs was found there, with many sculptured stones. On Holy Island, near Bamburgh, there was another missionary centre isolated at high tide, from which in the 7th century St. Aidan of Iona began the Christian penetration of Northumbria, the centre of the Angles.

These men who clearly thrived on solitude and loved natural beauty showed their aesthetic quality in sculpture. The splendid crosses of the Celtic church reveal a craftsmanship unrivalled by any other product of the period. Intricate but freely flowing lines, geometrically interwoven, form the basis of the designs carved upon the shafts, some of which were six to eight feet in height. Birds, beasts, leaves, flowers and human figures were worked into the pattern too. The Ruthwell Cross near Dumfries is the best known, but up and down the country there are cross shafts and stone slabs bearing fragments of this lovely sculpture, Scotland's finest tangible relic of the Celtic Church.

Of the buildings in which the new congregations worshipped, virtually nothing remains, because of the destruction wrought by Vikings later on. It seems that they were nearly all tiny, designed to shelter the altar where mass was celebrated, not the wor-shippers, who heard the preaching of the saints in the open air.

It is by place-names, by the dedication of later churches, by fragments of sculpture that Celtic foundations are traced.

The Celtic Church was monastic. It demanded poverty and obedience from its clergy, who were all monks. There were no secular priests, no organized parishes, no diocesan administration and no supreme authority at the top. Bishops were consecrated to ordain monks, but they were under the obedience of the Abbots to whose houses they belonged. Riches this Church never accumulated, uniformity it never demanded. Marriage took place among some of its monks and this was not considered wrong. Some of its buildings were so placed that the sanctuary faced east, some were not. Celebration of mass and of baptism varied in detail from place to place.

This lack of organized administration was both the strength and the weakness of the Celtic mission. Founded by men who had a passion for preaching and a natural gift for worship, sustained by the practice of prayer, hymn-singing, and study of the scriptures, it appealed to the Celtic people who responded to a personal approach. Some of the sordid by-products of wealth, orthodoxy and power, so marked in Rome and other influential centres, never developed in the Church of St. Ninian and St. Columba. But when it met with opposition from a much more highly organized body, with international affiliations, this smaller and weaker Church had no resources with which to fight back.

In the 7th century there appeared from the south men who owed their allegiance to Rome and who were briefed by the Pope and by St. Augustine of Kent to carry out the conversion of Britain. When their representatives met Christian communities in Northumbria they were horrified to discover unorthodox practices. And so bitter controversy broke out over the tonsure and the date of Easter, and an unedifying story it makes. Now was illustrated perhaps for the first time in British history, the ungodly capacity of Christians for mutual hatred. Bede, the historian of the Anglo-Saxons, admits in one passage that the Celtic Christian 'held in his heart and venerated and preached nothing other than do we: that is the redemption of the human race through the passion, the resurrection and ascension to the skies of the Mediator between God and men'. This should have

been the healing bond between two active and devoted branches
of the one Church. But to the Anglo-Saxon priests the calendar
which permitted Easter to fall on a date other than their own
seemed a barbarous contravention of the 6th century Roman
decree: as Bede, inaccurately and censoriously, declared—'The
Britons . . . wrongfully and from wicked lewdness set themselves
against the appointed Easter of the whole Catholic Church.'

In the year 664, when Britain was afflicted by an earthquake,
an eclipse of the sun and a violent epidemic of yellow plague, the
Synod of Whitby was called to discuss the problem of Easter's
date, by Oswy, King of Northumbria. He was a devout man who
owed his faith to Iona. His wife, Eanflaed, was a Mercian
princess, who followed the teaching of the Anglo-Saxon Church.
Thus the court witnessed the celebration of two Easters each
year. As Bede put it, 'when the King, having ended his fasting,
was keeping the Paschal Feast, the Queen and her retainers
would still be fasting and celebrating Palm Sunday'—certainly a
confusing situation. So Oswy called a conference and the
Queen's protagonists won the day. In humiliation the Celtic
representatives retreated to Iona to talk the distasteful situation
over at their headquarters.

The monks of Iona disagreed about it. In 688, Adamnan, their
Abbot and the biographer of Columba, accepted the new ruling
but failed to persuade the others. From 704 till 722, there were
rival abbots in Iona, upholding the two opposite systems, but
such dissension could not last and complete capitulation followed
very soon. Celtic customs however died slowly in northern
England and still more slowly in Scotland. It was not until the
12th or 13th century that the last resistance to the Roman ways
disappeared.

The achievement of the Celtic missionaries illustrates the
power of a living faith in the living Christ. These men were the
first to offer the satisfactions of a real religion to a pagan people
who were sensitive to spiritual forces. The collapse of their
Church is one of the many sad developments in Scottish history.
Roman organization was too strong for Celtic Christians and in
the 8th century they were subjected to new and uglier attacks
from quite a different quarter.

CHAPTER 4

Vikings and Normans

The Vikings began to attack Scotland towards the end of the 8th century. The resistance they met was weakened by the hostility between the Picts and the Scots, who had not yet merged into one Celtic block, while the Strathclyde Britons and the Lothian Angles were still separate communities and offered no concerted defence.

For a time the Norsemen swung between Norway where they wintered and the Orkneys where they spent their summers. Gradually they made permanent settlements in these islands and in the Shetlands. Their long houses were often built over the sites of Stone Age dwellings as at Sumburgh or of Celtic monasteries as at Birsay. In the 790s, they began to turn their magnificent ships towards the islands and coasts of Scotland.

Applecross, the most northerly Christian centre, took the first onslaught in 793 or 794; Lindisfarne on Holy Island was attacked immediately after. The Vikings at this stage were sea-raiders using their ships as their base, and because the Celtic Church had favoured islands and coastal sites, it suffered grievously. Iona was attacked in 795, 802, 806, 825 and at frequent intervals throughout the 9th and 10th centuries. The chroniclers throughout Britain were prolific in their lamentations. As one of them sadly wrote: 'There always were and there always will re-appear those that are spurred on by evil rage against the servants of the Lord.'

Christian communities were ravaged, monastic buildings sacked, valuable Church plate and illuminated manuscripts, often in pieces and shreds, taken back to Norway as keepsakes for womenfolk. The Celtic Church, already undermined by its controversy with the Anglo-Saxons, never regained its former vitality.

44

As time went by, the Vikings settled in the islands and also on the seaboard fringes of the mainland. Tangible evidence of their way of life is now much less than it should be, on account of the comparatively modern destruction of it, but records through the centuries give tantalizing hints. A late 17th century writer, for example, describes a ship-burial unearthed at Stranraer in 1681. It lay 'a considerable distance from the shore, unto which the sea, at the highest spring-tide, never comes. It was transversely under a little bourne and wholly covered with earth to a considerable depth, for there was a good yard with kale growing in it upon the one end of it. By the part of it which was gotten out, my informers who saw it conjecture that it was pretty large.'

We know most about the Norsemen who lived in the jarldom of the Orkneys, which for a long time included Sutherland and Caithness, and whose recorded history goes back to 880. The Orkney Earls were versatile, interesting and violent. One of them, Earl Rognvald, was the father of Rollo, the conqueror of Normandy and the ancestor of Duke William. Rognvald's brother succeeded him as Earl and in 995 forced a mass conversion to Christianity upon Orcadian chieftains. During the 11th century, the ideas of this religion were gradually absorbed and the persecution of Christian communities abated.

The Orkneyinga Saga of the 11th and 12th centuries suggests that the Orkneys enjoyed considerable if rather rugged prosperity, especially in the 12th century, when large farms were worked and much grain produced. A good deal of building was done on a grand scale for the times, since castles were made of stone and furnished with large drinking-halls for lavish entertainment. Vikings were good at enjoying themselves. Unlike the Icelanders, Norsemen in Orkney seem to have had little interest in prolonged lawsuits and did not indulge in family vendettas. Their poetry concentrated upon love-themes and seafaring ventures, with much less emphasis upon murder than appears in the Icelandic sagas.

We have little knowledge of how the Shetlands fared, though their rulers owed allegiance to the Earls of Orkney. Then, as now, less grain could be harvested in these windswept islands and they were always proportionately poorer. We know hardly any more about the Hebrides in early medieval times, except that here the Norse weakness for family feuds did much more harm than in the Orkneys. It seems, indeed, as if the best Viking adventurers were attracted to the Orkneys and that for a number of generations they made the most of their opportunities there. The racial background, the language, the customs, even the household gear and other implements in use on these islands, became Norse in character and remained so for many centuries.

In the 9th century, when the full onslaught of Norse attack was being experienced, a more unified authority began to emerge in Scotland. In 841, Kenneth McAlpin became King of Dalriada. This King, we are told by the chroniclers, 'led the Scots from Argyle into the land of the Picts, with marvellous astuteness', and 'reigned over the Scots for sixteen years, after destroying the Picts'. The Chronicle of Huntingdon tells us that after 'Danish pirates had occupied the shores and with the greatest slaughter had destroyed the Picts who defended the land, Kenneth passed over into and turned his arms against the remaining territory of the Picts and after slaying many, drove the rest to flight. And so he was the first of the Scots to obtain the monarchy of the whole of Albania, which is now called Scotia.'

It seems therefore that Kenneth's astuteness lay in descending upon a people already exhausted by other terrible enemies. He fixed his capital at Forteviot, the centre of Pictish territory. He transferred the relics of Columba to Dunkeld, which became a focal point of religious organization. He began the evil practice of Border-raiding, with a view to securing Lothian too. Kenneth died of a tumour in 858 and was buried in Iona, the traditional resting-place of Scottish kings.

How far Kenneth McAlpin really united his two peoples is uncertain, for though the Picts and the Scots were henceforth ruled by one King, and their land became known as Scotland, the differences between the two were not ironed out for many a long day. The mysterious thing is that recorded history has so little to tell us about the Picts, although these people had dominated most of Scotland for over a thousand years.

Kenneth's successors in the 9th and 10th century were unable to extend their frontiers because of the Vikings. During these years of insecurity, a strange sect called the Culdees developed among Pictish Christians and persisted for some two centuries at a number of centres—Monymusk, Abernethy, Scone, Dunkeld, Muthill, St. Andrews and Lochleven, for example. The name seems to have been derived from Célé De, Companion of God. Still less than the Celtic missionaries did the Culdees follow the orthodox rites of the Roman Church. The movement was spontaneous and it stimulated different rules of life in different places. Some of the Culdees were hermits, some lived in community, some were married, others celibate.

In 1005, Malcolm II became King of the Picts and Scots. He defeated the Angles at Carham in 1018 and made Lothian permanently part of Scotland, an event lamented by the English chroniclers. He was succeeded by a grandson, Duncan, who had already inherited the kingdom of Strathclyde through connections on the distaff side, and who therefore extended his rule south of the Borders into Cumberland, a larger sphere of influence than any earlier king in Scotland could claim. This was the Duncan slain by Macbeth in 1040, after six rather unhappy years on the throne. Macbeth's character has suffered unjustly at the hands of Shakespeare, as he ruled Scotland well for some seventeen years, and there is evidence that the country enjoyed some prosperity during his reign.

One result of Duncan's untimely death was the effect it had on his two young sons. Malcolm, known as Canmore or Bighead, was sent as a nine-year-old to England, to be brought up by his maternal uncle, Siward, Earl of Northumbria. This Siward was a man of influence with Edward the Confessor, King of England, and he took his young nephew to Edward's court, where the boy was influenced by men familiar with French culture. The younger brother, Donald Bane, was sent to the Hebrides, where his sympathies became identified with Norse chieftains and Gaelic islanders who were out of touch with European thought. The separate treatment of these two brothers was to cause trouble later.

Siward, Earl of Northumbria, fought against Macbeth on behalf of Malcolm Canmore, who was recognized as king in 1058.

Soon after this, Malcolm married Ingibiorg, daughter of Thorfinn the Mighty, Earl of the Orkneys, a man notorious for his annual expeditions each summer to plunder Scotland, Wales and Ireland. Thorfinn was described as the 'biggest of men in stature and the strongest; ugly in appearance; black-haired; sharp-featured; and large-nosed; and somewhat beetle-browed; and most soldierly . . . a great man of vigour and greedy, both of wealth and of honour'. Like many another Viking, Thorfinn visited Rome, where the Pope gave him an audience and also absolution for all his sins. In his old age he became milder and founded a splendid church at Birsay, where he was buried in 1065, after being Earl of the Orkneys for sixty years.

Perhaps Ingibiorg lacked the tough constitution of her father, for she died soon after he did, leaving her husband with three little sons. Malcolm then looked for another helpmeet, and found one, as a result, so the chroniclers say, of a violent storm in the Forth. The wind blew upon the Scottish shore a ship with distinguished passengers on board—Edgar Atheling and his sisters Margaret and Christina.

The background of this storm-driven family needs some explanation. Their father was Edward the Confessor's nephew and they had all been brought up in Hungary. They had arrived in England in 1057 when Margaret, the eldest, was only twelve and they then experienced life at the court of Edward the Confessor. Margaret was specially susceptible to that pious King's influence as she had been devoted to religious practices from childhood.

When Edward the Confessor died in January 1066, Margaret's brother, Edgar, had quite a convincing claim to the English throne, but he never seemed to regret his failure to secure it. 'Handsome, well-spoken and unmartial', a genial talker, a charming lightweight, Edgar lacked the moral fervour so characteristic of his sisters. They all found the atmosphere in England less congenial after William the Conqueror arrived, so they embarked in 1069 for the continent, and according to tradition were blown by contrary winds into the Forth. Malcolm III offered them hospitality and lost his heart to Margaret. He married her in 1069. Perhaps they found a bond in their sympathy for French people, their interest in French ideas, which they had both learned in childhood at the English court.

From 1069, the year of Malcolm's marriage to Margaret, until 1124 when David I became king, Norman influences began to affect Scottish society in the southern parts of the country. There was no military conquest, as in England, but a steady inflow of people and ideas, encouraged by Malcolm and Margaret and their sons.

When Margaret married Malcolm she was about twenty-four, little more than half her husband's age. She was determined to improve him, his friends and his country. With supreme assurance of her own rectitude, she devoted her considerable intelligence to this task. She had a continental love of splendour, so Malcolm and his courtiers had to fit themselves out with fur and velvet and jewellery; gold and silver dishes appeared on the royal tables; ornamental hangings were pegged up on the walls of the king's residences, serving the double purpose of decoration and draught exclusion. Manners and ceremonial were made more stately, and the King began to appear on special occasions with an official bodyguard. Margaret herself appreciated luxuries and encouraged her courtiers to do likewise, so that foreign merchants began coming to Scotland. These interests of the new Queen were not without economic significance, and they were fostered by the refugees from the south who came to Scotland when the Conqueror's policy became too oppressive for them.

It was in religious matters that Margaret's energies found the greatest scope. She was astonished to discover that in Scotland services were not conducted as they were in the south, that Sunday was not kept free from normal labour, that Mass was infrequently and variously celebrated. She could not approve of the way Lent was observed, she was dismayed that people did not communicate on Easter Sunday, and that the sacred rituals were sometimes conducted in the vernacular. With fortitude and singleness of mind the Queen laboured to bring the worship of her adopted country into conformity with Roman practice. She was lavish in her gifts to the churches where she worshipped, as she was in her charities to the poor, indeed there is a suggestion of exhibitionism in some of her almsgivings. She encouraged pilgrimages as means of promoting personal devotion, and established foundations at North and South Queensferry, on either side of the Forth, for the benefit of pilgrims to St. Andrews.

Queen Margaret made an impression on her contemporaries in south-east Scotland, because of her devoutly religious life. Her biography was written soon after her death by Turgot, who became Bishop of St. Andrews, and its records of her good works reflect the public opinion of the day.

Meantime, political relations between Malcolm III and William the Conqueror varied. Malcolm was not much involved in William's affairs, but was prepared to offer hospitality to his brother-in-law Edgar, and to anybody else from the south who cared to visit him. He was mainly interested in retaining a hold on the large, indeterminate Border country which sprawled across the hills of Cumberland and Northumberland. Raiding in the vicinity of this unfortunate area was already frequent: both cattle and slaves were regularly rounded up and driven off by marauders from both sides, and the Scots did not lose on these illegal projects.

William for his part early realized that to conquer Scotland thoroughly would be impossible. He satisfied himself with a demonstration of strength. Like the Romans almost exactly a thousand years earlier, he organized in 1072 an immensely complicated movement of his army and his navy to the Firth of Tay and there Malcolm became 'his man'. Exactly what this involved in general is hard to say, but Duncan, Malcolm's eldest son by Ingibiorg, discovered that for him in particular it involved a long journey. He was sent to England as a hostage, and there remained for some fifteen years.

In 1080, William's eldest son, Robert, arrived in Scotland with an army, soon after the harrying of northern England by his father's troops. Although his business was to punish the Scots for raiding over the Border, there was no fighting. Amicable conversations were followed by the surrender of more hostages and a christening service in which Robert became the godfather of Malcolm's infant daughter Maud. On his way home Robert established a New Castle on the Tyne, perhaps to mark the northern limit of his father's kingdom.

Things changed for the worse when the Conqueror died and his second son, Rufus, became King of England. Malcolm refused to pay homage to him, on the grounds that allegiance was owed only to the eldest brother, Robert. William Rufus therefore launched an attack upon southern Cumbria, planted the district with 'a great multitude of churlish folk', and built a castle at Carlisle. Later he invited Malcolm III to journey into England and discuss things with him, and on receipt of a safe-conduct, Malcolm set out. On his way south, he assisted in a foundation ceremony at Durham Cathedral. But when he arrived at Gloucester, Rufus refused to see him, an insupportable insult to Malcolm's dignity.

Hitherto any incursions into English territory made under Malcolm III had been in the nature of Border raids. Ordericus Vitalis, a 12th century English chronicler, gave an account of Scottish character not endorsed by later historians. 'Though they are fierce in battle,' he wrote, 'yet they love ease and quiet, decline to let themselves be troubled by neighbouring kingdoms and are given to the practice of the Christian religion rather than of arms.' In 1093, bruised in spirit from the shock of insult, Malcolm III gathered up his forces for an attack upon England which hardly justified the words of Ordericus Vitalis. It was to prove his last undertaking, for at Alnwick Malcolm was killed in ambush, by a Norman called Morel, with whom he was on close terms of intimacy. The news of the disaster shocked the English court, where Malcolm was a popular figure.

The Queen heard of his death, and that of her eldest son Edward, when she herself was ill in bed. Characteristically, she composed herself to die also, having no desire to survive him, and within three days she had passed away, firm to the last in religious faith and in wifely affection.

When Turgot wrote Margaret's biography in the early 12th century, he obviously thought of her as a saint, though her canonization did not take place till 1249. The force of her character is strikingly shown because almost all of her eight children held the same view, and most of them shared her religious convictions. Between them all, these eight won considerable worldly success, which was in keeping too with their parents' example. The two eldest were the least distinguished. Edward died with his father at Alnwick, Edmund by political intrigue became the black sheep of the family; Ethelred was an Abbot, Edgar, Alexander and David all Kings of Scotland. The two sisters, Maud and Mary, after rather a stormy childhood, both achieved distinction, for the former married Henry I of England and became Queen of England, while the latter married Eustace of Boulogne.

On Malcolm's III's death, his brother Donald Bane was elected King, in accordance with an ancient Celtic tradition called tanistry, by which a brother's claim was stronger than a son's. Donald Bane, now sixty, had always been doggedly resistant to his brother's ideas and he instituted a complete change of policy. There followed a reaction against French, English and Norman ideas.

Four of Malcolm III's sons were despatched to England forthwith and there experienced a Norman upbringing, directed by their uncle, Edgar Atheling. Their sisters were already being educated at Romsey Abbey in Hampshire, a foundation for nuns where many Norman ladies spent their childhood. The stern Christina, Margaret's sister, was one of the senior members of the community and *in loco parentis* she beat her little nieces and cowed them with rebukes. Meantime Duncan, son of Malcolm and Ingibjorg, had spent some fifteen years at the Norman Court as a hostage. Medieval parents of royal status sent their children away to alien and even enemy courts with strangely little compunction. In the case of Malcolm's family, the results were very satisfactory, odd though the whole régime may seem to us.

William Rufus did not approve of Donald Bane and sent Duncan, Ingibiorg's son, now in his early thirties, to dethrone him by force. This Duncan did, but he was murdered almost immediately; not long after this, in 1097, Malcolm III's son Edgar was made King. Edgar's success was achieved with Anglo-Norman assistance, and he rewarded those who had helped him: so more Normans than ever passed over the Border to settle in Scotland.

Edgar recognized the loss of the Hebrides by formally ceding them to Magnus Barelegs, King of Norway. The terms stated that Magnus could claim all land west of a line that a galley could pass over, so the Norse King seated himself at the helm of his ship, while his sweating henchmen hauled it from Tarbert, at the north-east end of the Kintyre peninsula, across to the sea on the west. This haulage of sea-going ships was fairly common, in fact the name Tarbert is believed to be derived from a word meaning 'Draw-Boat', and it is to be found at various narrow necks of land in Scotland. By this device, Magnus secured a good slice of the mainland in addition to the islands. Iona became Norse territory, and the degraded Donald Bane was the last king to be buried there.

Edgar, who never married, was succeeded by Alexander, perhaps the least attractive member of this gifted family. Chroniclers describe him as 'generous beyond his means to newcomers', a man 'who wishes to do everything in his kingdom alone, by himself, and will not suffer any interference from any authority whatever', 'devoted to clerks', 'severe towards men of his own land'. Like most of his family, he was generous to the Church. He set up foundations for Canons Regular at Scone, at Dunkeld and on an island in Loch Tay, and also on Inchcolm in the Forth. He appointed Turgot, prior of Durham, as Bishop of St. Andrews, after rather a long vacancy; he restored the bishopric of Dunkeld and founded a third in Moray.

Alexander, Edgar's brother, probably exercised royal control only over the land between the Forth and the Spey. Argyll, Ross, and even Moray, were too remote to administer effectively, and they were almost independent of his authority. Cumbria was ruled by Alexander's brother, Earl David, according to the terms of Edgar's will, and Ayrshire and Galloway were included in his sphere also.

Alexander assisted Henry I of England in a brutal invasion of Wales. Did he ponder the question why his own land was spared such treatment? It was of course because his sister Maud, emancipated from her Aunt Christina's discipline, had married Henry I, the only Scottish princess who ever became Queen of England and one who was dearly loved. Henry was father-in-law as well as brother-in-law to Alexander, by the latter's marriage to one of Henry's numerous illegitimate daughters, Sibylla. She was a lady of royal tastes, who liked splendour and stateliness.

She enlarged Alexander's corps of personal attendants, and court life in Scotland continued to grow more like that in England.

When Alexander died, without a legitimate heir, he was succeeded by David, the most vigorous and original of the brothers. He was Earl of Cumbria in his own right, Earl of Northampton and Huntingdon by his marriage to a rich Norman heiress. In fact this Scottish prince, Henry I's brother-in-law, was one of the most prominent barons in England, holding a place of honour in Henry I's court. He was gifted and popular, capable of holding men's loyalty, well equipped for kingship, and like his mother devoted to organized religion and stately services. Because he was a good Norman, hunting was his favourite sport, litigation his hobby, rule by charter an accepted habit. His friends in England were mainly Norman or Breton in origin. Of these Robert de Brus was one, son of a man of the same name from Cotentin, who had fought at Hastings. Bernard, Lord of Bailleul in Picardy, was another—he built Barnard Castle in Teesdale and became known as Baliol or Balliol.

David came to a land where people still lived and worshipped in buildings made of wattle and woodwork, where towns hardly existed, where industry was primitive, where men bartered goods and services because they had no metal currency. The feudal system was hardly known in Scotland as yet, allegiance was given to local chieftains who were reluctant to recognize the claims of higher authority. Different parts of Scotland were separated from each other by uninhabited hills and moors, the elk was still found in the north, wolves, bears and lynxes were common enough in most places. There were dialects which were incomprehensible to travellers who went too far afield from home. The influence of the Church was superficial because the organization of parishes, each with its church and its priest, had not yet taken place, there were only three bishoprics for the whole country, and monasteries were few and far between.

David ruled from 1124 to 1153. In these three decades, permanent changes were effected, so that by the end of the 12th century, Scotland south and east of Norse territory was completely different from the kingdom won by force of arms for Malcolm III in 1058.

CHAPTER 5

David I

ACistercian historian, Ailred of Rievaulx, knew David I and his court well because he had been brought up with David's son Henry, whom he dearly loved. Ailred could have become the King's trusted counsellor, but in 1135 he underwent an experience akin to conversion which led him to join the abbey of Rievaulx in Yorkshire. When Prince Henry died years later, still a young man, Ailred unburdened himself about his long separation from his royal friends. 'In the body but never in mind or affection, in order to serve Christ, I left him in the full bloom of his prime, as also his father, now flourishing in hale old age, whom I have loved beyond all mortals.'

Ailred had more to say in 1153 when David I also died. 'O desolate Scotia, who shall console thee now? He is no more who made an untilled and barren land a land that is pleasant and plenteous, who adorned thee with castles and cities and lofty towers, enriched thy ports with foreign wares, gathered the wealth of other kingdoms for thine enjoyment, changed thy shaggy cloaks for precious raiment, clothed thine ancient nudity with purple and fine linen, ordered thy barbarous ways with Christian religion.' Graeme Ritchie, author of *The Normans in Scotland*, says of this passage that 'for all its rhetoric, it is a singularly exact epitome of David's achievements.'

During his long residence in England, David had seen much that he admired, and when he became King he introduced into Scotland many features of Norman society and government. The Norman state was feudal and its principles required that land should be managed by people responsible to the King, with recognized obligations; that the royal revenues should be efficiently administered, and accounts inspected; that justice should be enforced by royal officials, themselves under supervision; that defence should be organized from castles under the King's direct control. David shared the Norman respect for the Church too, because he was personally devout, but also because religion, properly organized, gives society stability.

When he arrived back in Scotland, David awarded large areas of land to his Anglo-Norman friends, and to tenants from his English estates, and in doing so introduced a much more strictly feudal system of ownership. For the first time in Scottish history, land grants were now generally confirmed by Charters, set out in Latin and signed by witnesses. The earliest of David's charters still extant, a document measuring 6½ by 3¾ inches, confirmed the grant of about 200,000 acres in Annandale to Robert de Brus, who already owned 80 manors in Yorkshire. De Bourneville, de Morville, de Graham, de Sommerville, Oliphant, Fitzalan, de Bailleul, Comyn—these are some of the names among the new Norman tenants-in-chief. David gave them lands, because they understood administration and were used to the responsibility involved in running big estates. By education and upbringing, David was at one with these Anglo-Normans, whose traditions were his and whose reactions he could predict and understand. Their obligations to him were sacred because of the vows they took as his liegemen. Such people he felt he could trust.

The former landowners in Scotland seem to have objected little to David's arrangements because they lost little by them. They continued on their accustomed holdings as tenants of the new Norman overlords rather than directly of the King. The lower social orders included various ranks of free landholders and also serfs. These serfs were considered part of the property and they were not allowed to go elsewhere. They probably detected little change in their lives, except that they had to work harder, since the new nobility were quick to begin building castles, to intensify agriculture and to develop home farms and gardens.

David's land policy caused far-reaching changes which later created difficulties. The ordinary folk of Scotland still spoke Gaelic, the new nobility French, the literate classes, which were largely ecclesiastical, Latin. Thus Gaelic hardly made its way into written literature at all. This meant that a language barrier developed which emphasized class barriers, always a harmful situation.

Another ominous feature was that powerful men in Scotland owned land on two sides of the Border and paid homage to two Kings. David himself owed allegiance for his English territories to the English King. So later on, when war broke out between the two countries, the leading men in Scotland hardly knew where their first loyalties lay. Worst of all was the radical defect which bedevilled all feudal countries. The overlords became too powerful for any monarch to hold them. The purpose of government on a national scale is to eliminate private wars: the effect of a feudal organization is to stimulate private wars between the great family factions of which feudal society is composed. National and feudal systems are incompatible, as medieval Kings in France and England discovered, as well as those in Scotland.

In the twentieth century it is easy to look back and to criticize David I. This is mistaken. National feeling as we understand it was unknown then in Europe. David had to handle a country in which tribal and local disorder was chronic and in which the King's writ ran only within a limited sphere. The land organization he worked out met the difficulties as he knew them and gave Scotland a chance to build up a better way of life.

Anglo-Norman overlords were quick to build castles. Castles were at once the means of maintaining feudal authority and the symbols of feudal power. Dark, dirty and damp little erections they were, constructed of wood, with outside staircases and few amenities, perched on the top of artificially raised earthern mounds and surrounded by water-filled, stagnant ditches. Below the mound, each castle had an enclosed area, also entrenched and palisaded, for stables, smithy and garrison quarters. Beyond this again were enclosed fields, and, generally, gardens. The men who did the work were local peasants such as Gillepatrick, Ragewin and Ulchil, whose names we know because they were the personal property of David himself and presented by him to the Church of the Holy Trinity at Dunfermline.

A multitude of minor officials was required for the maintenance even of small castles and domains. In *The Normans in Scotland*, Graeme Ritchie lists clerks, bailies, falconers, fletchers, foresters, lorimers, porters, sergeants, tailors, taverners and others. As with the more stately officials of David's court, many of these were Norman by origin, though they identified themselves with the country of their adoption. Their designations gradually became surnames.

Administration had been developed on Norman lines to a certain extent by Alexander, David's brother. He had appointed such officials as Chancellor, Constable, Chamberlain, Marshal and Steward to supervise the various departments of the royal household. David continued all these offices and added others, again giving them to Anglo-Normans. From these officials, he selected some, along with certain bishops, to form a central governing body, which was always at hand to give him advice and to receive his instructions. It could handle at high level the awkward and difficult problems of administration and justice. It was particularly concerned with financial matters, now of increasing importance, though later these came to be dealt with separately in the Court of the Exchequer. To central headquarters also came justiciars, those barons whom David appointed to travel on circuit, hearing judicial cases and settling other problems too. The justiciars carried the King's authority further afield than he could go himself, and they heard appeals from the Sheriff Courts.

David appointed Sheriffs, although there were as yet no shires. These officials administered the King's personal domains from the royal castles, summoned juries to give evidence in civil and criminal cases, collected feudal dues and supervised defence. Their judicial work was scrutinized by the travelling judges, their financial records by the Exchequer Court, their military arrangements by the Constable.

David therefore established the beginnings of a rule of law, not only in central and southern Scotland but also as far away as Moray. Unfortunately, this did not develop in the turbulent centuries which followed. In medieval Scotland local law-courts under feudal barons and sheriffs pursued their own way, with little reference to central authority and small interference from it. In England the King's judges gradually established control over civil and criminal procedures and the mighty authority of the common law was there based on the precedents accumulated by these judges. In Scotland on the other hand, decisions made in the local courts affected only the people involved in each separate case, and no common law was evolved. This meant that ordinary people had much less chance of securing reasonable justice than in England, especially as the powers over both baronial and sheriff courts often became hereditary, vested in one family of great local prestige, while rights of appeal were scanty and very hard to put into effective action.

David I was aiming at a national system of justice and administration, in which the King should be no mere figurehead. He and his advisers and officials were constantly on the move from one royal castle to another, because he wanted to keep in touch with his people everywhere. There was also the economic factor: feudal dues were paid in kind, so the court had to move away from any one centre when the perishable goods there stored up for the King had been consumed.

David was a devout man. He realized that the Celtic Church had been under-organized, particularly in its lack of parishes, and also in its lack of dioceses which could be supervised by bishops. The origin of the Scottish bishoprics is obscure. All that can be said for certain is that, by the end of David's reign, the country had been divided into nine dioceses—St. Andrews, Dunkeld, Moray, Glasgow, Ross, Caithness, Aberdeen, Dunblane and Brechin. The bishops he appointed were Anglo-Normans, who were valuable to him as members of his court and participants in his work of government.

During David's reign some parishes were established, but this work was of slow growth and a long time passed before there were enough to serve the needs of the country. There must have been many people living far away from the nearest church, untended by any priest and therefore ignorant of the Christian religion.

The 12th century was a time of renaissance in Europe. One manifestation of revitalized thinking was the Cistercian movement which reformed monasticism. This was started at Cîteaux and much influenced by St. Bernard of Clairvaux. His understanding of the gentleness of Christ brought fresh religious insight and new ways of expressing it. Though he may not have been the author, his characteristic piety finds expression in 'Jesus, the

MAP 5.
XII CENTURY RELIGIOUS FOUNDATIONS

Urquhart

Kinloss

R. Spey

R. Don

Monymusk

R. Dee

N. Esk

S. Esk

Restennet

Coupar Angus

Scone

R. Tay

Lindores

Arbroath

St. Andrews

Isle of May

Lochleven

Cambus-kenneth

Dunfermline

Inchcolm?

Holyrood

New Battle

Paisley

R. Clyde

Kilwinning

Melrose

R. Tweed

Kelso

Selkirk

Dryburgh

Lesmahagow

Jedburgh

Soulseat

Glenluce

Dundrennan

Whithorn

Φ.Γ.

0   10 20   40   60   80   100 Miles

0 10 20   40   60   80   100   160 Kilometres

very thought of Thee with sweetness fills my breast', and other
hymns written originally in beautiful Latin, sung by Christians
to this day in many other languages. St. Bernard also preached
the poverty of Christ. One historian has described the Cistercian
movement as 'an outcome of the mighty but ever-changing
influence of the idea of renunciation'.

Cistercian abbeys were built on sites far from human habitation
and the buildings were austere. All physical comfort was forbidden so that men might discipline the flesh and dedicate the
spirit, garments were made of undyed wool and designed without
ample folds, monks were not allowed to wear shirts under their
habits, food was of the simplest. The daily routine was divided
between prayer, meditation, reading, corporate worship and
manual labour. The services were stripped of all aesthetic appeal.
Ailred of Rievaulx expressed the Cistercian views when he
denounced sculpture, wall-paintings, engravings, choral and organ
music. The latter he described as 'that terrible blast of bellows,
simulating rather the roar of thunder than the sweetness of the
human voice' and he also condemned in one sweeping sentence
'the tinkling of cymbals, warblings, superfluous beauty, pleasure
of the ear and lust of the eye'.

Self-abnegation always makes an appeal to idealistic people
and the Cistercian movement attracted some of the finest and
most thoughtful men. The abbeys became centres of religious
inspiration, and also of enlightened agriculture, for manual
labour was done in the fields and on the pastures. The Cistercian
foundations, designed to divorce the monastic movement from
wealth, ironically enough, created yet more wealth by their
excellent farming methods. They also promoted scholarship in
their libraries. It has been said that the one luxury permitted
was the enjoyment of perfect Latin prose.

During the 12th century, many Cistercian foundations were
established in Scotland, where valleys remote from human
habitation were plentiful. Fergus of Galloway, his successor
Roland, Reginald of the Isles, Hugh de Morville, Walter Fitzalan,
the Earls of Mar and of Buchan were among the many landowners who endowed abbeys. Often they handed over parishes
recently formed on their estates to some monastery as an

endowment combined with responsibility. The Order of Tyron and various Orders of Regular Canons were popular as well as that of Cîteaux.

David I naturally supported this trend. Of all Scottish Kings, he did most to enlarge the influence of the monasteries. In some cases he introduced Cistercians to places where there had been earlier foundations, as at Melrose and Newbattle, elsewhere he gave them new sites. To Dunfermline, where his parents were buried, he made generous gifts; he granted Lesmahagow and Kelso to the Tironensians, Holyrood and Lochleven to the Augustinian Canons. All these he endowed with land and to many of them Anglo-Norman abbots were appointed. The old Culdee foundations David uprooted. He brought them to an end because to him they represented an unorthodox element of dissent.

The enrichment of the Church helped Scotland at the time, when Scotland was, as Ailred said, 'barbarous' for lack of Christian organization, 'untilled and barren' for lack of agriculture. Later generations suffered however. The King's domains were reduced by David I's generosity to the Church, and because of their diminished capital, his successors had to impose unpopular taxation. The parish churches were not always faithfully administered by those monasteries to whose care they had been entrusted, and as time passed, Church lands became more and more valuable. The temptation to misuse accumulated wealth later proved too much for both bishops and abbots.

The 12th century was a period when many little parish churches were built. They had solid stone walls, massive round pillars, tiny round-headed windows and arched doorways. They usually had no aisles, but consisted simply of a small nave and a smaller chancel, sometimes with a rounded eastern apse, sometimes with a western tower. At Leuchars and Dalmeny near Edinburgh are almost unspoiled examples of these smaller churches, at Muthill and Dunning in Perthshire fine western towers, and the little chapel in Edinburgh Castle attributed to Queen Margaret is also 12th century in origin. You can see fragments of Norman work still in a number of churches, for example Monymusk and Tyninghame, and in quite deserted places such as the Craignish peninsula you come across ruined remains showing the characteristics of this time, when stone was reserved for religious purposes and handled with loving care. Kirkwall and Dunfermline, larger and more splendid in design, show how Scottish craftsmen made this beautiful and dignified style of building their own. Perhaps the richest example of their ingenuity in decoration is the archway at Whithorn Priory, which is enfolded in layer upon layer of sculpture.

The renewed vitality of the Church in Europe at this time was shown in the enthusiasm for Crusading. Not so many people went from Scotland as from England because the population was limited, poverty-stricken and remote, but enough did for William of Malmesbury to note laconically: 'Then the Welshman gave up poaching and the Scot fraternising with fleas.'

Some of the most enthusiastic of the northern Crusaders were Orcadians. Earl Hakon went early in the 12th century and on his return built a round church at Orphir, of which unfortunately only the apse remains. Only five similar churches were built in the British Isles; a perfect example is still used for public worship in Cambridge.

Another famous Orcadian Crusader was Earl Rognvald. He set out in 1150, and was delayed by a snowstorm, from which he sheltered with his men in the sombre Megalithic tomb-chamber called Maes Howe, then some 3,000 years old. They rifled its contents and made doodles and drawings on its interior walls. To this day you can see their runes and their delicately executed emblems. His party must have found Maes Howe a gloomy shelter, indeed two later Jerusalem-farers went mad there. They enjoyed the rest of their adventures however, especially in France and Spain, where they made love and wrote love poems. They called at Crete, survived 'the tempestuous wind called Euroclydon', reached Acre, visited Jerusalem and bathed in the Jordan. They had little fighting to do as most of the Holy Places were now in the hands of Christian rulers. They came home by Constantinople and sailed up the Danube with all their sails spread before a beam-wind, to impress the local inhabitants on both sides of the river. When he got home, Rognvald built St. Magnus Cathedral in Kirkwall. It still stands, some of the arches and columns in choir and nave unspoiled since the 12th century craftsmen worked upon them, a solid, dignified, beautiful building.

Interest in the Crusades lasted well into the 13th century. Walter Fitzalan went, and so did his brother John, who was killed at Damietta in 1249. Among others were the Earls of Atholl and Carrick, both of whom died abroad.

The 12th century renaissance in Europe found expression partly through the stimulus given to town life at this time. Kings and nobles in France, Germany and England favoured the growth of towns where men with goods for sale could gather and do their business.

Hitherto there had been little buying or selling in Scotland except through primitive forms of barter. David I tried to make a standard system of weights and measures for the encouragement of internal trading, and it is amusing to find that the inch was to be reckoned by setting three grains of bere end to end, or by measuring the width of the masculine thumb. Three men, it was said, were needed to get an average result—'a mekill man, and a man of measurable stater' and 'a lytil man'. The king also established two royal mints, one at Berwick, one at Roxburgh, to issue silver pennies, the first metal currency officially sanctioned in Scotland.

At least fourteen towns claim that they were originally granted burgh status by David, who enjoyed referring to 'my burghs' and stayed frequently in them on his journeys. Among the more important were Stirling, Perth, Dunfermline and Edinburgh.

A burgh enjoyed valuable rights, for its burgesses were granted freedom from tolls throughout the kingdom, they could hold markets and fairs at regular intervals, they had monopolies in the making of certain goods for sale, such as bread, beer, cloth, and they also had exclusive rights in the export of local products.

The opportunities thus opened up appealed to foreigners. Flemish wool merchants settled in burghs on or near the east coast, particularly in Berwick and Aberdeen, Anglo-Norman and French craftsmen made homes in various other burghs and the business they promoted improved prosperity. Commercial travellers also toured the fairs. Such was a Lincolnshire trader called Godric, who journeyed in England, France and Denmark, buying local products cheap and selling them elsewhere at higher prices. He came often to Scotland. His business career had an

unusual climax, for he was so impressed with the traditions of
the Northumbrian St. Cuthbert that he entered the religious life
and was afterwards canonized.

In later years, the burghs became a hindrance to the nation's
economic progress, because of their monopolies and restrictive
practices, but in the 12th century they stimulated the accumulation of wealth. Although they were always defended by ramparts
or palisades, they must have looked rural enough, as they had
gardens and orchards within these walls, and their burgesses
farmed the burgh fields outside. Unfortunately, being built of
wood, the little towns were susceptible to people's carelessness
and dreadful fires were frequent. In 1244, eight burghs were
burned to ashes.

David's rule of nearly thirty years was on the whole peaceful.
Three major controversies arose, all in connection with problems
that remained unsolved for a long time.

The Archbishop of York wanted to control the new Scottish
bishoprics and this provoked a long wrangle which lasted till
1192, when Pope Celestine III declared that the Scottish Church
was to be directly subject to Rome. Even this ruling did not
prevent later English archbishops from trying to interfere in
Scotland.

Another perennial source of discord concerned Northumbria.
This controversy became involved in a third and bigger cause of
friction in 1135, when Henry I of England died. His son had been
drowned in the English Channel, and the English throne was now
claimed by his daughter Matilda, who had to contend with the
rival claim of her cousin Stephen, son of William the Conqueror's
daughter Adèle.

For David the affair was very awkward. Henry I had married
his sister, Maud, and Henry's heiress was his niece. Stephen had
married another niece also called Maud, daughter of David's
sister Mary. Thus family relationships were much disturbed, and
it was difficult to know which side to support.

In the event, David invaded England on behalf of Matilda,
Henry's daughter. His forces captured a number of valuable
castles, including Alnwick and Newcastle, but while this was
going on, David's son was negotiating with Stephen under his

father's instructions, so that the Scottish King had his foot in both camps. What did he really want? Undoubtedly Northumbria.

In 1138, David assembled a great army and prepared for an engagement at Cowton Moor in Yorkshire. The chroniclers set out the tradition that Robert de Brus and Bernard de Bailleul, both arrayed on the English side, came out to parley with David for the sake of peace. Moving speeches are recorded, in which the aged Brus pointed out that there were old friends on both sides and that David owed everything to the support of men he now proposed to slaughter. It was the first major occasion when the clash of loyalties became intolerable for men whose associations were strong on each side of the Border. It is said that David wept when he heard Brus speak. But he went on with the fight.

It is known in history as the Battle of the Standard, because the Archbishop of York lashed to a wagon a tall ship's mast, on which was elevated the Sacred Host and the banners of the patron saints. In David's army, the men of Galloway caused confusion at the eleventh hour because they insisted on their ancient right to lead the first attack, although they were unmailed. David had ample numbers of feudal knights and men-at-arms properly protected, but he gave in to the Galwegians. The result was described by Ailred: 'The southern flies swarmed forth from the caves of their quivers and flew like closest rain; and irksomely attacking the opponents' breasts, faces and eyes, very greatly impeded the attack.' An English historian put it differently: 'The Scots were preceded by actors, dancers and dancing girls, and we by the Cross of Christ and the relics of the saints.' The Galwegians wore the kilt—though not the tartan kilt we know—and it proved an inadequate battle-dress, despite the wild war-cries and leaping movements of its wearers.

Though David was defeated in this battle, he got what he wanted. His son's negotiations with Stephen were so successful that Northumbria was ceded as a fief and the Scottish frontier extended south to the Tees. When David died in 1153, Scotland was in a stronger position with regard to the state of the Border than ever again.

Critics analysing David's work from a modern point of view find fault with him, because of his Norman interests and his

David I

neglect of the Celtic and Gaelic background of his country. It is worth asking what Scotland needed in the 12th century and whether the tribal organization of the Celtic peoples could meet that need. There is no evidence that the Celtic way of life could promote law and order, business, peace, security or worship. These benefits were stimulated by David's feudal policies and they produced immediate results. Judged by the standards of European civilization in his day, David was a very great ruler, who vastly improved conditions of life for ordinary folk. Ailred's admiration for him was well-founded.

CHAPTER 6

A Time of Hope : The Thirteenth Century

David I lost his only son, Henry, the prince whom Ailred had missed so much. The crown therefore passed in 1153 to Henry's eldest boy, Malcolm, a child of eleven, but he survived only until 1165. He has followed by his brother, William, who reigned until 1214, and who was known as William the Lion.

During the sixty years of these two brothers, the controversy about Northumbria moved into a new stage; the Celtic lords of Galloway and Argyll tried to break free from the Scottish Kings; the burghs flourished and so did the Church. In the main, it was a time of peace and promise.

The year after Malcolm IV's accession, Henry II became King of England. He was powerful enough to insist that Northumbria should be restored to him, a loss which William the Lion deeply resented. William organized a grand invasion of England in 1174, a well-chosen moment when Henry was facing the consequences of Becket's murder and when the disloyalty of his sons was a dreadful humiliation for him. Henry must always have recollected William's invasion with pleasure however, for only a few hours after he had completed his humiliating penance at Canterbury, the Scottish King was captured at Alnwick. The thick east coast mist which helped the English on this occasion was regarded by them, and also by William himself, as evidence that God had forgiven the penitent Henry.

William was taken to Normandy, and there forced to accept the Treaty of Falaise. Scotland was laid under feudal subjection to England, the Scottish Church under the English Primate, Northumbria was confirmed as English territory, castles in southern Scotland were invested with English troops.

William was released after some months. He had to wait nearly fourteen years before events took a more promising turn for Scotland.

In 1192, Pope Celestine III made his pronouncement that the Scottish Church was to be directly under the jurisdiction of Rome, not under that of English archbishops. In 1189, Richard Cœur-de-Lion, desperate for money to finance his Crusade, ceded to William the castles surrendered in 1174 and renounced his feudal superiority in Scotland. In return William was to pay 10,000 marks. The fact that this sum could be raised shows that Scotland was growing wealthier, and aware of the value of freedom.

From 1174 until 1292, no warfare interrupted the peaceful relations between England and Scotland.

Meanwhile the Celtic chieftains took advantage of the set-backs suffered by the Scottish royal house. Three times Fergus, Lord of Galloway, rebelled against Malcolm, whose forces finally defeated him; royal officials then built castles in his territory and colonized the districts round them. Fergus, a great founder of monasteries, at last retired to Holyrood Abbey, and there died in 1161. His sons rebelled again, when William the Lion was Henry II's captive, and slaughtered the Anglo-Norman garrisons and colonists. When William the Lion returned to Scotland, he built, and fortified with castles, burghs at Ayr, Lanark and Dumfries upon which to base his defence against Galloway. It was a long time before this inaccessible and entirely Celtic province was pacified. The last of the old Celtic Lords was Alan of Galloway who died in 1234; he was succeeded by three daughters, all of whom became the wives of distinguished Anglo-Norman lords—Roger, Earl of Winchester, John Balliol of Barnard Castle and William, Earl of Aumale.

Argyll was the other centre of Celtic resistance. During Malcolm IV's reign, Somerled was its Lord, and he had Norse blood in his veins. He was never induced to accept the King's rule. In his last outbreak, he sailed up the Clyde in an effort to destroy Malcolm's power, but he was defeated and killed by the men of Walter Fitzalan, the Steward of Scotland and Lord of Renfrew. Norse influence always encouraged the native lords of Argyll to resist Scottish Kings, who had trouble to face from this quarter until the Norse rule was ended in 1263.

In spite of these conflicts with English kings and western chieftains, Scotland's prosperity developed while David's sons were on the throne. The well-trodden routes leading north over the Border still attracted southerners and foreigners who wanted to make good, and while some were ne'er-do-weels escaping from debt or disgrace, others were sound men. There was a considerable colony of Flemings, for example, who settled in upper Clydesdale; their names may be traced in the villages of Lamington, Symington, Thankerton, Wiston and others, all situated on rich farming land where their flocks of sheep contributed to the wool trade briskly pursued in the royal burghs. The monasteries already founded did not suffer from the barbarous warfare which afflicted them later on and their numbers increased throughout the final years of the 12th century.

Scotland enjoyed a stability in the 13th century which contrasted sharply with what was to happen later on. After William the Lion's death in 1214, his son and grandson, Alexander II and Alexander III, covered between them seventy-two years. Both were capable men, and the administration they inherited from David I was a good one.

Alexander II's reign was disturbed by rebellion in Galloway, Argyll, Moray and Caithness, but these outbreaks were crushed and they were the last major attempts by the remote regions to divorce themselves from the rest of Scotland. Alexander II wanted to regain Northumbria, but fortunately accepted a settlement of the controversy which proved permanent and which gave him five estates in northern England in compensation. This closed one source of war danger.

The kingdom Alexander II left to his son, the third Alexander, was full of promise. Although he died in mid-life when his heir was a child, there was no setback because the system of government was sound enough to survive a ruler's boyhood.

The second part of the 13th century was a brief but long-remembered golden age for Scotland. Medieval kingdoms needed above all else strong personalities to rule over them. Given long periods of continuous leadership by Kings of integrity, law and order could be maintained and normal life for ordinary people could be tolerable. In the mid-13th century, these conditions did obtain in Scotland and but for a few sharp and localized interruptions there was no warfare to wreck the nation's economy. Never again was Scotland independently to enjoy a similar stretch of years in which to build up prosperous and civilized ways of life.

Alexander III experienced only one threat to his kingdom, in 1263. In this year, the aged King Hakon of Norway brought a great Viking fleet south to punish Scotland for its encroachments into the Norse domains on the Hebrides. He delayed too long in the Orkneys and in Skye however, and Alexander III put off engaging battle until the October storms broke and did most of the work for him. Hakon's fleet, the largest host ever to have left Norway, was destroyed off Largs, with little loss on the Scottish side. Hakon died at Kirkwall on his way home. The Hebrides submitted to Scottish rule and Alexander III's daughter, Margaret, went to Norway as the bride of the new King, Eric.

Meantime Alexander was enjoying friendly relations with England. Henry III's daughter Margaret was his wife, and the two royal families respected each other and corresponded as amicably as any relatives could wish to do.

Statisticians judge from the meagre records available that the total population of the Scottish mainland at this time numbered only about 400,000, of whom far the majority lived south of the Highland line. Alexander's authority over this scattered and thinly spread population was exercised through sheriffs and justiciars, operating from the royal castles which were the centres of administration even in distant places like Cromarty, Dingwall, Inverness and Nairn. In 1264, the King's revenue from feudal dues and customs reached over £5,000, a sum five times larger than the same sources could produce forty years later.

Prosperity developed most of all in the burghs of the east. Berwick was described in 1266 by the chronicler of Lanercost as 'a city so populous and of such trade that it might justly be called another Alexandria, whose riches were the sea and the water its walls. In those days, its citizens being most wealthy and devout gave noble alms.' Norse writers confirm that Berwick was the richest Scottish town at this time, commanding control over much of the Baltic and north-European trade. Exports consisted mainly of wool, but included also furs, skins and salted fish: imports were wines, woven materials, spices and corn.

Burgh life was only one manifestation of increasing wealth. Much building was done in the 13th century. Between 1240 and 1249, the Bishop of St. Andrews consecrated 140 churches in various parts of the kingdom. This was a time when men wanted to create beauty to the glory of God and the symbolism of tall pillars and vaulted roofs was used to draw people's thoughts away from themselves and upwards to God. Even the ruins of Elgin Cathedral, now a wrecked skeleton, show that its proportions were as splendid in balance and scale as those of many continental buildings of the same period. At the cathedrals of Dunblane and Glasgow, you can see 13th century Scottish work at its best and almost unspoiled. The massive lines of these buildings do not show the slender grace of the contemporary Early English style, but their strength is expressed with reverence, their dignity is vigorous rather than solid; and there are subtle varieties in the structural design and in the sculpture which give light and fluency without the disturbance of over-decoration. Dornoch Cathedral is another 13th century work and there were many monasteries built at this time too—Pluscardine, Deer, Culross, Beauly, Sweetheart are among them.

Architects and craftsmen were employed in castle-building too, since barons wanted more durability in their strongholds than the wooden structures of David's day could provide. Instead of the old earthworks, stone walls were built round a new castle with towers to defend the entrances. The great keep within had immensely thick walls, with slits of windows which were shuttered but not glazed. The main hall on the first floor was larger than formerly, the staircases were indoors, the defence works more imposing, but living conditions must have been as damp and squalid as ever.

Personal calamities ultimately wrecked the happiness of Alexander III and brought disaster to his country. In 1275, his wife Margaret died; he lost a little boy in 1281; not long after, his daughter, the Queen of Norway died, and so did his eldest son. In an effort to stabilize the succession, he married again in 1285. The following year, when his young wife was staying at Kinghorn,

Alexander made a night journey from south of the Forth to see her. His horse slipped in the darkness. The great King was thrown over the cliffs and killed.

CHAPTER 7

A Time of Desolation

Alexander's death at the age of forty-five was a national disaster. Had he lived another twenty years, he could have guided his country through a time of acute danger from England. Had he been spared a prince to succeed him, that young man would have inherited not only the kingdom but probably also the fine qualities of an admirable family.

Six Guardians of the realm were appointed to carry on the government for Alexander's heiress, the three-year-old daughter of the Norwegian King. Almost immediately, Edward I of England suggested the little girl's betrothal to his own young son, and in 1290 a marriage treaty was signed at Brigham. Its carefully drawn terms show that Scottish barons understood the risks involved. Scotland was to remain a separate and independent kingdom, with its own Parliament and laws, Scots were not to do homage to an English King and if the Queen died childless a Scottish heir was to succeed her North of the Border.

Responsible Scotsmen respected Edward I, but they saw the iron hand slip out of the velvet glove for a moment when he suggested that castles in southern Scotland should be garrisoned by English troops. This they hotly refused. It was agreed, however, that the Queen should be brought up in Scotland; a ship was sent to fetch her and Edward offered a consignment of sweetmeats and raisins. Everybody felt satisfied except one old man, Robert de Brus, the sixth of the name, a descendant of William the Conqueror's knight.

This Brus, or Bruce, had been heir-presumptive in 1238, when it seemed that Alexander II's Queen would bear no children. The birth of Alexander III had been a personal disappointment for Bruce, the death of the great King had raised his hopes. But he had to content himself with being one of the Guardians and he reluctantly agreed to the Treaty of Brigham.

And then came the shattering news that the Queen had died on the journey from Norway.

Thirteen lords forthwith put forward claims to the Scottish throne. The two strongest were those of John Balliol and Robert Bruce, both descendants of David I's youngest son, of whom Balliol was great-grandson, and Bruce grandson. Balliol's grandmother had been the elder daughter, Bruce's mother the younger. By modern law, Balliol's was the better case, but medieval Scotland gave some weight to Bruce's closer proximity to David.

Both were powerful men. Balliol's father had owned half Galloway by his marriage to Devorguilla, daughter of Alan of Galloway, and by inheritance he had Border lands, thirty English manors and rich French properties. He had founded Balliol College in Oxford as an act of penance for assaulting the Bishop of Durham; his widow, Devorguilla, was the devoted and loving woman who founded Sweetheart Abbey in memory of her husband and who took more care than he to give his College a sound endowment. Their son John was a man to be reckoned with, especially after his sister married John Comyn, Lord of Badenoch and Guardian of the realm. The powerful Comyn interest always supported Balliol in the troubles that followed.

Robert Bruce, the former heir-presumptive, was Lord of Annandale. He too owned land in England, and he had married the daughter of the Earl of Gloucester. He had been Sheriff of Cumberland and governor of Carlisle and had often served on the English King's Bench. His son, the seventh Robert Bruce, married the widowed Countess of Carrick and so acquired her title and inheritance.

Balliol, Comyn and Bruce knew each other well and were all well-known to Edward I, because they frequently visited their English estates and because all three had fought for Edward and his father during de Montfort's civil war.

When the quarrel between Balliol and Bruce over the inheritance began, the Bishop of St. Andrews wrote to Edward I and begged him to come north at once and assist the Scottish barons to settle the matter. All the claimants seemed willing to let Edward decide for them, nor apparently did it occur to them that he might abuse his powers.

So Edward came and presided over the convention at Norham-on-Tweed in May 1291, a gathering attended by bishops and barons, and conducted with scrupulously judicial procedure. Twenty-four English and eighty Scottish auditors were appointed to scrutinize the claims. On November 17th, 1291, in the great hall of Berwick Castle, Edward announced the award to Balliol. Old Robert Bruce therefore laid upon his son, the seventh Robert, now Earl of Carrick, the duty of pursuing the family rights.

Edward began at this point to claim feudal superiority over Scotland. He insisted that Balliol should pay homage, proclaimed his right to hear appeals from Scotland, summoned Balliol to London to answer charges brought against him by his own subjects, demanded money contributions for English military projects and in 1294 ordered Balliol to join him with feudal vassals and hosts in an invasion of France.

What is the explanation of Edward's hardened attitude, his deliberate goading, his legal fictions invented to justify aggression? Edward concentrated the whole weight of his administrative and military machine upon the task of reducing Scotland to the condition of an English shire and an evil fever of hatred seemed to possess him. Perhaps he was corrupted by power, for he exercised enormous authority in England: possibly his bloody conquest of Wales had given him a lust for further military glory. Whatever the reason, from 1292 onwards his attitude towards Scotland was that of a dictator, insatiably hungry for domination. It was infinitely sad. For almost a hundred and thirty years no serious controversy had broken the peace between England and Scotland, but now future relationships were poisoned.

Balliol, exasperated beyond endurance, renounced his allegiance to Edward and in 1295 negotiated an alliance with France and prepared an invasion of north England. Balliol has been vilified by historians, and nicknamed Toom Tabard, Empty Coat, a man with the trappings but not the reality of kingship. Nonetheless, it was he who took this desperate initiative and launched the alliance with England's fiercest enemy, an alliance renewed by subsequent Scottish monarchs over a period of three hundred years.

Edward's agents always gave him prompt information about Balliol's activities. In good weather a mounted knight, travelling at speed, required about a fortnight to reach London from Berwick. Yet Edward almost always knew his enemy's movements ahead, in spite of the difficulties created by Scotland's forests, rivers, estuaries, bogs and horrible storms. Only two days after Balliol's army crossed the Border, Edward's entered Scotland, bent upon punitive revenge. This was in the spring of 1296.

The feudal barons in Scotland were now faced by an insoluble conflict of loyalties. Many were Edward's vassals because of large estates owned in England; they had no respect for Balliol; they had no experience of political controversy or what happens to countries in time of invasion: as yet, national feeling in western Europe was almost non-existent. Taken by surprise and confused, more than eighty met Edward at Wark Castle and gave him their homage as if he were the King of Scotland: amongst these were the seventh Robert Bruce, and his son the eighth Robert Bruce, who later became King. When Balliol heard this, he confiscated all the Bruce properties in Scotland and conferred them upon his brother-in-law, John Comyn.

From this moment onwards, the struggle in Scotland became a three-cornered one. Edward was fighting to bring Scotland under his direct control. The Balliol-Comyn interest was contested by the Bruces, and both of these powerful family groups believed that the downfall of the other would secure the throne for their own representative. Each therefore sought the policy best cal-culated to further personal advantage. Ordinary people did not understand the issue at all, but they soon learned to dread English authority. As for the Church, whose leaders were some of the most experienced and best-educated men in the country, its influence was at first paralysed because it was sharply divided. The Bishop of St. Andrews stood by Balliol, the Bishop of Glasgow by Bruce.

After he had received the homage of the nation's leaders at Wark, Edward moved with his great host to Berwick. This town's inhabitants, long accustomed to peaceful commerce and civilized business, simply did not believe that war was coming to them, and no preparations were made for defence until long past the last moment. The destruction of Berwick, carried out under Edward's instructions, was one of the most outrageous affairs he was ever responsible for. Many hundreds of people were slaughtered, including almost the entire Flemish colony, buildings were sacked, for days the licence of soldiers was unchecked. The horror of the whole affair made the deepest impression on Scotland. By this one preliminary action, Edward implanted that bitter hatred for all things English which was to be nourished so consistently by English policy during the next three hundred years.

Edward intended to rebuild Berwick as an English base and asked the citizens of London to select four skilful men who knew how to 'plan, order and lay out a new town'. Its commercial status was never recovered and Edinburgh became the principal trading centre for Scotland. The customs of Berwick, which, according to some historians, had totalled £2,000 in Alexander's day, yielded £120 by 1305.

The bloody affair at Berwick was followed by a military engagement at Dunbar, in which Edward's forces, considerably strengthened by contingents from Bruce and other Scottish lords, inflicted immense slaughter on Balliol's. John Balliol gave up his crown, and after three years in the Tower of London, retired to the family estates in France and died in 1313, a broken, forgotten failure.

From Dunbar, Edward proceeded on a triumphal tour through Scotland, taking possession of castles all the way from Roxburgh to Elgin and even further north. In August 1296, he returned to Berwick, where a massed act of allegiance was staged in which great numbers of Scots swore fealty to him. Many of their names are recorded in documents which still exist and are known as the Ragman Rolls. Some key nobles were taken south with Edward to serve in his French wars, but apart from these, it was proclaimed that no Scot was to leave the country. Quantities of charters and official records were confiscated and either destroyed or taken to London, along with what was believed to be the Stone of Destiny, upon which Scottish Kings had always been invested with their royal authority. The stone which Edward took was placed in Westminster Abbey, but some people think that he was duped and knew it. If so, the whereabouts of the real stone is still a matter of conjecture.

English officials were left to govern Scotland in Edward's name. English garrisons held every castle of importance. Edward was well satisfied and considered that the conquest of Scotland was complete.

In reality, it had not yet begun. So far the Scottish people had had no chance to organize themselves against the English incursion, nor indeed any special motive for doing so. The slaughters they experienced in 1296, the iron dictatorship established thereafter, the barbarity of the English garrisons, all these hardened Scottish national feeling. This change in the situation was masked by the jealousy between the Balliols and the Bruces, which delayed the nation's awakening, though the Comyn family was consistent throughout the worst years in its determination to drive the English out.

The first warning Edward had that all was not as he thought came with the news of William Wallace's sudden action at Stirling Bridge in 1297, when by excellent strategy perfectly carried out, the Scots annihilated a great English force. This isolated action led to little practical result, except a terrible renewal of Edward's punitive measures. Its significance was incalculable however. Wallace's army had included men from every part of the country, Galwegians, Highlanders, contingents from the north-east, and from central Scotland. It was an expression of national fury and its dramatic success proved to the Scots that the dreaded English were not insuperable. The importance of the affair may be gauged by the treatment given to Wallace when at last he was captured by Edward's agents in 1305. He was one of the first people to be tried as a traitor in the great hall at Westminster. All the medieval love of colour, drama and climax must have been gathered up in the setting of that scene, when Wallace was condemned to death by some of the most revolting barbarities known to medieval people.

The years 1298 to 1305 were some of the most miserable in Scottish history. While Edward's officials, agents and soldiers were in command everywhere, the Comyns did what they could to turn the tide, but resistance was always followed by fresh ravaging. In 1298, 1300, 1301 and 1302 and 1303, Edward sent his armies north for this purpose. Here and there, a well-provisioned castle held out for some months, as at Bothwell, which lasted for a year and nine weeks, and at Stirling, which was defended for three months. Always however it seemed that Edward's immense resources, and the thorough way in which he used them, must inevitably overcome Scottish endurance. His campaign in Galloway, for instance, was supplied from a fleet of sixty vessels, manned by 1500 men, based on Kirkcudbright. In 1303, he had two elaborate, fortified bridges constructed at King's Lynn, at a cost of over £1,000. Thirty ships carried them north, and they were assembled below Stirling, to enable the English forces to get across the Forth. For the siege of Roxburgh in 1303, between ten and twelve thousand men were mustered, including contingents from Ireland. Scotland's limited resources could not stand up to such large-scale organization, amply financed and administered by a nation five times her strength in population.

Much courageous resistance was organized by John, the Red Comyn, nephew of John Balliol and the accepted leader of the Balliol-Comyn faction. He considered himself the rightful heir to the throne and, with this in mind, he struggled on until 1304. But then he seemed to give up hope: he made his peace with Edward and became his liegeman.

Many others had done this during the bad years and Edward was diplomat enough to treat these high-ranking nobles with some generosity, and also to use them. The eighth Robert Bruce served him both as Governor of Carlisle and as Sheriff of Lanark, and his men were often conscripted to fight beside English soldiers. Edward's motive was to make it worth these men's while to yield. By 1305 it seemed as if Scottish resistance were spent.

The eighth Robert Bruce, now the head of his house, was restive however, despite his long record of service to Edward I. There are no records which reveal his thoughts and one can only guess at his motives, but it is known that from 1304 onwards he was in secret league with the Bishop of St. Andrews and others, waiting for the time when he could at last and finally renounce his feudal obligations to Edward I, assert himself against the Comyns and assume the crown which he believed should be his.

He asserted himself sooner than he intended and in a quite unpremeditated fashion. In February 1306, he and the Red Comyn and other nobles were in conference at Dumfries. An acute altercation arose, nobody can tell exactly how or why. In the physical violence that followed, Bruce killed the Red Comyn, in the sanctuary of the church at Dumfries.

Though Bruce almost certainly had no intention of such a shocking outcome to the old family feud, he instantly took what advantage he could of the situation. He went to Scone and there arranged the strangest coronation ceremony in recorded Scottish history. He was supported by four loyal younger brothers, by his very able nephew Thomas Randolph, by the Bishops of Glasgow, St. Andrews and Moray, and by a limited number of powerful nobles. In his favour were the facts that the Comyn family was practically ruined already, that Edward I was old and failing, that the young Edward of England was a foppish weakling.

His position was most unenviable. All Scotland was horrified by the sacrilegious nature of his crime. As soon as the news of it became known, Bruce and all connected with it were excommunicated. In a savage burst of fury, Edward I again gathered his forces to punish Scotland, with devastating success. Bruce was defeated at Methven and he became a hunted refugee. For months he was in hiding, in Kintail, in Kintyre, in an island off the Irish coast, possibly also in Orkney or even Norway. During these terrible months, three of his brothers were captured and executed, his wife, his young daughter and his two sisters taken prisoner, and some twenty of his principal supporters hanged.

Early in 1307, the tide turned. In the spring of that year a great band of Yorkshiremen and Borderers were slaughtered by Bruce's men in Glentrool. In May, Bruce won a bigger engagement at Loudon Hill. On July 7th, Edward I died.

CHAPTER 8

Robert Bruce

T he new English King, Edward II, had no stomach for war. Perhaps he had sublimated his martial instincts by making a pet of a tame lion, which he took about with him on a collar and chain. He found the Scottish project dreary, and soon called it off, leaving the English garrisons to manage as best they might, seriously short of provisions.

From 1307 onwards, therefore, Bruce had a better chance. He first planned a campaign north of the Forth and Clyde, which took some time to complete. By summer 1309, only Dundee and Banff remained in English hands north of the Tay, only Perth, Stirling and Kirkintilloch between the Tay and the Forth-Clyde line. It took him rather longer to dislodge English influence from Galloway and Lothian, but by 1311 he was strong enough to invade England. The richest farmlands in Scotland had been disastrously harried by the English, Scottish monasteries and churches often desecrated, but from now on people living as far south as Appleby in Westmorland and Richmond in Yorkshire learned to dread the Scots as if they were agents of the Devil himself. This perpetual harrying of people who lived within striking distance of either side of the Borders was a *damnosa haereditas* for almost three centuries.

Bruce made a special point of destroying castles in his own country, for it was by means of these administrative strong points that the English power had been consolidated, and he wanted them permanently levelled to the ground.

His progress was hindered by the family feuds which had been nurtured by English interference. All Comyn's supporters, such as the Earl of Buchan, the Ross interest in northern Scotland, the men of Argyll and Lorne, the McDowalls of Galloway—these and many more hated Bruce worse than they hated Englishmen.

By slow stages, with pitiless disregard for the life and property
of plain folk, Bruce beat these family factions down.

In 1313 Bruce captured Perth, Roxburgh and Edinburgh. In
central Scotland, there remained only Stirling, which was still
held by the English, though its defenders were now in desperate
straits. Edward II at last bestirred himself for the relief of his
troops within this almost impregnable fortress. Enormous supply
trains and large engines of war were assembled on the old scale,
far beyond anything that Bruce could rival. In 1314 the two
armies met in an engagement which is probably better remembered
in Scotland than any other in her history.

The success won by the Scots at Bannockburn, below Stirling,
in 1314, was due to Bruce's superior generalship. His army was
on higher ground than the English, who tried to advance over the
almost water-logged stretches of land through which the Bannockburn flowed. The heavily mailed, mounted knights found their
horses collapsing under them because of the spiked pot-holes
prepared by the Scots. Worse still, the English archers had no
room for deployment. All battles between medieval English and
Scottish armies were conditioned by the freedom with which the
English could use their dreaded archery. The Scots never
produced anything comparable to the English or Welsh bowman,
against whom they had no adequate defence. But archers did
need room to move freely. Bruce knew this, and chose his battle
site in such a way that the English bowmen were virtually useless.
Bannockburn was such an overwhelming triumph for the Scots
that the English gave up all pretence of maintaining any hold in
Scotland, and many Scotsmen hitherto disaffected from Bruce
came over to his side.

The next objectives were Berwick and Carlisle, the two gate-
ways for armies crossing the Border. Bruce organized large-scale
attacks upon both, meeting with success at Berwick and complete
failure at Carlisle. The two campaigns spread over several years
and were supported by great invasions into Yorkshire and
Westmorland. In 1320, Edward II tried another invasion of
Scotland, but had to retreat, pursued by Bruce to Rievaulx.
Edward's personal baggage and a number of distinguished
people were captured and then, as Bain puts it, 'Bruce roamed

MAP 6.
THE WARS OF INDEPENDENCE

Elgin

Banff

R. Spey

R. Don

R. Dee

N. Esk

S. Esk

R. Tay

Scone

Dundee

Methven

Dupplin Moor

R. Forth

Perth

Stirling

Kinghorn

Dunbar

Bannockburn

Kirkintilloch

Linlithgow

Edinburgh

R. Clyde

Bothwell

Halidon Hill

Berwick

Norham-on-Tweed

Loudoun
Hill

R. Tweed

Roxburgh

R. Nith

Otterburn

Glen Trool

Wark

Kirkcudbright

Dumfries

R. Tyne

R. Cree

Carlisle

Ф.Г.

Sites of battles other than those of towns .... ✗

0 10 20   40   60   80   100 Miles

0 10 20 40 60 80 100   160 Kilometres

freely about Yorkshire, taking ransoms from Ripon, Beverley and
other places, and retired to his own country unmolested.'

At last, in 1327, the English were ready to negotiate. Edward II
was deposed in that year by the evil partnership of his wife,
Isabella, and a group of barons under Mortimer. Isabella and
Mortimer agreed to a treaty signed in 1328 at Northampton.
This document is still preserved in Edinburgh. It stated the
English recognition of Scotland as an independent country and
of Bruce as its King, with the provision that Scots who had
supported the English interest during the wars were to be given
back the lands Bruce had confiscated. As a guarantee of per-
manence, the treaty was supported by a device frequently used
in the Middle Ages. The young Joanna, Edward II's daughter,
was married to the five-year-old David, Robert Bruce's son and
heir. Thus after thirty-six years of unprincipled scheming for
each other's ruin, the royal families were to be united by the
matrimony of two children.

During the years following 1306, and while he was battling
through arduous military engagements and political negotiations,
Bruce himself became a different person. Brought up as an Anglo-
Norman baron, he had passed his earlier years like others of his
social class, fulfilling as best he might both personal ambition
and feudal obligation. In his younger days he apparently had no
conception of Scotland as a national entity or of any responsibility
towards his country and people. The extraordinary thing is that,
from the day when he committed murder with sacrilege, Bruce
began to see that he must create in Scotland a people united by
loyalties greater than feudal bonds could promote. His idea of
kingship steadily deepened as the years went by and as his
experience of private grief and physical endurance became harsher.

The murder of Comyn which started Bruce on this most
significant phase was a crime which Christendom could not for-
give. Bruce's excommunication was continued and renewed.
Nonetheless, he had the support of many Church leaders from
the day of his coronation onwards. They called a gathering
together in 1310, when by formal oath they bound themselves to
his support, in defiance of Christendom's laws. The most remarkable evidence of the stiffening of public opinion in his favour,

however, was the meeting which took place at Arbroath in 1320. It was a gathering of barons and clergy, who produced a Declaration, or a formal letter, which they sent to the Pope, in the name of the nobles and of the Community of Scotland.

The Declaration explained that the people of Scotland were devoted to Robert, their King, that they would continue to resist Edward while even a hundred of them were alive, that freedom meant everything to them. 'We fight not for glory nor riches nor honour, but only for that liberty which no true man relinquishes but with his life'—'libertatem solummodo quam nemo bonus nisi simul cum vita amittet'. Of Robert they wrote: 'By the Providence of God, the right of succession, those laws and customs which we are resolved to defend even with our lives, and by our own just consent, he is our King.' The extraordinary statement continued with words of great interest, words designed perhaps to carry a hint of warning to Bruce's successors. 'Yet Robert himself, should he turn aside from the task he has begun, and yield Scotland or us to the English King or his people, we should cast out as the enemy of us all, as the subverter of our rights and of his own, and we should choose another King to defend our freedom.'

The forthright statement of Scottish devotion to freedom and the uncompromising assertion of the will of the community require some explanation. Whose was the initiative in calling such a meeting and in drafting such a document? It is clear that the author of the ringing words must have been a man of intellectual distinction. Probably it was Bernard, Abbot of Arbroath. At any rate the man who reduced a profound political philosophy to such splendidly rhythmic phrases knew his Sallust, because there are interesting parallels between some of the sentences in the Declaration and some in *Catilina*.

The Declaration proves that Scottish national feeling, at least among some of the barons, was now aroused, and had been captured by Bruce. He had taken years to see what course to adopt in the complex circumstances of the times, but once he made the cause of Scottish national freedom his own, he evoked from certain of his people a loyalty and initiative of which this letter to the Pope is plain evidence.

Robert Bruce

There is so much to be guessed at in medieval history. Why is the original Declaration of Arbroath, with its many seals, still to this day in Scotland? Was it because of this document that the Pope annulled Robert's excommunication soon after 1320? Nobody knows.

One other gathering of Robert's reign must be described, the Parliament he held at Cambuskenneth in 1326. This is the first recorded occasion on which a Scottish King summoned clergy, barons and also representatives of the burghs to a Parliament. Two important matters were dealt with, one financial, the other political. A contribution of one-tenth on all rents was decided upon for Robert, to defray the expenses of government. To safeguard the succession, oaths of allegiance were paid to Robert's little son, David, with an additional vow of loyalty, in the event of his death without heirs, to the son of Margery Bruce. This Margery, a much-loved daughter of Robert, had married Walter Fitzalan, the Hereditary Steward of Scotland. He was known more briefly as Walter the Steward, or simply Walter Steward. The surname became Stewart, and Walter and Margery the founders of the future Scottish royal family.

Why was Robert concerning himself about the succession in 1326? Again we do not know—but by 1327 he was ill. The extreme hardships he had endured for so long, especially those of 1306, had probably taken their toll and Bruce was exposed like everybody else to diseases which 20th century Scotland never sees. He died in 1329—a leper, according to tradition. And his son was only six.

CHAPTER 9

Medieval Confusion

The strength of medieval kingdoms depended upon the strength of their rulers, for when the monarchy was weak, the barons could wage the private wars which were the curse of feudal societies. The Scottish barons degenerated into unprincipled opportunists once Bruce's strong hand was removed and they made full use of the English King's equally unprincipled opportunism. The result was decades of misery for ordinary people.

When Robert I died, Thomas Randolph, Earl of Moray, was made regent for David II. He was Bruce's nephew, a strong personality and a fine leader, steeped in the traditions built up by his King, but he flatly refused to carry out one part of Bruce's treaty with the English. It was more than he could stomach to restore large properties to Scotsmen who had collaborated with the Edwards, doing their utmost to bring ruin to Bruce. So the Disinherited, as they came to be called, angrily turned to Edward III for help.

Edward III resurrected the Balliol interest in the person of Edward, the son of Toom Tabard. After his coronation at Scone, this man paid homage for Scotland, as his father had done, and surrendered Edinburgh, Berwick and all the land between Linlithgow and the Solway; he even offered to marry Edward's sister Joanna, and 'to provide otherwise for her husband, David', a gallantry which was never carried out.

Moray, the only man who could have held Scotland together, died just when these troubles were beginning. There was now a dearth of able, vigorous patriots, partly because so many had been wiped out in earlier fighting. Resistance was made by Scottish armies, but under new and inferior generalship, by men who had neither the training nor the military scholarship needed.

They had not studied Bruce's principles of strategy. The English were supremely successful at the battles of Dupplin Moor and Halidon Hill, in 1332 and 1333, because their archery was allowed full scope for its destructive work.

The ugliest part of the whole business was that prominent Scottish barons and prelates changed sides without scruple, so that the English armies were assisted by men who had been the sworn vassals and trusted supporters of Robert I. The fine phrases of the Arbroath Declaration were forgotten and its lofty ideals passed out of men's minds. As for the young David and his adolescent wife, Joanna, they were sent to France for safekeeping. The Bruce interests and the government of Scotland passed under the guardianship of another Robert, son of Walter the Steward and Margery, the old King's daughter.

Soon however, Edward III became absorbed in his prolonged adventures in France. This gave the more resentful Scottish nobles their opportunity, and from 1340 onwards many went to France and spent their lives and fortunes fighting against England in these opening phases of the Hundred Years' War. The alliance between France and Scotland drew some of the best Scots into this profitless way of life for nearly three centuries.

During the 1340s, however, there were Scots who bestirred themselves in their own country to regain some of the lost strongholds and displayed something of the old spirit. Perth, Stirling, and Edinburgh were recovered; at Dunbar, Black Agnes, the Earl of Moray's stalwart daughter, conducted a defence which has become one of Scotland's sagas of courage. In 1346, David II himself made an effort to wear the mantle of his father. He invaded England and carried out horrible acts of cruelty in defenceless villages, only to be defeated at Neville's Cross and captured by the English.

Scotland was now left in a state of anarchy. Edward Balliol's friends seized what they could get. Scots allied to English interests were stronger than anybody else. Once again, Robert the Steward, David's nephew, was faced with the task of administration, but he could not restore order.

David II remained in England for twelve years and greatly enjoyed his captivity. The court life of Edward III was more palatable to him than the work of kingship, and even when his release had been bought by an enormous ransom, he and Joanna liked to go back to England. No more of a patriot than Edward Balliol, he did not mind the fact that much of Scotland lay in English hands. Robert, the nephew upon whom so much of his own responsibility had fallen, he cordially hated.

David II's inglorious reign ended in 1371. He was followed by Robert the Steward, whom he disliked so much. This King, Robert II, was little more than a crowned noble and could not check the baron's lawlessness. Of this period, a contemporary wrote: 'In those days there was no law in Scotland; but the great man oppressed the poor man and the whole kingdom was one den of thieves. Slaughters, robberies, fire-raisings and other crimes went unpunished, and justice was sent into banishment, beyond the kingdom's bounds.'

Once, indeed, decisive action was taken by feudal leaders against the national enemy instead of against their own country-men, in 1388, when the Border Douglases invaded Northumber-land and defeated their opposite neighbours, the Percys, at Otterburn or Chevy Chase. The miseries inflicted during this campaign were long remembered in England, especially at Appleby which never recovered its former prosperity; even in 16th century records, references were made to the losses sustained by this little town in 1388.

Robert II had to face the task of producing David II's ransom, which was never fully paid and which caused endless wrangles with the English. In his efforts to raise it, Robert was obliged to increase customs duties and to levy taxes. The sanction he needed for such unpopular decisions he sought and gained from Parliament. His handling of this political institution was to have long-term results and needs some explanation.

Parliament was one of the great developments in medieval Western Europe. Meetings of responsible people were summoned in one form or another in most countries from Bohemia to Iceland, during the Middle Ages, to discuss and to settle public problems. The chief landowners and higher clergy were normally the only people summoned and medieval Parliaments were quite unlike any modern gathering of the same name.

Medieval Confusion

In England, Parliament became as nowhere else a political institution. Under Henry III, and still more under Edward I, it was made an integral part of the administrative system, meeting regularly to solve the problems of government and to supervise the dispensation of justice. Occasionally the lesser gentry and the wealthy burgesses were required to attend Parliament, mainly in order to discuss proposed taxation. By Edward III's reign, these knights and burgesses were invariably summoned and Parliament became a means whereby royal funds, and therefore royal policy, could in some measure be controlled by those who represented the richer classes of society. The process took many centuries to reach its culmination, but the English Parliament eventually assumed at least the forms of democratic government and could no longer be used as an instrument of royal or aristocratic authority. The share in its deliberations taken by wealthy commoners was a most important feature of this development.

The Scottish Parliament also grew out of the advisory Council which met under early medieval Kings for administrative and for judicial business and, as in England, it was attended by the chief lords and higher clergy. Robert I had summoned lesser gentry and burgesses to it in 1326, and Robert II continued this practice, because he was in desperate need of financial assistance. This the gentry and burgesses greatly resented, because a country with so small a population could not afford the loss of such people for weeks at a time from their normal work. Parliamentary authority was therefore delegated to committees, so that citizens might be spared the irritation of attending throughout the sessions. In this way, the Scottish Parliament was strangled, for legislation passed under the control of a small group of senior clerics and barons. In the 15th century, the delegation of powers was so carefully worked out that Scottish commoners never exerted any real influence in their Parliament, which was therefore dominated by feudal overlords.

When Robert II died in 1390, he was succeeded by his son John, Earl of Carrick, who disliked the unfortunate association connected with Kings called John, and therefore adopted the name Robert III. This Robert was lamed by a horse's kick in 1385 and never became physically fit again, so he depended much, as his father the second Robert had done, upon the help of his brother, the Duke of Albany.

Robert III decided that his heir, Prince James, should be sent to France for safety against English interference and a ship from Danzig was chartered in 1406 to fetch the little boy from Bass Rock. The captain was set upon by pirates from the Norfolk coast, who seized the prince and sent him to the English court: and, only a month later, Robert III died. Eighteen years, all his boyhood and youth, James spent in England, while the Duke of Albany and his son, Murdoch, acted as Regents. All his life James believed that from personal ambition these two neglected negotiations for his release and he never forgave them.

The latter part of the 14th century was a time when ordinary people in Scotland had to face a bitter daily struggle for existence. Their troubles were due partly to the social organization of the country, partly to economic conditions, partly to the degeneracy of the Church. The lack of effective political leadership naturally enabled rogues of many varieties to ride roughshod over other people.

There were great families which managed to consolidate their estates and to build up kingdoms within the kingdom. Such were the Douglases, descended from Robert I's fine supporter, the good Sir James, but later tainted by their preference for the Balliol interest. The head of the family became Warden of the Marshes and Lord of Galloway, appointments of immense importance, awarded by David II, with cynical disregard of Douglas disloyalty. In 1358, the family's Earldom was created. By a series of well-planned marriages, the Earls of Douglas acquired the lands of other great lords, and two of them married into the royal family. At the end of the 14th century, the fourth Earl, Robert III's son-in-law, was a dangerous rival to the King, with an accumulation of properties sprawling over Galloway, Douglasdale, Annandale, Clydesdale, Lothian, Stirlingshire and Moray.

Meantime, an almost autonomous kingdom was developing in the Isles, whose people had always followed a separate way of life. In this, they were supported by West Highland interests. The Lords of Argyll and Lorne had been Bruce's deadly enemies

and although Highlanders and Islesmen had fought for the King
at Bannockburn, no tradition of loyalty was built up. The Lord
of the Isles had supported Edward Balliol and had refused out-
right to contribute to David II's ransom.

This was the period when the clan system became more clearly
defined. Its origins of course were very much earlier and are not
to be found in written records, which date only from about the
end of the 14th century. The clan was composed of closely inter-
related family groups, all owing loyalty to a chieftain whose
authority was unassailable. During the Middle Ages, chieftains
established judicial procedures in their own courts by traditional
rights which passed from father to son. They dealt summarily
with criminal and civil cases, without reference to Sheriffs or
other royal officials; their decisions were anything but impartial,
since it was considered a matter of honour to avenge all injuries
to the life or property of the family in no matter what circumstances. Vicious punishments were carried out, including death
by execution and by drowning.

The chieftains identified themselves with their people and
knew many of them individually and the clans held together as
social units, giving their members a certain sense of community.
But the chieftains maintained interminable vendettas against
each other, in the interests of which they called out their clans
for prolonged and bloody wars. Organized cattle-raiding and wife-
stealing were accompanied by murder, betrayal and cruelty, so
that for centuries tragedy was inseparable from the daily lives
of people who inhabited one of the most exquisitely beautiful
regions of Europe.

The clansmen lived in miserable conditions even during the
uncertain spells of peacetime. Autumn gales destroyed on
average every fourth harvest, the soil was either sour and thin,
or else water-logged. The patches of primitive bere and oats
which were cultivated could be ruined by raiders from other
glens, and the scraggy cattle were always in danger of being
stolen, especially in summer when they were pastured high up
in the hills. Families lived in long, low-built huts, made on the
Scandinavian model. The walls were piled up with stones and
pebbles held together by mud, the roofs were heather thatch,

there were neither windows nor chimneys, so the peat-smoke
hung about day and night. Draught was excluded better than
one might think by five-foot-thick walls; but damp and filth were
unavoidable, especially in winter, when animals shared the
dwellings with their owners. To all other smells was added the
acrid odour of stale manure which was saved up to be spread over
the little fields. The limited gear and equipment needed for such
a way of life were home-made, even to the plough, an instrument
of ancient design, known to historians as the caschrom. Caschrom
means crooked foot, and the instrument had a single curved
metal blade at the end of a long wooden shaft. It was really a
glorified spade and the ploughman himself dug into the soil with
it by pressing his foot on a small pedal above the blade: he
moved backwards as he drove his furrow, a slow laborious
progress which made for limited husbandry.

South of the Highland line, agriculture was still based on the
ancient run-rig system. The land round a group of dwellings was
divided into two parts, the infield close at hand on the more
fertile ground of the valley or the lower hill slopes, the outfield
further off and higher up. The infield was divided into rigs, or
strips, which ran up and down the hillsides across the contours,
separated by unploughed lines known as balks. On the infield
was bestowed all the manure collected during the winter months
and it was ploughed by an enormous, locally made contraption
of unwieldy bulk, which needed several oxen to work it in relays.
The rigs were shared out among the people, re-allotted at short
intervals, sometimes every second year, and they were planted
with bere or oats, season after season. It was a case of perpetual
tillage under communal ownership, a state of affairs unlikely to
stimulate initiative or farming skill. The outfield was used for
pasture, except once in a decade or so when a portion of it would
be put under cultivation for a couple of seasons; and it too was
communally held.

There was nothing in Scotland comparable to the English
manorial system, which enabled a class of copyholders to emerge,
men who had recognized rights in the land which could be
defended in the law courts. Scottish tenants could be ejected at
short notice by their feudal superiors and often were. Their

insecurity was the worse because they had no recognized rights
to common land; so that whereas English villagers enjoyed the
use of a common on which to pasture their beasts, Scottish
peasants had to drive them to the more remote outfield or the
mountain glens.

In a country whose people lived at such a low level of prosperity,
disease ran a terrible course. Leprosy, plague, agues and bowel
complaints, illnesses of a loathsome nature unknown nowadays
in western Europe, took toll of life in a way we can hardly
imagine. Plague found its way north of the Border amongst the
booty and prisoners captured on more than one Scottish invasion
of England; it is believed to have killed a third of Scotland's
people in the 14th century; it ruthlessly penetrated the dirt-
infested houses all through the 15th and 16th centuries, often
coinciding with famine. The last recorded outbreak in Aberdeen
was in 1648.

From the infection of leprosy, plague and the rest, wealthier
people were by no means free. The more spacious castles with
open court-yards of the 13th century had been destroyed under
Bruce's instructions, and 14th century lords lived in squat, solid
keeps which were square-built, almost innocent of drainage, and
so congested that there was personal privacy for nobody. Physical
well-being as we know it could not be maintained in any rank of
society.

The 14th century was of course a period when all western
Europe was afflicted by civil wars, plague, poverty, hardship.
That conditions in general were worse in Scotland than else-
where seems however apparent. The French historian of the day,
Froissart, puts revealing words into the mouth of French knights
sent to Scotland in 1385: 'What could have brought us hither?
We have never known till now what was meant by poverty and
hard living.'

The influence of the Church counted for little. Statutes passed
by a reforming synod of St. Andrews towards the end of the period
show why. Excommunication was threatened against people who
practised any out of a comprehensive list of sins—coin-clipping,
perjury, sacrilege, witchcraft, laying unwanted babies at church
doors, violence against parents or ecclesiastical persons. The

laymen thus warned were set a poor example by their priests. The same synod decreed that rectors were to stop living with women, they were to reside in their benefices and neither to engage in secular business nor to accept fees for saying masses.

Clergy were degenerate and they had little chance of being different. It was almost impossible to secure an education beyond the most perfunctory teaching by rote of liturgical routine. Some young men found their way to Oxford, others to France, where there was an endowment instituted by the Bishop of Moray to keep four poor scholars from his diocese at Paris University. On the whole, however, the clergy were an ignorant and depraved lot, and they were given no encouragement by their leaders to be otherwise. Bishops and abbots were often soldiers by choice and by habit, as indeed they had to be when armed attack was so common. Many fine buildings were wrecked in warfare and not always by alien hands. In 1390, for example, Elgin Cathedral was burnt out by 'wyld, wykkyd, Heland men' under the Earl of Buchan, a lord known to contemporaries as the Wolf of Badenoch. Private wars between barons caused much damage to church buildings and English armies on the Borders constantly desecrated such monasteries as Melrose, Jedburgh, Kelso and others that lay on their route. It was impossible for religion to flourish in such conditions.

In England, Wyclif's influence by this time had set men thinking and the Lollard movement he founded anticipated the Reformation in some ways. The Lollards reached Scotland too, though not in any great number; the first of their martyrs, an Englishman named Resby, was burned, by order of the Scottish government in 1407, an ugly omen of much that was to follow.

The high promise of the 12th and 13th centuries came to no fulfilment because of the disasters following Alexander III's death. Scotland desperately needed the chance to revive and rebuild and only a strong King could provide it. The chance came when at long last, in 1424, James I rode north, a free man.

CHAPTER 10

The Fifteenth Century

This chapter and the following one describe changes which influenced the lives of ordinary Scottish people for some three hundred years.

The 15th century opened in unpromising circumstances, for during the absence of James I in England, the great lords made unprincipled use of their opportunities to consolidate their own strength. There were other setbacks in the middle years of the century because James I, James II, and James III all died prematurely, but important traditions in local and parliamentary government were established: later on, James IV's vigorous leadership stimulated a new resilience among his people. A most unfortunate feature of the period, the last phase of unchallenged Catholicism, was the prolonged stagnation in religious affairs, at the very time when the leaders of the old Church could have done much to safeguard their principles and build up their spiritual resources.

James I spent a restless youth, fretting over his captivity, hating his lack of means to keep a decent wardrobe, fuming over the Albanys' reluctance to arrange his return; but Henry IV saw to it that he was educated, both in literary and knightly pursuits. The prince's lively mind and flair for poetry gave him a means of escape from his cramping circumstances and he was probably more widely read than any previous Scottish King. He took part in most of the great court occasions and accumulated much information about English institutions. He also kept in touch with Scottish developments, of which three must have especially excited him.

The first was a rebellion organized by Donald, Lord of the Isles. He wanted to seize the Earldom of Ross, and thus extend his authority over most of the northern mainland. Henry IV, who nurtured every dissension in Scotland, gave Donald promise of support, though being a cautious man, he offered him little else. The Earl's forces swept across towards Aberdeen, and were defeated at Harlaw in 1411 by the Earl of Mar, the Provost of Aberdeen and the Frasers. The battle was an incident in a mighty clan conflict, but its significance was national. Had Donald succeeded, Scotland would have been divided into two kingdoms.

The year 1411 was marked by a second event of national importance. Bishop Wardlaw founded St. Andrews University. It was a tiny institution and it passed through difficult times but it gave Scottish boys the chance of having some education in Canon Law and Theology before going abroad to French or Italian Universities.

James experienced personally the effects of a third development. In 1419, when Rouen was captured by Henry V, the French appealed to Scotland for armed assistance, and some six or seven thousand men were accordingly sent over. Henry decided that James had better come to France in person, hoping that the Scots might be persuaded by their prisoner-King's presence in the English army to go home. James did not take the nature of his mission very seriously, but he found the experience of English army life abroad exhilarating. He was impressed by the handling of siege engines and the use of archery, which he could now observe from an angle unusual to Scotsmen. He fretted more than ever when he returned to England. Some grim satisfaction he must have derived from the news of Scots' activities in France, for they fought along with the armies of Joan of Arc on behalf of the French King, and at Beaugé, in 1421, Scottish arms turned the tide. During the 15th century, the Scots Guards became famous for their services in France and drew many useful young men away from their own country. French soldiers and peasants, who did not much like their protagonists, termed them 'sacs à vin' and 'mangeurs de mouton'.

After Henry V's death in 1422, serious negotiations were set afoot for the release of James. Again, a crippling ransom was demanded, and a truce was agreed, which should have stemmed the tide of Scottish reinforcements to France. James returned to

Scotland in the highest spirits in 1424, the happier at this happiest moment of his life because he had with him Lady Joan Beaufort, whom he married for love, an unusual experience for a medieval King. He expressed his feelings about this in a poem called *The Kingis Quair*. He was unlike other monarchs too in his idealism, which he summed in words now famous: 'If God give me but the life of a dog, I will make the key keep the castle and the bracken-bush the cow.'

It was not easy for him. For almost a century, the Scots Lords had known no strong monarch: and they had been most ill-advisedly bribed by the weak Stewart Kings with enormous grants from royal properties, so that by 1424 crown lands had been reduced to relatively small proportions.

James I lost no time. He had hardly returned before the Duke of Albany was arrested to stand trial before Parliament, for treasonable neglect during the regency. On the eve of this trial, Albany's son instigated an unfortunate revolt which was soon crushed, but which hardened opinion against his father. Albany, his father-in-law and his two sons were all executed and the family properties annexed to the crown.

James followed up his ferocious beginning by enforcement of the rule of law. Even his most important subjects were punished for resisting it, and the powerful Earl of Douglas was imprisoned in 1428. James penetrated the north and west as no earlier King had dared and he recovered some of the lost crown lands. He also confiscated a number of wealth-bearing properties, especially in the Lowlands.

In order to raise his ransom, James instituted some unfamiliar financial measures. The whole kingdom was assessed for taxation with an efficiency which omitted no moneyed class, customs duties were increased, the export of gold and silver stopped. Everybody groused about it and James himself grudged sending instalments of his hard-earned resources to England, theoretically in payment of expenses incurred during his imprisonment, though he had been kept so short of necessities. The taxation lapsed and so did the payments, but James continued to extract money by every other means he could think of and he also borrowed it from his richer subjects.

Within his first year, James summoned Parliament and presented it with a legislative programme designed to improve economic conditions and defence measures. No detail was too small for his attention. Salmon-fishing in the close season was prohibited, rooks and wolves were to be destroyed, peas and beans cultivated, corn marigolds weeded out of the fields. Football and poaching were forbidden, hostelries were to be built in the burghs, prices were fixed, even clothing was regulated to prevent extravagance by the citizens. Scotsmen have always resented this kind of interference with private affairs, and although all these measures would have improved the general standard of living, they were neglected and James had not sufficient executive power to insist that they should be carried out. His instructions that sheriffs should inspect people's arms and enforce regular practice, especially in archery, would also have been good for the country had they been effective.

It was offensive to James to discover that Parliament was overloaded with judicial work which should long since have been disposed of. The sheriff courts and the courts of the travelling justices were giving no satisfaction; because Parliament was the highest court of appeal, all sorts of complaints were being laid before it and left unsettled from one session to another. It took the King no time at all to decide that the traditional methods of securing justice in civil disputes were inadequate and early in his reign he made Parliament legislate about the matter. 'Certane discret personis of the thre estatis' were to be chosen, nine in all, to sit under a Chancellor three times a year and 'know, examyn, conclude and finally determyne all and sundry complayntis'. This was the origin of the Court of Session. Of course it did not meet regularly as James had hoped. It was another of his excellent ideas, one which ultimately materialized, but not during his lifetime. Much later, in the 16th century, the College of Justice evolved from his Court.

Unlike some of his contemporaries, James was moved to discover that some people were too poor to pay for actions at law; he had a statute passed that for the love of God, any 'pur creatur' so placed was to be given the help of 'a lele and a wys advocate', a poor man's lawyer in fact.

Religious matters were also much in James I's thoughts. Benedictine and Augustinian foundations in Scotland were ordered to reform their ways and to carry out the regulations of monastic life. To reduce the interference of Rome he tried to make it illegal to purchase benefices from the Pope, and it would have been well if this had succeeded, because the Pope's traffic in ecclesiastical appointments did much harm to the Scottish Church during the one century now left before the crisis of the Reformation. Already signs of restlessness were appearing which contemporaries could not interpret but which are significant to the historian. Heresy was shocking to James, whose legislation sanctioned its punishment by burning, and a Bohemian called Paul Crawar suffered this torture in 1433 at St. Andrews, later the scene of many similar executions.

Altogether, James worked Parliament hard. He would have liked to create a House of Commons, such as he had seen in action in England, as this would have helped him in standing up to the barons. It would also have enabled the Scottish Parliament to become gradually more representative of national feeling and to give the country a more democratic constitution.

Already, however, tradition had hardened against any such development and James was dismayed by the reluctance of any but feudal overlords and high-ranking clerics to attend. He tried to encourage as many free landowners as possible to come, but the feudal background was too strong for him. In 1428, therefore, it was arranged that tenants-in-chief were to be personally summoned by writ, and were to come, but lesser freeholders were to be excused if they appointed two commissioners from each shire to represent them: and only the royal burghs were entitled to choose members to speak for townsfolk. Even this was not fully implemented and later a Committee was formed, whose members became known as Lords of the Articles. This committee did all the real work of initiating and drafting legislation, so that Parliament itself became an institution which merely ratified the decisions of an executive council, and its members often had only the haziest idea of what they were sanctioning. As it continued to meet in one assembly, the few burgesses and commoners who were there had little chance of expressing opinions contrary to those of the great lords. So Parliament excited little interest in Scotland, until the end of the 17th century when reforms made it much more effective.

For thirteen years, James worked to achieve his ideals, with superb confidence and small concern for the many people he offended. In this comparatively short time, he went a long way towards making the key and the bracken-bush more reliable custodians of property.

He also built up the prestige of royal authority, at the expense of much else, for James exasperated many whom he had also humiliated and people were angered by his personal extravagance. When Linlithgow Palace was burnt out in 1424, the King spent over £2,000 rebuilding it on a splendid scale although at that very time he was legislating for heavy taxation. He dressed magnificently, spent freely on himself and his family, apparently with no idea that he could be in any personal danger. Horrible vengeance came in 1437, when Sir Robert Graham burst into the presence of James and his Queen, and murdered him. By this crime, Scotland lost the strong leadership the country had needed so long and once more the wrangles of unscrupulous family groups bedevilled the country's affairs.

The Earl of Douglas was made regent for James II, who was only seven. In addition to the French lordships of Touraine and Longueville, Douglas owned more estates in Scotland than anybody and it seemed possible that he might establish supreme control, but he died in 1439, leaving two young sons. Their implacable enemy was the Earl of Crichton. It was Crichton who became the King's guardian and he rejoiced in his chance to break the hated Douglas power. By a thoughtfully planned and brutally exercised plot he had the young Earl and his brother murdered at a dinner-party: the little King saw how it was done, and remembered. The great Douglas estates were divided up, but the eighth Earl, a cousin of the murdered boys, set himself to consolidate them again. In 1452, James II, now nearly twenty-three, himself stabbed and killed this rival to his own power and the house of Douglas never recovered its influence. The violent way in which it was humbled reveals 15th century morality at its worst, but for James II it meant increased security, since no comparable family group could threaten his position.

During the mid-15th century, England was suffering from the baronial feuds which flared up into the Wars of the Roses, so English invasions abated, and in Scotland town life had a chance to revive. New burghs were founded, known as burghs of barony. They were not entitled to send representatives to Parliament, and they were never given any trade monopoly nor were they allowed to share in export and import trade. They could however hold markets and fairs and their burgesses began to make money.

Within the burghs, a new class of society began to emerge, the craftsmen. Their Incorporated Associations gradually became powerful enough to rival the older Merchant Gilds. The craftsman was a speeialist, skilled in making shoes, saddles, garments, household gear or implements of various kinds. The merchant did international business, selling raw materials and buying foreign wares wholesale at such centres as Bruges and Middelburg. The craftsmen, who lived by manual skill, were regarded by the merchants as socially inferior, nouveaux riches, and every effort was made by the merchants to exclude them from office on the burgh councils. In 1469 an act was passed to prevent the 'gret truble and contentione', the 'clamour' of 'sympil persons', which occurred in open elections. Retiring councillors were now to choose the new ones, so that local government fell into the hands of small but powerful family groups. Burgh representatives to Parliament were chosen exclusively from the councils and these families therefore exercised a most undemocratic influence on national as well as municipal affairs. The effect of this unfortunate act was the more damaging because the only burghs which enjoyed even this restricted franchise were those holding royal charters. One of the strangest features in Scottish constitutional history is that this defect was not dealt with until the 19th century, so that for nearly four hundred years townsmen were inadequately represented in Parliament.

The burghs were very small. In the mid-15th century Glasgow had about 1,500 inhabitants; in the early 16th Aberdeen had less than 3,000. Most houses were still made of timber, and the narrow streets were always dirty because of the middens which people piled up at their doors. Tiny as the communities were, they jealously guarded all their rights and so villages were prevented from holding markets and fairs, and village crafts and industries were discouraged, to the great disadvantage of the country as a whole. Not until the 17th century did people realize that trade and industry were a national concern which should be liberated from medieval privilege and parochialism, and even then this idea was strenuously opposed by the burghs.

Landowners in the 15th century interested themselves in making their homes more comfortable. Experience in the French wars had given many of them new ideas about architecture and they began to enlarge their castles. Courtyards were added, with defensive towers at the corners and additional sets of buildings surrounded these courtyards, which therefore formed quadrangles. So more domestic apartments were provided, kitchen quarters became more spacious, banqueting halls larger: and as windows were at last designed to admit light, family life must have become more comfortable. James III employed an unpopular Scottish friend of his to build him a magnificent hall in Stirling Castle, which you can still see. French masons designed the royal apartments there and they were among the first to bring Renaissance ideas of architecture into Scotland. But defence against enemies was still the main purpose of castle-building, even though artillery had by now made large stone-built establishments less secure than in earlier days.

While richer men's homes were more spacious, fittings and furniture were still of the simplest. In the hall, the dining-table was a trestle, removed at night, so that servants could sleep on the floor. Only the service-table by the wall would be a fixture. There were no carpets or cupboards; one oak chair would be placed at the head of the table for the lord, everybody else sat on backless benches or stools. People ate off wooden trenchers or pewter, men carried their own knives, forks were hardly known; good manners demanded that food should be carried to the mouth with two fingers and a thumb only, and not in fistfuls.

In Scotland, neither burgesses nor landowners accumulated riches on the scale of the English wool merchants, in fact wealth was concentrated in the great monastic estates. Many of these, and especially the Cistercian ones, were managed better than those of any lay landlord in the period. Records of Cupar Abbey, for example, show that its great properties were drained, fertilized and cropped by methods which ensured excellent harvest, and the Cupar monks also developed something akin to ley-farming, a six-year rotation of crops designed to produce first-class grassland. Many monasteries planted orchards and herb gardens too.

It seemed as if the monasteries possessed almost unlimited means, but 15th century developments made this wealth largely illusory. The ecclesiastical dues extracted from Scotland by Rome became steadily heavier. In 1483, Arbroath had to pay 3,000 gold crowns to buy the Pope's confirmation of their newly elected Abbot, and this kind of thing reduced the Church to desperate straits at a time when Scottish Kings were learning fresh ways of extracting cash grants from religious foundations. By the end of the 15th century Abbots, and Bishops too, were beginning to feu large properties in an effort to balance their accounts. Feuing was a form of heritable land tenure based on a fixed rent, but though the feus brought the Church an immediate income, the cost of living was rising steeply and so the value of the fixed rents soon became nominal. Historians living in the 16th century all agreed that the Church was alienated from the people by its riches, and this was the common opinion, but the fact was that its capital assets were steadily dwindling.

That there were enlightened religious leaders at this time is proved by the history of Scotland's universities. Bishop Turnbull founded Glasgow University in 1451, and his Cathedral was closely involved in its progress for many years. The previous year St. Salvator's College in St. Andrews was set up, a residential centre of corporate life which afforded its students many advantages. Its founder was Bishop Kennedy of St. Andrews, a man of ability and patriotism who gave the Church excellent leadership. In 1495, Aberdeen University was established by another great churchman, Bishop Elphinstone. These three fine men were however exceptional and on the whole the leading ecclesiastics did nothing to stem the abuses which were becoming flagrant in church life.

When James II took over the direction of affairs in the 1450s, he proved to be a man of some energy. Ambitious to drive the English out of Roxburgh and Berwick, their last two strongholds in Scotland, he took a personal interest in the military preparations, particularly in a new type of cannon which was to be used at Roxburgh. The ill-luck which dogged the Stewart family now appeared again in a ghastly accident. The machine exploded while James was examining it and he was killed on the spot, in 1460, his thirtieth year. Roxburgh was taken by the Scots a few days later and destroyed to the point of obliteration. Berwick was also regained by the Scots, but in 1482 the English captured it again and it has remained English territory ever since.

Bishop Kennedy of St. Andrews, a real statesmen and a strong personality, became regent for the nine-year-old James III, but he died in 1465. During his few years in office, Kennedy negotiated successfully with the English who had now reached a critical stage in the Wars of the Roses, so that both sides wanted peace on the Border.

James III grew into a man whom 15th century people could not understand. He was a poor horseman, he was bored by athletic pursuits, disgusted by warfare, unsuccessful in knightly skills. He preferred his own company to that of other people, avoided men of noble birth, made friends with musicians and interested himself in architecture and necromancy. One interesting political achievement he did carry through in 1470, when he exchanged royal estates in Fife for the islands of Orkney and Shetland and thus became Earl of Orkney. This was confirmed by the Scottish Parliament in 1472, and these remote places became legally part of Scotland. The year 1472 saw the fulfilment of another semi-political success when the Pope made St. Andrews a metropolitan see, which freed Scotland at last from the interference of English Archbishops.

James III's nobles became alienated by his morose, suspicious nature and his tactless ways. They unscrupulously captured the sympathy of his young heir, who was about fifteen, and organized a revolt in 1488. During the rout of his troops from Sauchieburn, James III's horse bolted. The King was thrown to the ground. An unknown, but possibly priestly hand stabbed him as he lay helpless in the kitchen of a local miller's wife.

CHAPTER 11

James IV

People who knew James IV personally, even those who did business with him by correspondence, were always impressed by him. He had phenomenal energy of mind and body, an infectious zest for the enjoyments of life, an invigorating approach to everything. The great scholar Erasmus, who tutored one of his many illegitimate sons, mustered an imposing sequence of superlatives. 'He had a wonderful force of intellect, an incredible knowledge of all things, an invincible magnanimity, the sublimity of a royal heart, the largest charity and the most profuse liberality. There was no virtue which became a prince, in which he did not so excel as to gain the praise even of his enemies.' Pedro De Ayala, for several years Spanish Ambassador in Scotland, knew the King better than Erasmus and understood his faults, partly no doubt because they spent many long dark evenings playing cards together. But De Ayala had good things to say about him too. He admired the physical courage of the King, his self-confidence, his willingness to hear what his Council had to advise and then to make his own decisions. De Ayala was amazed at James IV's regularity in worship, his habit of fasting twice or three times a week; he was impressed also by his consistently moderate appetite for food and drink in the midst of a gluttonous society, and by his facility in picking up foreign languages.

James IV was certainly the most popular King Scotland had had for a long time and also the best known to his subjects. His extraordinary restlessness has been recorded by many writers. There seemed no limit to his energy. A fortnight here, two or three days there, a weekend somewhere else and then a prolonged journey to the far North and back to where he originally started from—this kind of programme constituted his normal way of life.

Everywhere he went, he had time and interest for ordinary people, he talked to everybody and was easy to approach, he enormously enjoyed all forms of sport, he loved horses and dogs, and he spent freely. His habitual extravagance and personal ostentation appealed to the people of his day, who liked him for his love of fine clothes and jewels and gear, as well as for the generosity he showed to such an unusual degree. The kitchen boy who broke his leg, the beggar woman on the roadside, the blind man 'be the gait', the man whose corn was trampled down by the royal horses, the sailor who fell from the rigging—these and many more received money gifts from him and all appear in the records of his personal expenses. His pleasure in dancing, in dicing, in playing cards, in watching guisers and taking part in all kinds of recreation endeared him to people too. That he founded a large family of illegitimate children and constantly sought and enjoyed the company of his mistresses seems to have been taken as understandable and perhaps even as another point in his favour.

For all his enjoyment, sensual, aesthetic and personal, the King could never rid himself of a devastating sense of guilt for his father's death. Though James IV had not actually killed him, James III's tragedy had been due in part to his son's collaboration with traitors. The prayers and pilgrimages and penances which impressed people so much were probably all carried out because of this sense of guilt, and the King's almost abnormal search for diversions and his distaste for relaxation may have stemmed from the same thing. All his life he wore a metal belt under his clothing to remind him of his shame.

The celebrations which took place at James IV's wedding in 1503 show what he could do when he really meant to stage a splendid show and they made an enormous impression at the time. The bride was Margaret Tudor, daughter of England's King, Henry VII. The marriage of course had its political significance, as the long preliminaries in negotiation and the carefully worded treaty show. It was to ensure for Scotland and England 'a good, real, sincere, true, entire and firm peace, bond, league and confederation on land and sea, to endure for ever'. Special clauses made new safeguards for the peaceful control of the

Borders. The Pope's sanction was invoked and whichever King broke his vows was to be excommunicated.

James rode out to meet his bride in splendid state and showed her dramatic gallantry. He accompanied her on the last leg of the journey into Edinburgh where money had flowed unceasingly in the preparation of pageantry, music, decoration, feasting and general jollification. Hundreds of pounds had gone to the King's own wedding garments and to those of his pages, thousands more to purveyors of food and wine, masons, builders, armourers, jewellers, joiners, minstrels, players and many more. Cloth of gold seemed to be in plentiful supply in Scotland that year, and at one of the royal feasts the menu included some sixty dishes, of which roast swan was one.

At the wedding itself, the King wore a white damask gown, crimson sleeves in his jacket, a cloth of gold doublet, scarlet hose. The crimson was taken up in the velvet border and lining of the Queen's robe, her train was carried by the Countess of Surrey, she wore her long hair loose under a rich coif and a little gold crown, specially made for her in Edinburgh by John Currour from eighty-three Treasury coins.

The modern reader cannot help feeling some sympathy for Margaret Tudor, then only thirteen years old, facing life in a strange country fully fifteen days' uncomfortable travel from home, with a man seventeen years her senior, already experienced in sexual relations, and reluctant to part with his mistresses. As time went by, however, she proved herself a true sister of Henry VIII, a virago of a woman, well able to impose her wishes on the people with whom she had to do.

The King perhaps understood that Margaret was bound to be frightened and homesick. He let her sit on the arm of his chair because she found her allotted stool too low, he had the walls plastered in the palaces at Stirling and Holyrood, he was patient about her luggage—twenty-four carts were required to carry her dresses on one occasion from Linlithgow to Edinburgh. Quite soon however, thirteen-year-old Margaret was writing to her father to complain that she was not being sufficiently considered, because her husband and his advisers were overriding her wishes.

The Queen generally stayed in or near Edinburgh, which now became the accepted capital, and James often made it the headquarters from which he set out on his interminable journeys to and fro in his kingdom. Margaret's share in these journeys was necessarily hindered after a while by her child-bearing. Between 1507 and 1514, she gave birth to six children, of whom only the future James V survived infancy. How lonely and disillusioned did these experiences make her feel? We do not know.

Music was a necessity to James. When he travelled, he sometimes sent Currie the Court Fool ahead, but journeying with him, he invariably had an odd collection of guisers, bards and Italian musicians. These accompanied him even when he was on pilgrimage to St. Ninian's shrine at Whithorn or to St. Duthac's at Tain. He played the lute himself, and the court baggage always included lyres, pipes, stringed instruments, and sometimes even a collapsible organ, which was actually hauled over the Mounth and re-assembled at the King's destination. One can safely guess that James enjoyed the songs which people sang in the fields and steadings. R. L. Mackie quotes some of their titles in *James IV of Scotland* (1958)—'Broom, broom on hill', 'The Frog cam to the Mill Door', 'Be yon woodside' and 'Late, late on evenings'.

James took an interest in religious music too. He endowed his Chapel Royal with sixteen canons and 'as many prebends skilled in song, with six boy clerics . . . trained in song or fit to be instructed therein'. The Royal Musical Association published in 1957 *Music of Scotland* 1500-1700. In this, a collection of 16th century choral and instrumental works has been assembled. It includes religious music, composed by Robert Carver of Scone in 1508, in a style described as 'massive yet vigorous'. James must have known Carver and listened to his works.

The King enjoyed poetry as well as music and this was a pleasure shared by many of his subjects. It was stimulated by local minor poets, of whose work little now remains in identifiable form, and also by some who have become famous. The best known are Robert Henryson, Gavin Douglas and William Dunbar.

Robert Henryson lived in the last part of the 15th century and died when James IV was still a young man. He wrote poems, ballads, metrical forms of Aesop's Fables, and a longer work called *The Testament of Cresseid*, designed as a sequel to Chaucer's *Troilus and Criseyde*. People liked his work for its vivid, rhythmic lines, its good, earthy vernacular and its undertones of melancholy. Henryson's narrative poems were full of chivalry and drama and they appealed to men and women whose lives offered little that was romantic. Like many Scots, he was fond of pointing the moral and some of his versified fables had a topical reference. His best gift was perhaps descriptive. Country scenes familiar to rural people, country folk, animals, birds, stand out in lyrical but pointed phrases, touched both with humour and with pity. His understanding, his capacity indeed for identifying himself with other people, sometimes stirred him to write poetry of the highest quality. R. L. Mackie says of his *Testament* that there are passages in it 'that Chaucer would have been proud to call his own', which in fact Chaucer could not have bettered. But though Henryson's work may have something of Chaucer's quality, it is necessarily different in character, for Henryson was born and nurtured in Scotland: and so his poetry reflects the mind and emotions of a people Chaucer never knew.

Gavin Douglas was a son of the Earl of Angus and he became Bishop of Dunkeld. He was more of a scholar than Henryson. He too wrote allegories, but they were long and involved and too heavily moral in tone to appeal to most readers; they are redeemed by his gift of description, especially of natural scenery, though even this was often devoted to wintry, shadowed beauty. Douglas undertook the astonishing task of translating Vergil's *Aeneid* into Scots verse, and here he was breaking new ground, for no Scottish writer had attempted such a thing before.

The most prolific writer in James IV's day was William Dunbar, known in contemporary English society as 'The Rhymer of Scotland', a sort of Poet Laureate really, for he had an annual pension from the King, which he himself considered very niggardly. In his poems, Dunbar described many of the great occasions of the day, tournaments, city functions, the royal wedding, the Queen's visit to Aberdeen. He also wrote about the King's illicit love affairs, about the merchants of Edinburgh, about James Dog, the Keeper of the Queen's Wardrobe and Currie the Court

Fool. Like the others, Dunbar loved allegory and, in the elaborate poem called *The Golden Targe*, he described a dream, in which he witnessed the triumph of Love in a conflict with Reason. *The Lament for the Makars*, an elegy, pays tribute to poets such as Blind Harry, Shaw, Kennedy and some forgotten authors whose works have been lost. 'Timor mortis conturbat me' was the sobering refrain of this lament, which invited its readers to grieve over the shadows closing round us all. There is a strange undercurrent of religion in some of Dunbar's work, a religion relieved by little hope, rather perhaps an obsession with death than a confidence in redemption. He wrote humorous and satirical verse too however and at times descended with lusty enjoyment to the bawdy. He had none of Henryson's gift of pity, except for himself and his own grievances.

Modern readers are bound to have difficulty in understanding the poetry of this time, written in archaic language and expressing the contemporary mood. You get the impression that people lived under a cloud, of which they were not always consciously aware. Storm, rain, cold evening shadows, the flight of bats, sombre though often majestic manifestations of natural beauty, seemed to focus men's attention more than the sunlit uplands. Were they afraid? If so, what did they fear? Of joyous gaiety, of contemplative poetry there was apparently little. Nonetheless, these writers opened a new world to their contemporaries and secular literature began to count for something at last.

De Ayala was impressed by the King's love of reading and by his knowledge of Latin, French, German, Flemish, Italian and Spanish. R. L. Mackie suggests that James had a nodding acquaintance rather than real knowledge of these languages, and that, while he bought books from time to time, there is not much evidence of his reading them frequently. Nonetheless, James was interested in literature and he could not fail to be attracted to the new printing technique, known in London since 1476. Two burgesses of Edinburgh, Walter Chapman and Andrew Myllar, were granted a patent by James IV in 1507, to establish a printing press operated with movable metal types, the first of its kind in Scotland. The King thought it would be useful for the printing of statutes, mass-books and chronicles. So indeed it was. The Church and the Universities were almost immediately able to secure better supplies of professional literature.

But the introduction of printing was far more important than the King could guess. Now, for the first time, relatively cheap books could be produced quickly. The printers at once realized that they could command a market far exceeding clerical or academic limits if they catered for other interests as well. Printing made a more significant and immediate effect on popular thought than any modern invention prior to radio. It brought to Scotland ideas profoundly exciting and disturbing. Ten years after Chapman and Myllar began printing Dunbar's poems, Luther made his explosive protest against Indulgences, and the Reformation began. Its work was done in the printers' establishments quite as much as in the pulpits, for books were now produced so that they could be read by the many rather than looked at by the few.

Under different circumstances James IV would have enjoyed the new vitality of Renaissance writers and he was enthusiastic about Bishop Elphinstone's university at Aberdeen. As he pointed out to Pope Alexander VI, people in northern Scotland lived too far away from St. Andrews and Glasgow to make proper use of them for their sons' education. He was delighted when King's College, named in honour of himself, was built in Aberdeen: its first principal, Hector Boece, knew Erasmus and was in sympathy with the new Greek studies of the day, though he did not succeed in revitalizing Scottish students or their teachers.

In the early 16th century, European and English Universities were much influenced by the humanism of the Renaissance scholars, such as Erasmus, Colet, Melancthon. 'Literae humaniores' constituted a study of the best Greek and Roman classics in the original text and not in bad translations. The new humanists tested long-accepted ideas by examining afresh all the available evidence, and they thought of the old-fashioned schoolmen with much the same impatience that certain schools of scientists have recently adopted towards defenders of a classical education.

This enjoyment of classical literature, with its stimulus to bold thinking, informed criticism and fluent, beautiful writing, unfortunately hardly touched the Scottish Universities. Here the traditional disciplines of the Middle Ages were carried on, although their vitality was now outworn. Medieval scholasticism, based on logic, had afforded genuine intellectual life to the best minds of the 13th and even 14th centuries, but it had degenerated into a pointless and sterile system by this time.

The most renowned Scottish scholar in the early decades of the 16th century was probably John Major, a man of massive learning, who wrote the old, pedantic Latin and enjoyed the fruitless logical disputations of former years. Of him, Melancthon wrote with a venomous exasperation which still rings across the centuries: 'He is now, I am told, the Prince of Paris divines. Good Heavens! What wagonloads of trifling! What pages he fills with disputes whether there can be any horsemanship without a horse, whether the sea was salt when God made it.'

For seventeen years in the mid-16th century, Major was Provost of St. Salvator's College in St. Andrews, upholding the outworn ideals of the past and resisting ideas of his age both in religion and in learning. Major's *History of Greater Britain* is a work of great interest as it reflects so clearly the attitude of its author and the climate of thought in which he lived. It can be read in an English translation published by the Scottish History Society. Not all his statements may be taken at their face value, emphatic and vivid as many of them are.

James was determined that the three Scottish Universities should serve the country in a practical way, rather than continue as training centres exclusively for professional ecclesiastics, because he believed that if the sons of the nobility were properly educated, responsible secular officials would do their work more effectively. As early as 1496, he had a statute passed by which the eldest sons of all freeholders were to be sent to grammar schools and thereafter to a university, a most original measure, unprecedented in a country where literacy had been almost confined to the church. Perhaps because so many boys arrived on their doorsteps at the early age of thirteen or fourteen, the universities developed the unfortunate system called regenting.

By this, one master or regent saw a whole generation of students through the entire academic course of several years. This had the advantage of giving wild adolescents continuous handling by one man who knew them well, but it prevented specialization, limited original research and made for uninspired teaching. It continued in the Scottish Universities until the 18th century.

During James IV's reign, life became easier and conditions better. The ledgers of Andrew Halyburton, a prosperous Scottish merchant, illustrate this. At Middelburg and other European centres, Halyburton bought damasks, silks, velvets, writing-paper, feather beds and pillows, jewels, tombstones, carts, wheel-barrows, groceries, especially spice, olives, figs, almonds and raisins. In return, he exported the traditional products, namely hides, wool, furs, and salted fish. Europe was still Roman Catholic and consumed quantities of red herrings and similar fare during the frequent fasts, and people were still so exposed to furious winter winds that much clothing was made of leather and fur.

Halyburton's books reveal important facts. Scotland was unable to make at home goods which a well-developed country should have produced: she had no skills with which to manufacture articles for export: her balance of trade depended on raw materials of a primitive kind which foreigners could make into saleable articles. It is significant too that most of his imported luxuries were bought by ecclesiastical dignitaries and not by Scottish nobles or burgesses.

What these 15th century ledgers do not reveal is probably more significant than anything else. Where trade moves, ideas move. Not only the men of business themselves, but also their servants must have observed strange ways and talked of this and that in the cities of Europe. A new vitality of thought began to develop in Scotland among people who had had little formal education.

There were however no wealthy cities with capital to spare, no citizens rich enough to patronize the arts. This is one reason why the Renaissance did not influence Scotland so much as other European countries. There seems little evidence that Scotsmen of this period were interested in painting. Even James IV seems neither to have sought out artists nor to have bought their pictures.

But Scotsmen were interested in architecture. Now that methods of warfare had changed, the old solid towers and keeps were not so easily defensible and their discomforts therefore became intolerable. Men who had travelled realized that the new culture had material as well as aesthetic merits, with its emphasis on the individual's right to enjoy being himself, a person entitled to dignity, beauty and even some physical comfort in his surroundings. So nobles enlarged the living apartments in their older castles, sometimes by adding new wings, sometimes by ingeniously exploiting upper storeys. New buildings were more generously constructed, with finely decorated exterior façades, imposing outer doorways and larger windows, while indoor rooms were designed to dignified proportions, and fitted with large ornamental fireplaces. Much of Linlithgow Palace as you see it today dates from this period and the same is true of Falkland Palace. Many other castles were also partially rebuilt, Craigmillar for example, Huntley, Caerlaverock, Crichton, to mention only a few. French designs in structure and decoration were still sought after, but Scottish craftsmen were not enslaved to them. Their work was conditioned by the nature and site of the buildings they worked on, each with its individual character.

De Ayala, writing home to Ferdinand and Isabella, said that Scottish people lived in stone-built houses with glazed windows, that they burned coal in their hearths, had fine collections of continental furniture, and cultivated charming gardens. Susceptible to ladies' fashions, De Ayala specially admired the headdresses worn by Scottish women, the handsomest in all Europe. As he mixed only with court society and knew little about districts beyond central Scotland, we need not interpret his comments too generally, but he recorded accurately enough a rising standard of living in the south-east. On what it was based remains something of a mystery. De Ayala himself noted the deficiencies in Scottish husbandry, which on the whole failed to extract as much from the soil as should have been possible, except on some of the Cistercian properties. The burghs were still pursuing their traditional policies which tended to restrict rather than to enlarge trade. There is room for much research still into this field, for it is clear that the King and his nobles could not have spent money so freely as they did if there had been no solid foundation to the nation's economy.

James' interests were not confined to cultural and recreative activities. He made courageous efforts to reduce the country to law and order. These indeed were needed in a land where it was possible for David Drummond to organize in 1490 the burning of a Strathearn church packed with his personal enemies. Drummond was executed, and so were a number of other trouble-makers. In the Border regions, disorder was continual and James established courts at Dumfries and elsewhere, with instructions that marauders were to be brought to trial and hanged.

He took more active measures in the Highlands and Islands than any of his predecessors, and actually made journeys in person right into the heart of this wild, uncivilized country, whose language, surprisingly, he could himself speak. No other medieval Scottish ruler is believed to have had the Gaelic. James abolished the Lordship of the Isles and forfeited to the crown all the properties of the fourth and last man to hold this title. He repaired and strengthened castles in key positions, such as Tarbert and Urquhart, he built new ones, at Loch Kilkerran and Inverlochy: these were to serve as bases for the administration of law and order. He revised the arrangements about Sheriffs and Sheriff Courts, increasing their number, so that the west and north-west should be adequately covered for judicial purposes. He used his fleet to intimidate those who disliked all this inter-ference and he made a point of showing friendship towards as many Highland chiefs as he could, while sanctioning merciless punishment of those who were unruly.

His energetic and bold attempts, unequalled by his pre-decessors, did little permanent good. The Highlands were too inaccessible for any medieval King to bring them under control. The Highland line continued, therefore, as a frontier between two peoples who lived completely apart from each other and who developed quite different traditions. James IV has been criticized as 'ineffective' because he failed to make his writ run permanently in the Highlands and Islands. This seems hard criticism, as no

Government really succeeded in this difficult assignment until the second half of the 18th century.

What was James IV's measure as a political thinker or leader? He was sound enough in his efforts to control the uncontrollable within his own realms, but he seems to have had little discrimination when he came to consider political relationships with other countries. He believed Perkin Warbeck to be a genuine claimant for the English throne and risked a major war with England in 1497 with the purpose of dethroning Henry VII. Mercifully, war on the grand scale at this time was averted, though not because of any good sense on James IV's part. A later enthusiasm was to go on Crusade against the Infidel Turk, an out-dated ambition, which suggests that James' abnormal boyhood had prevented him from becoming fully adult in his approach to European problems. He was perfectly serious in his desire to go Crusading and it was with this in mind that he built his famous fleet. Wood was felled on Loch Lomondside, especially at Luss, and also throughout Fife, and it was bought from Norway and France. Seacoast towns were ordered to build twenty-ton vessels and James took a personal and furiously energetic interest in the whole business. The ship which gave him the greatest pleasure of all was the *Great Michael*. James told the English ambassador that she carried more weapons than the French ever brought to a siege, a remark which the Englishman considered 'a great crack'.

Some of James IV's admirals and sea-captains were of the first order. Sir Andrew Wood, who commanded *The Flower* and *The Yellow Carvel*, served James until he was an old man, always with distinction. There were three seafaring brothers who were equally celebrated—Andrew, Robert and John Barton—sons of a fine sea-captain who was ultimately taken prisoner by the Portuguese. They all carried out punitive measures against English pirates, also against Dutch and Portuguese marauders, and themselves indulged in a good deal of fairly successful piracy. At no period in medieval history did Scotland's maritime strength reach such a pitch as under James IV's direction.

The end of James IV and all that he stood for is the saddest story in all the tragic history of medieval Scotland. In 1511, almost all western Europe joined in a Holy League under the Pope and against France. Henry VIII, James' brilliant young brother-in-law, a king of immense promise at this time, joined the Holy League. Because of the long alliance between his own country and France, James decided, against the advice of some of his best counsellors, to take active part on behalf of the French: he hoped too that victory in this campaign would help him later in his Crusading plans. It ended in the horror of Flodden Field in 1513. James was killed in action, with thirteen Scottish earls, two bishops, two abbots, the dean of Glasgow, the provost of Edinburgh and thousands of Scotland's best young men of all ranks.

Since 1295, Scotland had known no reasonably long period unbroken by warfare. Repeated efforts had been made to secure peace by the negotiation of royal marriages; Malcolm III, his daughter Maud or Matilda, Alexander II, Alexander III, David II and James IV all married members of the English royal family. David I and James I married distinguished ladies of the English nobility and the Maid of Norway was betrothed to Edward I's son before her early death. In spite of these marriage treaties, designed to make peace assured, the two countries fought each other unmercifully, and the wars, which afflicted the least prosperous part of England, wrecked the towns, villages, monasteries and farmlands of the districts most vital to Scotland's well-being. They also killed many of the best leaders and finest young men of a country so limited in population that such personalities were greatly needed and hard to replace. And they left Scotland with a deadly hatred for England.

Almost more essential to a medieval kingdom than consistent peace was the continuity of strong authority on the throne. It is startling to count up the protracted royal minorities which crippled the power of medieval Scottish monarchy. Malcolm IV was eleven when he came to the throne; Alexander III, eight; the Maid of Norway three; David II six; James I eleven; James II seven; James III eight. James IV was fifteen, by comparison quite a mature young man, but when he was killed at Flodden in 1513, James V was a baby a year old and this James died less than a week after the birth of his daughter and heiress, Mary. She became famous as Mary, Queen of Scots, and she was forced to abdicate when her son, James VI, was not yet two.

During the years between 1286 and 1513, there were therefore only brief intervals when an adult King of any strength was on the Scottish throne. So the great baronial families were able to pursue their selfish race for personal aggrandizement and grievously to retard Scotland's development. When the 16th century opened, Scotland was quite unprepared for the impact of the religious revolution which swept Europe, or for the redoubled efforts of England to reduce her to servitude. She was still a feudal country, with only a tiny middle class, and a limited share in international trade. Worse still, she had only the beginnings of a national culture, Renaissance thought had made little impact on her Universities, most of her people were illiterate, her religious leaders were corrupt, her constitutional machinery was controlled by vested interests.

The plain truth is that Scotland was about three-quarters of a century behind the times. In England, parliamentary institutions and local government by the early 1500s had given the lesser gentry and the leading burgesses some experience of responsibility, town life had prospered sufficiently to produce an influential middle class, feudal controls had been curbed by the economic changes of the 14th century.

Had James IV lived to bring up his son himself and to consolidate the improvements he had set going in his kingdom, Scotland's experience in the next hundred years might have been vastly better. The battle of Flodden was the worst tragedy the nation had known since Alexander III's sudden death.

PART TWO

———

The Reformation and the Covenant

CHAPTER 12

Religious and Political Turmoil

During the early 16th century, Protestantism was born and the Roman Catholic Church met the challenge. Luther's Theses against indulgences were published in 1517, Zwingli founded his Reformed Church in Switzerland during the 1520s, Calvin produced his *Institutes of the Christian Religion* in 1536. By 1541, Ignatius Loyola secured the Pope's recognition for his Society of Jesus and four years later the Council of Trent began a long campaign to strengthen the Roman Catholic position. Rivalry between the old and the new religions plunged all Western Europe into bitter controversy.

Nowhere in Europe was the Church so degraded as in Scotland. In 1549 and 1552, the Scottish Bishops held reforming Councils in a belated effort to set their house in order, and these openly admitted that the root of heresy had been 'the corruption of morals and profane lewdness of life in churchmen of almost all ranks, together with crass ignorance of literature and of all the liberal arts'. Archibald Hay, a relative of Beaton's, warned him that clergy were being ordained 'who hardly knew the order of the alphabet' and that priests 'come to the heavenly table who have not slept off last night's debauch'.

The priests knew Latin sufficiently to hurry through their offices by rote, but many of them could hardly repeat the Lord's Prayer or the Creed intelligibly. The dignity of worship which the ancient liturgies had been designed to foster could not exist in churches without educated or even reverent clergy, without choirs, without instructed worshippers. Churchgoers were observers of mangled rites which neither they nor the celebrants understood, they took no part in response, in prayer or in singing. So people went to Mass reluctantly or not at all.

The leaders of the Church were not fit to handle the situation. They blatantly ignored the rule of priestly celibacy, and this undermined their influence. Bishop Hepburn, 'the great dilapidator of the See of Moray', had nine children for whom he provided at the expense of the Church, and almost all his colleagues founded illegitimate families too. They were following the royal example in this.

James IV had several illegitimate sons. One of them, Alexander Stewart, he made Archbishop of St. Andrews at the age of twelve. This boy was also Abbot of Dunfermline and Prior of Coldingham. The properties which went with these appointments were held for him *in commendam*, a form of trust much in use, which gave the commendators all the financial advantages and none of the responsibilities attached to clerical life. Barons and bishops secured valuable properties *in commendam* for their protégés too, and the system encouraged pluralism. It became common for one cleric to hold several benefices simultaneously and to put in curates to do the work. These were some of Archibald Hay's men who scarcely knew the order of the alphabet.

Monastic communities were now very small. In the early 16th century, Melrose numbered twenty-three, Kinloss twenty, and these were comparatively high figures. Abbot Thomas Crystall of Kinloss was in fact a fine man, who had high ideals and improved the standards of his house. He was however an exception. Most abbots and priors were primarily concerned with economic problems and spiritually the monasteries were lax.

It was difficult for religious institutions to uphold the disciplines for which they had been founded, and it was also difficult for them to administer their properties wisely. In order to raise ready money which it badly needed, the Church let out its estates by feuing, and so bore all the odium of capitalism without retaining its advantages, since the rents steadily depreciated in value. At the same time, the Pope sanctioned heavy ecclesiastical subsidies to the Scottish crown. A corrupt State therefore became indebted to a corrupt Church and there remained no supreme authority untainted by abuse.

Religious leaders economized on current expenditure by neglecting to repair their buildings. All over the country, church walls crumbled and roofs leaked. By 1512 the little Cathedral on Lismore had become so ruinous that James IV suggested the See of Argyll should be moved elsewhere. Many other examples could be quoted. Protestant zeal of the wrong kind has been blamed for the destruction of many Scottish churches which had begun to collapse long before the new religion was known.

Ordinary people could not understand that the financial position of the Church was fundamentally unsound when they saw how some clerics lived. Adam Colquhoun, parson of Stobo, represented a type of priest who did untold harm. He lived with his two sons and their mother in luxurious comfort. His house in Glasgow was stocked with expensive furniture, feather beds, velvet, damask and silken hangings, gold and silver valuables, magnificent suits of clothes, armour and archery outfits, his kitchen with quantities of preserved meat, fish, groceries and wine. Besides being a collector of silver plate, he was a connoisseur in up-to-date novelties. He possessed the first cupboard recorded in Scotland, a striking clock, a set of Flemish carving knives, a fork, a silver toothpick and in his bedroom he had a parrot in a cage. When Colquhoun died, in 1542, his nephew claimed the inheritance, but in the legal case which followed, Adam's sons were formally legitimated, and they secured his entire fortune.

This was a time when plain people in country and town were living in poverty, when a bad harvest or an epidemic brought not hardship but starvation. Though Colquhoun's wealth was exceptional, many priests had private establishments where they brought up their children more comfortably than their parishioners could and it made for cynicism and embitterment among the laity. Most parish priests however were very poor, because they received only a pittance from the monastic houses or cathedrals which had appropriated the parishes and which absorbed most of the tithes and other revenues for other purposes. One effect of such poverty was that ordinary priests were often very ignorant, with the unfortunate result that the Church was weakest precisely where it ought to have been strongest—at the parochial level where it was most in touch with the people.

The Reformation and the Covenant

The inevitable consequences of a royal minority created harmful complications. After the débâcle of Flodden in 1513, intrigues among the nobles were fomented by James IV's unscrupulous widow, Margaret Tudor. The young James V was given no sound upbringing and in childhood was exposed to evil influences. In young manhood he thought himself a sincere Catholic, but he had an irresponsible attitude to religion and scant regard for integrity.

Sincere religious people were at a loss to know where to turn for the leadership they needed. It was the tragedy of the Church that it could not offer some of its best members the spiritual direction they were seeking. And there was a strong desire for purer spiritual teaching, for genuine worship at this time, as if, despite all the corruption they had seen and all the faulty teaching they had received, people had a spontaneous and natural hunger for religious truth.

Many of them found what they wanted in the Bible. This had not been studied in a scholarly way or used in personal devotions for hundreds of years. Within a decade of James IV's death in 1513, Scotsmen were eagerly absorbing it in a language they could understand. At first, a 14th century Wycliffite translation was used, with the archaic words altered by a Scot called Murdoch Nisbet. Much more easily assimilated was the New Testament secretly printed at Worms in 1525, by the Englishman, William Tyndale. The Scottish Parliament made it illegal to handle this publication, but in spite of this copies were smuggled into the country.

One of the earliest leaders in the new Protestant movement of Scotland was a great-grandson of James II, a young man of much personal charm, named Patrick Hamilton. He met Lutherans in Paris and in Marburg and returned to St. Andrews in 1527, an active supporter of the new doctrines. He was the author of a Latin commentary, known as *Patrick's Places*. Like Tyndale's Testament, it became a best-seller, especially after its translation into English by John Frith.

Lutheran teaching therefore made its impact upon Scotland largely through print. Those who could read found refreshment of spirit in the beautiful prose of Tyndale's translation and in Patrick Hamilton's commentary. The purity of Christ's love, the transforming effect of the Crucifixion and the Resurrection, the

126

assured promise of redemption for believers gave people an experience of new light, new freedom in the power of Christ.

Patrick Hamilton was a rich man with powerful connections, recently married, enjoying apparently every prospect of a successful career. Archbishop James Beaton of St. Andrews determined to make an example of him and he was arrested and ordered to recant. The Archbishop was forthwith faced not with submission but with a declaration of faith. 'As to my confession, I will not deny it for awe of your fire, for my confession and belief is in Jesus Christ. I will rather be content that my body burn in this fire for confession of my faith in Christ than my soul should burn in the fire of Hell for denying the same.'

So they burnt Patrick Hamilton in their fire at St. Andrews. Unfamiliar as yet with the technique of building such fires and hampered by squalls of rain, they took six hours to kill him. His serenity throughout the long torture shattered the complacency of everybody who saw it, hardened as people were to brutality. Somebody offered the Archbishop advice which he should have taken seriously. 'My Lord, if ye burn any more, except ye follow my counsel, ye will utterly destroy yourselves. If ye burn them, let them be burned in deep cellars, for the reek of Master Patrick Hamilton has infected as many as it blew upon'.

The people infected by the reek of Hamilton's fire were far more numerous than the Archbishop and his advisers could guess, nor did they know that members of the Augustinian and Dominican orders, also of the nobility, some of Scotland's keenest thinkers, were strongly attracted to the faith for which Hamilton had suffered.

The King himself never failed to encourage those who made open fun of religion. By 1537, when he was only twenty-four, James V was looking for a tutor to direct the education of an illegitimate son, a child called James Stewart. He chose George Buchanan, a scholar of prodigious learning, steeped in the new humanism, who had so far spent most of his life in Europe. James was enchanted by Buchanan's gift of satire, and urged him to publish his poems. These made mock of the Franciscans, and they were skilfully written, in no sense great poetry, but full of sarcasm and deadly invective. At this time, Buchanan was not much attracted to Protestantism, but he helped to inflame hostility against the Roman Catholics.

One of James V's Gentleman-ushers, named Sir David Lyndesay, also diverted him with poems in which the vices of the clergy were made amusing. In 1540, the King and the Court, with a number of Church dignitaries, assembled during Epiphany, at Linlithgow, for the first performance of Lyndesay's famous dramatic piece *Ane Pleasant Satyre of the Thrie Estaitis*. Richly entertaining, highly dramatic and pointed with topical reference, this play ridiculed the clerics who hated Chastity, revered Folly, faked relics and exploited paupers. James V and his entourage found it entirely delightful.

By this time, James V's uncle, Henry VIII of England, was the bitter enemy of the Pope, bent upon breaking the power of Rome in England. He wanted James V to marry his daughter, to give up the French alliance and to turn against the Pope. James V understood in no way the gravity of the religious crisis breaking upon Europe, but he disliked Henry VIII, and preferred the old links with Rome and with France. He married Madeline, the French King's daughter, and after her early death, Mary of Guise. This second wife belonged to the most powerful family in France. Of her seven brothers, the best known was the Cardinal Duke of Lorraine, who organized vigorous persecution of religious reformers in his own country, and for whose judgment Mary had sisterly respect. She was herself a woman of ability, endowed with the Guise brains and well accustomed to political intrigue.

When he discovered that James did not intend to oblige him, Henry enticed many Scottish noblemen into his own service, and used them in his efforts to wreck their country's wellbeing. He found it easy to do this, because James had alienated a number of them by his pro-French policy and by his readiness to depend on French armed assistance. Furthermore, Henry's dissolution of the English monasteries had enriched land-hungry subjects and there were Scotsmen who could hardly wait to enter upon similar good fortune. Secular greed for monastic property had much to do with the political disloyalty and the religious intrigue that were ugly features of this period.

Henry VIII was now possessed by a fanatical passion to dominate Scottish affairs by armed force and he was a formidable enemy. Exasperated by James' French sympathies, he organized an invasion of Scotland in 1542, which James wanted to arrest by a counter-invasion of England. The Scottish nobles saw in this merely a manoeuvre to support France and they refused to cross the Border. On November 24th, 1542, James' small army was defeated at Solway Moss. Two weeks later, his daughter and heir, Princess Mary, was born. Six days after that James suddenly died, aged thirty, and the baby was proclaimed Queen.

So Mary of Guise was the Queen Mother. She was confronted by an English King who now intended to absorb Scotland into his own domain, and who was not only an excommunicated man but also a megalomaniac. She was committed to Roman Catholicism, while Scotland was already shot through with the explosive forces of Protestantism. She was supported by powerful French interests, while many Scottish nobles were in the service of Henry VIII. The situation was complex and dangerous enough to tax the resources of the most gifted ruler.

Her most trusted adviser was David Beaton, Abbot of Arbroath and Bishop of Mirepoix in Languedoc. He had succeeded his uncle James Beaton as Archbishop of St. Andrews and, thanks to French influence, he had become a Cardinal. He was a man of the times, unscrupulous, immoral, but very able, and set against allowing Scotland to be swamped by England. He and the Queen Mother were disgusted by Henry VIII's proposal that the baby heiress of Scotland should be married to the English prince Edward, and especially by the conditions attached to the plan. Henry VIII wanted the little girl to be sent to England and brought up under his care: he demanded that he should be recognized as Lord-Superior of Scotland, and that key fortresses should be handed over to English garrisons. He was acting as if the evil genius of Edward I at his worst had found re-incarnation in himself and, like Edward, he had at his back a number of Scottish lords who were residing in England.

Enraged by the refusal of the Scottish government to accept such proposals of marriage, Henry launched on Scotland in 1544 and the following year the cruel invasions under the Earl of

Hertford which became known as the Rough Wooing. Leith was captured, the Border Abbeys destroyed, the Lothians ravaged, 243 villages and five market towns laid in ruins. The cruelties of the English in these campaigns did ineradicable harm. The Protestant cause became identified in many people's minds with Henry VIII's policy, people were revolted by all that he stood for: patriotism demanded subservience to Beaton, support of the Roman Catholics, adherence to the French alliance. Worse still was the legacy of hatred. The traditional hostility of Scots against Englishmen which spoiled the Union of 1707 and survived the 18th century had long roots in these terrible years from 1544 to 1547.

Henry VIII died in 1546, but his policy was continued by the Duke of Somerset on behalf of Edward VI and in 1547 the English victory at Pinkie Cleugh was the climax of the whole bloody business.

Meantime the Protestants were struggling to understand the new faith and to adjust themselves to its claims. Some of their leaders suffered Hamilton's fate, all of them lived in danger, and as many as could manage it went abroad. George Wishart for example left in 1538, under grave suspicion because he had started teaching from the Greek New Testament in Montrose Grammar School. After six years in England and on the continent, he came back, in 1544, when Cardinal Beaton's persecution of reformers was at its height. He preached then in Dundee, in Ayr, in village churches, in the fields. The theme he best loved was the liberation of the believer in Christ, as it is expounded in Romans 8.

When plague broke out in Dundee, he went back and ministered to the people who were suffering; then he moved to Leith. In 1546, Beaton's agents arrested him in Haddington. It was a time of acute political tension, when Protestants were considered traitors, working in the interests of the English. In March 1546, two weeks after Luther's death, Wishart was burned in St. Andrews, in the presence of the Cardinal.

Two months later, Beaton was murdered in his own castle. No news could have delighted Henry VIII more. He hated this active and intelligent statesman, because he thought that only Beaton could organize Scotland sufficiently to withstand him. The

Cardinal's murderers were young noblemen acting like gangsters
and to secure themselves from retribution they fortified themselves
within St. Andrew's Castle, where they remained under siege
until July. During these weeks they were joined by a strange
selection of sympathizers, one of whom they made into a kind of
garrison chaplain. This was John Knox, a young priest who had
met George Wishart two months before his death and had been
greatly impressed and disturbed by him. Knox, like others who
were interested in the Protestant view, could not help rejoicing
over the Cardinal's death, although he had nothing to do with it,
but he did not like the company he found in the castle, a rough,
immoral crowd of ill-disciplined soldiers and hangers-on.

Mary of Guise was shocked by these events. She sent for help
from France and in July 1546 the French fleet attacked St.
Andrews Castle, overcame its defenders, and carried the leaders
away to the horrible punishment of rowing in the galleys. John
Knox was one of those who suffered.

The Queen Mother's policy was now concentrated on beating
off the English, crushing Protestantism and safeguarding the
future of her daughter. All three aims were wrapped up in the
third. The little girl had been kept on Inchmahome island in the
Lake of Menteith and then in the Castle on Dumbarton Rock.
In 1548, she was sent to France.

The French King was well pleased with this arrangement. The
child would be brought up at his court, and married to his son,
Scotland would become a French dependency. Meantime the
English were being beaten out of France and they were recalling
their troops from Scotland, so that the Auld Alliance seemed
firmer and more successful than ever. The Roman Catholic
Council of Trent was making progress with its reforming decrees,
the Protestant Princes in Germany were being beaten by the
Emperor, Henry II of France was preparing edicts to crush the
Huguenots. All seemed set for a Roman Catholic Europe under
the domination of a French King who controlled Scotland and
would soon absorb England too. The English King, Edward VI,
was sickening for the tuberculosis which killed him, his sisters
were illegitimate according to Catholic doctrine, the Queen of
Scots was the next heir to the English throne.

Henry II of France was so reassured about the situation that early in 1549 he released the St. Andrews prisoners. John Knox therefore made his way to England, the only country except Switzerland where Protestantism seemed to have a chance of survival.

CHAPTER 13

Protestant Scotland

When John Knox left his forced labour early in 1549, it seemed that the Roman Catholic pro-French régime was permanently established in Scotland. In England, the security of all reformers depended upon the boy Edward VI, whose Protestant principles were as strong as the Roman Catholic loyalty of his elder sister and heir, Mary Tudor, but whose health was already undermined by a 'tough, strong, streining cough'.

The decade between 1549 and 1559 proved one of the most important in all Scottish history. The year 1560 was a turning-point which changed the whole course of events. In that year Mary of Guise died, the French alliance abruptly ended, permanent peace was made with England. Above all, the Protestant Church was established in Scotland. Even in the highest moments of faith, no reformer living in the 1550s could have anticipated such an outcome.

In this chapter, the developments which led to this extraordinary climax are described, the nature of the new Church discussed. The terrible débâcle of Mary, Queen of Scots, which followed the reformers' triumph and caused repercussions of incalculable significance is also recorded here. The dominant personalities of the period, so far as Scotland was concerned, were John Knox, Mary of Guise and Mary Queen of Scots.

In John Knox himself, a finely wrought, conscience-ridden and mentally tortured man, the tensions of the age were concentrated.

For almost five years after his release in 1549, Knox lived in England, where the Protestant Edward VI was King, and where he met all the leading reformers and especially Cranmer. He was highly thought of, appointed to a royal chaplaincy and offered a bishopric. When Mary Tudor came to the English throne in 1553, dedicated to the recapture of her country for Rome, Knox was one of many who left England. He went to Frankfurt-on-the-Main and then to Geneva. Already he had thought with fierce concentration about the meaning of Christianity. Now, in Calvin, he met a reformer whose powerful and logical mind helped him to work out his revolutionary ideas. Not until 1559 did he permanently settle in his own country. The foundations of the new church there were laid by other hands than his.

He was a man 'in spiritual torment', as Lord Eustace Percy puts it. There was agony in breaking loose from strong and even yet hallowed tradition; the revolt from the old faith cost him years of intellectual strife; his European outlook forced him to identify himself with problems from which men of the parish pump were spared.

Everywhere Knox saw ruin for the young Protestant Church. Reformers were being driven under by Mary of Guise in Scotland, by the Emperor in Germany, by Henry II in France, and after 1553 they seemed doomed to extinction in England. Only in Switzerland, a tiny island of resistance, embraced by almost impassable mountains but surrounded too by mighty Roman Catholic powers, did there seem any hope of Protestant survival. Within the ranks of the Reformers themselves there was no unanimity but stark disagreement, and they were weakened by the influences of those fellow-travellers who wanted to exploit religion in the interests of materialism. This background of agonizing tension and vicarious pain must be remembered when one reads of Knox's later policies in Scotland.

Mary of Guise was not only a Roman Catholic, but also, naturally enough, a French patriot, and like Knox at least to the extent that she saw the international significance of national policies. Logical, courageous, resourceful and infinitely hardworking, she co-operated with her brother, the Duke of Lorraine, to establish French control at all key-points in Scotland. Why? Because her daughter was to marry the Dauphin and become Queen, not only of Scotland but also of France, and ultimately of England too, for Roman Catholic Europe recognized her as heir to Edward VI's crown.

While Knox was battling his way to theological assurance and Mary of Guise was preparing for her daughter's future, Roman Catholic and Protestant leaders were trying to consolidate the faith of their supporters.

The Archbishop of St. Andrews summoned in 1549 and 1552 Reforming Councils. Their most impressive achievement was the production of a Catechism for priests to use when they were instructing their people. It dealt especially with the Ten Commandments, the Creeds, and the Sacraments, and it was reverently and beautifully expressed. Such a document in the hands of sincere priests could have done much to save the old Church, if only it had been produced half a century earlier. Its late appearance, under a French ruler, its association with corrupt and cynical men of immoral habits meant that for the time being it could do little good. By the 1550s, the damage was too severe, the political exploitation of the religious issue too far advanced for calamity to be prevented.

Meantime, the Protestants in Scotland were needing an order of worship in their own language, with which inexperienced religious leaders of no great educational background could replace the old Latin liturgy. They found what they wanted in the English Book of Common Prayer, published in 1549 and revised in 1552. This included large portions of the Bible, which were read or sung as a central part of every service and which enabled people to become familiar especially with the Psalter, the Gospels and the Epistles. It set out orders of service and also many short prayers suitable for use in public and private devotions, prayers collected from ancient sources and translated by Cranmer into English of unsurpassed beauty. The Sacrament of Holy Communion was the central act of worship and the Prayer Book stated clearly that while people were to receive the Bread and Wine kneeling, 'no adoration of the sacred elements is intended or ought to be done.' So the men who held to the Roman Catholic belief in transubstantiation could not join in the English celebration of Communion. But the Prayer Book at this stage imposed no rigid uniformity and it left both priests and laymen a certain freedom in worship. People of widely differing thought could join in the services with sincerity.

It is impossible to exaggerate the importance of the English Book of Common Prayer. Its dignity and reverence, its ordered rhythm and lucid prose so close to poetry, its spiritual insight and the depth of meaning in its prayers gave strength to generations of believers. In Scotland it was lovingly and reverently used for many years and it helped to shape Scottish Protestant thought, the first Service Book ever handled by Scottish laymen, who learned from it the central doctrines of the Christian faith.

Another work much loved by Scottish Protestants at this time was compiled by three brothers, James, John, and Robert Wedderburn. It was called *A Compendious Booke of Godly and Spiritual Songs*, or *The Gude and Godly Ballatis*. This was a collection of Lutheran hymns, with some metrical Psalms and some rather scurrilous poems, almost doggerel in nature. The Saltire Society has recently published a small volume containing a selection of these verses which influenced 16th century Scotsmen so much. In his book, *Worship in the Church of Scotland*, Dr. Maxwell shows the significance for Scottish Protestants of the Prayer Book and of the Wedderburns' hymns and psalms. 'For the first time in centuries, the voice of the people was once more heard in praise and worship of God. Except in great churches, the metrical psalms did not replace plainsong, they replaced silence.'

The tension between the old Church and the new grew more acute during the 1550s, for in spite of the Queen Mother's efforts, Protestantism was becoming stronger. The leadership came from the nobility, who were inspired by motives far from wholly religious, for political and economic advantage was clearly to be derived from a breakdown of the old religion. In 1557, a group of Scottish Lords drafted a document which has become famous in Scottish History. This was the First Covenant.

It was designed to promote 'the most blessed Word of God and His congregation', to provide 'faithful ministers', to defend both congregations and ministers from interference. The Lords proposed to persuade their Government to authorize the Book of Common Prayer, they emphasized the need for Bibly Study and private worship and, above all, insisted that when the Sacraments of Communion and Baptism were celebrated, the Scots tongue must be used. By 1558, this Covenant was being taken round Scotland for signature by gentry and burgesses. It created an immense sensation because the procedure was unprecedented and much more because the proposals were revolutionary.

One explosive event followed another in 1558, while Scotsmen were signing the First Covenant. Mary Tudor died and the English throne passed to her half-sister, Elizabeth, who set about establishing a Protestant state religion, based on the Book of Common Prayer. The burning of Protestants therefore ceased in England. The last of the martyrs in Scotland died that year in St. Andrews—old Walter Myln or Mill, aged eighty-two. The citizens in St. Andrews were so shocked at his sentence that nobody would provide fuel for the fire or ropes to bind him to the stake and the Provost flatly refused to have anything to do with the affair. In the end the Archbishop's personal servants had to carry it through as best they might, and it caused a scandal throughout Scotland.

Four days after Myln's death in 1558, Mary Queen of Scots married the Dauphin. She was sixteen. Her subjects at home did not know that she had pledged her kingdom to France if she had no heir. They did know that her young husband had demanded the Crown Matrimonial, that he boasted himself King of Scotland, and they knew also that Mary of Guise was preparing to suppress the Covenant by force.

The country was now worked up to a fever of excitement. The danger was an outburst of violence such as had swept Germany in the early days of Luther's movement. Even the Queen Mother underestimated this risk and the Lords of the Congregation were totally unprepared for it. But the Protestants knew they needed a leader to weld them together and urgent messages were sent to John Knox to return. He came back to Scotland in 1559 and at once became the inspiration of Protestant activity and the architect of Protestant thought. His incredible capacity for concentrated, rapid work astonished everybody and during the next few months he helped to bring about profound changes in the Scottish way of life.

He was an inflammatory preacher whose prophetic message was not understood by people whom fear and hatred had embittered.

His sermons at once touched off an orgy of desecration, in which angry mobs, excited beyond all control, burst into action, and began senselessly smashing the altars, pictures and furnishings of monastic buildings and even parish churches. The extent of these outbursts has been exaggerated and much destruction wrought by other hands has been attributed to Knox's followers, but they were responsible for outrages in Scone, Perth, St. Andrews, Stirling, Linlithgow, Edinburgh and Holyrood—a sufficiently black indictment.

Knox and the other Protestant leaders were horrified. It was clearly the beginning of civil war. The Queen Mother had ample strength to annihilate the rebels, if she could mobilize her forces, and the outlook was very black. And then the incredible happened, so quickly that people could hardly keep up with events.

Henry II of France died from an injury received in a tournament in July 1559. His son Francis II therefore became King of France. He quartered on his arms the devices of Scotland and also, most misguidedly, of England. All Roman Catholic Europe supported him in this. His wife, Mary Queen of Scots, the great-granddaughter of Henry VII, was deemed by Rome to be the only surviving heir to Henry VIII whose claim was legitimate. Elizabeth, according to Catholic doctrine, had been born out of wedlock. Thus, for the first time in hundreds of years, the English sovereign had cogent reasons for seeking alliance with Scotland against the French, because both countries were now threatened by France. In an agony of suspense Knox supported negotiations for assistance from Queen Elizabeth.

Elizabeth was reluctant. She strongly disapproved of rebellion, as indeed did Knox himself, and she was deeply alienated by his recent publication of a most unfortunate work. This was *The First Blast of the Trumpet against the Monstrous Regiment of Women*, which denounced the notion that women were fit to be crowned monarchs. But it was plain that, now or never, the French claims to Scotland and to England must be refuted. So the irony of history brought about this strangest of partnerships. In January 1560, the English fleet appeared in northern waters to assist the Protestant Scots, a sight incredible to men who remembered the Rough Wooing. The Queen Mother's forces retired to Leith, where they were besieged by an English army co-operating with Scottish nobles. In the early summer, the Treaty of Leith or Edinburgh finished the business, and all French troops were ordered out of Scotland.

This would not have been the end of the story however, but for the death of Mary of Guise in June 1560. The significance of her hold on affairs is shown by the rapid changes which followed her death.

The Scottish Parliament was called. To it there came a better representation of lesser freeholders than ever before. Not until the 1690s was so much popular interest shown in any Parliament.

By a rapid succession of statutes, the authority of the Pope in Scotland was abolished and the celebration of Mass forbidden. Knox, with five other ministers, was asked to draw up a definition of the new beliefs, and they produced a document in four days. This was the Confession of Faith, an intellectual statement of Christianity as he understood it, which became the basis of Scottish Protestantism until 1647. That even Knox's dynamic mind could work so rapidly is surprising, though he was prepared for the sudden need by the years he had spent with Calvinists. There followed in a matter of weeks *The First Book of Discipline* also the work of Knox and his colleagues. This set out the principles upon which the Scottish Church should be organized and though it bore the marks of haste, it was expressed in terms of such authority that it was accepted almost without question, except as regards its far-reaching financial proposals.

Knox has been much misinterpreted and so has the Church which he helped to found. The Confession of Faith and *The First Book of Discipline* show clearly that he believed whole-heartedly in the sacramental nature of worship. Shocked as he had been by the degradation of the Mass, Knox wanted Communion to be the central focus in the life of the Church. He found authority for this in the New Testament, and believed it to be the principal means of grace for the Christian. Knox, like Calvin, believed in frequent Communion, but shortage of ministers and the prejudices of people who had been in the habit of communicating only once a year at Easter made this impossible, and the general rule in Scotland was that Holy Communion should be celebrated quarterly in burghs and twice yearly in country parishes. There were long periods, however, when in many places even this frequency was not attained. The celebration, however, was always recognized as a corporate action, in which the faithful should share, and all communicants were encouraged, after examination, to receive at every Communion service. Worshippers were seated at long tables, because this was believed to be nearer the Apostolic practice than kneeling.

The Bible was the basis of the Confession of Faith. Because people must not only know but understand the Scriptures, preaching was to be an important part of worship. Ministers were told to speak in Scots, in a loud clear voice so that all could hear

The First Book of Discipline set forth the way in which the Church should manage its business. It gave laymen responsibility in religious matters which was quite new. Each parish was to appoint a Kirk Session of lay elders, whose task it was to assist the minister in oversight of the people and in all parish concerns. Superintendents, or itinerant ministers, were appointed, each with a district which coincided more or less with one of the old dioceses, and these superintendents had status and authority similar in many ways to that of bishops. From the first, a General Assembly met once or twice a year to settle matters affecting the whole Church.

This bold scheme to enlist lay responsibility led later to the formation of district Presbyteries, composed of ministers and elders representing the parishes. They dealt with some of the work which proved too difficult for the Sessions. The Presbyteries were given power to ordain ministers, and this was one of the most important breaks with Roman Catholic tradition, for in the Old Church, clergy were ordained by bishops. Between the Presbytery and the General Assembly came the Provincial Synod, composed of several Presbyteries. The Supreme Court was the General Assembly which eventually came to be composed of commissioners from the Presbyteries both ministers and elders.

This whole system of Church Government became exceedingly precious to Scottish Protestants, who ultimately did away with the office of Superintendent, but clung most tenaciously to the Sessions, Presbyteries and Synods.

Protestant Scotland

The General Assembly flourished from the beginning. People took the liveliest interest in it and it gave them a means of expressing public opinion long needed in Scotland. In fact it took something like the place in national life which the House of Commons came to hold in England, though it was a far more representative and democratic body.

The Book of Discipline demanded that the wealth of the unreformed Church should be used to provide Scotland's parishes each with a minister's manse and salary, a fund for poor relief and a school. Knox was well aware that already much of the land formerly owned by monasteries had been secured by lay lords and commendators, often in collaboration with the abbots and priors themselves. 'With the grief of our hearts, we hear that some gentlemen are now as cruel over their tenants as ever were the Papists, requiring of them whatsoever before they paid to the Church, so that the Papistical tyranny shall only be changed into the tyranny of the lord or the laird.' This was what Knox wrote. Years earlier the poet Henryson had put it more succinctly: 'The worst wolves are lords that have lands as a loan from God.' In the introduction to the *Register of the Privy Council of Scotland* 1625-27, a list of the principal abbeys and priories with the names of their lay owners is set out, showing how well Scottish lords exploited the Reformation for their own material benefit.

It is essential to the health of both Church and State, that those who take decisions must have some education. In the Protestant Church, which bases its teaching on the Bible and calls upon laymen to take their part, it is necessary for Church members to be at least literate. *The Book of Discipline* therefore stated that every parish was to have its school. Knox and his colleagues in fact wanted a free, compulsory, national system of education.

Nobody in Scotland had ever suggested such a revolutionary idea before. It was typical of these early Protestant leaders, who believed with Calvin that it was a moral duty to train the mind. The scheme never succeeded because Protestant nobles had effectively secured so much of the old Church's property and the new Church had no chance to share adequately in the spoils.

141

Many parishes in fact had no school till the second half of the 18th century. But do not let 20th century complacency overlook the astonishing originality of Knox's educational policy, unmatched in any contemporary society.

Knox's third great literary production was delayed until 1562. This was the Book of Common Order, a Service Book designed for laymen as much as for ministers, and based on one used in Geneva by English refugees. It took some time to supersede the English Book of Common Prayer, which was popular in Scotland until the 1570s, but once people became used to it they liked it and it passed through seventy editions between 1562 and 1637.

Later generations of Scottish Protestants cut completely adrift from this Service Book. It repays study. It sets out the Lord's Prayer, the Creed, the Ten Commandments, the Magnificat, the Nunc Dimittis and the Veni Creator. Strangely enough, unlike the English Book, it includes no Scriptures. No celebration of special festivals in the Christian year was allowed, so that even Christmas, Easter and Whitsun were passed by without recognition. This was of course in reaction against the Holy Days of Rome, but Scottish Protestants suffered spiritual loss in their neglect of these special periods of worship and recollection.

It is odd that 1314 is the best known date in Scottish history. Although the Battle of Bannockburn was glorious for Bruce, it heralded decades of frustration and fighting. The year 1560 is surely a much more momentous one. It ended three centuries of warfare with England. It saw the foundation of the Presbyterian Church. A nation's thoughts were radically changed by all that Parliament did in those brief weeks of 1560. And for those who grieve over the divisions among Christians, 1560 is a year of tragic significance, for then the breach between the old Church and the new was made permanent in Scotland.

There was one final shock in store for Europe before 1560 ended. When Christmas preparations were afoot, Francis II, King of France, died suddenly from a mastoid. Mary, Queen of Scots, not yet nineteen years of age, was widowed. There was nothing for her now but to return to Scotland.

By character and training Mary was hardly fitted to deal with what she had to undertake. Deprived since earliest childhood of her parents' company, of normal family life and of home security, she was almost uninstructed in the history and traditions of her country. She was more French than Scottish. She had even adopted the French form of her own surname, which she spelt Stuart. Famous for her beauty, strongly sexed, conditioned to gay court life, delighting in pleasure and also in intellectual stimulus, she was at home in the atmosphere of high-powered intrigue: devout according to her own light, she understood less readily the religious dedication of the spiritually-minded Protestants than the self-interest of the worldly ones. And when she came to Scotland this eighteen-year-old girl felt her isolation from the sunshine, the warmth, the palace life, the court festivities she had known during her childhood in France.

Her return to Scotland in 1561 was a moment of crucial opportunity. Had Scotland ever needed a balanced, wise, experienced monarch more desperately than then? Enlightened patience, mature judgment, firmness of purpose and tolerance of mind in the Scottish ruler could have preserved the nation in its wholeness and inaugurated the new era of religious growth without excessive embitterment or partisan politics. People are ready enough to recollect Mary's personal tragedy with hot resentment or cold criticism, according to their outlook. Not enough has been said about the nation's tragedy at this time of new beginnings when the very springs of national thought became poisoned at the source.

The middle-aged Protestant divines by whose courage the new beginnings had been shaped were nonplussed by Mary. The wonder is that for nearly five years a modus vivendi was somehow found. She insisted on hearing Mass regularly in Holyrood. Knox and the other Protestant leaders were deeply shocked by this. They were desperately afraid that such a royal example might bring a reaction in Scotland, and indeed in Europe, which would undo all their work and let loose again the evils they had striven to crush. And certainly Roman Catholic Europe did regard their Queen as a kind of Joan of Arc, a Crusader in a pagan land, fighting a lonely, holy war.

Mary was at a loss to understand why people in Scotland disapproved of her so much. Probably some of her happiest hours

were those spent in the company of George Buchanan. He had
returned to Scotland after many years on the continent, in 1561.
He was more interested in humanist thinking than in religious
controversy at this time, although he was by now a Protestant
thoroughly trusted by Knox and a member of the General
Assembly. He had a great love for France and the Queen used
to read the classics with him, no doubt also enjoying his reminiscences of the country they both knew so well.

In 1565 she fell in love. Henry Darnley was the grandson of
James IV's widow, Margaret Tudor, by a later marriage. He
was about nineteen, attractive in appearance and very tall. They
were married before Mary discovered his third-rate mind and
total lack of perception. So for intelligent companionship Mary
looked elsewhere, and within ten months of the marriage, Darnley
was jealous of David Rizzio, an Italian musician.

Rizzio was murdered in Mary's presence by Darnley and a
group of others. She was six months pregnant, and the next day
she almost miscarried, and she became very ill. Her baby, the
future James VI and I, was born three months later. Darnley's
brutality had only just missed depriving two kingdoms of a
monarch.

After that, Mary could not get over her repugnance for this
odious second husband and one disaster followed another. He
fell ill of smallpox in 1567, and while he was slowly convalescing,
his house at Kirk o' Field near Edinburgh was blown up: next
morning, amongst the wreckage cluttering the garden, his body
was found—and his neck had been wrung.

Nobody knows exactly what happened, or how many agents
were employed in the crime. Scotland was in no doubt as to who
organized it however—James Hepburn, the fourth Earl of
Bothwell, a Protestant of notoriously bad character. Within
eight weeks, Mary had married this man.

What could have possessed her? Beautiful, sensitive, high-
powered—why did she twice tie herself up with a contemptible
character? The union with Bothwell cost her everything. Roman
Catholics throughout Europe were scandalized by it, the Scottish
Protestants outraged, George Buchanan no less than the rest.
It brought about immediate war, for the nobles had no difficulty

in raising troops to fight both the Queen and Bothwell. In June 1567, her soldiers retreated from Carberry Hill and she was forced to sign her own abdication. The baby James was crowned, Knox preached the Coronation sermon and Mary's Protestant half-brother James Stewart, Earl of Moray, one of James V's abler illegitimate sons, was made Regent.

Mary was imprisoned in Lochleven Castle, from which she made a dramatic escape in 1568, but another defeat followed, at Langside by Glasgow, and she made one more desperate decision. She appealed to Queen Elizabeth, secretly crossed the Solway and appeared on English territory as a suppliant for hospitality and assistance.

This was the last development Elizabeth wanted and it distracted her. She did not know what to do with such a guest, the heir-presumptive to the English throne, who had already made free to consider herself Queen of England; a Roman Catholic, the wife of her husband's murderer, a woman whom Scotland no longer wanted and whose presence in England was an acute danger. A hundred years later, in 1668, Henry Savage, Master of Balliol College, made the following comment on Mary's decision to go to England: 'The circumstances of her suffering, 'tis not my business to dispute or relate, but the event gives way to this note upon it, viz: How dangerous a thing it is, first to lay claim to a crown and afterwards to fly for succour to the head that wears it.'

Elizabeth kept Mary imprisoned in country castles and her advisers organized careful scrutiny of all her correspondence, which often contained incriminating documents. Meantime, it took the Protestant Lords almost five years to achieve a stable government in Scotland, and James VI was subjected to the most rigorous discipline ever endured by a Scottish King in childhood. The Protestants were determined to leave no stone unturned to ensure that this time they would educate their ruler in the way of their own choosing.

This final royal minority did Scotland endless harm. At a time of bold new thought, it is disastrous to have weakened leadership, because career-minded climbers, materialists, people devoted to intrigue of all kinds have such unusual opportunities.

The Reformation and the Covenant

The fight between Mary of Guise and John Knox for the nation's soul, followed by the anti-climax of Mary Stuart's personal calamities, set the scene for sordid developments during the childhood of the new King.

CHAPTER 14

Prelude to the Seventeenth Century

James VI was crowned in the summer of 1567, when he was thirteen months old. By the time he was four, his studies were being directed by George Buchanan, who had formerly made his conversation acceptable to the little King's mother.

When he began tutoring James, Buchanan was sixty-three, an advanced age for those times, his health was poor and his temper short. Although he had tutored a number of boys before, including a Stewart prince, he was unsuited to the care of small children. He could not stand noise and as the years went by he found schoolboy wit intolerable. He had learned his pedagogy in schools where thrashing was a normal part of each day's work and he did not change his method. Worse than this was his habit of making embittered reference to James' parents, especially his mother. James hated him and was afraid of him.

The King was systematically overdriven at books, for which he showed unusual ability. He quickly absorbed Latin and Greek, committed long passages of the Bible to memory, mastered much Calvinist theology and became probably the best-educated prince of his day. But it was a precocious learning, acquired during a lonely, abnormal childhood. Although a library of some six hundred books was collected for him during his childhood—probably a unique personal possession in those days—money was so short that James' royal apartments were shabby and by modern standards he was neglected. It occurred to nobody that the King should have any training in consideration of other people or in understanding the mentality of those with whom he would have to deal.

Buchanan vigorously drummed his political ideas into James' head. Kings were answerable to law, their authority was derived from the people, if they failed in their responsibilities their subjects were entitled to get rid of them. These were not original views. John Major and John Knox and many others had voiced them before. Because James was afraid of Buchanan he came to hate his political doctrines and, although he was never particularly loyal to his parents' memory, he resented the crude way in which Buchanan justified the Scots' rejection of Mary.

James grew up with fear on the doorstep. From 1563 till 1573, nobles who supported Mary Stuart's cause waged active war against those who wanted a Protestant régime and peaceful terms with England. There was a succession of Regents, who had impossible difficulties to contend with. The Queen's friends, and others too who wanted power, were always trying to get possession of the King's person. As a boy James more than once witnessed physical violence between his guardians and their enemies in his own home. The experience frightened and humiliated him.

One can understand James and his legacy best by considering his reaction to all this boyhood misery. In self-assertion against the adults who overruled him, he developed a brazen self-conceit. Starved of loving companionship as a child, he began in his early teens that series of emotional attachments with specially favoured men which caused scandal till his old age. Esmé Stuart, Seigneur d'Aubigny, was the first to awaken this side of James' nature and his was a wholly harmful influence, for he was both evil and charming.

More serious for both Scotland and England was James' reaction against Calvinism. He hated Presbyterian principles so much that in later life he could not think logically about them, and this hatred he bestowed also on Puritan ideas. All his adult life, he laboured to destroy the power of the Kirk and to force Scotsmen to adopt the ritual worship he came to love in the Anglican Church. And he became set on Episcopacy. The establishment of bishops in Scotland was one of his dearest ambitions from very early days.

Equally disastrous was James' reaction against Buchanan's political philosophy. It must have been a positive release of the spirit for James to realize, as he did in adolescence, that one need not believe in the sovereignty of the people. It was perhaps from Esmé Stuart that he first learned how some continental thinkers approached political philosophy, and how differently from himself continental rulers were trained to work out their responsibilities. One wonders whether old Buchanan realized how dangerous were the volumes of Jean Bodin which had been included in the King's library. They are difficult, indeed exasperating to read, but to James they were meat and drink. Bodin was a French philosopher of the late 16th century. The general purport of his teaching was that law is nothing else than the command of the sovereign, that sovereignty in fact consisted in the right to make law. From Bodin, James deduced that men are anything but equal and that democracy is a rebellion against nature because it encourages belief in an equality of man which does not really exist. True sovereignty, in fact, was only to be found in monarchy.

In defiance of Buchanan, James embraced the doctrines of Bodin and worked out his own theory of the Divine Right of Kings. This he explained in various books which he published, but especially in *The Trew Law of Free Monarchies*. His son Charles I adopted this book's teaching with a seriousness of purpose that led him to antagonize the most powerful classes in his kingdom. So James' revolt against Buchanan's political philosophy produced long-term results which did infinite harm.

Some writers have suggested that not even the most enlightened handling in childhood could have made James into a wise or balanced personality. But it is almost impossible to conceive of an upbringing more likely to bring out the worst in his nature.

James never knew his mother personally. She was imprisoned in England until his twenty-first year. In theory, he wanted to stand up for her, but he resented the inconvenience she caused him by her implication in plots against Queen Elizabeth. For James desperately wanted to be King of England. Only by this means did he see any chance of eluding forever the poverty and the humiliation he endured in Scotland. Anything Mary did to endanger his succession to the English throne irritated and even alarmed him. When at last she was executed in 1587, he was in a sense relieved, though of course he took it as a personal insult to himself that such a thing should have happened.

Queen Elizabeth had been most reluctant to allow this execution, which affronted all her sensibilities and was contrary to all her principles. Her ministers had the greatest difficulty in persuading her to agree to the measure, even though they were all sure that it was essential to Elizabeth's own life, for they had damning evidence of Mary's dealings with traitors.

The result of Mary's execution in Scotland was an emotional upheaval which Englishmen could never have foreseen and certainly never have understood. Though Mary Stuart had shocked Scottish public opinion and offended Scotsmen's religious scruples, though she had been forced by her own subjects to abdicate and few people had wanted her back, now that English hands had been laid upon her and she had been done to death by an English Queen's orders, a surge of loyalty to her and hatred against England swept through the country. People clamoured for vengeance and could not understand James' embarrassed inactivity about the matter. Border raids were organized and the whole thing became a national scandal. The execution of Mary Stuart, like the Rough Wooing organized in the 1540s by Henry VIII, left deep roots of bitterness.

For the first thirty years of James' reign, Scotland suffered cruelly from the lawlessness of the aristocracy. As a young man, James could no more assert his authority over the nobles than he could keep on good terms with the Kirk, and he was so desperately short of money that it was a problem even to meet tradesmen's bills. In the last decade of the century, James' position was so humiliating that he had to put up with bare-faced insolence from those about him.

The country was tormented by the feuds and wrangles between Protestant and Roman Catholic lords. Of the latter, the Earl of Huntly was a principal leader. He was for awhile one of James' favourites and he pretended to take an interest in Protestant services, in order to earn more favours from the King. He was a barbarous, double-faced man, who conducted treasonable correspondence with Spain, to Queen Elizabeth's indignation, but James could hardly bring himself to disgrace Huntly, even when this was discovered. Later, Huntly carried out a dreadful murder. He killed the young Earl of Moray, a popular Protestant, and burned out the castle of Donibristle on the Forth where his victim was staying. Public opinion was utterly shocked by this and James himself had to bear much of the odium.

Huntly's chief enemy was the fifth Earl of Bothwell. This disreputable, and probably deranged, man was a nephew of Mary Stuart's third husband and a grandson of James V. He hated Huntly and the other Roman Catholic Earls and for years he made orderly government impossible. James was terrified of him, because he believed that Bothwell was endowed with supernatural powers. Three times, this extraordinary man made personal attacks on James in an effort to kidnap or injure him, twice in the King's own palace quarters.

At last in 1595, Huntly and Bothwell were both driven out of Scotland as exiles, and from this time onwards, James' position improved. His adviser Maitland died in that year and he took over the direction of affairs himself, showing a new and dogged determination to be master in his own land and to quell disorder.

In the midst of the worst upheavals, James had enjoyed a short spell of romance. He became betrothed to Anne of Denmark. In October, 1589, he went to Oslo, where she was stormbound on her journey to Scotland, and there he married her. He really enjoyed this episode, anxious though he was about the reception he would receive on his return, for there was as usual no money to spare for suitable celebrations. 'For God's sake' he wrote to a friendly minister, 'take all the pains ye can to tune our folks well now against our homecoming lest we be all shamed before strangers. Thus recommending me and my new rib to your daily prayers, I commit you to the only All-sufficient'. The arrangements worked out well enough to spare his blushes, and he really loved his new rib. Unfortunately, she proved to be silly and quarrelsome and she did not help him much. James found her most tiresome when their children were born because she wanted to have them under her own care. This he considered unsafe, owing to the very real risk that treacherous nobles might do them harm and he insisted that they should be brought up in other households of his own choosing. That was common practice amongst the aristocracy at the time, but the Queen disliked it and it estranged her from her husband.

One of the few encouraging events of these difficult years was the foundation of Edinburgh University in 1582. James liked to think himself responsible for this, but in fact the initiative and the endowments came from the capital's own citizens and the University was organized and controlled by the Town Council, which retained considerable authority, even to the appointment of Professors, until the 19th century.

While James was still at the very threshold of his troubled reign, Presbyterians began giving fresh thought to the organization of their beloved Kirk, and in doing this they accelerated the pace of controversy. In 1581, the *Second Book of Discipline* was declared authoritative by the General Assembly. This was inspired by the thinking of Andrew Melville, formerly Principal of Glasgow University, now Principal of St. Mary's College, St. Andrews. He was much more definite than Knox had ever been on the question of Episcopacy, which he condemned with the forthright severity James disliked so much in Presbyterians. Melville went so far as to urge that church courts should instruct civil magistrates in their jurisdiction 'according to the Divine Word'.

James naturally was much displeased by this development. In 1584, he persuaded Parliament to pass statutes which confirmed the appointment of bishops, and forbade convocations of ministers except with the King's consent. This legislation made James most unpopular. It was a shock to Presbyterians, the first in a long series of crises which aroused such emotions that it became difficult for people to think rationally about episcopacy. Within two years, James had to modify his position, and though bishops still held office, Presbyteries, Synods and General Assemblies were again allowed to meet.

Frightened by the possibility of losing their hard-won religious liberty, hardened by their hatred for all things Roman, ministers and laymen in the Kirk began to adopt a more extreme Calvinism. They insisted that, as God is no respecter of persons, all the elect are equal in His sight and they began too to depart from the dignified forms of worship set out in the Book of Common Order, adopting instead more extempore prayer. Many serious-minded Protestants were concerned about this change. John Spottiswoode was one of these, and his views are worth quoting. 'My judgment is and has been that the most simple, decent and humble rites should be choosed, such as is the bowing of the knees in resaving (receiving) the Holy Sacramente and others of that kinde, prophannesse being as dangerous to religion as superstition; and touching the government of the church, I am verily persuaded that the government episcopall is the only right and Apostolique form. Paritie among ministers is the breeder of confusion, as experience might have taught us, and for these ruling elders, as they are a mere human devise, so they will prove, if they find way, the ruin both of church and estate.'

Melville and Spottiswoode represent the two militant and opposed bodies of Scottish Protestants, now fully conscious of their beliefs and determined to stand up for them. The issue was not simply the virtues and defects of one form of Church government over against another. It was complicated by the fact that the King saw in bishops appointed by himself an essential instrument of his own royal supremacy. This complication was intensified by the conflicts of the 17th century and it drove the cleavage between Presbyterian and Episcopalian so deep that its healing could not even be attempted until the 20th century.

The late 16th and early 17th century saw a strange revival of belief in witches. It is difficult to understand this hysteria or its causes, nor can one explain why Scotsmen were much more afflicted by it than Englishmen, prevalent as it was in England too. They attributed any sudden death of man or beast, and especially any suicide, to an alliance with the Devil on the part of some withered, senile woman. Witchtrials gave the men who conducted them ample chance to satisfy and even to stimulate sadistic impulses: the poor old crones often became demented under the prolonged interrogation and confessed to impossible sins before they were finally burned alive in public.

The King was fascinated by sorcery because he was afraid of it. Like other leading men of his day, he believed it was a Christian's duty to root out witchcraft and he published a treatise on the subject. It was called *Daemonologie* and described in some detail the techniques by which the Devil established his hold upon those who became enthralled to him. There were of course warlocks, male devotees, as well as witches, in this bondage to Satan, but

James declared that, because of Eve's surrender, the Devil had always been on 'homlier' terms with the female sex.

But the King was more enlightened than many Scots and he knew that delusion and hysteria could produce extraordinary states of mind. Unlike most people at that time, James could distinguish false from genuine evidence. He followed many cases in detail, with the result that he was able to expose a number of malicious attempts to incriminate defenceless victims, and he secured their release. He discovered that physical causes often explained strange behaviour and he was known to recommend rest and proper food and on one occasion, marriage, as the best cure. Some people think that James ultimately abandoned his belief in sorcery as a result of his investigations. However this may be, Scotsmen in general did not, and the torture of witches remained an ugly feature of the 17th century Scottish life.

It was unfortunate that in the closing years of the 16th century James not only set the tone for religious controversy, but also acquired a dangerous skill—the management of the Scottish Parliament. Because of the 15th century developments, described in chapter 10, it was relatively easy for him to establish complete mastery over the whole Parliament. He himself selected the Lords of the Articles. A full meeting of Parliament was of course summoned to 'elect' them, but the men chosen were his nominees. James then had all the ordinary members dispersed while the Lords of the Articles were at work, drafting legislation according to his instructions, and a full meeting was once more convened to vote for the statutes en bloc. So ordinary Scottish members could not influence the course of legislation at all, and indeed hardly understood its significance. All this was of course more or less in keeping with 14th and 15th century tradition, but it gave James a false sense of security and a very bad training for handling the totally different English Parliament.

During his adolescence and young manhood, James was much concerned about the succession to the English throne. He wanted it more passionately than he wanted anything else and he thought about it continually, sometimes with anxious doubt, sometimes with confident hope. There was in fact no other heir for Elizabeth and when at last the great old Queen died on March 24th, 1603,

James was proclaimed King of England without any opposition at all. He set forth for the magic south on April 5th, happy at last, delighted by the welcome he received at every stopping point along the Great North Road. His Queen followed later with the children and the Court became permanently based in England.

James positively basked in his new way of life. He appreciated the deferential, not to say obsequious, manners of English courtiers, who quickly learned that he could digest any amount of flattery: he was delighted with all the opportunities for hunting, and he found his large and gracious palaces entirely satisfying. At last, too, he was among people who had a proper regard for bishops, and he enjoyed the aesthetically pleasing ritual and the formal tone of the services he now attended. In a recent biography of James, David Harris Wilson says that he 'took the Church of England to his heart in a long rapturous embrace that lasted the rest of his life'. He continued to talk his broad Scots to the end of his days, but he was not in the least homesick: on the contrary he felt released from an unloved bondage, and he only visited Scotland once during the remaining twenty-two years before he died.

He devoted some thought to Scottish affairs however. For one thing he was determined to unite the two Kingdoms in name and in fact. He introduced the title 'Great Britain', against strong opposition from his English subjects, who had no wish to sink their ancient identity in a new political creation. They also bluntly refused to contemplate organizing a joint Parliament with Scottish representatives at Westminster and still less would they consider allowing trade concessions to their brothers across the Border. James was disappointed about this. As a Christian King, he said, he did not want 'to be a polygamist and to have two wives . . . as God hath made Scotland the one half of this isle to enjoy my birth and the first and most unperfect half of my life, and you here to enjoy the perfect and last half thereof, so can I not think that any could cut asunder the one half of me from the other'. But he had to accept polygamy. It was perhaps a pity, for real union, together with parity in trading privileges, might have prevented many later troubles—but few people, apart from James and perhaps Francis Bacon, saw the matter in this light.

The King now succeeded in establishing a remote control over Scottish affairs which was more effective than the authority of any of his predecessors. He worked the Scottish Privy Council hard, sending them sharply worded instructions, which on the whole they faithfully carried out. 'This I must say for Scotland, here I sit and govern it with my pen, I write and it is done, and by a Clark of the Council I govern Scotland now, which others could not do by the sword'. This boastful remark was not far wide of the mark.

James' orders to his Council dealt frequently with the problem of lawlessness, which reached lengths one can hardly nowadays imagine. In 1612, for example, some of the Neish clan raided the Macnabs as they were about to enjoy Christmas dinner, and were able to escape with the roast to an island on Loch Earn, because they owned its only boat. Macnab's four eldest sons, urged on by their mother, carried their own boat from Loch Tay over to Loch Earn, caught the Neishes unprepared and in vengeance killed the whole family except two small children. They decapitated the corpses and took the heads back to their mother in a sack, to her great satisfaction, though they felt too tired to carry back their boat as well.

This was the kind of thing James was determined to stamp out. The Clan Gregor was possibly one of the worst hornets' nests: its neighbours, especially in the Loch Lomond area, had suffered endless misery from it. James authorized the complete extinction of this clan, whose name was abolished, and whose members were driven away from their homes by fire and slaughter, willingly carried out through the agency of traditional foes.

The Southern Hebrides were reduced to quiet in similar fashion; the Macdonalds of Islay suffered frightful punishment; and the notoriously evil 'Earl Pate', Patrick Stewart of the Orkneys, a cousin of the King who had ruled these islands with injustice and violence for years, was hanged. James' methods would hardly stand scrutiny from a constitutional or judicial point of view, except perhaps his treatment of Earl Pate, but he made Scotland a more peaceful and orderly country.

James' other aim in Scotland was of course to break the power of the Presbyterian Kirk. After 1603, for a number of years, the

General Assembly was forbidden to meet. In 1606, Andrew Melville and seven other leading Scottish ministers were summoned to England to discuss the religious situation in their country. They were subjected to insulting cross-examination and exhortation, which Melville would not suffer mildly. He was therefore imprisoned in the Tower for three years and then, like his nephew James, forbidden to return to Scotland; and the other six ministers were delayed in England much longer than they wanted to stay.

After this suppression of the Presbyterian leaders, James increased the powers of the Scottish bishops and also their numbers. By 1610, there were eleven of them and two Archbishops, one of whom was John Spottiswoode. They could enforce ecclesiastical law through the two Courts of High Commission, established for them in 1610 on the English model.

That Scottish people put up with such interference is surprising. It was partly because Andrew Melville was safely out of the way and their other leaders intimidated, partly because some of the Scottish bishops, Forbes of Aberdeen for example, were men of tolerance and wisdom. Mainly, however, it was because so far congregational worship had not been tampered with, and so ordinary people found their Sunday services unchanged and did not realize the new power of the bishops in Scotland.

In 1617, the King decided to come north himself and deal with religious matters. His visit did not endear him to his subjects in Edinburgh, who were angered by an organ and surpliced choristers suddenly appearing in Holyrood. James tried to make a representative group of ministers accept five considerable changes. These were that Communion should be received kneeling, that the festivals of the Christian year should be observed, that confirmation should be administered by bishops and not by ministers, that private Communion and private baptism should be allowed in the case of serious illness.

A General Assembly was summoned on the King's orders for 1618, and met in Perth. It was subjected to all the bullying that James could devise. So his Five Articles of Perth were sanctioned by the Kirk's highest authority. There was a furious reaction up and down the country. People were specially incensed by the order to receive Communion kneeling. Congregations and ministers boycotted the innovations so systematically that not even the Courts of High Commission could do anything to enforce them. Some twenty years were to pass before the General Assembly met again.

James' policies south of the Border do not fall within the scope of this book, but it is relevant to say that his experience of Scottish life and institutions, his vanity and his weaknesses of character made him ill-prepared to deal with the English situation.

When he met the English Puritan leaders at the Hampton Court Conference in 1604, for example, James assumed at once that they were of the same stamp as the Presbyterians he had hated in childhood, especially as they used some of the same religious terminology. He handled them with angry contempt and the Conference ended in recrimination. English Puritans had so far been milder in spirit and less extreme in principle than Scottish Presbyterians, and under more moderate guidance than James could give that Conference could have initiated a period of comprehensive tolerance. It was a tragedy for 17th century England that their new King's prejudices should have made him miss this unique opportunity.

In similar fashion, James fell foul of the English Parliament. He was indignant when he discovered that the Commons, meeting quite separately from the Lords, felt free to debate all legislation at leisure and openly to critize royal suggestions. The King was poles apart from his new subjects too, in that he had no personal pride in the seamanship of Elizabeth's great admirals like Sir Walter Raleigh, nor did he feel as they did towards Spain. Englishmen had never shaken off their fear of Spain and the Armada tradition was their great pride. James' idea that he would hold the balance of power in a peaceful Europe by negotiating both with France and with Spain suited his own vanity excellently but it horrified Englishmen who remembered the old days.

Possibly things would have worked out better had James' eldest son Henry survived, but this promising young man died before his father. By 1624, James was mortally ill, and affairs

were under the control of his second son, Charles, and the royal
favourite of the King's old age, the Duke of Buckingham. In
1625 he died. The Scots had gained nothing by the fact that they
had given Great Britain her first King, except a complexity of
problems which his successor was even less capable of interpreting
wisely.

CHAPTER 15

The Making of the National Covenant

When Charles I became King, his subjects in the Highlands probably remained unaware of the fact for many months. Mountains and sealochs separate the north and west from the rest of the country and there were then no roads fit to carry wheeled traffic. The northern and western shires were unmoved by controversies which disturbed people elsewhere in Scotland and they were not even represented in the Scottish Parliament until the middle of the 17th century. Chieftains exercised their ancestral hold on their clans and administered their traditional forms of justice, clan loyalties were strong, clan feuds unforgotten, in spite of James I's strong hand. Economic conditions were primitive and standards of living much lower than people in the south realized.

In sharp contrast to the Highlands was the north-eastern area of Scotland. The people of Aberdeen consciously enjoyed the sense that theirs was the capital city of this prosperous district. In the mid-17th century the population in Aberdeen was probably about 8,750. They were relatively well-to-do people, because of their east coast sea-trade. They imported taffetas, calicoes, looking-glasses, swordblades and much else. They were proud of the peaceful and orderly way of life that was normally theirs, and proud too of their University.

The Border shires enjoyed more peaceful conditions after 1603. The old Border feuds abated, raiding became less common. In southern and central Scotland, in the north-east too, the landed gentry established at this period a prosperity they had not known earlier, a rough and homespun prosperity, but nonetheless enjoyable. It was based on traffic in Church properties and carefully planned marriage alliances, which enabled the Lords to live more spaciously, as one can see by the domestic architecture of the times. It is significant that in the Western Highlands there was apparently no such change in building as one can detect elsewhere and no improvement in personal comfort.

Agriculture was the chief means of making a livelihood. People lived as their forbears had done, by subsistence farming. For ordinary people, poverty was necessarily still a continuing nightmare. Village life was stifled by the jealous way in which the little burghs guarded their medieval monopolies, trade played only a small part in the national economy except on the eastern coastline, industry was hardly established at all. There was no banking system and currency had a very limited circulation. Scotland's middle class was a relatively small element in the nation.

At this time there seemed to be little conscious national feeling. So far as it existed, it was dormant, or perhaps masked. While Highlanders thought of clan before country at this time, many Scotsmen were more international than national in outlook. The nobles were in the habit of sending their sons to France and to the Netherlands for university and also for legal training. But the travelling Scot was to be found at every level of society. In particular, the armies of Sweden and France attracted all types of Scotsmen who joined up as professional soldiers in foreign service. A violent political or religious crisis was needed before a specifically Scottish national spirit would emerge once more.

There was no religious unity. Protestantism had reached Caithness and the Orkney and Shetland Isles through the traffic by sea, but it had not penetrated old Drumalban. The Western Highlands knew little of it, except in the Earl of Argyll's domains. Even the medieval Church had failed to establish an effective hold on parts of the north and west, so difficult were some of the glens to reach, and there were districts where the inhabitants must have been living in a state of near paganism. Early in the 17th century, however, priests from Ireland began a mission to the Islands and Western Highlands, and its success is marked by the devout and loyally Roman Catholic population which survives in certain districts to this day.

The strongholds of the Presbyterian Kirk were in southern and central Scotland. Here the ministers exercised an influence far beyond anything we can easily realize today. So long as they

satisfied Calvinist consciences on matters of principle, all
Protestant laymen were prepared to support their ministers
staunchly. This was especially noticeable, when the Kirk was
in danger. And danger seemed always near at hand. Ministers
and laymen alike were obsessed by horror of Rome and fear of
anything akin to Roman practice. They thought the Church of
England was only a step removed from Rome, and bishops they
resented as the agents of a supposedly romanizing King.

Only in one part of Scotland was Episcopacy firmly rooted. This
was in and around Aberdeen, where a strong Episcopal tradition
grew up. It is rather difficult to explain this. Perhaps it was
partly geographical. Today it takes almost four hours to reach
Aberdeen from Glasgow by train, and in the early 17th century
the city was far removed from the militant Presbyterians of the
south, and still farther from the sphere of Anglican interference.
The bishops of Aberdeen generally maintained harmonious
relations with the university officials and they were on good
terms also with the local Kirk leaders. This goodwill was extended
even to the Roman Catholic families and priests of the neighbourhood, who, fostered by the Gordon family's influence, were
able to practise their religion without incurring hostility.

The way in which Presbyterians and Episcopalians and Roman
Catholics maintained their way of life in the north-east suggests
that religious intolerance need not have developed so acutely as
it did later in the century. Possibly, if James I and his son had
not tried to make church organization uniform throughout their
kingdoms, members of these three Churches might have accepted
each others' existence more readily.

There is ample evidence that spiritual issues meant everything
to many of the militant Presbyterians in southern Scotland. It
has sometimes been fashionable to decry piety of the 17th
century Presbyterian type, on the grounds that it was skin-deep,
a device to secure worldly advantage, a hypocrisy in fact. This is
far from being true. Many ministers were imbued with the spirit
of Samuel Rutherford, minister of Anwoth in Galloway. 'I desire
not', he wrote in 1631, 'to go on the lee-side or sunny side of
religion, or to put truth betwixt me and a storm: my Saviour did
not so for me, who in His sufferings took the windy side of the

ill'. This spirit of devotion was nurtured by prayer and Bible study and it bought no worldly advantage for those who cultivated it. Ministers were not alone in seeking this living relationship with Christ. Burgesses, lairds, shopkeepers, countryfolk, nobles—many of them were inspired by a faith, unostentatious but genuine, which enabled them ultimately to face almost impossible strain. Like Lord Warriston at the height of his success in the legal profession, they could say: 'God's consolations never run drye, ar ay tastye, and keeps men ever fresh, for they are a fountayne, not a pudle or a pond.'

Presbyterians were at one in believing that their religion should be the supreme influence in the land. They thought, as Andrew Melville had inspired them to think, that secular officials should be guided in matters of principle by the leaders of the Kirk. Only so could they hope for security in their faith. They were reluctant to accept episcopacy, partly because they knew that bishops were appointed by the King, and that the King would give the bishops political authority, which could mean the infiltration of Roman Catholic practices.

Into this situation in 1625 there came a King utterly incapable of understanding it. Charles I was more divorced from his Scottish subjects than his father had been. He spent all his life after his fourth year in England. He never even visited Scotland until 1633. He made friends with hardly anybody, least of all Scotsmen. He did not know what other people's thoughts were and it never occurred to him that there was any reason why he should. He lived in a world of his own, a cultivated, fastidious world, where painting, literature, formal manners and serenely conducted religious services were the things that mattered. If only Charles had been a reasonably wealthy country gentleman, with a well-appointed country house, a good-sized garden, a library, a stable, a quiet wife and a large family, he would have been happy and successful, a man with few friends perhaps, but enjoying widespread respect and upholding valued principles.

As it was, Charles I could no more understand Scotland than he could guess at the existence of nuclear energy. The pattern of Scottish life and the climate of Scottish opinion remained foreign to him all his days. He knew little about the Kirk and disliked what he knew. He had no notion of the hold the General Assembly had on people's affections, even though its meetings had been proscribed. He did not understand Highland clan loyalty, nor did he grasp the fact that traditional alliances held certain great Lowland families together. That Scots regarded England as a rich and ruthless neighbour, that they had bad memories dating back to Tudor invasions of Scotland, that they were deeply afraid of Roman Catholicism—none of these things occurred to this serious-minded, highly cultivated grandson of Mary, Queen of Scots.

Charles inherited his father's suspicion of democratic assemblies and by 1628 he had deeply offended the English Parliament. So incensed was he with this organ of the English body politic, that he ruled without it from 1629 until 1640, a feat which put him in a difficult position with regard to money matters. He had to finance his very expensive court and administration by methods which shocked people who had every wish to remain loyal to him.

Charles I was devout. And his religion was the religion of William Laud.

Laud was Bishop of London, later Archbishop of Canterbury. He had a great reverence for the authority of the Church of England, which he enforced through the Court of High Commission. He loved ritual and orthodox Anglican principles. He began a carefully planned campaign of church reform to bring even obscure parish priests into line with his own practice.

For English Puritans, this was a time of terrible difficulty. They were repulsive to Laud, because of their indecent insistence on the individual's right to interpret Christian doctrine and the Scriptures according to his own light. They condemned certain things in the Prayer Book as dregs of popery and they put great stress on the necessity of preaching. Their courage in the face of persecution became notorious and the Court of High Commission was busy with them continually. Their ministers were removed from their churches; open-air preaching was forbidden; physical torture and imprisonment were inflicted on them. Among these Puritans, who also hated Episcopacy, there grew up a lively sympathy for the Scottish Kirk.

Although Charles had no love for Scotland, he devoted serious attention to its affairs. The most sincere of all Stuart kings, with the possible exception of James II, Charles was forced by the logic of his own thinking into a policy of imposing religious uniformity. Like his father, he believed himself to be invested with Divinely given authority. He thought he must use it to foster true religion: and he believed that political loyalty to the Crown could flourish only when all its subjects were united under one form of Church government. So he set himself to complete his father's task of bringing the Scottish Kirk into line with the Church of England. Within a dozen years, the leaders of the Scottish Kirk in their turn were trying to force the English nation to come into line with Presbyterianism. It was typical of the age to see no way but the one way, no safety other than the safety of uniformity.

Charles began by planning a re-organization of all the old Church properties, which had been for some eighty years in the hands of the Scottish gentry, and of the old Church tithes, which were also being enjoyed by laymen. These capital assets he proposed to use as provision for the maintenance of the clergy in Scotland.

Later, in 1633, Charles made a royal progress into Scotland and held a coronation service in St. Giles, Edinburgh. This service was conducted with full Anglican rites, which Charles believed the Scots would find so impressive that they would be completely won over to a Laudian view of ritual ceremony. In the same year the King founded the bishopric of Edinburgh. Not long after, he appointed Spottiswoode, Archbishop of St. Andrews, to be his Chancellor in Scotland.

The General Assembly had not been allowed to meet since 1618. Charles decided that the other democratic elements in the Kirk must be brought to an end too, and therefore he planned to abolish Presbyteries. At the same time, he and Laud took up with fresh vigour a problem which had troubled them both for some time—the Scottish form of Divine Service. It was clear to them that the English Book of Common Prayer was not acceptable in Scotland, though they could hardly see why, so they appointed a Commission to draw up a Revised Prayer Book for use in the Northern Kingdom. They thought they had offered a big concession in doing this, especially as a number of Scots were included among those who worked out the new Liturgy. They compiled a very fine Prayer Book.

One can never quite become accustomed to Charles I's ignorance of his own people or to his life-long habit of giving offence unawares. He did not know that his schemes to redistribute Church properties had enraged the Scottish gentry. He did not know that his coronation service had seemed like an act of paganism to Edinburgh people. He did not know that the Scots hated the thought of bishops being endowed with political authority. Least of all had he the slightest idea of how the Prayer Book would affect the situation.

The new Liturgy was read for the first time in St. Giles, Edinburgh, on July 28th, 1637. The Dean had hardly begun the service before there was an uproar of shouts from the congregation. Angry worshippers flung stools and Bibles about, and after they had been forced by armed guards to leave the cathedral the rioters banged on the doors and threw stones at the windows.

The outburst of fury was an expression of hatred against high-handed interference with religious liberty. As somebody wrote later, 'This new Book of Common Prayer is introduced and urged in a way which this Kirk hath never been acquianted with.' It was a beautiful Liturgy and its adoption would have been to the advantage of the Kirk in many ways, but it was doomed to rejection because it was identified with autocratic, remote control and it became a symbol of Roman Catholicism in thin disguise.

Public demonstrations were so violent that the Privy Councillors did not know what to do. They shut themselves up in Holyrood, which at a pinch could be defended against physical attack. They announced that the rioters were guilty of treason and worthy of death, but they also suspended the use of the Prayer Book. And then they composed a report of the matter to send to the King.

Charles had much else on his mind, and little attention to spare for Edinburgh's reaction to decently conducted public worship. He wrote his instructions to the Privy Council and they were perfectly straightforward. All who had protested against the Prayer Book were to be punished and the Book itself was to be taken into regular use.

'This I must say for Scotland, here I sit and govern it with my pen, I write and it is done, and by a clark of the Council I govern Scotland now . . .' So wrote James I. So thought Charles I. But this was one stroke of the pen too many. The Privy Councillors could not even begin to enforce the King's will in the matter.

Wild disorder continued in Edinburgh. In her book, *The King's Peace*, C. V. Wedgwood describes 'the Bishop of Brechin, tough and formidable, who glared at his congregation over a pair of loaded pistols while he conducted the service'. It became a risky proceeding for a bishop, or even a bishop's sympathizer, to appear in the Edinburgh streets. Of course, the rabble which chased and insulted these people was drawn from the barbarous vennels and closes of the city slums. It was headed as often as not by street women, harridans who understood nothing at all about orders of worship, but who loved to goad their men into a spirited fight. At the same time, however, petitions against the Prayer Book were appearing from many parts of the country, written in dignified incisive prose, the work of men who were fully capable of leading responsible opinion. The anger which inspired them was no emotion of the mob, but a new political fervour. But Charles persisted in sending orders that the petitioners should be dispersed and punished.

During the autumn and winter, representatives of the opposition formed a committee in Edinburgh known as The Tables. It was led by men with powerful connections, the Earls of Rothes and of Montrose. They had the support of many influential laymen, Lord Warriston for example, and ministers of first-class ability, such as Alexander Henderson of Leuchars. In sympathy with them were Lord Lorne, heir to the Earl of Argyll, and Sir Thomas Hope, both members of the Privy Council. Their hold on public opinion became very powerful.

When February 1638 came, the King decided to go off on holiday to Newmarket and enjoy some hunting. He did so with a relatively easy mind about Scotland, because, before setting out, he had despatched yet another proclamation. It was to be publicly announced in Edinburgh and other cities, that all the nobles who had resisted the Prayer Book were to submit to the King's will and to conform.

The proclamation was the spark that fired a totally unexpected explosion. Hundreds of demonstrators gathered at the Mercat Cross in Edinburgh in such a threatening temper that the only way of getting them to disperse was by asking their own leaders, Rothes and Montrose, to send them away. Even Charles was forced to see how slender his authority in Scotland had become when news of these scenes reached him in early March.

Far worse news however was to follow. On February 28th, in the Greyfriars Kirk at Edinburgh, the nobility of Scotland signed a document of which copies were soon made and signed on the two following days by many ministers and other delegates assembled in Edinburgh. The National Covenant was the document and it represented, in Lord Warriston's words, 'the great marriage day of this nation with God'.

The National Covenant had been drawn up by Lord Warriston and Alexander Henderson and other leaders, after months of thought and prayer. It incorporated a Confession of Faith, signed in 1581 by the twelve-year-old James VI; it detailed many Acts of Parliament for the establishment of the true religion and the maintenance of the Church's liberties; it included a protest against all the recent changes forced upon Scotland's Kirk; it ended with a vow of loyalty. 'From the knowledge and conscience of our duty to God, to our King and country, without any worldly respect or inducement——we promise and swear by the great name of the Lord our God to continue in the profession and obedience of the aforesaid religion; that we shall defend the same and resist all those contrary errors and corruptions according to our vocation and to the utmost that God hath put into our hands, all the days of our life.'

When Edinburgh's civic act of faith had been completed, copies of the Covenant were taken by mounted messengers to every part of Scotland and signatures were collected from all over the country, except the Catholic Highlands. It was then carried to Europe, to be signed by Scottish soldiers serving in foreign armies. It was supported by men of all classes and all ranks.

Cynics can claim that for political reasons skilled rascals whipped up the emotions of simple people and forced them to support the Covenant. Unquestionably many did so without in the least understanding what it was all about. We, who live in the 20th century, have every reason to appreciate that there are always people willing to sign documents in complete ignorance of their contents. And we know too that every movement attracts some knaves as well as a good many fools. But these were by no means the only influences behind the Covenant. Sincerity, courage, agonizing anxiety about the future, integrity, all went into its making. Among its authors and their best supporters were men who really loved their country and their religion. Charles had in fact precipitated exactly the crisis which could unite the Scottish people against him and he almost made the nation a unity. But he did not know this.

The Covenant expressed loyalty to the King and this was deliberate. The Scottish people had no wish to go against their sovereign, but they did think he was badly advised and they were desperate that he should know their thoughts. They probably did not realize that they had faced Charles with a challenge he could not ignore, but did not know how to meet.

CHAPTER 16
Scotland and the Civil War

The religious crisis of 1638 nearly achieved the impossible. For a few months it seemed as if the Scots were caught up in an all-embracing national purpose. From Edinburgh and the Lowlands there surged a wave of enthusiasm for the Covenant.

The driving force which inspired this movement came in large measure from James Graham, fifth Earl of Montrose. He was a Calvinist, but not at all a conventional one, for his was a tolerant, gay and generous spirit, he loved life and savoured its happinesses in friendship and in experience. By his personal charm and uncommon gift of leadership, perhaps too by his irrepressible sense of humour, he created a tremendous enthusiasm for the Covenant. His family seat was at Kincardine on the Ochil Hills and his influence extended through much of Perthshire and the east, but he carried the Covenant into Aberdeenshire too, the heart of Episcopalian territory, and even there he gathered a number of signatures.

In the west, the overwhelming power was that of Archibald Campbell, eighth Earl of Argyll, a different type of Scot, although he too was a single-minded Calvinist and as such distrusted all that Charles had been trying to do. His headquarters was at Inveraray and he controlled great stretches of the beautiful mountain country from Loch Awe to Loch Etive and across to Islay. While he was a dangerous enemy for Charles, he was also a dangerous colleague for Montrose, though this did not come to light in the early stages of the conflict.

Copies of the Covenant soon found their way to London, where nonconformists of all persuasions were stirred to great sympathy with the Scots. Charles realized that he was faced with a resistance that would yield to no persuasions, and in July 1638 he told his English Council that he would have to use force. This was easier said than done, as he had no standing army and his administration was riddled with inefficiency.

To give himself time for preparations, and hoping that his Scottish critics would quarrel with each other, the King sanctioned a meeting of the General Assembly, which was summoned in November 1638. A good many Covenanting Lords arrived, representing their congregations as elders. With them came bands of armed retainers. None of Aberdeen's Episcopalians dared to show face at all, nor were any bishops present, so the ministers of the kirk were well pleased. The King's Commissioner was the Duke of Hamilton, a London Scot who was most unpopular in his own country.

The Assembly of 1638 proved one of the most important in the century. So violent were its debates that after only a week Hamilton tried to dissolve it and he himself stalked out of it, but it continued in session without him. The Assembly deposed and excommunicated all the bishops, rejected the Service Book and appointed a Commission to enquire into abuses. The King declared that none of its decisions carried weight because in the absence of his Commissioner it was not a properly constituted body.

Enthusiasm for the Covenant received fresh impetus as a result of the 1638 Assembly, and the leaders found people eager to help in the preparations for war, which were now openly going ahead. Scottish officers and soldiers who had seen long service in continental armies returned home, and recruiting in the Lowlands and elsewhere was most successful. In Alexander Leslie the Covenanters had a first-class general whose experience had been gained under Wallenstein in Germany.

The King made two attempts to reduce the Covenanters by force, one in 1639, the other in 1640, and each was a humiliating disaster for him. On the second occasion, the Scottish army crossed the Tweed at Coldstream, led by Montrose, who waded the river in full kit three times to show the troops that it could be safely forded: they then marched in triumph to Newcastle, where they met with no resistance.

The failure of his efforts to crush the Scots forced Charles to summon his English Parliament. The members seized their chance to set out all their criticisms of the King's government since 1629 during which time he had ruled without any meetings of Parliament at all. Scottish commissioners, who were in London at this time, came to the premature conclusion that the English were pleased to have the Scottish army in their country and that they would be glad to adopt the Covenant.

Already, Covenanters in Scotland were falling foul of each other. A vindictive, intolerant spirit was abroad by now amongst some who wanted to enforce the Covenant, to make signature compulsory and to excommunicate any who stood out against it. Others were most uneasy about this bitterness, and saw that it could lead to religious tyranny of a very dangerous kind. At the same time, Argyll was making use of every chance to build up his own power. He was even talking of deposing the King, and it seemed that he wanted to organize a military dictatorship. Round Montrose a more moderate group was gathering, and it was known that he was out of sympathy with Argyll. He signed a pact with some of his supporters at Cumbernauld in Lanarkshire, re-affirming his belief in the Covenant but also his loyalty to the King.

In an effort to play off one faction against another, and to enlist Scottish support for himself, Charles agreed late in 1641 to all the decisions of the General Assembly of 1638. He was becoming more and more of an opportunist, and he still believed his enemies would quarrel so bitterly with each other that he would be able to re-assert his authority. Charles over-estimated his powers of intrigue. As he had never studied other people's thoughts, he did not know how their minds worked and he was wrong in thinking he could manipulate the factions arrayed against him.

He was not far wrong however in diagnosing disharmony among his enemies. When Civil War broke out in the harvest season of August 1642, there was friction in both his kingdoms among the people who hated him. The English Parliament and Army were hearing more than some people liked from the Independents, men of strong and sincere religious conviction who wanted much more individual freedom in religion than anybody else could approve. The Scottish Covenanters were divided less on principle but much more in practice. Montrose had no doubts as to his duty. Though still unchanged in his religious outlook and still loyal to the Covenant as he understood it, he was disgusted by the idea that he should take up arms against his King, and there were many like him, who had come to distrust the dogmatic views expressed by extremists. Argyll on the other hand was implacably hostile to the King and identified himself with the Parliamentary point of view: he too commanded support from many Scotsmen.

During the opening months of the war, events went ill for Parliament, whose leaders became desperately anxious. In 1643, therefore, they began to negotiate for active help from Scotland. Here was the chance for which Covenant men had been seeking. They consented to give Parliament military assistance by attacking the Royalist positions from the North, in return for which they were to be paid £30,000 a month for expenses. It was also agreed—and this was the marrow of the matter for the Scots —that there should be 'a reformation of religion in the Kingdoms of England and Ireland in doctrine, worship, discipline and government, according to the Word of God and the example of the best reformed churches, and that popery and prelacy should be extirpated'. The Scots hoped that by this treaty, which was called the Solemn League and Covenant, the English might be induced to bring their Church into conformity with that in Scotland, but the English Parliament interpreted the matter rather differently.

The Scottish Covenanters had been shocked when Laud had tried to impose his kind of religious uniformity throughout the land. They saw nothing inconsistent now in trying to enforce their own. This was because they believed that the Law of God must be supreme over the law of men, and throughout the 17th century the Covenant seemed to them to contain the Law of God. The Solemn League was a serious setback for Charles as it led to war on two fronts, which his forces could not sustain.

Meantime Parliament was giving attention to the spiritual wellbeing of the country, which in their view had been so gravely damaged by Laud, and it appointed the Westminster Assembly to give it advice. This Assembly, which in later days would have been described as a Parliamentary Commission, consisted of 121 English clergymen and 30 laymen, some of whom were Members of Parliament. Once the Solemn League and Covenant was ratified, the General Assembly was invited to send five ministers and three laymen to represent Scottish opinion in these deliberations.

The Westminster Assembly, despite a good deal of wrangling among its members, produced four documents of great importance. The Confession of Faith set out religious principles which were Calvinist in nature; the two Catechisms, known as the 'Larger' and the 'Shorter', were designed to help ministers and elders in their duty of instructing the young in Christian belief; the Directory of Public Worship gave orders of service which were to replace the English Book of Common Prayer. It was expected that England, Scotland and Ireland would all adopt these publications and so the desired uniformity throughout the three kingdoms would come about.

In fact, the Westminster Assembly's work exercised little influence in England except among the Congregationalist and Baptist Churches, but it did have a lasting effect in Scotland. For many generations Scottish ministers and Church members based their religious thinking and their worship on the Westminster documents, which have indeed become part of the Scottish Presbyterian's inheritance, though many devout members of the Church of Scotland would be astonished to realize that English influence predominated in the drafting of them.

Another publication which, after it had been revised, received the approval of the Westminster Assembly, was a metrical version of the Psalms by Francis Rous, a Cornish Member of Parliament, who was Provost of Eton. Further revision was carried through in Scotland over a period of several years, with the result that the Metrical Psalter, which came into use in 1650 with the authority of the General Assembly, bears little trace of Rous. The metrical Psalms have become an essential part of Presbyterian worship and they are still used too in some of the English Nonconformist Churches.

After the Solemn League and Covenant was signed, Parliament reorganized its army, under Cromwell's direction, and from 1644

onwards it was clear that Charles was doomed. With Scottish
help—and it was worth much, because the Scottish soldiers were
experienced and well-disciplined—Parliament's forces defeated
the King's at Marston Moor in 1644. The following year, Charles
met with fresh disaster at Naseby.

The only thing Royalists could rejoice over in 1644 and 1645
was the news from Scotland. Montrose had taken up arms for
the King and was gathering a formidable army in his support.
The story of his year of victories has become one of Scotland's
sagas. He defeated the Covenanters at Tippermuir and captured
Perth in autumn 1644. He campaigned in Speyside and caught
Argyll unawares at Fyvie. He went to Blair Atholl and thence, in
dreadful winter weather, forced his way over the barren mountains
westwards and attacked the Campbells at Argyll's own stronghold
of Inverary, so unexpectedly that Argyll himself only escaped by
rising from his dinner table, embarking on his boat and sailing
away down Loch Fyne to the sea. After an appalling winter's
march, Montrose defeated Argyll's people once more at Inverlochy and here again their chief left them to their fate and made
off by boat. Nobody who has even the slightest knowledge of all
this wild country or of winter conditions in the Highlands, can
fail to marvel at Montrose's generalship and at the physical
endurance of his troops.

The Covenanters in Scotland were in despair by 1645 and they
sent for English help. But Montrose captured Dundee, won fresh
victories at Alford, near Aberdeen, and at Kilsyth, and finally
established his hold both on Edinburgh and also on Glasgow. He
met with his first defeat in September 1645 at Philiphaugh, but
he still hoped to redeem the King's fortunes in Scotland, when
he heard that Charles had surrendered to the Scottish army at
Newark, in England. A condition of this surrender was that
Montrose should disband his followers and leave the country.
This was in May 1646.

It was a frightful blow for Montrose. Charles was at his old
game of playing off one set of enemies against another and he
was now seeking the support of Argyll. He thought he could do
this because the Independents in the English army had become
so hostile to Presbyterianism that there was no chance of Parlia-

ment honouring the promises the Scots considered they had made in the Solemn League.

Montrose went to Norway, deeply disillusioned, but with his personal reputation high, and his hold on Scottish affections extraordinarily strong, even in the districts where he had carried out his already legendary campaigns. Only amongst Campbells was he unforgiven.

The Scottish army in England was unfortunately placed. Since Marston Moor, their services had become less necessary to their allies, and the Covenant was most unpopular among the English soldiers. Moreover, the Scots were short of money; their expenses had been heavy, in the region, they estimated, of half a million pounds, and they had not yet received the payments promised in the Solemn League. Though they held Charles I, they could not make him accept the Covenant. Had he done so, they could have raised enthusiastic and effective help for him in Scotland, but it was more than he could swallow, even in his extremity. Stalemate had been reached, and so the Scottish leaders handed him over to the Commissioners of Parliament, accepted a promise of £400,000 towards their expenses, and made their way back to Scotland. They were dismayed when Charles declared that they had sold him.

And then, most curiously, there was a reaction among some of the Scots, who began to think that if Charles were re-instated things might improve. The Earl of Lauderdale, and others, visited him secretly and assured him of Scottish military aid if he would undertake to make England Presbyterian for a trial period of three years. Charles agreed, though with some modifying conditions. The treaty was called the Engagement, and the lords who negotiated it became known as the Engagers. Many Covenanters were bitterly angry with the Engagers, who seemed to be diluting the implications of the Covenant.

Meantime, Montrose was still abroad, much cast down in spirit because of all that he had seen and suffered and because he knew very well that the end was not yet. He was in Brussels when he learned, in February 1649, of the King's execution. When he was told of this, the shock was such that he fainted.

His great enemy, Argyll, was also profoundly moved. It had seemed logical enough to him that he should fight against Charles in collaboration with the Parliamentary leaders, but when Englishmen executed his King, Argyll was incensed. Like Montrose, he at once offered his services to Prince Charles, who was then eighteen years old, and he had him proclaimed King in Edinburgh. The Prince was not at all like his father in character, but unfortunately he believed, as Charles I had done, in playing one set of people against another. So he negotiated both with Argyll and also with Montrose, perhaps without fully realizing how furiously the former longed to bring about the downfall of the latter.

Montrose went to Orkney as the Prince's representative and thence crossed to Thurso to begin recruiting in Sutherlandshire, well aware that the cause was now almost hopeless. At Assynt he was betrayed by a laird who had offered him hospitality. He was then taken in miserable and humiliating circumstances to Edinburgh and put on trial for treason to the Covenant. In June, 1649, he was hanged, drawn and quartered. This horrible climax may have given Argyll some satisfaction. It established Montrose forever in the affections of those Scots who saw in him a man without bitterness or self-pity, capable of selfless devotion to a King unworthy of such service. His sentence was ordered by the Edinburgh Committee of Estates, men of his own country and his own religion.

After Montrose's disaster, Prince Charles had no option but to trust to Argyll. He came to Scotland and accepted the Covenant, a gesture which was not misunderstood by the Scottish leaders, for they knew that he did not intend to fulfil his word. But a coronation ceremony was arranged for him in Scone and it was Argyll himself who placed the crown on his head. Everybody present knew that not one of the principals in this stately scene trusted any of the others.

Already Charles II's supporters had been defeated by Cromwell at Dunbar, in 1650. The following year they met with an even worse disaster at Worcester. So the newly crowned King went on his travels and lived abroad for nearly nine years. During this period, Cromwell set up the most efficient, just and successful government Scotland had experienced in centuries. It was also the most hated.

It took Cromwell's troops from twelve to eighteen months to establish the military control which he considered a necessary beginning. By August 1652, resistance was at an end and already the Scots were becoming accustomed to the idea that their country had been united with England in a Treaty of Union. Thirty Scottish members were later selected as representatives in a national Parliament at Westminster. This startling departure from history and habit seemed perfectly natural to Cromwell, who had no patience with illogical or cumbersome political arrangements. He was in no doubt that a full Union would make for better administration, more effective control over those who might wish to make trouble, and also considerable economic benefit for Scotland.

Sir Thomas Urquhart of Cromarty, a most odd individual who translated Rabelais and wrote books on Trigonometry, offered some advice about this Union. He recommended that 'it be not heterogeneal (as timber and stone upon ice stick sometimes together) bound by the frost of a conquering sword, but homogeneated by naturalisation and the mutual enjoyment of the same privileges and immunities'. Urquhart had some attractive ideas. He begged the English not 'to maintain the charge of an everlasting war against the storms of the climate, the fierceness of discontented people, the inaccessibility of the hills and sometimes universal penury, the mother of plague and famine; all which inconveniences may be easily prevented without any charge at all, by the sole gaining of the hearts of the country'. Cromwell's officers in Scotland had difficulty in gaining the hearts of the country however, and one wonders what effect such a miracle would have had on the inaccessibility of the hills, let alone the storms of the climate. Robert Blair made a shorter and sadder comment. 'As for the embodying of Scotland with England, it will be as when the poor bird is embodied with the hawk that hath eaten it up.' This was the general view of the Scots. One of Cromwell's officers wrote with naive surprise, when the Union was proclaimed at the market cross in Edinburgh: 'Soe senceless are this generation of theire owne goods that scarce a man of them showed any sign of rejoycing.'

Cromwell appointed seven Commissioners, four English and three Scottish, to supervise the administration of justice. Their work surprised the Scots. 'To speak treuth, the Englisches were more indulgent and merciful to the Scottis, nor was the Scottis to their awin countriemen and nychtbouris, as wes too evident, and thair justice exceidit the Scottis in mony things, as wes reportit. They also filled up the roumes of the justice courtes with very honest clerkis and members of that judicatery.' New sheriffs were commissioned for all the Scottish counties, and special care was taken to put an end to violence and disorder in the Highlands. After some three or four years, it was said that 'a man could ride all over Scotland with a switch in his hand and £100 in his pocket, which he could not have done these 500 years'.

Cromwell deeply offended the General Assembly with whom he had little patience. He wanted to allow freedom of worship to all except Episcopalians and Roman Catholics. This new idea, and others too, shocked the Assembly, which was set on the Covenant's principles first and foremost. 'In the bowels of Christ', Cromwell wrote, 'think it possible you may be mistaken.' As the Assembly could think no such thing, Cromwell forbade it to meet. Small wonder that he was hated by Presbyterians.

The administration of Scotland, both during the Common-wealth, which lasted till 1653, and also thereafter under Crom-well's Protectorate, was based on military authority. At one time there were as many as nine regiments in Scotland. Five large permanent garrisons were established at Inverlochy, Inverness, Perth, Ayr and Leith; and a great many much smaller garrisons occupied old castles and country houses. The cost was so great that the most crushing taxation Scotland had ever known was laid upon a people already suffering from poverty which moved the English officers to pity. The Generals were appalled by the 'multitudes of Vagabounds, masterfull Beggars, strong and idle persons' wandering over the country, unemployed and without hope of finding material security. General Monck, who was Cromwell's commander-in-chief in Scotland, saw that most of the

£10,000 per month that he was supposed to raise in taxation must come from the struggling little burghs. He objected to it all very much. The burghs he said should be 'tenderly and carefully cherished', not bled white by such terrible exactions. This financial burden hit the common people very hard.

Naturally enough, Scottish people deeply resented the new arrangements which cut across precious traditions and subjected everybody to a discipline sanctioned by armed force. Cromwell's political idealism was too much for his contemporaries: believing in toleration and democracy, he was driven by the tensions of his day into establishing a rigidly enforced dictatorship. People in Scotland did not realize that their English neighbours disliked it all as much as they themselves. Anglo-Scottish relations, already much poisoned by bad memories of James I and Charles I, deteriorated still further under Cromwell.

The Marquis of Argyll was one of the few who made the best of it. Typically, and ingeniously, he came to satisfactory terms with Cromwell, despite his dealings with Charles II in 1649. On all his wide domains, only at Dunstaffnage and at Dunnolly were English soldiers posted, and he managed to maintain a certain independence which gave him a more comfortable existence than any other leading noble.

When Charles II was restored to his father's throne in 1660, there was a wave of emotional rejoicing all over Scotland. People irrationally believed that at last things would settle down, and that there would be an end of military dictatorship, interference with normal daily life, civil war and all the other evils. There was to be terrible disillusion.

CHAPTER 17

The Persecution of the Covenanters

C harles II was not vindictive and he was no religious fanatic. Bloodthirsty revenge on his family's opponents did not appeal to him and he disapproved of religious persecution. But he was determined not to offend those upon whom his security in England depended. He therefore agreed that fifteen of the surviving leaders who had been responsible for his father's execution should themselves suffer the same fate.

Argyll, whom Charles had made a Marquis in 1649, expected to be honoured when the man he had crowned in Scone was restored to the throne. Charles' advisers meant to get rid of him however, and the ingenuity of the great Marquis was at last defeated. They could not convict him as a regicide, but they executed him for treason. He received much more considerate treatment during his trial than Montrose had been allowed.

During the whole twenty-five years of his reign, Charles II never visited Scotland. He appointed a Privy Council, as his father and grandfather had done, which worked in Edinburgh, but whose Secretary was a London Scot, always based on the English capital. At the beginning of his reign, this Secretary was the Earl of Lauderdale, the Engager. Once an ardent Covenanter, he now held very different views.

The Scottish Parliament was summoned to meet in Edinburgh in January 1661, and the King's agents saw to it that this Parliament was efficiently packed with men of Royalist views. It cancelled all legislation carried through since 1633. This implied the restoration of bishops and also of the system of patronage, abolished in 1649, whereby ministers were chosen by the landowner and not by the congregation.

Ministers admitted to the parishes since 1649 were required to seek out their patrons and ask to be formally presented and then to secure admission to their charges from the bishop of the diocese. About 300 ministers refused to submit to the regulations and abandoned their churches and manses. They formed almost one-third of the total number of ministers and the authorities had some difficulty in finding substitutes for them. The main centre of opposition was in the south-west where, in many places, the people forsook the parish churches and resorted to their former pastors in kitchens and barns, and later in the open fields and on the hillsides.

The Privy Council began to fine people who refused to attend the services in the parish churches, and to encourage parish ministers to make lists of absentees, so that these fines could be enforced. It also decreed that 'outed' ministers were not to live within twenty miles of their former parishes or within three miles of any royal burgh, so that it became difficult for their supporters to keep in touch with them. And then troops were quartered in the areas where resistance was strongest, especially in the shires of Ayr, Lanark, Dumfries and Galloway.

Meantime the newly appointed bishops were trying to make the best of a very awkward situation. Some of them, like Patrick Scougall in Aberdeen and Robert Leighton in Dunblane, were men of real piety and much wisdom, but on the whole they had not the qualities or the leadership to make Episcopacy any more palatable than formerly. Most unpopular of them all was Archbishop Sharp of St. Andrews.

By 1665, the illegal services in the farms and fields, known as conventicles, were so numerous that the Government made absurdly severe efforts to crush them by force. The punishments were made steadily harsher, until the Covenanters were goaded into raising a pathetic and ill-organized little rebellion. A number of them marched in pouring rain and squelching mud through Ayrshire and Lanarkshire to Rullion Green, on the outskirts of Edinburgh. Here in November 1666 they were hopelessly routed. Fifteen leaders were hanged in Edinburgh, others in Glasgow and Ayr, many more were imprisoned and subjected to torture by an instrument known as the Boot.

In 1669, Lauderdale himself came north as the King's Commissioner and tried a new policy of winning the Covenanting ministers by issuing Letters of Indulgence which offered them parish appointments on rather less stringent conditions. While some of the ministers accepted them, others refused, on the grounds that Covenant principles were still in danger and the Government had no right to legislate for the Church. Those who continued their resistance were treated more severely than ever. By armed force they were hunted out and rounded up with their lay supporters and put in specially prepared prisons, such as that on the Bass Rock, where many of them died in great misery. For years and years the odious oppression went on and so did the resistance.

At last violence produced the inevitable reaction. In 1679, Archbishop Sharp was shockingly murdered by a group of Covenanters who came upon him driving home to St. Andrews in his coach. Shortly after the King's troops, commanded by John Graham of Claverhouse, a relative of the great Montrose, were surprisingly defeated by an armed mob of Covenanters at Drumclog, on the borders of Ayrshire and Lanarkshire. This led to terrible retribution. Charles II's illegitimate son, the Duke of Monmouth, was sent to quell the disorder, and at Bothwell Bridge he carried out his mission. The Covenanters were mown down by the Government troops, and after the battle was over, twelve hundred were taken prisoner. They were herded into an improvised concentration camp in the churchyard of Greyfriars, Edinburgh, for many weeks on end. About a third of them were cowed by this and took oaths to submit to the Government, and so were sent home. Others obdurately refused and of these many died and some were executed, but about two hundred and fifty were condemned to slavery in the West Indies and loaded onto a transport ship. Perhaps fortunately for them, this vessel sank in a storm near the Orkneys and they were drowned. After another Indulgence, the policy of repression was renewed, the persecutions were accelerated, and the early 1680s became known as the Killing Time.

The stories of Covenanters who underwent all this shocking misery have been told and re-told. Descendants of these people naturally accord them the highest place in family regard and tradition. The fundamental point is overlooked very often however.

How, why, did men and women stand it? And how, why, did they do so for such long years? Unquestionably, their strength was derived from their Calvinist faith. They believed that they were predestined to grace and that they would be given the blessings of those who had 'come out of great tribulation', who would be 'before the throne of God' to all eternity. Many of them died, not with Spartan fortitude, but with joy.

Relief came at last in an absolutely unexpected way. When Charles II died in 1685, he was succeeded by his brother James, Duke of York, who became a Roman Catholic. So bitter were the controversies in which he involved himself with his English subjects that, late in 1688, he threw in his hand and left the country. The English at once declared that this 'abdication' meant that he had forfeited all right to the throne. They invited his Protestant daughter Mary and her husband, William of Orange, to become the rulers of the country in his place, and this great change is known in English history as the Glorious Revolution. In England it was almost a bloodless revolution. Though William III was never much liked, Protestants were thankful to have him, and they saw to it that he came on conditions thoroughly understood and well hedged about by sanctions.

For Scotland, the Revolution meant an abrupt end to the Killing Time and to all the miserable hounding of Covenanters that had bedevilled everything for so long. Early in 1689 a Scottish Convention of Estates agreed that William and Mary should become King and Queen and declared that there should be no more bishops. Later the same year, Episcopal government was in fact abolished and in 1690 the Westminster Confession of Faith was once again adopted: the Presbyterian government of the Church by General Assemblies, Synods, Presbyteries and Kirk Sessions was confirmed; and patronage was again set aside.

A most important constitutional change was also brought about in 1690, one which had been long needed in Scotland. The Committee of the Lords of the Articles was abolished. This meant that the Scottish Parliament was at last free to discuss legislation as a Parliament should, and in consequence its work became more vigorous and influential, because the King could not interfere so effectively as hitherto. Not enough emphasis has been laid on this side of the Revolution Settlement in most histories of Scotland.

It was impossible for the Revolution to be 'bloodless' north of the Border. Stewart loyalties were strong in the Highlands, and Graham of Claverhouse raised enthusiastic support for James among the clans. General MacKay was sent with Government troops to suppress this outburst, but unfortunately for them their route took them through the deep, narrow gorge of Killiecrankie, to this day a grim, wild spot. Claverhouse waited for MacKay at the head of the gorge, with his men in an advantageous position in the cliffs above. The success of the Highlanders was complete and in a matter of hours MacKay's forces had been almost annihilated. But Claverhouse himself was killed, and without his leadership, his forces were ill-handled, and soon after were themselves defeated in the grounds of Dunkeld Cathedral beside the River Tay.

William III's position was now assured in Scotland. On the whole people were thankful for it, though the country was too exhausted and poverty-stricken with the results of three terrible decades to show much enthusiasm. Apart from certain West Highland clans, only the most extreme Covenanters grudged William his success. They formed a hard core of implacable and obstinate dissent, the nucleus from which sprang a number of splinter groups in the 18th century Presbyterian Church, and to them the Revolution meant nothing but the betrayal of their principles. In their view a State-sponsored Church was a disaster: and the Covenant should have been made compulsory by the supreme authority of the Kirk. But there were too few of these fanatics to hinder the establishment of William's authority.

Of the Highland clans, the Glencoe Macdonalds were the most reluctant to accept the inevitable. The horrible tragedy that befell them spoiled the success of the Revolution and made one more black and disgraceful memory for Scotsmen of the 1690s.

The Chiefs who had fought against the Government were offered pardon on condition that they took an oath of allegiance before January 1st, 1692. For this purpose, MacIan Macdonald of Glencoe arrived at Inveraray, his nearest point of civil administration, on January 2nd. His lateness was due partly to his own procrastination, partly to the snowstorm which held up his difficult journey from Fort William. By January 2nd, the Sheriff-depute had temporarily left his Inverary headquarters. But he returned on January 5th and took Macdonald's submission.

The Master of Stair reported to the authorities that by January 1st the Macdonalds had not subscribed the oath. Hereditary enemies of the Macdonalds now seized upon the moment as a chance of wiping out old grievances, which were numerous, because this family had indeed been a lawless, marauding lot. William III was therefore induced to sign a document authorizing the annihilation of the Glencoe Macdonalds. His defenders have always alleged that he never read it—and certainly he had the bad habit of allowing correspondence to accumulate and then rapidly going through it, signing papers he had not digested.

In February, 1692, Campbell of Glenlyon was instructed to go to Glencoe and billet his men on the Macdonalds, which he did. For a week, the Campbell troops lived on good terms in the small Macdonald community of that exposed mountain glen, and then at 5 o'clock one morning, they turned upon their hosts and began, under stringent orders, an attempt to murder them all. Tradition tells many tales of Campbells evading the horrible task, warning individuals up and down the glen to escape while the going was good, but thirty-eight of the one hundred and fifty adult men living there were murdered and others lost their lives afterwards in the snowbound mountain region where they tried to hide.

The scandalous affair created angry reaction up and down the country from Ballachulish to London. No public disaster, no official or semi-official crime, had ever made people so furious or so disgusted before. Some historians have suggested that the Glencoe massacre was no worse than earlier attempts to liquidate unruly clans, such as James I had perpetrated against the Loch Lomond MacGregors. But the betrayal was unforgivable to a Highland people, where proper treatment of those who are admitted to one's home was traditionally matched by the principle of respect for the man who has given another his hospitality. Nor could public opinion overlook the fact that the Macdonalds had taken their oath, and a four days' lateness seemed a minor matter

in those unpunctual days, so that there was left no excuse for
justifying the massacre as a punishment merited by disaffection.
The whole affair blackened the reputation of William's government in Scotland for many years.

As one thinks about the thirty years following the Restoration
of Charles II in 1660, one realizes that it formed one of Scotland's
most unhappy periods. Irreparable harm was done. Charles II's
Government was afraid of treason, afraid that if legal regulations
were disregarded, the State would be endangered. It was influenced
by men who were unfitted to form a reliable judgment either on
the state of public opinion in Scotland or on the right way to
handle religious dissent, and so the policy of barbarous repression
was adopted and nobody had the wisdom or courage to stop it.

Had there been wiser counsels in Westminster and in Edinburgh, the Presbyterians and Episcopalians might have found a
modus vivendi and their divisions would thus have been much
less damaging in the following centuries. As things worked out,
however, the results of religious persecution made it impossible
for Presbyterians and Episcopalians to trust each other. The
bitterness between them had been artificially inflamed to such a
point that religious intolerance seemed almost a moral duty.

The sadness of it all becomes more poignant when one recalls
that at this time the two parties had much in common. In order
of worship and in religious principle they were more similar than
people nowadays realize. Both preferred to receive Communion
seated at long tables; neither as a rule observed the Christian
festivals of the year; both upheld Sabbatarian principles, and
administered severe moral discipline; each was suspicious of organ
music but devoted to the metrical Psalms. As an English army
chaplain stationed in Scotland put it—'The difference between
the Episcopalians and the Presbyterians can scarcely be discerned
in their worship and therefore we the more admire that the two
parties so much disagree between themselves when they appear
to the world so much like brethren.'

The brotherliness detected by the English chaplain did not
survive the Killing Times. In revulsion against the authority
which had sanctioned all that terrible suffering, Presbyterians
developed a bitter hatred for everything English, forgetting that

the persecution had been approved and largely administered by Scots. Anger and pain make for irrational judgment, and it is not surprising that the children of Covenanters identified Anglican and Episcopalian principles with the English way of life. They adopted the mistaken idea that everything Anglican was hostile to their own traditions and to spiritual wellbeing. So Presbyterians now became narrower in outlook than the founders of their Reformed Kirk had been, and they came to regard the Creeds and Doxologies as liturgical devices that should be expurgated from their services and many even rejected the Lord's Prayer as an 'obnoxious prelatic superfluity'. In the 18th century services were composed of long sermons and extempore prayers, with Bible readings which were too often selected from the Old Testament and expounded with emotion rather than scholarship. There was little in all this that was in keeping with the Book of Common Order and with the principles of John Knox and his associates.

The 20th century has seen a growing desire among many Christians for union between the Churches. In Scotland, this ecumenical movement has been impeded by the long-term results of controversies now three centuries past, inaccurately recollected and emotionally rather than rationally interpreted. It is difficult to exaggerate the harm done by those who directed the religious policy in Scotland of Charles II and James II.

The King who came to power as a result of the Revolution in 1688 and 1689 was unaware of all these tensions. He was a European and he thought in continental terms. To William III, the separate political and economic administration of two such small countries as England and Scotland seemed absurd. Like his predecessors James I and Cromwell, William believed that there should be full union. Pre-occupied with his international worries, he could not carry through even the preliminary steps towards such a change, but as he lay dying in 1702, he sent a recommendation to Parliament: 'Nothing can contribute more to the present and future peace, security, and happiness of England and Scotland than a firm and entire union between them.'

The way in which this unlikely event was achieved is described in the following chapter.

PART THREE

The Eighteenth and Nineteenth Centuries

CHAPTER 18

The Union of 1707

That Scotland and England became united in 1707 is one of the oddest facts in British history. In the last decade of the 17th century everything seemed to be militating against any such event; yet thinking people were beginning to realize that political and economic union would indeed offer both partners real benefit. This opinion was encouraged by two strange and unconnected developments—the Darien scheme and the ill-health of Queen Anne's son.

The Darien affair was largely the work of a Dumfriesshire man named William Paterson, who had a flair for associating himself with novel projects, and had amassed a fortune in London. He was one of the original directors of the Bank of England, founded in 1694, and he took a hand in organizing North London's new water supply, led from the Hampstead and Highgate hills. He had also travelled a good deal in the West Indies and New England.

In June 1695, Paterson helped to found the Scottish Africa and India Company. He advertised it with such zest that he secured £300,000 from English investors, and subscriptions from Hamburg and other European centres, besides promises of £400,000 in Scotland. High hopes were centred upon the project amongst Scotsmen, who believed it would bring them a trade revival, and there was furious indignation when the English government suddenly repudiated it and all English contributions were accordingly withdrawn.

To Paterson such a setback was merely a goad to further effort. He now made Scotland his headquarters and began to charter Dutch vessels, to buy stores and to accumulate goods for export. The scope of his endeavours had to be reduced because of the English withdrawal, and so the Darien isthmus was selected for its beginning. The company directors planned a settlement there for colonization and trade. They pictured it as a world emporium, for did not the isthmus command access both to the Pacific and to the Atlantic Oceans? Here a new Caledonia would retrieve Scotland's economy, provide markets for world trade, careers for the young, dividends for the old and glory for everybody.

One wonders whether Paterson was unaware that Darien belonged to Spain, that the English government was negotiating with the Spanish, that any Scottish success in the isthmus would lead to hostilities. Had he no knowledge of Darien's swamps, flies and fevers? Did he really expect customers for the bonnets, serges, huckabacks, stockings, bobwigs, periwigs and gridirons which were loaded onto his vessels?

The three ships of Paterson's first Darien expedition sailed in 1698 and he himself was a member of the company. Before news of the disasters encountered by this advance party had reached Scotland, a second expedition was on its way. On arrival, this new group of 300 settlers found that famine and disease had almost obliterated the first contingent, that there was nowhere to live, nobody to sell to, and no protection from fever. A few months later, a third expedition set forth, still without information about the calamities of the first two. There were brief hostilities with Spanish forces, after which a handful of survivors managed to struggle home, despite shipwrecks and other distresses.

Scotland had subscribed almost a quarter of a million, nearly a third of her total cash circulation. Every penny of this was lost, all the ships and their cargoes squandered. Two thousand young men had died.

The disaster brought it home to Scotsmen that even though Scotland and England were ruled by one sovereign, as had been the case since 1603, the Scots would never be able to develop their material wellbeing properly while their country remained economically separated from England. The Darien tragedy had used up all Scottish capital and it would be years before any more could be available. Sheer want drove men with business knowledge to a new political viewpoint about union. They realized that

Scotland, with limited resources and little influence, needed what England, strong and alienated, was determined not to give.

Queen Anne's personal tragedy provided the smaller country with the only bargaining power which could modify the larger country's policy. She had given birth to seventeen children: only the Duke of Gloucester survived. In 1700, at the age of eleven, he also died. England therefore had to face the prospect of Anne's own death, without a direct heir.

The principal danger, of which English statesmen were acutely aware, was a second Stewart Restoration, and this the ruling Whigs were determined to prevent. The country was now predominantly Protestant, and James Edward, the son of James II, was a Roman Catholic. Parliamentary institutions had become essential to the English way of life, and Stewarts had proved themselves to be evasive of constitutional limitations. In 1701, therefore, the Act of Succession was passed, to ensure that the crown should go to Protestant George, Elector of Hanover, and the great-grandson of James VI and I. The next and urgent step was to secure the agreement of Scotland in order, as Bishop Burnet of Salisbury put it, that 'the back-door' might be 'shut against the attempts of the pretended Prince of Wales'.

Here was Scotland's weapon. The English so little understood their neighbours that it was a matter of conjecture whether the Scots would prefer a Roman Catholic or a Protestant succession. This was because they knew that loyalty to the Roman Church and to the Stewart family was assured in the Highlands, also among many Scottish nobles; on the other hand the strength of the Reformed Kirk in the Lowlands and among townsfolk was not fully understood in London. And political leaders in Scotland played for time so that English anxiety about the 'back-door' was aggravated, especially when war began against France in 1703.

The Scottish Parliament, lately released from the paralysis formerly laid upon it by the Lords of the Articles, acted with spirit. Most of its members were Presbyterian and most of them knew that a Stewart succession would lead to disaster. They were not prepared, however, submissively to follow England's lead and for months heated debate raged over the questions of succession, separation and federation. Andrew Fletcher of Saltoun declared that if union under one sovereign must continue, it should be much modified. Burnet said that his proposals amounted to 'setting up a commonwealth, with the empty name of King'. These proposals included automatic royal consent to parliamentary bills, the appointment of all highly placed officials by Parliament, and parliamentary sanction for declarations of war and peace.

At last, the Scottish Parliament showed how far they were prepared to collaborate with the English over the succession, by the Act of Security, passed in 1704. This stated that the Scots would not decide who was to be their next sovereign during the lifetime of Anne, and that while they would give the crown to the nearest Protestant descendant of the royal line, in no case would Hanover be acceptable without safeguards for Scottish political institutions, religion and trade. It also made provision for a military force to be trained in defence of the country. This Act aroused furious reaction in England, and at first the royal assent was refused. Two other Acts emphasized the new strength of Scotland's bargaining powers. One embodied Fletcher's suggestion of parliamentary sanction for declarations of war and peace, which in effect took foreign policy out of the control of the sovereign; the other legalized the import of French wines, duty-free.

England was now deeply involved in hostilities against France, and as an incentive the Scots flung in the threat to withhold supplies for maintaining strongholds and defences along their coasts. The back-door seemed to the English half-open already, and, reluctantly, Anne's ministers conceded that she should give her assent to the Act of Security, because of the danger if French ships were allowed access to Scottish ports.

In March 1705, the English produced their counterblast, the Aliens Act, by which Scotsmen were to be treated as aliens, unless they agreed to the Hanoverian succession by Christmas Day the same year. This meant that Scots would be forbidden to send their linen and cattle over the Border, and they would be cut off from supplies of English horses, woollen goods and weapons. Such a situation would naturally have led to even more deplorable poverty in Scotland. The Aliens Act was a vicious move, but it suggested that Commissions should be appointed to discuss 'firm and entire union'.

Less than a month after this Act had inflamed Scottish feelings to a pitch of hatred, an English sea-captain called Green, with two of his crew, was executed on the sands of Leith, on a charge of piracy. This was partly because a short while earlier a Scottish ship called the *Annandale* had been seized in the Thames by the London authorities for trespassing on East India Company preserves; still more potent an incentive was the common belief in Scotland that Green had been responsible for atrocities inflicted upon another Scottish vessel, ill-named *The Speedy Return*. Storms of anger convulsed the Edinburgh mobs, who were determined to have blood revenge on Green, although the charge against him was substantiated only by false evidence, so that soon after his execution his innocence became a well-established fact.

In the heat of this crisis, while London opinion was seething over the tragedy of Captain Green, while Edinburgh was letting loose a spate of anti-English pamphlets, while many serious-minded people were dreading bloodshed, the Commissioners were appointed. The atmosphere could hardly have been worse. Yet the moment had arrived when at least each side had something to offer and something to sacrifice. If Scotland would agree to the Hanoverian succession, and if England would concede commercial equality, Union would have some chance of success. By the end of 1705, responsible opinion on both sides was aware of this fact.

Once it was agreed that negotiations should be undertaken, thirty-one Scottish nobles and thirty-one English Commissioners were without delay appointed by the Queen. It is to their great credit that they approached the difficult work seriously and decisively, each side making adjustments in order to find a feasible compromise where opinions clashed, because at this late date each side believed that the Union was essential to the future peace of both countries.

The two Commissions worked separately, except for one meeting, and they communicated with each other in writing. They completed their draft of the Treaty in rather less than three months. In October 1706, the final session of Scotland's last Parliament met to consider the terms in an Edinburgh seething with anti-unionist mobs. Violent scenes occurred also in the streets of Glasgow and Dumfries, while hostile addresses flowed in from many shires and also from royal burghs. But there was support for the measure too, from the nobility, from businessmen and from ministers. With only slight modifications, the Treaty was finally passed in the Scottish Parliament on January 16th, 1707. Thereafter the measure was debated at Westminster in the final English session of the last English Parliament, with much less heat and much less delay. Finally the Act of Union received royal assent on May 1st, 1707. It was described by Mar as 'a solid fundation for putting the countries on one bottome to all posterity.'

The two Parliaments were both brought to an end, and the newly constituted Houses of Lords and Commons were created to form the new supreme legislative body for the United Kingdom. The question of representation was complicated, because England was not only the larger partner but also much the richer. The ratio of wealth was probably about 38:1, and of population about 5:1. In the end it was agreed that there should be 513 English members to Scotland's 45 in the House of Commons, a ratio of 11:1, and that there should be 16 Scots peers to England's 190.

The Treaty made no change in the religious systems of the two countries. Statutes were passed for the purpose of recognizing the Churches of Scotland and England, and these were incorporated in the Acts which ratified the Union. Without this safeguard, designed to make sure that their religion was 'effectually and unalterably secured', Scottish Presbyterians would never have allowed the Union to come to pass.

The legal traditions of the two countries were also safeguarded. Scottish law courts were to continue as before, the heritable jurisdictions and legal rights enjoyed by clan chieftains were unaltered, nor was any adjustment suggested for royal burgh privilege. Appeal from Scottish courts to certain named English courts was forbidden, but no reference was made in this regard to the House of Lords, an evasion which was to cause trouble later on.

Scottish ships, whether foreign-built or otherwise, were classed as British, so that the old sting of the Navigation Acts was removed forever. Standardized coinage, weights and measures were adopted, on English lines; although English customs and excise were to become the basis of future British tariffs, Scotland was exempted for the duration of the war from any increase of the malt tax, and for seven years from higher impositions on salt.

The most complex of the Articles of Union dealt with financial matters, and they illustrate, as do those dealing with commerce and trade, the effort made by the Commissioners to negotiate a fair deal for the Scots, now that the Union had become essential. By 1697, England had a National Debt of some £14½ million, which increased year by year until in 1714 it amounted to over £36 million. This money represented loans, or investments, made through public subscription, largely by such privileged organizations as the East India Company and the Bank of England. The loans were regarded as permanent, and annual dividends on them were paid by the Government, on the security of national taxation. The system marked a considerable advance in financial policy and offered reasonably safe investment for capital, and great convenience to the Government. On the other hand, by the time of the Union the Scottish public debt was less than £200,000. Thus Scottish taxation would in the following years be partly devoted to the payment of annuities on National Debt, for which the Scots had no responsibility. The Commissioners agreed therefore that trusted Scottish mathematicians should be employed to work out an assessment of Scottish loss from this source. A figure of almost £400,000 was finally arrived at. The sum, termed the Equivalent Money, was sent up to Edinburgh in bullion and exchequer bills. It was used to compensate Scottish merchants for private losses caused by the change in coinage, to discharge the public debts of the Crown in Scotland, to encourage Scottish industry and fisheries, and also to repay as far as possible those who had suffered loss through their Darien investments.

There was little enthusiasm for the Treaty. One historian has stated that 'most of the subjects of the new united kingdom were ignorant of the Union or unmoved by it'. Even the Equivalent Money made a bad impression. The dragoons detailed to guard the waggons dragging this curious load northwards were abused and pelted by Northumbrians, who were enraged at the sight of

English gold crossing the Border, and abused and pelted again in Edinburgh because people thought the great sealed boxes contained only stones and useless paper. The mud slung at those unfortunate soldiers from both southerly and northerly critics perhaps symbolizes a good deal of later abuse. Certainly it was not long before the habitual mistrust between the two sections of the new United Kingdom found fresh means of expression.

Critics of the Union have often declared that the Scottish Commissioners were bribed by the English government to accept it. In fact, these thirty-one Commissioners spent four months in London during 1706 and they were given handsome grants to cover their expenses, which must indeed have been considerable, while various state officials had arrears of salary made up. Almost all who received such reimbursement were fully committed to the Act before any payments were agreed, and the whole transaction was publicly debated in Parliament. By 18th century standards of public integrity there was no question of bribery and even by modern standards it would be hard to prove the charge.

In recent years, it has become fashionable to belittle the Treaty of Union, to dwell upon its more irksome consequences and to question the motives of those who worked to achieve it. Some 20th century Scottish Nationalists regard the whole thing as a great betrayal. But as one reconsiders the circumstances in which it was worked out, one can see that the Commissioners on both sides acted in good faith to establish what was essential for the future welfare of both nations. And they had no precedents to help them. Inexperienced as both Scots and English were in handling the problems which arise when two nations seek a common way of life, they could look to no other similar union for enlightenment. Thus they had to concentrate upon what seemed to be of fundamental importance, and to work out as best they might a daring and unusual political experiment, whose consequences could only be surmised. Some of their decisions show insight and wisdom—the recognition of the Scottish Church and the maintenance of the two separate legal systems for example, also the assessment of the Equivalent Money. More impressive still is the fact that, both to England and to Scotland, Union was now a fundamental necessity. For the sake of its assured continuance, the English abandoned the commercial monopoly they had so tenaciously maintained hitherto. For the same purpose, and also to rescue their people from economic disaster, the Scots embarked upon organized collaboration with a people whom they had formerly found hostile and unyielding.

Those who decry the Treaty and criticize its makers would do well to consider the only available alternatives. These were renewed warfare at worst, ill-defined and uneasy federation at best. Each of these expedients would have made Stewart restoration more likely and so would have led to fresh religious conflict, and probably also to economic disaster. Each would have deprived both nations of the stimulus produced by partnership with a vigorous and gifted neighbour. The Treaty of Union, on the other hand, gave Scots and English alike the chance to develop economic stability during the 18th century and at the same time to foster their own special characteristics.

But the question still remains, why has the Union aroused angry, even emotional criticism amongst Scottish people from time to time since 1707 and especially in the 20th century?

Perhaps this may be explained by its two most serious defects. Included in its terms there was no scheme for altering the balance of representation in Parliament, should the balance of population or wealth become changed. Thus when Scottish contributions to the Treasury increased, and when Scottish people formed a larger constituent in the total British population, it did not occur to the Government that there should be more Scottish members sent to Westminster, until 1832. Even then no rational principle of increasing the Scottish membership was worked out, and only in 1884 was the northern partner in the United Kingdom adequately represented. The other defect was more fundamental, more difficult to rectify and even less readily understood in England. Sovereignty is a precious thing. The Scots now lost it. However well they might be represented at Westminster, in terms of numbers they would necessarily always be in the minority. So decisions about Scottish affairs, the spending of national resources on Scottish administration, would always be controlled by a legislature overwhelmingly English.

CHAPTER 19

Jacobites

The half-century from 1695 onwards formed a wretched period in Scottish history. There was the Darien disaster. Then there was James Edward's rebellion of 1715. Thirty years after that, the families who had already suffered so much endured the terrible losses of Culloden, and the privations caused by Cumberland's policy of suppression. Much hostility and some hardship came through the Government's financial measures. Religious animosities were once more aroused. The Scottish people were insufficiently represented both in the House of Lords and also in the House of Commons.

The troubles began with misunderstandings about religion. In 1711, an Episcopalian clergyman called Greenshields was punished by the Court of Session for using the Book of Common Prayer. This man set off an explosion by appealing to the House of Lords, now by implication the supreme court of appeal for the whole country. So soon therefore was the test case launched which the framers of the Treaty had hoped to evade. The House of Lords reversed the findings against Greenshields, put through a Toleration Act in support of Episcopalians, and ordered all Presbyterians and all Episcopalians to take an oath abjuring the Pretender.

Worse aggravation followed in the Patronage Act of 1712. This restored the right of landowners to appoint the ministers to churches situated on their properties. No piece of legislation could have contravened more flagrantly the spirit in which the Treaty of Union had been drawn up, no misunderstanding of Presbyterian principle could have produced more resentment. The religious emotion evoked by this Act aroused both hatred of the English arrogance in handling ecclesiastical affairs, and much dissension within the Church of Scotland itself. Not until 1874 was it abolished.

Scottish anglophobia was stimulated by other insults to Scottish pride. In 1711, the Duke of Hamilton was given the additional and British title, Duke of Brandon. He expected a seat in the House of Lords as a peer of the realm, but it was decreed that no British title should give a Scottish peer the right to this honour, also that Scots who became peers of Great Britain should thereby lose their right to vote for their sixteen representatives in the Upper House. Thus the most distinguished members of the Scottish aristocracy were disfranchised.

There were economic grievances too. The tax on salt was increased and this damaged Scottish fisheries. The Malt Tax was re-assessed in 1713, in order that the excise on Scottish malt might be brought more into line with that of the much richer English product. Home-brewed ale was produced all over the country at that time, when tea and coffee were hardly known, wines and spirits far too costly. The uproar caused by the proposed increase in the excise on malt was so great that the regulation was allowed to remain a dead letter for a dozen years, but Scottish anger was not lessened by this procrastination.

There were repercussions all over the country. As early as 1710 Parson Wodrow of Eastwood wrote: 'The Jacobites are mighty uppish . . . They talk of nothing but Resignation, Restauration and Rescission, their three R's, and they talk their King will be over, either by Act of Parliament or by invasion by August nixt. They boast mighty, which I hope will ruin their cause.'

The only people in the United Kingdom who were consistently against these three R's were the English Whigs and a proportion of the Presbyterian Lowlanders. In fact most of the Tory leaders were in touch with James Edward, even though they affirmed their loyalty to Anne. So strong was Jacobite feeling that, when Queen Anne fell ill in 1714, there was danger of the Hanoverian Succession being annulled by a coup d'état. The proclamation of George I was due to the rapid and cool-headed action of Shrewsbury, a Whig leader who was appointed Lord Treasurer by Anne only a few hours before her death. 'A wonderful dash to the

Jacobites' wrote Wodrow of this proclamation. 'Had the Queen lived a little longer they think their schemes would have taken effect. However the Lord hath broken the snare and we are escaped.' George himself, like his English advisers, knew the escape had been by a narrow margin.

At this time James Edward was twenty-six years of age. All his life had been spent abroad, mainly on French territory, and as his father died when he was thirteen, he was much influenced by his Italian mother, Mary of Modena. Had James Edward become King, therefore, he would have seemed as foreign to the British as did George I. If he had been willing to renounce his Roman Catholicism and to declare himself a Protestant, the crown would have been his, probably without bloodshed, but he was not prepared to secure his inheritance on such terms. Further he must have imagined that a second Stewart restoration was feasible without resorting to any such policy, for malcontents of all parties corresponded with him, and as he never visited either Scotland or England he could hardly have realized the odds against him.

By the time George I had been on the throne a year, he had inspired little affection for himself among his new subjects, while James Edward could boast many supporters in south-west England, in Oxford, in Northumberland, in London itself, as well as in Scotland. The failure of the enterprise on the English side was due to the well-timed action of the Government in arresting prominent Jacobites. The sudden departure of the Duke of Ormonde, who went abroad at the critical moment, had a good deal to do with the collapse of the movement too, as he was its acknowledged leader. His failure of nerve, or lack of judgment, in going off at this point left James Edward's supporters without a commander-in-chief on the spot, so that few of their movements were co-ordinated.

The Scottish rising was led by the Earl of Mar. He summoned a gathering at Braemar, ostensibly for 'hunting', and there on September 6th, 1715, he proclaimed James VIII and III as King. At the same time he made a public statement to the effect that the Union had proved a blunder, by which Scotland's 'ancient liberties were delivered into the hands of the English'. The ideals he had entertained eight and a half years earlier, when he had supported Queensberry and acted as Commissioner for the Treaty, Mar thus publicly renounced and thereby gave his critics one more reason for nicknaming him 'Bobbing John'.

A large number of chieftains came out to join Mar from the shires of Ross, Inverness, Banff, Aberdeen and Perth, also from parts of northern Argyllshire, from the Lothians and from Galloway. The burghs of Inverness and Inveraray remained Government strongholds, as did Glasgow, with most of the central Lowlands and Fife. Late in September, the Pretender learned with some surprise of the Scottish developments, for he had expected the main effort to come from south-west England.

'Bobbing John' proved himself to be no leader. In the early weeks of the revolt he commanded far more men than the Government. He captured Perth almost at once, and made it his headquarters. Had he then advanced upon Stirling, he could have secured the road to England, and with an immediate move across the Border, or a concerted drive on Edinburgh, he could have won further success before winter set in, and this would have brought him more supporters. However he chose to remain in Perth, and to divide his army, part of which he sent to Galloway.

Meanwhile Argyll was organizing Government forces in Scotland. This very able soldier made sure of Stirling, with the help of a contingent from Glasgow and Paisley, and immediately afterwards consolidated the defence of Edinburgh. On November 14th, 1715, the forces of Mar and Argyll met in battle on Sheriff-muir, a desolate upland above Dunblane. The Jacobites outnumbered their opponents, but the battle ended indecisively, as each right wing scattered its immediate enemies and flung itself into disorganized pursuit. A Jacobite officer summed it up as follows: 'Thus ended the affair of Dumblain, in which neither side gained much honour, but which was the entire ruin of our party.'

Sheriffmuir did prove to be virtually the end. Within a few days of the engagement, the half-hearted efforts of the Jacobites in northern England were crushed at Preston. From now on, with winter's ordeals threatening their families, short of many necessary supplies and without effective leadership, the

Highlanders began to go home. Desertion depleted the Pretender's armies so much that when at last James Edward arrived at Peterhead in mid-December, he found that Mar had lost about half the troops he was believed to command. James Edward's late arrival and pessimistic outlook depressed his followers. He had every reason however to be depressed himself by the attitude of his undisciplined and unco-ordinated supporters. On February 4th, 1716, he left again for France, accompanied by Bobbing John, who preferred not to await events in Scotland.

Many Jacobites believed things would have been different had French help been forthcoming, and these regarded the death of Louis XIV, in September 1715, as a major disaster. In fact, Louis XIV would certainly not have given effective help, at least until James Edward had proved himself supreme, as France could not have faced the renewal of war with England which this policy would have brought about. The true causes of the failure in 1715 lay in the Jacobites' lack of a leader, who could both co-ordinate the scattered resources and also exact loyal obedience. In short raids and guerrilla tactics the Highlanders excelled, but in strategic movements on alien ground over a period of several months, they were not reliable. Further, there could be no unanimous support for James Edward in a predominantly Protestant country while he continued in his Roman Catholic loyalty. The same difficulties were to arise again thirty years later.

The aftermath of the revolt makes dreary reading. Some hundreds of Scottish Jacobites were transported to the plantations, and nineteen peerages were forfeited by Act of Attainder, so that although only two of the leaders were executed, many Scotsmen had to go into exile. An attempt was made to disarm the Highlands, with the result that loyal clans handed in their arms while those who had supported James Edward successfully hid most of their more efficient weapons for future use. Throughout all these proceedings, Scotsmen resented the fact that their whole nation was stigmatized, although George I had been loyally supported by many of the clans and by most of the Lowlands.

The influence of Sir Robert Walpole on the affairs of the realm did nothing to improve the situation. His long tenure of office lasted from 1721-42. During this time, he set himself to extract more national income from customs and excise and he never troubled to study Scottish ideas or traditions. In 1725 he determined to put into effect the changes in the assessment of salt which had been made statutory in 1713. The result was an outburst in Glasgow, where so far the support for the new régime had been consistent since 1707. The mobs destroyed the magnificent mansion of Daniel Campbell, the member of Parliament for the Glasgow group of burghs, and put up a spirited fight against the town guard.

Such an outburst could in no way prevent the law from being fulfilled, but this one was long remembered as a patriotic display, and it caused even more popular sympathy with smuggling. From now onwards, French wines were regularly brought to inlets all along the East coast and even to the Solway, and so were brandy, tea and cambrics. The nation's attitude to smuggling was well illustrated in 1736, when the Edinburgh folk yet again broke out, this time to lynch Captain Porteous. The cultured and broadminded minister, Alexander Carlyle, described Porteous as a man 'elated' by being 'admitted to the company of his superiors' proud of his 'skill in manly exercises, particularly the golf', insolent, rough and of violent temper. When he was in charge of the execution of a well-known smuggler, Porteous was insulted and pelted with mud by the crowd, a common enough occurrence when these odious hangings were carried out. Losing his temper, he fired on the densely packed mob, and a number of people were killed. Although he was imprisoned for this outrage and condemned to death, rumours got round that he might be reprieved. In consequence 'Persons unknown, with the greatest secrecy, policy and vigour', forced his prison, 'executing his sentence upon him themselves, which to effectuate cost them from eight at night till two in the morning; and yet this plot was managed so dexterously that they met with no interruption, though there were five companies of a marching regiment lying in the Canongate'.

The affair became a public scandal. In Parliament, the view was taken that Edinburgh should be disgraced, because of the disorder which the authorities had possibly countenanced and certainly failed to quell. In the end, the Lord Provost was expelled from his office, never to be allowed to hold a public position again, and Edinburgh was fined £2,000. Scottish public opinion was enraged by these decisions, just as English public opinion had been enraged by the lynching of Porteous.

All things English were now under suspicion, but more harmonious relationships might have developed through the increased travel and trade between the two countries. Charles Edward however hankered to proclaim his father as King. He landed in July, 1745, on the island of Eriskay, with two Scotsmen, four Irishmen and one Englishman. The enterprise was a hopeless one from the start, although in the early stages Charles Edward brought to it an enthusiasm and an assurance which almost made it seem feasible.

As usual, the Jacobites hoped for French help. In 1744, France had declared war on Britain, already deeply involved in the War of the Austrian Succession, and Louis XV had invited Charles Edward to Paris, for discussion about a Stewart restoration. Shortly before the Prince embarked, the British had met with defeat at the Battle of Fontenoy. Louis XV was prepared to follow this up by creating a second front, for the embarrassment of his foes, in Scotland. Charles Edward's interpretation of the events was optimistic in the extreme, and he expressed his hopes in a letter to Louis XV. 'May I not trust . . . that this signal victory which your Majesty has just won over your enemies and mine (for they are one and the same) has resulted in some change in affairs; and that I may derive some advantage from this new blaze of glory which surrounds you?'

Scottish Jacobites were reluctant and dubious. Soon after Charles Edward's arrival in Scotland, Macdonald of Boisdale begged him to go home. 'I am come home, Sir,' was the reply, 'and I will entertain no notion at all of returning to that place from whence I came; for that I am persuaded my faithful Highlanders will stand by me.' The Prince managed to persuade Lochiel, Chief of the Cameron clan, to join him, and this had an immediate effect on others; indeed, but for Lochiel's decision, the whole project might well have petered out. On August 19th, the standard was raised at Glenfinnan, James VIII and III was once again proclaimed King, and the Prince set forth towards Edinburgh, gathering supporters as he went.

Sir John Cope was in charge of the inadequate Government forces and, knowing that it would be some time before he could be reinforced, he determined not to risk another Killiecrankie. His withdrawal was sensible enough, but he chose an odd direction for his retreat, making for the north and leaving the road to the capital open. In mid-September Charles Edward marched exultantly into Edinburgh where he was 'mett by vast Multitudes of people, who by their repeated shouts and huzzas express'd a great deal of joy to see the Prince'. Cope meantime reached Aberdeen, embarked his men on board ship and brought them south to Dunbar, whence he gloomily set forth to recover what lost ground he could, although he was still short of supplies, arms and even cash to pay his troops. The Jacobites, who were at their best in these circumstances, came out from Edinburgh in strength and on 21st September met and routed Cope's army after a brief engagement at Prestonpans. This victory elated the Prince's supporters and brought him many reinforcements. 'The Prince', recorded Lord Elcho, 'from this Battle entertained a mighty notion of the Highlanders, and ever after imagin'd they would beat four times their number of regular troops.' In a triumphant letter to his father, Charles Edward wrote: 'The men I have defeated were Your Majesty's enemies, it is true, but they might have been your friends and dutiful subjects when they had got their eyes open to see the true interest of their country, which I am come to save and not to destroy. For this reason, I have discharged all public rejoicings.'

Had this campaign been staged half a century later, the Prince would probably have made an immediate drive over the Border. These however were days of slow motion warfare, inevitably, because communications were so poor. As Mar thirty years earlier had remained in Perth during the precious autumn weeks, so Charles Edward now stayed in Edinburgh for well over a month. In the first week of November, a bad time of year for starting a war, he began his march southwards with nearly eight thousand men. They came from the same areas and the same clans as those who had supported his father, with some additional groups, such

The Eighteenth and Nineteenth Centuries

as the Frasers of Lovat. Old Simon Lovat, the head of the clan, refused at first to commit himself, and negotiated with both sides, waiting to see who would win before acclaiming or disowning his heir, who went out under his instructions.

Many clans were firmly hostile to Charles Edward throughout the affair. These included Campbells, Mackays, Munros, Macphersons, Grants, McLeods, MacNeills and some of the MacDonalds. Of those who joined the Prince, few could have understood the issues at stake. These men marched because their chieftains told them to, and perhaps also in hope of booty. Years later Lord Cockburn recorded the story of a Highlander who was asked whether he had not always considered it absurd even to try to dethrone the Hanoverians. 'Na, Sir!' was the reply, 'I ne'er thocht aboot it. I just ay thocht hoo pleasant it wad be to see Donald riflin' London.'

On November 8th, the Prince's army reached Carlisle and then pushed on to Preston. By a feigned advance upon Wales, they shook off the pursuit of Cumberland, who had been sent to intercept them. Once again a road to a capital was open, and the Jacobites made use of it, but by the time they reached the Midlands they were suffering from familiar difficulties. When was French help going to materialize? Why had only about 300 Englishmen joined them? What would the Londoners do? With these questions in mind, Charles Edward's advisers fell to quarrelling, while his Highlanders decided that winter in England offered little reward, that 'riflin' London' seemed a remote possibility and that they would be better at home.

The decision to retreat was taken against Charles Edward's wishes. Lord Elcho, who was present, said that he 'fell into a passion and gave most of the Gentlemen that spoke very Abusive Language, and said that they had a mind to betray him.'

His instinct was to press on. Many historians have believed that his instinct was right and that, had he gone on to London, his immediate campaign might have been successful, though ultimately his cause could hardly have survived. Once the Jacobites turned north, their luck was out. People who had been friendly when the army was marching south were now hostile, supplies were not to be had, the wintry weather impeded everything, discipline weakened and desertion increased. The army retreated to Dumfries, then to Glasgow, where they forced the merchants to supply them with quantities of clothing. In January 1746, Charles Edward won his last success at Falkirk, where he dispersed a Government force, but he did not follow the victory up and he made no effort to get back to Edinburgh. Instead he went further north.

Only misery now lay ahead for the Jacobites. They had served their turn as far as Louis XV was concerned, for large numbers of British and Continental troops had been withdrawn from Flanders. These troops were sent to Scotland under the Duke of Cumberland, George II's favourite son. This Prince, now twenty-five years of age, was enjoying a reputation described by Horace Walpole: 'The soldiers adore him, and with reason; he has a lion's courage, vast vigilance and activity and, I am told, great military genius.' Later, Walpole changed his opinion, as did many another.

Cumberland made for Aberdeen, where he spent six weeks in methodical preparation. With him was his aide-de-camp, young Wolfe, later famous as the conqueror of Quebec. In April 1746, with a well-armed and experienced force, they caught the Jacobites on Drummossie Moor, east of Inverness, near Culloden House. Charles Edward's men were exhausted with forced marches and lack of food and sleep. They were taken by surprise and cornered, to face driving wind and rain. Their divided leadership and inadequate weapons made them easy prey for their enemies and they suffered a devastating defeat. Duncan Forbes, the Laird of Culloden, was the Lord President of the Court of Session, a man of justice who valued peace and had devoted himself at great personal cost to the Government. That the ghastly slaughter carried out came to be known by the name of his family home must have been bitter indeed for Forbes. He loathed bloodshed, and he did all he could to restrain Cumberland from the brutal excesses which followed.

Cumberland on the other hand detested Jacobites, with almost pathological fervour. After the battle he ordered that all stragglers were to be killed and that no mercy was to be shown, even to the wounded. As one contemporary record baldly puts it, 'everybody that fell into their hands gott no quarters, except a few who they reserved for public punishment.' The Duke organized a systematic burning of homes, including remote hovels, and he had thousands of cattle rounded up for confiscation. The disaster he inflicted on the Highlands caused terrible destitution. Duncan Forbes he described as 'that old woman who spoke to me of humanity'.

Charles Edward made his escape towards the west, while Cumberland's butcheries were inflicted on those who went north or north-west. The Prince was given such wonderful help on his sad journeyings at this stage that in songs and poems and historical romances the story has been made a classic, and justifiably, for the £30,000 reward offered to the man who captured the Prince represented untold wealth.

Flora Macdonald's share in his adventures won her respect and renown. After she had secured his embarkation at Portree, she was arrested and sent to London, for her Highland boatmen talked injudiciously, even though many of their countrymen were silent. She spent some months in the Tower, was released, and later lionized in London, whose inhabitants had a good eye for the spectacular. Her head was unturned by this publicity, and she went home again, to marry Alan Macdonald of Kingsburgh. When Samuel Johnson met the two of them at their own home in 1773, he was immensely taken with her personality and he deeply regretted her emigration to North Carolina the following year. She and her husband made a stand for the Hanoverians during the American War of Independence, and experienced as exciting adventures in support of George III in the New World as Flora had gone through for the Stewart Prince in Skye: ultimately they got back to Kingsburgh. Her portrait by Allan Ramsay may be seen in the Bodleian Library at Oxford; the painter's sure touch has revealed the gentleness, the sympathy and the courage which in youth had comforted the Prince and in middle age had stolen old Johnson's heart.

After 1746, Jacobitism was finished, although the authorities in London did not realize it. The Government had been so shocked that every effort was now made to crush the already moribund movement. One hundred and twenty people were executed, including the 78-year-old Lovat, whose foxy behaviour brought him no advantage and caused him to be mourned much less than the rest. Over eleven hundred were transported or exiled, and nearly seven hundred died in filthy gaols. The Highlands were disarmed, this time with scrupulous and undiscriminating care; the confiscation of weapons and bagpipes was imposed throughout the Highlands, to the exasperation of the many clansmen whose loyalty to the Government had been consistent. The most absurd ruling of all was that the wearing of the tartan was forbidden—'no more than a chip in the porridge', and 'not worth a halfpenny', as Forbes contemptuously exclaimed, but none the less an unrealistic and silly prohibition devised by distant Englishmen and calculated to exacerbate bitter feelings. The estates of the Jacobite chieftains were confiscated for administration by the Government, until 1784, when heirs of the families were reinstated.

A more telling piece of legislation, which had permanent results, was the abolition of heritable jurisdictions, in right of which civil and criminal justice had been summarily dispensed by the heads of certain Highland families for many centuries. The abolition of this anomaly was a necessary prelude to establishing the King's Courts and the normal judicial routine in the Highlands. As G. M. Trevelyan put it: 'The King's writ must run in the glens.' Contemporary letters suggest that the Judges found their new spheres of activity exacting and bizarre, not least because of the misadventures which befell them as they journeyed over rough tracks and negotiated fords across the rivers which swirled through their enlarged circuits.

The two rebellions poisoned the relationships between England and Scotland just when there was some hope of improvement. The inept interference from London with Scottish religious problems and the equally unfortunate fiscal policy caused a lot of resentment, naturally enough, but in spite of these mistakes, economic conditions in Scotland did gradually improve in the early years of the 18th century and confidence in a supposedly equal partnership might have been established. But the repressive measures carried out in Scotland after the rebellions, and especially the presence of English soldiers on Scottish soil, made a permanent and a very bad impression. The whole thing smelt of conquest. Popular sentiment and popular literature—both powerful forces—romanticized the Jacobites, not so much because the Scots really wanted the Stewarts back as because they hated the English. The Union of the two countries would have been far more successful but for this.

After about 1750 however there came a marked change in the Scottish scene, because now, for the first time since 1286, when Alexander III's horse stumbled in the darkness and flung his master over the cliff-edge, Scotland was relieved of the nightmare of war on her own territory. At last, long-stifled vitality found outlet, in original and vigorous form. From about 1750 onwards, the Scottish share in British and in imperial developments became more and more significant. This may be illustrated from the history of agriculture, industry and transport; it is apparent in Scottish literature, art and architecture, in religious thinking and educational planning: almost more strikingly so in exploration, missionary work and colonial enterprise.

Too often it is assumed that Scotland's true greatness may be found in medieval times or even in the more remote past, to which periods sentimentalists are inclined to attribute romance of an altogether fictitious nature. The truth is that, in facing the demands and seizing the opportunities offered by the new way of life opening out from the mid-18th century onwards, Scottish people entered upon a renaissance not always accorded its rightful emphasis. Certainly it was tarnished by the grim and materialistic squalor in which it was nurtured, marred by much physical and mental suffering, vitiated by greed and heartlessness. This dark side of modern history must be admitted: and it must be recognized as characteristic of many countries other than Scotland. It was the price at which was bought the adjustment to unprecedented tensions, the growing-pains of modern society; gradually it became recognized as such and then men gave their minds to this challenge also, with results which are not yet fully realized in the 20th century.

In the following chapters the bold achievements of Scottish courage and intelligence are set out and the record shows that, once freed from the fear of crippling internal warfare and of foreign invasion, Scotsmen could take a leading place on many frontiers, physical and intellectual.

CHAPTER 20

Agriculture

Scotsmen living in the Lowlands and the Borders enjoyed a rather better standard of living even as early as 1707 than those in Argyllshire and the north and west. Even so, their families, like those of all other agricultural workers in Scotland, were held in chronic bondage to unrewarding labour. This was because medieval techniques were followed with little adaptation and so the soil yielded poor results. Malnutrition sapped people's strength and burdened their lives.

Traditional designs in domestic architecture did not help matters. People lived in one-roomed cottages, built of loose stones, turfs and clay, thatched with heather, ventilated by one door but no window and no chimney. Such hovels were in use till the end of the 19th century in the Highlands, though elsewhere rather better homes began gradually to appear. Admirers of the poet Burns will recall that his father, William Burnes, himself built the cottage where in January 1759 he was born; and that the little building collapsed in a violent storm less than a week after the baby's arrival. William then rebuilt it, and the second structure withstood all subsequent gales and today is one of the most frequently visited centres of tourist traffic. It represents a more roomy and comfortable style of living than agricultural workers could afford at the time of the Union.

The terrible poverty of the Scottish countryside, caused by unenlightened farming methods, was suddenly worsened at the end of the 17th century, because in 1696 there began a dreadful series of bad summers. For seven consecutive years there were destructive rainstorms in July, August and September, the harvesting months, and in each of these years winter came early and proved severe. This calamity coincided with the financial disasters of the Darien scheme.

The Eighteenth and Nineteenth Centuries

The destitution in Scotland at this time was vividly described by many writers, both Scottish and English. In 1698, Andrew Fletcher of Saltoun expressed his bitterness in terms somewhat confused by emotion. 'There are at this day in Scotland, besides many poor families very meanly provided for by the church boxes, with others who by living on bad food have fallen into various diseases, 200,000 people begging from door to door. These are not only in no way advantageous, but a very grievous burden to so poor a country. And though the number of them be perhaps double to what it was formerly, by reason of the present great distress, yet in all times there have been about 100,000 of those vagabonds, who have lived without any regard or subjection either to the laws of the land or to those of God and Nature.' An anonymous author wrote in 1747: 'If we cast our Eye over all the counties in Scotland and look into the wretched and low Condition of the Common People and Poor, we will find some famished for want of Bread; others dispirited for want of Employment; not a few starved with Cold and Nakedness; and many whole families throughout every County, especially in and about Villages, commonly remain in a languishing, nasty, slothful and useless condition, uncomfortable in themselves, and unprofitable to the Proprietors of the Grounds.'

Even the men who were not dispirited for want of employment in the early 18th century were short of many necessaries, because wages were so low. Labourers in 1730 were earning 40/- a year and by 1760 this figure had risen only to 60/-, so that although food was cheap, standards of life were miserable. The lairds were also hard put to it to maintain reasonable comfort in their families, since much of their rent was paid in kind and, being perpetually short of cash, they had nothing to invest and no means of undertaking improvements.

One fundamental and rarely acknowledged reason for such continuing poverty was that Scottish soil lacked lime. Even nowadays, the value of lime is probably not fully appreciated. In the 18th century, few landowners understood how badly their acid soil needed calcium in one form or another: and transport was so difficult that not even the best-intentioned farmers could have carried lime to their properties in sufficient quantity.

Agriculture

The collapse of the monastic system had done away with the landowners who were best able to make a success of their farms. Their properties had fallen into the hands of lairds who knew little or nothing themselves, while until the mid-18th century their tenants persisted in the run-rig system of early medieval times. The outfields were alternately scourged and neglected; the infields were divided into hump-backed rigs; and each man had to tramp around his neighbour's intervening rigs in order to reach his own scattered holdings. Seed was still broadcast by hand; winnowing was done out of doors on windy days; grinding continued as a daily chore for the women, who used querns, unless there was a local mill, in which case the tenant always had exorbitant dues to pay. The old, heavy, Scottish plough pursued its slow progress until the 1790s or even later, surface-scratching half an acre a day to a chorus of shouts and yells from the four or five men and women who directed it and controlled its eight or ten oxen. The astounding fact is that these underfed and ignorant people did for many generations somehow succeed in supporting their families. It is equally astonishing to realize how rapidly in some areas the transition from the outmoded run-rig system to more adequate methods of production was effected.

For these improvements, better transport was the first necessity to make proper manuring possible, and drainage a strong second, since much of Scotland's best soil was lying waterlogged in the channels between the rigs, or in uncultivated valley marshes. Along with these could be listed afforestation on a national scale, for Scotland had built and burnt her woods away, with the result that rain and wind had done much deadly work in shifting topsoil and laying bare the rocky structure of the Scottish hillsides.

Clearly initiative in the use of fertilizers, the planning of drainage, tree-planting and the like could be undertaken only by moneyed landowners, or by wealthy tenants enjoying the security of long leases. Most Scots leased their holdings on uncertain tenure for one or two years at a time: such men could not undertake longterm improvements, for if they did so, their rents were raised in proportion to the increased prosperity, or else they were turned off their holdings when their leases expired.

Soon after the Union, landed gentry began to realize the scope for agricultural developments. As early as 1723, the Honourable Society of Improvers in the Knowledge of Agriculture was founded, the first organization of its kind in Scotland. Its members planned to collect and publish information, to give advice and to support all enterprise in agricultural projects. From this time onwards, Lowland and Border landowners began to take a more active interest in farming techniques, and numerous other societies were founded by enthusiastic agriculturalists. They pooled their information, discussed their experiments, criticized what they had observed on their continental travels, and often found occasion to comment unfavourably on the work being done by landowners over the Border. These Scottish pioneers in agriculture were spared some of the delays which their English contemporaries had to face, because tenant rights in Scotland were not buttressed by traditional or legal safeguards. At the end of a man's lease, the tenant could be turned off with scant ceremony, so that the term 'enclosure' north of the Border came to mean merely the process of building dykes or walls around the owner's land, and it should not be confused with English 'enclosure' which involved sanction by Act of Parliament.

A considerable literature on farming topics naturally began to develop. James Donaldson was the first of such Scottish writers. In 1697 he published his *Husbandry Anatomised*. Donaldson suggested enclosure of the rigs, so that people's property might become geographically compact, he wanted more fertilization, with a regular system of resting the fields between crops, and he believed in potato culture. He also said that far too many head of cattle were being maintained on indifferent pasture, and he therefore suggested reducing livestock.

Donaldson's book was followed in 1699 by Lord Belhaven's *The Countryman's Diary* and, during the next century or more, by a quantity of pamphlets and other publications, all dealing with agricultural improvement. In some districts the new methods were ignored or despised, in others this literature was eagerly sought, even by people struggling against adverse conditions with little or no capital behind them. One such was the poet Burns, who found himself in 1784 responsible for a family of brothers and sisters, on the death of his father. Burns moved them to a new holding, at Mossgiel in Ayrshire, where he threw himself into the task of making the little farm pay, and he read all the agricultural literature he could lay hands on. Sixty years earlier nobody in such a position would have dreamed of reading anything.

One of the first individuals who began practising new methods was the Earl of Peterborough's daughter, who married Lord Huntly in 1706. She took the bold step of bringing English ploughmen with their ploughs all the way up to the Gordon estates, and began a campaign of draining, tree-planting, fallowing and haymaking. Her enterprise proved infectious, so that some of her neighbours began to undertake similar improvements.

A contemporary of Lady Huntly was Sir Archibald Grant, son of Lord Cullen. In 1717, on the occasion of his marriage, Grant's father presented him with the poverty-stricken estate of Monymusk, twenty miles from Aberdeen. This was no fatherly gesture, as Lord Cullen had been regretting his recent purchase of these lands. Grant was an Edinburgh advocate and a Member of Parliament, so he could not settle on his new property until 1734, but he corresponded with his factor and other responsible employees.

In his first year, Grant spent £1,200 on enclosing his fields, building dykes, draining and tree-planting, with such success that between 1726 and 1731 his nurseries provided, for sale or transplantation, over a million trees of various kinds. The cultivation of trees improved his property, for the plantations acted as windbreaks. This prevented wholesale erosion of the soil by gales and so enhanced the value of the adjoining fields. At the same time, valuable supplies of Scottish timber were developed, in a period when Scandinavian wood was being imported at high costs.

In 1726, Grant brought an English farmer called Thomas Winter to his estate and this man supervised the cultivation of turnips by the drill, and also instituted hoeing. Turnips provided winter fodder for the undernourished cattle, so that the stock began to improve. At the same time better grain could be produced

on fields where turnips had recently been grown, because
the hoeing dealt with weeds. Monymusk was one of the first
Scottish estates where turnips were properly used, and Grant
was well ahead of many English improvers in this matter. The
English prophet of turnip culture, whose preaching was rapidly
adopted in progressive areas, was Jethro Tull, author of the
classic, *Horse-Hoeing Husbandry*. This book, privately issued in
1731, was published in 1733. Grant bought a copy for 10/6d in
1736, by which time he had little to learn from it, and neither
he nor his Aberdeenshire friends accepted all its findings.

Grant was one of the earliest Scottish improvers to insist upon
regular use of lime. In adopting this method of improving his
soil, he was doing his country a significant service, as it enabled
him to grow wheat, a crop hardly known in Scotland before the
Agricultural Revolution, although afterwards it was successfully
produced on many Border and eastern farms. Grant's success in
wheat production was also due to his rotation of crops, in which
turnips were followed by wheat, beans and oats.

Grant made time to talk freely with his tenants and by personal
conversation to stimulate their own initiative. Gradually he
parted with those who were obstructive, while to those who were
enthusiastic he gave long-term leases. In studying Grant's work,
one is reminded of the great Coke of Norfolk, whose similar
achievements a century later have attracted much wider publicity.
Grant left in Monymusk one of the best-farmed and most
beautiful estates of Scotland, and Lord Cullen's wedding gift
proved to be more valuable than the donor himself would have
dreamed possible.

Many other landowners transformed their estates by similar
methods during this century, for example the Earl of Stair, who
had property in West Lothian and in Galloway. He concentrated
on roots, grasses, sainfoin and lucerne, all pioneer crops, but his
most famous achievement was his great scheme of afforestation
in Galloway, where he planted half a million trees, and where
his woods still remain, a living testimony to his foresight, and a
most beautiful heritage. Later in the century, Lord Kames
became famous for the work he did in Berwickshire, and also in
Perthshire. These two counties gained almost more than **any**

others by the changes introduced, although throughout the Borders, in extensive areas near the east coast, in Morayshire and in Aberdeenshire, the new methods brought about a dramatic transformation. For the last two centuries some of these estates have been hard to rival in standards of husbandry and quality of output.

As rents and profits increased, small landowners and lairds took to enjoying spells of Edinburgh life, and so the more luxurious city ways spread into the countryside and provincial towns. After about 1760, Lowland farmers' wives began buying china dishes to replace pewter and wooden ware. By this time too, tea was used in all classes of society, to the disgust of Duncan Forbes, Alexander Carlyle and others, who regarded it as a demoralizing drug. About 1765, George Robertson noted that farmers were looking for carpets, exchanging their old boxbeds for four-posters with pleasantly checked curtains, furnishing their apartments 'in a more dashy style', purchasing sofas and elegant pianofortes. In 1790, the minister of Kilsyth reported a change in fashions. 'Formerly the most respectable Scottish farmers used to wear nothing but Scotch cloth of their own making, plaiding, hose and bonnets. Now the servant men on holidays wear nothing else than English cloth, cotton and thread stockings and hats ... Every maid servant wears silk bonnets and cloak, and generally muslin or printed gowns and thread stockings. So that the men and women are more gayly dressed than their masters and mistresses were formerly.'

From medieval times there had always been a demand in England for Scottish cattle. There were famous cattle trysts at Crieff and at Falkirk, to which beasts were driven incredibly long distances. The drovers maintained a nomadic way of life as they journeyed over the Borders towards the south, following the ancient drove roads, and their story is admirably told in A. R. B. Haldane's *Drove Roads of Scotland*. English dealers bought Highland cattle eagerly, because although they were small, skinny animals, and although they lost weight on their long marches, a period of fattening on the richer southern pastures transformed them: their beef carcases had a particularly succulent flavour which was much appreciated in London dining-rooms. In the early stages of their journeys, the cattle were saved many miles of land travel because they swam some of the estuaries, such as Lock Fyne, but the rough wayfaring was so hard on their feet that they had to be shod. North of Cambridge, on the Huntingdon Road, there is a little public house called the Travellers' Rest. It was one of many stopping places for the Scottish droves, and in the field behind it hundreds of small cattle shoes cast by the beasts have been unearthed.

The quality of Scottish stock greatly improved towards the end of the 18th century. This was partly the result of enclosure by dykes, which enabled owners to keep their herds separate from those of other people, but much better winter fodder became available as more turnips and grasses were sown, and this naturally improved the quality of the animals. The demand in England increased towards the end of the 18th century. Fully 100,000 beasts were driven over the Border each year during the Napoleonic wars, and the trade was well maintained after the wars came to an end.

Much information about 18th century Scottish farming may be found in the famous *Statistical Account of Scotland*. This massive work was planned by Sir John Sinclair, the owner of large estates in Caithness, a man with a fanatical love of statistics, who had carried out improvements on his own property and accumulated an encyclopaedic knowledge of agriculture. The Statistical Account was a national survey, based on information extracted from parish ministers, each of whom was issued with a questionnaire and asked to provide a description of his parish, its economic background and its contemporary conditions. The Account ran to twenty-one Volumes, published from 1790 onwards. It contains vividly expressed evidence of the agricultural advances made in the parishes where enclosure had been carried out, also of the consequent rise in expenditure and improvement in living standards.

Sir John persuaded the Government to constitute the Board of Agriculture in 1793, and he became its first President. He made himself rather unpopular, as he was a bombastic man with little sense of humour and he was always harrying people to undertake grandiose schemes; indeed Sir Walter Scott nicknamed him Cavaleiro Jackasso. But he did a great deal for the nation's food production during the war and he was the first person to understand the value of statistics in public investigations. His immense labours proved so valuable that in 1845 a second Statistical Account was published in 15 volumes; and now, during the 1950s, a third and much more comprehensive one is in process of publication.

Farm implements were slow to change during the 18th century. It was not until 1764 that James Small, a Berwickshire man, invented a swing plough which could be manipulated by one man with a pair of horses. Progressive farmers were quick to see its advantages, because the furrows it cut were deeper and cleaner than those of the old Scotch plough. Nonetheless, the old model died hard and was used in remote corners of some counties until the 19th century was well advanced. During the 1770s, Andrew Meikle of Dunbar produced a horse-drawn threshing machine, which was soon adapted to water power. The notion of artificially creating a wind shocked a number of people who declared that Meikle's invention was of the Devil, but by the end of the century it had been adopted on many farms. Early in the 19th century, a Scots minister called Patrick Bell devoted his engineering tastes to the construction of a mechanical reaper. This entirely novel machine cut the grain and bound it into sheaves which were flung out into a line as the reaper made its way across the field. The original models were pushed, not pulled, by horses.

During the Napoleonic wars, Britain needed much more home-produced food, so that progressive Scottish farmers who made use of new methods and new machines were sure of ready markets and high prices. The incentive to modernize all husbandry made a great difference south and east of the Highland line.

In the Highlands however the picture was very different. The Statistical Account shows that by 1790 little enclosure had taken place in the north-west and west of Scotland, where indifference to new-fangled ways persisted throughout the 18th century. Indeed to cross the Highland line was almost like entering another country. The crofters carried out their ancient agricultural rites on scattered pockets and patches of land, and in some places, Arrochar for example, people used the ancient Highland digging-stick, or caschrom, until 1810 and even later.

Cut off from all but immediate neighbours by boulder-strewn hills, long narrow sea-lochs, and sodden peat mosses, the Highland people were lethargic in mind and slow in movement, partly because they and their families suffered chronically from the agues, rheumatisms and skin diseases of the ill-housed and the ill-fed. Ironically enough, part of the trouble was that in those glens that were populated at all, there were too many of these peasants, whose primitive methods of cultivation could not produce sufficient food to maintain their large families. Statistics concerning prisoners captured during the Forty-Five show that the average Highlander in Charles Edward's army was a man of poor physique, about 5 feet 4 inches in height, though he had proved himself capable of enduring excessive fatigue when campaigning in his own country.

That some of the least promising districts could be made to prosper was proved after the Second Jacobite Rebellion. By an Act of 1752, some forty Jacobite estates were forfeited and annexed to the Crown, to be administered by a Board of Commissioners. The hanging of James Stewart on account of the Appin murder has probably become the most widely known event connected with these proceedings, which is regrettable, however much one may enjoy the stirring narrative in *Kidnapped*, because enlightened work was done by the Commissioners, who were entitled to more recognition than they were accorded.

The forfeited properties varied in economic conditions from the potentially wealthy Breadalbane estates in Perthshire to the beautiful but unproductive possessions of Lochiel and Lovat in the west; the people who lived on them were wretchedly poor, but such was their loyalty that many of them paid their rents twice over, as they insisted on sending money to their exiled chieftains, although they also had to pay rent to the Board.

The Commissioners astonished the people at the start by paying all the proven debts of the banished owners. Sheafs of claims remain in the records, and they reveal, often in poignant detail, the miserable conditions in which the people were living. The

Glasgow Cathedral: Robert Paul, Foulis Academy, 1760.

By courtesy of the Mitchell Library, Glasgow.

Commissioners carried out surveying, roadmaking, bridge-building, and much afforestation. They even built schools, because the people were illiterate and their homes remote from those already in existence. Gradually the estates were given back to the heirs of the families; in 1784 all the remaining ones were returned, on condition that the money spent by the Government in meeting debts was repaid. In the end the total sum came to over £90,000, all of which was given to public works and charitable organizations in Scotland.

It was demonstrated, therefore, that the adoption of enlightened methods could bring much advantage, but Highlanders by temperament and by habit resisted change. Famine recurred in 1740, 1756, 1766, 1778 and, with sharply increased severity, in 1782, but only in the last two decades of the century did turnip cultivation, the key to all farming progress, become at all general in the Highlands.

Meanwhile resistance had been made with similar obstinacy to potato culture. Potatoes were grown in Ireland, and also in England, long before they were adopted in Scotland. R. S. Salaman has dealt with this subject in his fascinating book entitled *The History and Social Influence of the Potato*. It was not until after the Second Jacobite Rebellion that potatoes were much cultivated in Scotland, though some Lowland farmers had introduced them rather earlier. Salaman shows how popular this cheap, easily produced food became in a relatively short time, particularly when the food shortages of the Napoleonic wars became acute. By the second decade of the 19th century, potatoes formed 'the main food for nine months of the year in some parts of Scotland.'

Sinclair's Statistical Account has many references to the changes effected by turnip and potato culture. Where these two roots were cultivated in alternation with grain crops, prosperity steadily developed, indeed proper use of turnips and other roots was the hallmark of the up-to-date farmer by 1790. But there are also depressingly consistent reports that in backward and poverty-stricken places, such as the majority of Highland villages, people were substituting potatoes for grain in their fields, a retrograde policy. Sir John Sinclair, like many other experts of the day, probably failed to see the danger. 'It is difficult to conceive', he wrote, 'how the people of the country could have subsisted, had it not been for the fortunate introduction and extensive cultivation of this most valuable plant.' 'This most valuable plant' was too much relied upon among the really poor however.

While therefore the century following the Second Jacobite Rebellion was a period of much advance in the south and east, there were ominous developments in the Highlands. The chieftains, deprived of old privileges and stripped of power, tended to become absentee landlords, interested only in the extraction of rents. Many of these men were faced with an almost insoluble problem. The mountainous regions in the west and north-west cannot produce good arable crops, and they have always proved difficult as pastoral areas because cattle cannot survive a winter on some of those storm-wracked hills. In the latter part of the 18th century, landowners began to realize that Blackface sheep can stand up to such conditions, while Cheviots, which are not quite so hardy, do well in the glens. And so the fashion set in for sheep-farming.

In order to clear large areas for sheep-walks, these landowners forced their tenants to give up their holdings, and the most popular method at first was the simple one of raising rents. The naturalist Thomas Pennant was one of the many travellers in Scotland who remarked on this. He wrote in 1771: 'The rage of raising rents has reached this distant country . . . Here the great men begin at the wrong end with squeezing the bag before they have helped the poor tenant to fill it by the introduction of manufactures. In many of the isles this already shows its unhappy effect and begins to depopulate the country, for numbers of families have been obliged to give up the strong attachment the Scots in general have for their country and exchange it for the wilds of America.'

The higher rents forced some tenants to reduce their plots and to live almost wholly on potatoes, but many thousands, driven to despair, sought the more drastic alternative of emigration. Johnson was horrified by the numbers of people preparing to emigrate when he toured the Hebrides in 1773, and he shrewdly pointed out that generous landowners, 'of more prudence and less rapacity', caused no such 'epidemical fury of emigration'. It is believed that between 1760 and 1808 some 12,000 people left the Highlands for America and at least 30,000 for the Colonies. The depopulated farmlands they left behind became vast sheep-walks, which the chieftains found much more advantageous, because of the reduction in wage bills, and the existence, especially during the wars, of ready markets for meat and wool.

Some crofters were able to keep going at home during the Napoleonic wars by working at kelp. Largely used in the manufacture of soap and glass, kelp is an alkaline ash, one ton of which could be made by burning twelve or more tons of seaweed. During the wars the demand for kelp was much increased by the difficulty of importing the foreign alkaline substances, such as barilla, which were preferred in peacetime. By 1800, kelp was priced at £22 a ton; an enormous, though unskilled, labour force was needed both on the west and east coasts to collect the seawrack, lay it out to dry and burn it. An industrious family could earn about £7 a year at this unattractive work, the main profits of which went to the owners and employers. The boom outlived the wars which produced it by eight years. In 1823, the import tax on barilla was removed and the price of kelp dropped from £22 to £2 per ton. The wretched families who had been relying on the artificially high price were ruined and could no longer put off the only alternative to starvation at home and so they too emigrated.

The practice of driving out the crofters became so common during the Napoleonic wars and the following period that almost every county has sad and sometimes shameful records of such procedure, undertaken by landowners who saw in sheep-farming the only solution to their problems. You can still come across pathetic little mounds of grass-grown rubble which mark the sites of old villages. Hounam in Roxburghshire is an example, but far more frequently one finds such relics in the Highlands.

Of all the clearances, those of Sutherlandshire have become the most notorious. They have been described by many writers and they have provided material for furious controversy. From 1811 to 1820, some 15,000 people were evicted by the second Duke of Sutherland, through his factor James Loch. Eyewitness accounts of the unsavoury process make distressing reading. Donald Sage, minister of Achness in Strathnaver, saw the evictions, which were followed by the burning of the people's cottages. His grief and anger may be understood because at least 1,600 people were turned out of Strathnaver in one day at short notice. 'On the Sabbath, a fortnight previous to the fated day, I preached my valedictory sermon in Achness, and the Sabbath thereafter at Achnabuiaghe. Both occasions were felt, by myself and by the people from the oldest to the youngest, to be among the bitterest and most overwhelming experiences of our lives.'

It should be emphasized that the Sutherlandshire hills are enormous structures of rock and boulder, with patches of soil fit only for sheep farming, so that the crofters living among them had been for generations hopelessly poor. Their removal by Loch was organized thoroughly and ruthlessly, in an effort to turn the land over to more profitable use. Literally thousands of the families were transferred to the coast, where they built themselves fresh hovels and lived on the products of the potato plots which were allotted to them there. They made the best of it by working at the kelp on the seashore, but when this industry collapsed in 1823 great numbers of them embarked in the emigrant ships.

The steady flow of Scots to the New World received sharp acceleration in 1846, when the Potato Blight spread its poison into the crops of farmers all over Scotland. This brought about specially serious results in the Highlands, where within a few months whole districts were stripped of food resources. Relief schemes were organized by the Government, by the churches, by citizens of Glasgow and Edinburgh, by public-spirited chieftains such as Macleod, Mackenzie and Mathieson, but none of these efforts could prevent a national disaster. Faced with starvation, embittered by the death through famine of the weakly members of his family, many a Scot gave up all hope of making good at home. Thus the tide of emigration swelled and, in a year, 106,000 people left Scotland. The less adventurous crowded into the cities of the industrial belt, in search of relief. along with many thousands of Irishmen who were suffering from the same calamity and who believed that on Clydeside they would find work and wages.

Meantime, in Scotland's richer and more prosperous areas of the south and east, men were able to develop a material security such as they had never known before. Shorthorns, Ayrshires and Galloway cattle became well-known for their quality and commanded high prices. In 1829 the Royal Highland and Agricultural Society began to hold its shows, and dealers came from far and wide to make purchases and to study the improved breeds. First and foremost among these was the Aberdeen Angus. Magnificent specimens of the most famous herds were exported to the Argentine and to other foreign markets. This was the period too when Clydesdale horses made their name.

The golden age of Scottish agriculture was in the mid-19th century, when ley-farming began to be adopted. The great Border farms, and also many of those in central Scotland, were particularly well suited to this system, which is profitable only in areas where rich grass can be successfully laid down. The rotation of crops is extended to a cycle of six or eight years, of which half are given to consecutive seasons of grasses, carefully selected and nurtured. How astonished the advocates of this system would have been, had they realized that it was regularly practised by the Cistercian monks of Cupar Abbey in the 15th century!

Scottish owners and farmers developed some of the richest land in Britain to such a pitch of husbandry that their grain, seed-potatoes and fatstock became famous literally all over the world. Carefully constructed byres, comfortable farmhouses, extensive woodlands and, above all, the fields of first-class crops testified to the success of the new ways; so did the crowded stock-markets, the dignified bank-houses and the well-run county academies for the younger generation. The historian of Scotland's 19th century could make a heartening narrative of material progress if he neglected consideration of the emigrants huddled together in those overcrowded sailing ships which beat their way across the Atlantic. Those thousands of Highlanders left the land they loved, the way of life they knew, bitterly resentful. Nobody knew how to deal with the desperate problems which drove them away.

The tide of emigration was not stemmed until the once over-populated glens of the north and west had become almost deserted, so that the problem of depopulation became one for 20th century economists and politicians to solve. The Scots who made their way into Canada and America concentrated all their gifts of endurance and courage, all their mental and physical energy, on the task of building a fresh way of life in the cities and on the prairies. That they succeeded so well, and made such a magnificent contribution to the growth of the new communities, should not mask the calamity which destroyed a whole section of Scottish society.

CHAPTER 21

Transport

One result of the Roman failure to make permanent settlements in Scotland was that roads only appeared by gradual stages in medieval times, as a result of the passage of men and beasts. Road maintenance was never the responsibility of any reliable body of people until the 17th century, and when repairs were carried out, methods were perfunctory. Ruts and pot-holes were filled with loose stones or sand, and the ridges roughly levelled off. The whole operation was rendered useless by the next rainstorm.

The Tweed was crossed by only two bridges, one at Peebles, one at Berwick, with forty miles of unspanned river flowing between them. The further north you penetrated, the less you were likely to find any means of crossing water, other than ford or ferry. On one of his preaching tours, Wesley was nearly drowned with his horse in the Tay, while on another he took a severe ducking in the Solway, and in 1784 Lord Braxfield, who was riding his circuit, had to go twenty-eight miles up the Findhorn before he could find a safe place to cross. Lord Cockburn wrote from personal experience: 'There was no bridge over the Tay at Dunkeld, or over the Spey at Fochabers, or over the Findhorn at Forres. Nothing but wretched, pierless ferries, let to poor cottars, who rowed or hauled or pushed a crazy boat across, or more commonly got their wives to do it.'

Goods were transported on horseback, because wheeled traffic was not to be had, and even coal was carried in panniers by horses. In the 1750s and 1760s, horse-drawn, wheeled carts were an exciting new development, but their expense seriously affected prices. Coal costing 10d. per cartload at the Monkland pits commanded twice that sum when it reached Glasgow, twelve miles away; and the poor condition, both of horses and of road

MAP 7.
SOME ROADS AND CANALS IN THE EARLY INDUSTRIAL REVOLUTION

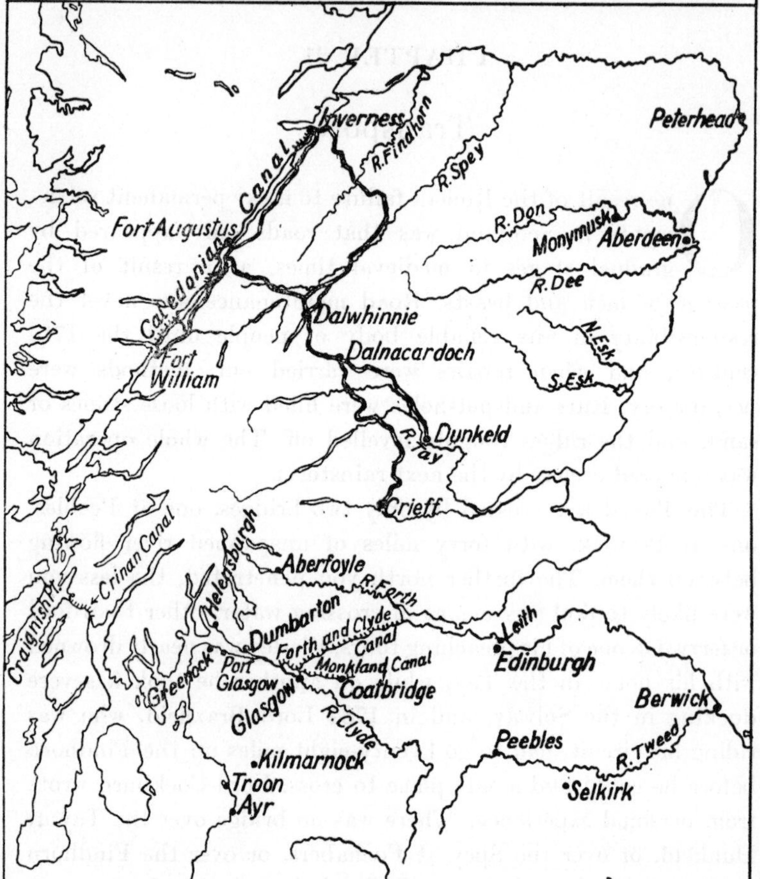

Inverness
R.Findhorn
R.Spey
Peterhead
Fort Augustus
R.Don
Monymusk
Aberdeen
R.Dee
Caledonian Canal
Dalwhinnie
N.Esk
Dalnacardoch
S.Esk
Fort William
R.Tay
Dunkeld
Crieff
Crinan Canal
Aberfoyle
R.Forth
Helensburgh
Dumbarton
Forth and Clyde Canal
Leith
Craignish
Greenock
Port Glasgow
Monkland Canal
Edinburgh
Coatbridge
Glasgow
R.Clyde
Berwick
Kilmarnock
Peebles
R.Tweed
Troon
Selkirk
Ayr
Carlisle
R.Eden
Φ.Γ.

Canals.............   Wade's roads.............

0 10 20   40   60   80   100 Miles

0 10 20   40   60   80   100 120 140 160 Kilometres

surfaces, is revealed in the fact that a cartload was only seven hundredweight. One carrier working the forty miles between Selkirk and Edinburgh took two weeks to complete his return journey; he found that he made the best progress by wading his horse and cart along the bed of the Gala River, a safer and easier route than was afforded by the main road. He used to be seen off by all his neighbours coming out to cheer. Landowners on the North-East coast found it more profitable to ship their grain to London than to transport it even ten miles inland, and when wealthy Scots made their way to London they sent the heavy luggage by sea with the servants. Scottish literature of the 18th and early 19th centuries is crammed, both with references to the frustrations of inland travel, and also with ample evidence that, one way or another, anybody who meant to get about did so, whatever the inconveniences involved.

The first large-scale scheme of road-building was initiated for military reasons. The misadventures of government troops during the First Jacobite Rebellion compelled the authorities in London to believe that something must be done. To General Wade therefore was assigned the task of constructing highways in central and north-east Scotland.

Wade began in 1725 and during eight consecutive summers he worked with some 500 soldiers, who were paid in Royal Bank notes, carried to them at regular intervals by clerks on horseback. His problems of discipline and commissariat in the remote and wild hills were as complex as any faced by contemporary officers serving in European areas, but despite all obstacles he completed forty bridges, also 500 miles of roads, most of which were about sixteen feet wide.

Wade's two points of departure were Crieff and Dunkeld; the two lines he carried north from these points met at Dalnacardoch, whence he drove a single road over the mountains to Dalwhinnie. There he divided the route again, making one branch towards Fort Augustus, and a second, by the Spey Valley, to Inverness; a third road linked Inverness, Fort Augustus and Fort William. The scheme covered mountainous areas and precipitous heights hitherto never crossed by properly surfaced roads.

Wade's achievement is rightly famous, and his hump-backed bridges, and narrow, steeply graded highways, now generally bypassed, are considered a national heritage. His work did not however solve the real problems of the day, as, with military rather than economic or commercial concerns in mind, he penetrated the Highlands at only two main entrances. The beginnings he made were followed up after the Forty-Five by another scheme of military roads, which covered almost 800 miles and included something like 1,000 bridges. The inhabitants of the areas thus opened up thought poorly of the whole enterprise. Ramsay of Ochtertyre recorded a typical countryman's view: 'In 1761, I was in company with Peter Graham of Rudivous, a lively man, past fourscore. The conversation turning upon roads, he said he saw no use of them but to set burghers and redcoats into the Highlands none of whom in his father's time would have durst venture beyond the Pass of Aberfoyle.'

With the rising ambitions of landowners and farmers, and also the increasing population in the towns, public irritation over the poor communications began to be aroused, in spite of Peter Graham and his kind. In 1751 the first effective Turnpike Act was passed, for the district of Edinburgh, and some 350 other local Turnpike Acts followed. This development led to hundreds of miles of roads being built. They were financed largely by the tolls taken from travellers at the regularly placed turnpikes, those five-barred structures which straddled the new highways and were supervised from little toll-houses—there were no less than ten turnpikes on the thirty-four mile stretch from Glasgow to Ayr. The roads were administered by trusts or companies, which employed distinguished engineers like Rennie and Macadam. Their well-metalled surfaces enabled wheeled traffic at last to travel with relative speed and safety.

In 1802, the Government commissioned the great Telford to report on roads, bridges and fisheries in the Highlands. This was part of a campaign to arrest the steady emigration which had already reached alarming proportions. Telford's survey did nothing to lessen public anxiety. He recommended schemes far more ambitious than anything undertaken elsewhere and he urged that the cost should be met largely by the State, as the works in question were 'exceptional and extraordinary.'

The Government accepted most of Telford's recommendations, with the result that 920 additional miles of roads and many bridges were made, while at Wick, Aberdeen and Peterhead, and at other harbours, there were big reconstructions. All these projects were directed by Telford, expenses being met half by the State, half by local assessment, with the help of some considerable gifts from the Duke of Gordon, the Duke of Atholl and other landowners.

During the second half of the 18th century, as a result of road-building, the great days of the mail coach began. In 1749 the first vehicle to run between Glasgow and Edinburgh set out twice a week, and it covered the forty-four miles in just under two days. In 1760, after the introduction of the turnpike system, the journey could be achieved in a day and a half, by a coach affectionately christened 'The Fly', so delighted were its proprietors with its speed. Passengers from Edinburgh reached Holytown on the first evening, where they had 'as comfortable quarters as double-bedded rooms in the inn could afford, there to repose and recover their breathing after the fatigue of twelve hours' jolting on a solid hand-made road, a little rough no doubt from the stones being somewhat of the largest, and having travelled no less than 33 miles. . . The two Flies made out very correctly three journeys betwixt them in the course of a week; that is thrice going to Glasgow, and thrice to Edinburgh; six journeys in all.' These recollections from the diary of George Robertson were offset by some less flattering passages. 'In wet weather' the tracks became 'sloughs in which the carts and carriages had to slumper in a half-swimming state, whilst in time of drought it was a continued jolting out of one hole into another.'

It was not till 1760 that an Edinburgh coach service to London became regularly available and then there was only one service per month. Glasgow folk had no direct contact with London till 1788, so that for nearly thirty years they had first to make the two days' preliminary run to Edinburgh and then, duly rested no doubt by a night in a double-bedded room, set out for the south. When the first Glasgow coach trip was advertised the cost was

£4 16s. 0d., and the time sixty-five hours. In 1798, Aberdeen followed on with an independent service to London.

These facts show how isolated folk in Scotland were, alike from each other and from their English neighbours. The same thing is illustrated by the postal arrangements, which were re-organized after 1707 on a more business-like basis. A general Postmaster was appointed in Edinburgh at a salary of £200 a year; with the help of an accountant and two clerks he was able to handle easily all the mail entering and leaving the Capital, and for ten years deliveries were distributed by one letter-carrier. Even as late as 1780 only six post-boys were needed. The arrival of a letter was an event worth comment, and in Glasgow a gun was fired when the daily quota of letters had been sorted and was ready for distribution.

Ambitious commercial firms soon began to press for better use of Scotland's numerous inland waterways and for the construction of canals. Such goods as china—now in demand because of the new-fashioned coffee and tea—did not improve by being hauled about on horseback, while coal and manufactured goods soared in price as one horse-drawn mile dragged after another.

A canal connecting the Forth and Clyde was proposed in the times of Charles II, but the idea was dismissed because of the cost. After the Union it was revived, and Defoe was greatly taken with it and looked forward to the time when men 'shall not only feel the want of it, but find themselves inclinable as well as able to effect it'. In 1764 Smeaton drew up two alternative plans and in 1768 work was begun. By 1775, the proprietors of the scheme had spent all their money, the American war had started, the tobacco trade was collapsing, a financial panic had undermined confidence, and work on the canal came to an end. In 1784 however, the Government made a grant of £50,000 from the revenues of the Forfeited Estates and at last, in 1790, the whole magnificent venture was completed. In the 35 miles of the canal, which was eight feet deep, there were thirty-nine locks to negotiate the rise from sea level to a summit of 156 feet; and vessels of 19 feet beam and 68 feet keel could pass through it. The 80-ton sloop *Agnes* sailed from Leith to Greenock to celebrate the inauguration of the new waterway.

Transport

In the same year, 1790, a shorter but almost more important canal was opened. This was the Monkland Canal, designed to make available the rich supplies of coal in the Coatbridge area, because hitherto there had been no suitable transport to carry them to Glasgow. James Watt undertook the construction of the Monkland Canal, at a salary of £200 a year, with a staff consisting of one clerk, who assisted him in the tasks of surveying, planning, costing and supervising. After years of delay, it was completed and joined at Port Dundas to the Glasgow branch of the Forth and Clyde Canal. To-day, in 20th century conditions, this twelve-mile stretch of waterway is not only useless, but a positive menace to the safety of the children at play, who are the only people interested in it, but a century and a half ago it brought much financial gain to landowners and industrialists on the Lanarkshire side of Glasgow.

In 1803, another famous Scottish canal was designed by Telford, as part of his general scheme to improve Scottish transport. This was the Caledonian Canal, a gargantuan undertaking upon which almost a million pounds were spent over a period of seventeen years. In the end, this canal was 60 miles in length and no less than 40 of these miles were provided by the great inland lochs which form a diagonal rift across north-west Scotland. At the western end there were eight miles covering a drop of 90 feet; Telford built 8 locks for the negotiation of this gradient, dubbing the completed series 'Neptune's Staircase'. At the other end of the canal, a huge lock extended for almost half a mile into the sea. The purpose of the Government in undertaking all this was to make the dangerous passage round northern Scotland unnecessary. Samuel Smiles put it as follows: 'The Pentland Firth, which is the throat connecting the Atlantic and German Oceans and through which rolls its long majestic waves with tremendous force, was the dread of mariners.' A case was quoted to Parliament of an Inverness vessel sailing for Liverpool on Christmas Day, which reached Stromness Harbour in Orkney on January 1st there to be storm-stayed till mid-April. Another witness told of two vessels setting forth on the same day from Newcastle, one for Liverpool via the Pentland Firth, the other for Bombay via the Cape of Good Hope, and the latter reached her destination

235

first. Thus the Caledonian Canal was much desired and Telford
spent many years with hundreds of labourers working upon it,
but financially it never paid, a fact which nearly broke the heart
of its designer: his cheerful, optimistic nature suffered no more
hurtful experience than the failure of this tremendous enterprise.

There were a number of other canals constructed during this
period in Scotland, of which perhaps the Crinan Canal is best
known, because it shortens the dangerous run from the Clyde to
the Western Isles. All the canals were used for transport of
heavy goods, but almost all were regularly patronized also by
passengers who were encouraged to enjoy their trips by the
advertising agents of the day. In 1823, an Edinburgh publisher
produced a guide-book of 82 pages called *A Companion for Canal
Passengers betwixt Edinburgh and Glasgow*. It gave 'a complete
account of all the interesting objects that are seen along the lines
of the two canals; such as towns, villages, gentlemen's seats,
works of art, ancient structures and scenes of former wars.'
Tourist traffic was beginning to make its appearance and to be
recognized as a source of profit.

Of all the inland waterways developed at this time, the Clyde
was the most important, and the work done upon it has remained
as a permanent investment for commerce and industry. In 1755,
Smeaton made a report for the city magistrates on the state of
the river between Glasgow and Renfrew. He described twelve
large shoals, one of which lay 400 yards below Glasgow bridge,
leaving a depth of only 15 inches, while four others left only 18
inches. After nine years' delay, Golborne was commissioned to
make a similar survey, and his report showed that, owing to
neglect, the river was in 'a state of nature' and had spread its
meandering waters further still across the adjacent meadows. In
1773, Golborne was given a contract by the city and he undertook
to create a navigable stream giving a depth of six feet right up to
Glasgow itself. He constructed jetties and walls and he organized
regular dredging: by these means he gave the river a depth of
6 feet 10 inches, outdoing his promise by nearly a foot, but by
1781 the Clyde's own movement towards the sea in the narrowed
channel had produced a depth of 14 to 22 feet. The artificial
maintenance of this channel has been continued ever since. In

1809 the Clyde Navigation Trust was founded to keep the channel
clear. This organization still exists, and has carried out its
original function throughout its history by regular dredging and
excavation.

The results of these enterprises were soon apparent. In the
heart of Glasgow, there had been until 1773 a riverside meadow
where the broom grew so charmingly as to leave us the name of
the Broomielaw. Here people pastured cattle, hung out their
laundry, and shouted at boys wading over to the other side of
the river. All ships, shipping, quaysides and dock work were out
of sight at Port Glasgow, at least 16½ miles away. Visitors to
Glasgow in this enviable period were delighted with its pleasant
air, its gardens, fruit-trees, spacious streets, and the attractive
villages within reach for those who enjoyed an evening walk—
Govan for example, and Partick. The united efforts of Golborne,
Rennie and Telford were successful in inaugurating a transformation which was financially an overwhelming success. Quays,
docks, harbour equipment, warehouses and shipbuilding yards
were created so that the shipping brought to the Broomielaw
increased within Telford's own lifetime from nothing at all to
over a million tons a year. He died in 1834, long before the
steamer had ousted the sailing ship, and when each vessel was
incomparably smaller than would be the case to-day; these figures
illustrate the passing of the old, pleasant riverside city and the
emergence of the blackened, noisy centre of overcrowding we
now know.

The expansion of overseas commerce, which burst upon all
Scottish ports, but upon Glasgow with especial force in the early
19th century, was accelerated by the development of steamships.
For some twenty years William Symington and his partner,
Patrick Miller, laboured on their plan of building a steam-
propelled vessel and at last their dreams were fulfilled in 1802,
when they launched their *Charlotte Dundas* on the Forth and
Clyde Canal. Her performance astonished the crowds who turned
out to see, for she towed two barges, each loaded with 70 tons of
cargo, and she covered 20 miles in the record time of six hours.
The Canal proprietors objected to the 'agitation of the water'
created by her wash however and, in defence of their precious

banks, they put an end to her career as a substitute for the horse on the towing path.

Henry Bell, originally a wheelwright, was the second British engineer to succeed in this sphere. His Clyde-built *Comet* was launched in 1812. She had a three horse-power engine, she covered four miles per hour, she had on board a library of classical literature, and she was the pride of Helensburgh, whose school-master was her first Commander. Bell himself was Provost of the town, where with his wife's help he ran the Baths Hotel, now known as the Queen's Hotel; it commands a splendid view of the Clyde and the course taken by the *Comet*. The little vessel plied between Glasgow and Greenock, afterwards extending her run to Fort William via the Crinan Canal, until she was wrecked in 1820 off Craignish Point in Argyllshire. Two other very early paddle-steamers were the *Industry* and the *Trusty*, both of which were bought in 1815 by the recently founded Clyde Shipping Company. This firm has continued in business ever since and in 1956 published an interesting history of its services to Scottish transport.

The first steamship to cross the open sea was the *Marjorie*, one of nine similar vessels built on the Clyde in the last two years of the Napoleonic wars. By the end of 1823, 95 steamers had been built in Scotland, 72 on the Clyde; and 40 had been sold out of the country.

Shipbuilding therefore laid hold upon Scottish yards and soon iron began to be boldly incorporated in the great structures which carried goods all over the world. The crossing of the Atlantic under steam was achieved in 1838, by the *Sirius*, built the previous year at Leith, engined in Glasgow. She was 178 feet in length and she made the journey in eighteen days on 450 tons of coal, carrying forty passengers, of whom eleven were ladies. Her arrival in New York was celebrated by much publicity and by an official visit to the ship, at which the Mayor of New York made a speech. The excitement of the occasion was greatly increased by the arrival of the Bristol-built *Great Western*, a vessel of double the size, only a few hours after the *Sirius*.

The beautiful wooden sailing ships on the tea run to the East therefore had powerful rivals, but they held their own for many a year. Numbers of them were built in Aberdeen, such as the

Port-Glasgow from the South-East: Robert Paul, Foulis Academy, 1768.

famous *Thermopylae*, whose maiden voyage from the Thames to Melbourne was in 1868. The following year, the *Cutty Sark*, built in Dumbarton, began her long career. For twenty-six years she made journeys to the East and her speed became the talk of seafarers all over the world. From 1888 to 1893 there was a last magnificent boom in the construction of these ships, in which the Clyde took a leading part. One of the bold adjustments in design at this time was the use of steel for certain parts of the vessels. By the last decade of the 19th century, however, the tramp steamers had won the day and only fanatics could claim that there was any future for sailing ships. The beautiful *Cutty Sark* was sold away to Portugal, where, under the name *Ferreira*, she was used as a cargo-boat for nearly thirty years. She plied to West Africa during the 1914-1918 war and was still sailing in 1922, when she was bought by a British owner called Captain Dowman, whose widow presented her to the Thames Nautical Training College in 1938. In 1954 she was moved to Greenwich, where she may still be seen, the swiftest, the longest-lived and the last of a wonderful succession. Meanwhile, ocean-going steamers increased in number, tonnage and commercial profit. Scotland had a large share in the new shipbuilding industry, which became closely linked with the heavy metal industries, as more and more iron was needed in the construction of steamers, until steel replaced it.

Owing to the sudden development of the railway, inland waterways attracted less business from the 1830s onwards and finally became liabilities rather than assets. Wagonways for the transport of coal were in use both north and south of the Border for a long time before railways, as we know them, appeared. There was one at Alloa, originally constructed in 1771, and another at Little Govan which dated from 1778. The best known was the so-called railway from Kilmarnock to Troon, opened in 1810, and built at a cost of £50,000 to carry the Duke of Portland's coal from the collieries to the sea. This line was used by many business people in Ayrshire for the carriage of timber, grain, lime, and even passengers. On all these early 'railroads', the trucks were horse-drawn, and much better speed could be made by the horses than on the highways.

One year after the famous Stockton-Darlington line was completed, the first genuine Scottish railway was opened, from Monkland to Kirkintilloch. This line was 10 miles in length, with passing places here and there, and it linked the Monkland collieries with the Forth and Clyde canal. Other early railway lines were also built as feeders to canals, or as supplementary routes. The Glasgow-Garnkirk railway ran beside the Monkland Canal and was designed primarily for the haulage of coal. It was opened in 1831, with much flourish, as George Stephenson himself came to drive the first engine, which was named after him in honour of the occasion. The cost of carrying coal from Monkland to Glasgow was immediately halved, with the result that landed proprietors who were fortunate enough to find coal seams on their properties began to make enormous profits.

These early railways were designed for the carriage of goods, but, as in the case of the canals, passengers swarmed to enjoy this novel type of journeying. The 'carriages' in which they travelled had no covering and were provided only with the hardest of benches. All the same, people were eager to make use of the railways, boasting to each other of the incredible speeds at which they travelled, and enduring with apparent delight the smoke and smuts through which they rushed at 16-20 miles an hour: sixty-two thousand people travelled thus on the Glasgow-Garnkirk line in its first year, which shows what a complete change was taking place in the nation's habits, for even a decade earlier it would have been impossible to imagine so many people on the move. Passenger traffic was organized on methods similar to those used for highway coaches. People could hail the trains and board them where they wished; drivers blew their horns on approaching a road crossing; any owner of a wagon might hitch it on behind the train, for a given fee, provided it was clearly labelled with his name on the outside.

It soon followed that trunk lines were designed as well as a network of local routes and in 1835 citizens of Edinburgh and Glasgow began to interest themselves in a railway linking their two great cities. In their prospectus, they made the bold claim that such a railway would bring '200,000 persons more along its line into daily, nay, it may be said hourly, communication . . . It is impossible to see the extent to which it may go.' Sea-side holidays soon became a practical proposition for the Scot and his family. In 1836, a line from Glasgow to Paisley and thence to Ayr was proposed, partly to open up a fresh industrial area, partly for reasons set forth by the proprietors in their prospectus. 'A Railway to the sea-coast of Ayrshire would enable seabathing visitors to reach it with certainty in about one hour, in place of their spending as at present five to eight hours in an uncertain and tedious voyage. It is reasonable therefore to suppose that the sea-bathing quarters on the coast of Ayrshire which at present are considerable, would become still more fashionable resorts and in this way that a new traffic in the carriage of passengers along the line would also be created.'

Horse-traction was forgotten and locomotives were used on all railway lines by mid-century, the period of railway mania, when many small companies built short lengths of line, independently of each other and in suicidal competition. 'Britain is at present an island of lunatics, all railway-mad,' Lord Cockburn wrote in 1845. 'The patients are raving even in the wild recesses of the Highlands.' The absurd rivalries led to a number of bankruptcies and gradually to some amalgamations. A national gauge was then adopted, so that all railway lines were the same width apart and trucks could be used in any part of the country. A comprehensive system of safety regulations was also worked out, particularly for signalling, which in the earlier days had been primitive to a degree. By 1850, it was possible to travel from London to Glasgow and also from London to Aberdeen by train.

The Scottish contribution to the vast changes in transport throughout the kingdom in the 18th and 19th centuries was very considerable, particularly among roadbuilders and shipbuilders: John Rennie was the architect of the London Docks, the East India Docks and Waterloo Bridge; John Macadam invented a road surface which was universally adopted and his name has became part of the English language; Bell of Helensburgh, Scott of Greenock, Denny of Dumbarton, Robert Napier of Glasgow form only one group of many Scottish engineers, internationally renowned, on whose work Britain's lead in the new seafaring methods was founded.

Of all these giants, Thomas Telford was perhaps the most interesting. Laughing Tam was his nickname as a boy; Laughing Tam he remained all his life. His father, a shepherd in the little-known hills of Kirkcudbrightshire, died when his son was a baby. The boy began life as a working stonemason, doing odd jobs in the neighbourhood. When he died, in 1834, he was known all over Europe. He had been consulted in Sweden, Russia and Austria; he had built the Ellesmere Canal and rebuilt much of the Grand Trunk Canal; he had bridged the Menai Straits, the Clyde, the Tay and many other rivers; he had worked on harbours, docks and roads all over the United Kingdom. All his life Telford's sunny and compassionate nature made him beloved, and richly he enjoyed his friendships, particularly with Robert Southey, who gave him the nickname of 'Pontifex Maximus', because of his bridge-building. He was at heart a poet and a philosopher, for he read and wrote poetry all his days, and he always maintained an idealistic view of his profession. Shortly after the Battle of Waterloo, Telford wrote to a friend: 'During the war just brought to a close, England has not only been able to guard her own land, and to carry on a gigantic struggle, but at the same time to construct canals, roads, harbours, bridges—magnificent works of peace—the like of which are probably not to be found in the world. Are not these things worthy of a nation's pride?'

The changes in transport which took place north of the Border during this period are remarkable enough when we consider them in relation to Scotland alone. It is interesting to consider them in relation to Britain as a whole. Throughout the country, the pattern, though perhaps not the timing, is similar. In the early days of the great roadbuilders, people were able to take to the highways by coach, carriage and cart. Thus the inns and hostelries of the 18th century made their name. The second stage was the period when inland waterways were developed and a new race of British workmen came into being, the bargees and their families. After the turn of the century came the invention of steamer and railway engine. It followed that many of the fine old inns, with their dignified and bustling discomfort, fell into decay, for the railways passed them by, outmoding travel by road and also depriving the canals of much business; it also followed that by mass movements of goods and folk, by high speculation and huge turnover of capital, both countryside and city centre were utterly transformed. The home life, the business and recreative pursuits of Scottish folk were affected by the great changes in transport during these two centuries more than by any development other than the industrial revolution with which they were linked.

CHAPTER 22

Industry

The immediate effects of the Union upon Scotland's economic life brought about some unfortunate developments, because Scottish industries at once suffered from the competition of the more advanced and highly organized English producers, especially in the woollen business.

It was in commerce that recovery first began, because the Navigation Acts no longer excluded Scottish ships from the colonial markets, and a vast new sphere lay open to men of initiative. The almost chronic state of war between Britain and France during this period gave Glasgow its opportunity, as the Clyde was safer than the Mersey or the Bristol Channel, and it saved miles of uncertain sea travel. From the 1720s onwards, Glasgow merchants began to import quantities of tobacco from the New World in their own ships. In 1724, over four million pounds of it were brought up the Clyde, fully three-quarters of which were re-exported. It was largely because of this annually increasing commerce in tobacco that people began to insist that the Clyde must be made navigable so that ocean-going vessels could come right up to the city, instead of berthing at Port Glasgow.

William Cunninghame was the richest of all the magnates at this time. He secured the fine estate of Lainshaw, in Ayrshire, and for his Glasgow residence bought a site on Cow Loan, the old lane by which the city cowherd had hitherto driven the people's cattle to pasture each day. Here he spent £10,000 on the only one of the great mansions still to be seen in something like its original form. It is incorporated in the Royal Exchange, now used as a Public Library, and the old homely Cow Loan is Queen Street. Cunninghame realized that the American war, which broke out in 1775, would reduce supplies of tobacco and he bought up all that he could lay hands on, only selling when it reached the shattering price of 3/6d a pound. Thus, out of the utter ruin which because of the war fell suddenly and completely upon this trade, he made an even larger fortune; but he was the last to do so.

In 1771, Spenser published his *English Traveller*, a book which contains a description of such men as Cunninghame. 'Many of the merchants acquire vast fortunes and they have such an inclination to business that little besides it ever engages their attention. Those that trade to Virginia are decked out in great wigs and scarlet cloaks, and strut about on the Exchange . . . like so many actors on the Stage.' By 1777, this particular stage no longer existed. Instead of some 46 million pounds of tobacco, much less than ½ a million came up the Clyde that year and the city was faced with economic crisis.

The capitalists in Glasgow were quick to turn their wealth to other uses however. Already the staple industries of the 19th century had made beginnings, both in the west and in the east. After the collapse of the tobacco trade, five main types of enterprise were developed in Scotland, namely textile mills, iron foundries, coal mines, engineering shops and shipyards.

The textile industry was the first to become established. During the years when tobacco accounted for so much Scottish business, linen was steadily absorbing capital. Soon after the Union, and under the terms of the Treaty, steps were taken to foster the production of linen-yarns and materials. In 1727, a Board of Trustees for Manufactures was set up by Act of Parliament, with £6,000 a year to spend from government grants, to stimulate Scottish industry. To linen was allocated £2,650 per year.

Elizabeth Mure of Caldwell recorded in old age some early recollections, dating from about 1727. The following passage illustrates the state of affairs in linen production before and after the Board's early efforts. 'At that time there was little bread in Scotland; Manefactorys were brought to no perfection either in linnen or woolen. Every woman made her web of wove linnen and bleched it herself; it never rose higher than 2/- the yard, and with this cloth was everybody cloathed. The young gentlemen, who at this time were growing more delicat, got their cloth from

Holland for shirts; but the old were satisfied with necks and sleeves of the fine, which were put on loose above the country cloth . . . A few years after this wevers were brought over from Holland and manefactorys for Linnen established in the West.'

Elizabeth Mure's 'manefactorys' were started by the Board of Trustees, who brought in foreign weavers and flax-dressers, to give instruction about the methods best suited to the production of this difficult crop. Linen was successfully established in many places from Aberdeen to Paisley, and it began soon to be in demand abroad. In 1742 the first of a series of Bounty Acts was passed, to subsidize linen exports. As demand and profit consequently increased, so craftsmanship developed, with the result that linen of a much finer quality was produced in Scotland for sale to America, the West Indies and elsewhere.

The Scottish linen workers of the 18th century were cottagers and farmers, who carried out their craft on their own premises, with their own hand-made wheels and frames. It was a life of hard work and some financial anxiety, but it afforded them independence. Capital was provided by agents, who distributed flax to the spinners and collected the yarn, which they gave out to weavers. These agents were employed by men of small means, who had difficulty in securing credit, in maintaining steady markets and in accumulating sufficient supplies of currency. The Dukes of Queensberry and Argyll, with other leading gentry, therefore founded the British Linen Company, to assist these people with the organizing side of their business. This Company, founded in 1746, started branch banking in Scotland and later, when its other services were no longer needed, the banks were carried on: they are still familiar, under the original title, to all Scots folk.

The Statistical Account of 1790 shows that many hundreds of men and women were still employed upon the production of linen by hand, for craftsmanship resisted mechanization longer in this than in any other field of the textile industry. Stout Holland sheetings and shirtings, umbrella linens and linens for window-blinds, shawlcloths, calicoes and muslins, wide brown and white country linens 'chiefly used for hat-linings' are listed for Perth: fine lawns and damasks for Glasgow: coarse linens and bleached canvas, much needed by the Royal Navy, for Fife: 'bagging, canvas and osnaburghs' for Kincardineshire: muslin for Cambuslang, table-linen for Dunfermline, twisted thread for Paisley. But the prosperity in this characteristically 18th century craft began to decline soon after 1790 because mechanically produced cotton was soon to become supreme, both in home and in foreign markets. As early as 1814, Sir John Sinclair wrote of the great distress caused by the decreasing demand for linen. The minister of Colinton in Midlothian reported in 1840: 'Spinning has almost wholly disappeared. Thus the old are cut off from employment within the power of age and suited to its disposition . . . which used to keep time from becoming a burden and to supply the necessaries of life.'

This report was typical, and only in a few places, such as Dunfermline, did the linen industry survive after about 1820, for cotton soon became the 19th century's most successful textile. The *Annals of Commerce*, published in 1785 by Macpherson, show that already cotton had become popular and also much cheaper than linen. 'Women of all ranks from highest to lowest are clothed in the British manufacture of cotton, from the muslin cap on the crown of the head to the cotton stocking under the sole of the foot . . . With the gentlemen, cotton stuffs for waistcoats have almost superseded woollen cloths, and silk stuffs I believe entirely.'

The earliest ventures in cotton manufacture were made during the latter years of the 18th century in England. In 1765 Hargreaves invented his spinning jenny. Ten years later another Englishman, Samuel Crompton, completed his new spinning machine, known ever since as the 'mule'. His first one was fitted with 48 spindles, which could produce fine yet strong threads, suitable for weaving firm material of light texture. About the same time, Thomas Arkwright was at work upon the harnessing of industry to water power. The jennies and mules were hand-driven machines which could manipulate many spindles simultaneously: for some years they were used to make yarn for the weft, while Arkwright's water-frames produced the warps. Later the mules were adjusted to water-power too. During the last twenty years of the 18th century the cotton industry developed in

Lancashire and within a short time it made its appearance in Scotland.

The first successful Scottish cotton mill was opened in Rothesay on the island of Bute, in 1778, a two-storey building with machinery for a thousand spindles. In Renfrewshire and Lanarkshire, other mills were set up where cotton yarn was spun on jennies or mules, modelled on those installed south of the Border a few years earlier. At first the machinery was hand-driven, but soon in Scotland, as in England, water began to be used from swift-flowing hill streams; and factories began to invade the uplands. The old cottage industry was doomed.

Though most people knew little of what went on in these mills, it was plain that cargo upon cargo of raw cotton was coming up the deepened Clyde, also that quantities of cotton yarn were annually available for manufacture. New industrial magnates began to dominate the business world and thousands of workers' dwellings were rapidly built. Schools and churches were not provided in many of these industrial schemes, which consisted of meanly designed tenements, built as cheaply as possible without expensive amenities such as proper sanitation.

David Dale is perhaps the best known among many Scottish names associated with the early years of this industry. Dale began in Paisley as a linen weaver, later he became a dealer and employed large numbers of linen workers. In 1786 he entered upon a vigorous career in the new textile business, by founding his famous cotton mills at New Lanark, and afterwards he started similar works at Newton Stewart, at Catrine, by the Dornoch Firth and in Blantyre—it was at this last that David Livingstone was later to be employed during his toilsome childhood.

Like the tobacco lords before them, cotton kings lived luxuriously. Dale built himself a fine house of gracious and attractive proportions near Glasgow Green, which survived until 1954, when the City Council ordered its demolition, to make space for a neighbouring school's playground. Dale made this Glasgow home his headquarters and devoted his time to directing the mercantile side of his business, with managers to run the mills. At New Lanark, Dale employed William Kelly, a man of some distinction, for it was he who first adapted the mule to water-power

in Scotland. Later, another industrialist made his name at
this centre, Robert Owen of Manchester who became Dale's
son-in-law and bought the New Lanark mills. In a bold attempt
to run factory life on humanitarian lines, Robert Owen anticipated many reforms which were to be adopted in the 20th
century.

From 1795 onwards, spinning mules were constructed to work
over 150 spindles each, but weaving defeated inventors of
machinery for a surprisingly long time. Weavers therefore
continued to work by hand on the old-style frames and to command an enviable position even after the turn of the century.
They secured high wages and worked in their own homes,
employed by mill-owners, whose travellers distributed yarn and
collected in webs, just as was done in the old days. 'Then was
the daisy portion of weaving', wrote William Thom of Inverurie.
'Four days did the weaver work, for them four days was a week,
as far as working went, and such a week to a skilful weaver
brought 40/-. Sunday, Monday and Tuesday were of course
jubilee, lawn frills gorged freely from under the wrists of his fine
blue, gilt-buttoned coat. He dusted his head with white flour on
Sunday, smirked and wore a cane. Walked in clean slippers on
Monday, Tuesday heard him talk war bravado, quote Volney,
and get drunk. Weaving commenced gradually on Wednesday.'
Thousands of looms were worked by these aristocrats of industry,
but machinery was ultimately to prove too strong. In 1807, a
power-loom was set up at Catrine, and soon more appeared.

It was not until after 1840 that hand loom weaving was finally
ousted, because the early power looms could not make fine
materials, but during the '20s and '30s the competition of the
new machines reduced the weaver's wages, depriving him of
frills, cane and clean slippers, and finally in the '40s driving him
altogether out of business, after a period of acute distress. On
May 19th, 1848, the *Wiscassit*, an old whaling schooner, now
square-rigged for the merchant service, sailed from the Broomielaw for the United States. On board was William Carnegie, one
of the defeated weavers of Dunfermline, with his wife Margaret
and his sons Andrew and Tom, all in great distress over their
departure, but all perfectly clear that the Old Country could

offer them only penury. Of Andrew Carnegie, Scots all over the world were later to hear much. Thousands of his countrymen went to the New World in similar circumstances and there built up for themselves a new way of life.

For nearly three-quarters of the 19th century, cotton mills worked to capacity and commanded an enormous market, both at home and abroad. Their prosperity was in no way threatened by work done in other branches of the textile industry, important as some of them were. Galashiels and Hawick were ideally situated for the traditional woollen manufacture, because the great Border sheep farms gave good supplies of Cheviot wool, while the Tweed and the Gala provided water power. During the Napoleonic wars, this area was developed by industrialists who introduced machinery adapted from the cotton mills. Two pieces of good luck favoured the proprietors of these new woollen factories. One was that Sir Walter Scott, then at the height of his literary fame, liked to wear locally made shepherd's plaid, which therefore became fashionable. The other was the highly profitable inaccuracy of a London clerk, who substituted for 'tweel'—the accepted name of Scott's favoured material—the word 'tweed.' This accidental error was ingeniously exploited and the new name came to stay, and to give city men all over the United Kingdom a pleasant feeling of literary distinction when they sported suits associated with the poet's well-loved river. The Waverley novels also stimulated the demand for tartan, legalized since 1782, and a number of towns in the east of Scotland built up flourishing businesses in the production of tartans, commercially designed to satisfy the public.

Another interesting local industry was centred at Paisley, where in 1802 shawls began to be made, in imitation of those produced in India. At first cotton was used, later spun silk, later again, a mixture of silk and wool. Local craftsmen attained a wonderful skill in designing the intricate and exquisitely delicate colourings of these shawls, which were worn by ladies of wealth for many years. Such work could not be done by power looms and until the shawls went out of fashion Paisley remained one of the few successful strongholds of craftsmanship. Not until about 1880 was the day of this attractive garment over; thereafter the

Paisley workers had to concentrate once again on the making of twisted thread.

Throughout the formative years of these textile industries, that is to say from 1770 onwards, a new source of power was being examined. This was steam. The dominant personality in the story of steam as an agent of production was another Scot of world-wide distinction, James Watt. Telford referred to him affectionately as the 'steam-engine man from Glasgow', although he was born and brought up in Greenock.

This great inventor suffered all his life from the allied ailments of indigestion, indecision, self-distrust and pessimism. He was an only child and his boyhood in Greenock was rather miserable, owing to ill-health and failure to make friends. In his teens, Watt discovered Geometry, his first source of creative happiness. He spent his nineteenth year in London, training to become a mathematical instrument-maker, after which in 1757, at the age of twenty-one, he found work in Glasgow University. In 1763, Watt was asked by Professor Anderson to repair for use in the Natural Philosophy class, an 'atmospheric steam-engine', commonly known as a 'fire-engine'. This was a steam-driven machine which had been invented some fifty years earlier by Thomas Newcomen, a Devonshire man; it was used for pumping water out of mines. Watt realized when he examined Professor Anderson's model that its defect was in the loss of steam by condensation, indeed the engine could only be kept going for a very short time, because the boiler could not supply sufficient steam. It took Watt the best part of two years to find the remedy for this weakness and he finally reached his solution in the middle of a Sunday walk on Glasgow Green. To put his theory of a separate condenser into practice cost several more years of experiment, during which time he became well-known as a civil engineer. At last, in 1769, his patent was sealed for 'a new invented method of lessening the Consumption of Steam and Fuel in Fire-Engines'.

In 1775, when the American war was ruining the tobacco trade, and Crompton was completing his work on the mule, Watt went into partnership with Matthew Boulton, at the Soho Works of Birmingham. This firm began the manufacture of the new steam engines. They were first employed in the Cornish mines, for pumping water out of the way, and Watt had to visit Cornwall to supervise their erection and the training of the workmen who handled them. Boulton persuaded Watt during the 1780s to make further experiments on the use of steam power, in order that it might be used, not only in mines, but in the new mills, to drive machinery. The rotary engine was the result of Watt's busiest and most productive years, and this could be used to drive forge-hammers by steam power.

In spite of his chronic scepticism, Watt had succeeded in releasing a major force of incalculable importance. The industrialists of the English Black Country seized upon it. In Scotland, partly because of the almost unlimited supplies of water power, the steam engine was not taken into general use until after the Napoleonic wars. The subsequent changes in economic and industrial organization were largely conditioned by developments in the iron industry.

Until the mid-18th century, iron foundries in Scotland, as in England, burnt charcoal. This was one of the reasons why Scottish hillsides had been denuded of trees. The shortage of fuel became so serious that for some years iron ore was actually transported at colossal cost to wooded areas, so that the industry became very much dispersed. In the 1720s for example, furnaces were lit at Invergarry, Taynuilt and Inveraray, by Lancashire ironmasters, who leased considerable expanses of forest from Macdonell, Lochiel, the Duke of Argyll and the Earl of Breadalbane. Roads, wharfs, even boats had to be built for the transport of the ore to these remote places. 'The industry of smelting and refining was literally fleeing to the wilderness to escape destruction.'

The wilderness was not needed for this particular service after 1750, because in that year an Englishman called Abraham Darby discovered how to use coke for smelting iron. Foundries now began to be established near the coalfields, as people had become accustomed to carrying ore to the source of fuel supply, but it soon became evident that in many areas rich iron seams were to be found almost alongside the coal. The foundries expanded since demands for iron were increasing on every side, and the new method of smelting made production much more profitable.

Industry

The earliest Scottish iron foundry to use coke was the famous Carron Iron Works, set up at Falkirk in 1759, a strange development in a town hitherto chiefly remarkable for its enormous autumn Cattle Trysts. Although the Company had severe setbacks to face in its early years, it gradually developed into one of the largest ironworks in Europe and it still exists today. One of its founders was John Roebuck, an Edinburgh Doctor of Medicine, who became a captain of industry. He was an important influence in the life of James Watt, as he saw how immensely valuable steam power could be in working iron and through his influence one of Watt's engines was installed at Carron in 1767. 'The steam-engine man from Glasgow' was much encouraged by Roebuck, at a period when he was almost engulfed by his difficulties.

The Seven Years' War was in full swing till 1763, so that supplies of iron from Sweden and Russia were not available, when the demand for armaments was at its height. The forges and mills connected with the Carron foundries manufactured cannon, at first with small success, though later their productions became world-famous. It was cannon from these foundries which formed part of the armour of Nelson's *Victory*. Wellington's field guns in the Peninsular campaign were made there too; they were known as 'carronades'. Agricultural implements and household goods were also made for export to many European dépots and to the plantations. Iron-rod for nails was something of a side-line, but it enabled the 'naileries' to do a tremendous trade in these homely articles, with the result that the old hand-made heather pegs were superseded except in Highland districts, where they served their turn for at least another century.

In 1784, Henry Cort of Portsmouth worked out a system of forging iron with raw coal; he also invented a process of groove-rolling, which eliminated one stage hitherto essential to the preparation of forge iron. His work had immediate results all over the country. In Scotland, the Carron foundries increased in size and scope while new works were opened near Glasgow, in Lanarkshire and in Ayrshire. Within twenty years of Cort's success, there were twenty-nine furnaces at work in the Scottish Black Country. Almost all of them were blast-furnaces, employing engines similar to those designed by James Watt.

The demand for labour was enormous, but so was the supply of destitute incomers to the cities from the Highlands. The employees had to learn new skills and to live in unfamiliar surroundings and they handled dangerous equipment. No legislation protected them and suffering became an inevitable feature in their lives of their families.

During the early years of the 19th century, iron was in greater demand than ever before. It seemed impossible to produce enough for the manufacturers of components used in factory machinery, railway lines, engines of all kinds, bridges, ships, locomotives, and innumerable pieces of equipment for industrial and domestic use, let alone for the armament firms.

Some 20,000 tons of pig-iron were produced every year during the Napoleonic wars, and during the 1820s the output increased sharply. This was because the valuable blackband ironstone of the Monkland area was discovered and also a new process of working it, known as the hot-blast. James Neilson of Shettleston invented this in 1828 and it meant that the fuel consumption needed in smelting each ton of iron was reduced by about 75 per cent. William Baird's Gartsherrie works were opened in the same year, the first of a new series of firms almost all in the Monkland area, and by 1847 Scotland was producing 25 per cent. of all the pig-iron smelted in Great Britain. By 1857, Scottish mines reached the figure of $2\frac{1}{2}$ million tons a year.

This immense development, together with the adoption of steam power, created a new situation in the coal mines. Coal had been known and used in Scotland from medieval times. In 1790, a Stirlingshire minister recorded his belief that coal had been worked in his parish for 500 years, more or less continuously, and the Culross mines had a long history too. An English traveller visited them in 1618 and was astonished by what he saw. 'In the space of eight and twenty years, they have digged more than an English mile under the sea, so that when men are at work below, an hundred of the greatest ships in Britain may sail over their heads.'

During the 17th and most of the 18th century, coal-mining was confined to a few areas in Fife, Ayrshire and Lanarkshire where, for the most part, only surface coal was worked. A few thousand tons were sent annually by sea to London, a certain amount was used for domestic purposes in Glasgow and Edinburgh, but the main function of coal was the traditional one, dating from the middle ages—to provide fuel for the salt-pans. Colliers like salt-workers were 'thirled', that is, bonded to their tasks. Cockburn's Whig principles were outraged by this traditional curtailment of personal freedom. 'They could not be killed or tortured, but they belonged, like the serfs of an older time, to their respective industries, with which they were sold as part of the gearing.' Legislation in 1775 and 1799 put an end to this enslavement, which had gone on from one generation to another since medieval times.

The expansion of industry in the latter part of the 18th century naturally increased the demand for coal, so that new pits were opened and old seams deepened. It was to make more coal accessible that the early canals and wagon ways were constructed and, by 1790, ministers had a good deal to say about local mines when they prepared their records for the Statistical Account. The parson at Kilsyth for example wrote as follows: 'Coal has been wrought for ages and is still abundant, I trust inexhaustible . . . The coal in the west barony is one of the best I ever saw. It burns clear, lasts long, gives a good heat, and cakes so that the very dross of it is valuable . . . The manner in which the coals are wrought is by pick and wedge; boys and sometimes girls are employed to draw the skiffies below ground . . . The expences attending the work are very considerable . . . It is to be hoped that a great deal of this will be saved, for there is a small steam engine immediately to be set up. This will easily do the work of a number of men, and save an enormous expence.'

During the first half of the 19th century, many new mines were developed and old ones extended, in Ayrshire, Lanarkshire, the Lothians and Fife. By 1854, Scottish mines were producing $7\frac{1}{2}$ million tons a year and quantities of coal were exported. The output mounted steadily and in 1900 reached 33 million tons.

The wealth of coal and iron contributed to the establishment of the Scottish engineering industry. Machines and tools of all kinds for the factories and mills were manufactured, equipment for agriculture, transport, armaments, and later on locomotives.

Again, great quantities of these goods were sold abroad. They went to Europe, the Middle East, the Far East, and all parts of the Empire, and supplanted textiles as Scotland's major export.

The engineering industry was concentrated in and around Glasgow and by the Clyde, with important branches at the Carron works and in Fife—naturally enough, as it had to be as near the sources of coal and iron supply as possible. The Second Statistical Account, published in the 1840s, showed that one-third of Scotland's manufacturing labourers lived in Lanarkshire. Some 19,000 of them were in Glasgow; the overcrowding in the workmen's quarters of the city became appalling.

Shipbuilding on the other hand was more dispersed, indeed for a considerable period a greater tonnage was produced at Aberdeen, Leith, Port Glasgow and Greenock than in the Glasgow yards. In the 1830s however the balance began to change, because steamships were now regularly ordered by such firms as the P. & O. Company. The Cunard Company was founded, with many Glasgow shareholders, and the first four vessels used in its service were built on the Clyde, with engines made by Robert Napier. Soon after this, iron was adopted as a basic material for shipbuilding. Because Glasgow was a centre both of the iron industry and of engineering, it followed that the iron ships and their engines were built on the Clyde, which became a joint headquarters for many branches of heavy industry and for shipbuilding. In 1877, two steel paddle-steamers were built at Govan by John Elder and, during the next twenty years, steelworks began to take the place of the iron foundries.

By the year 1877, exactly a century and a half had elapsed since Elizabeth Mure's interest had been aroused in the 'manefactorys' established by the Board of Trustees. During this period, Scottish ways of life had been completely disrupted and a new society had evolved, a society which bore little resemblance to that in which Elizabeth Mure and her friends had been brought up. The Industrial Revolution which precipitated the upheaval caused many political repercussions and it was also accompanied by a quickening interest in ideas, in art and in literature, which gave Scotland, and especially the capital, a decisive influence in Western Europe.

CHAPTER 23

Cities, Citizens and the Arts

Defoe described Glasgow in 1727 as 'one of the cleanliest, most beautiful and best built cities in Great Britain'; nine years later McUre said it was 'surrounded with cornfields, kitchen and flower gardens, abounding with fruit of all sorts, which, by reason of the open and large streets, send forth a pleasant and odoriferous smell'. Barely 13,000 people lived there, in the small area between the Cathedral at the upper end of the High Street and the College at the lower. Close to the College buildings were the meadows, with their fringe of broom by the riverside, and the Clyde was a placid and beautiful stream, crossed by only one ancient bridge, below which fishermen were able to pursue successful sport, and children to go paddling. The absence on Glasgow streets of drunkenness and brawling was attributed by an 18th century Professor to the people's religion, which 'though of a gloomy and enthusiastic cast makes them tame and sober'.

These 'tame and sober' Glaswegians were satisfied with homes of primitive simplicity. While the well-to-do rented small, badly lit flats, the poor lived in hovels, and for everybody the daily carrying of water from the city's wells was an accepted piece of routine. There were no clubs, no coffee-houses, few public functions and little organized pleasure. Going out at night was not attractive when the streets were unlit, garbage collection spasmodic, and social enjoyment so limited in scope.

Over in Edinburgh, people lived in similar conditions, though here there was less space, less fresh air and no pleasantly 'odoriferous smells' from orchard or garden. The capital was confined within the area of the old city walls, for the North Loch was not completely drained until 1820 and it was a barrier to expansion. About the time of its disappearance, Lord Cockburn described this 'loch' as a 'nearly impassable fetid marsh, a stinking swamp, open on all sides, the receptacle of many sewers and seemingly of all the worried cats, drowned dogs and black-guardism of the city'.

For lack of ground space, Edinburgh people made their homes and did their business in tall and narrow houses, sometimes twelve storeys high. The close-packed dwellings were crowded together on each side of the High Street and the Cowgate, from which branched off cobbled wynds and stone-paved vennels, all incredibly filthy.

Many authors have made acid comments on the dirt of the capital. After the uncomfortable months he spent there in 1707, Defoe summed up the situation rather more charitably than most: 'Were any other people to live under the same unhappiness, I mean as well of a rocky and mountainous situation, thronged buildings from seven to ten or twelve storeys high, a scarcity of water, and that little they have difficult to be had, and to the uppermost buildings far to fetch, we should have as dirty a London or Bristol as Edinburgh; for though many cities have more people in them, yet I believe there is no city in the world where so many people live in so little room.' Over a century later, Lord Cockburn dropped a characteristic remark, 'Though standing in a rainy country, Edinburgh has always been thirsty and unwashed.'

The overcrowding led to a genial if insanitary way of life, in which everybody knew everybody. The two or three storeys above street level were occupied by titled and professional families, while huddled in the upper ranges were the poorer working people. The narrow stone staircases, ill-lit and never cleansed, were shared by all and sundry, judges, aristocracy, children, coal-porters, clerics, water-carriers, Musselburgh fish-wives, sweeps, message-boys and many more. Unceremonious pushing and jostling became natural to Edinburgh citizens on these staircases and on the narrow, mile-long thoroughfare of the Canongate and the High Street. This cobbled road was the city's spinal cord, the very centre of its life, linking Holyrood Palace at the lower end with the great battlemented, rock-founded Castle which still towers above everything else. 'Upon this street, twice every day

Glasgow from the South: Robert Paul, Foulis Academy, circa 1758.

By courtesy of the Mitchell Library, Glasgow.

there are seldom fewer than 1,500 people walking' was the evidence of Forbes of Culloden, when he was speaking in the House of Commons about the Porteous Riots. Most of the City's few shops were concentrated here, in the Luckenbooths, near St. Giles, where shopkeepers used the street itself for their stalls and counters.

Throughout Scotland people suffered from malnutrition, from the all-pervading filth and from the lack of piped water. Tuberculosis, fevers, epidemics and smallpox ran riot in the towns and also invaded rural areas, so that bereavement was a constant affliction. In Kirkwall, the principal town of the Orkneys, there lived in the latter years of the 17th century a sculptor, much in demand for rectangular grave slabs, which he decorated with skulls and crossbones and what he deemed suitable verse. One of the jingles reads as follows:

> '*Agnes nine children boor unto hir mate,*
> *Six died befor their sire, by cruel fate.*'

These lines seem crude enough, but the craftsman's obvious horror of death is plainly revealed in the pathetic phrases he selected for his many clients, and the tragedy of Agnes was characteristic of an age when people had no knowledge of how to safeguard children's health. And things did not improve as the 18th century wore on. From 1790 until about 1851, child deaths in Glasgow accounted for over 50 per cent. of the total.

For many years, Edinburgh remained the most populated city in Scotland, but gradually linen and tobacco began to attract more people to Glasgow. New streets were laid down, colourful and creaking signboards appeared to advertise the increasing number of shops and by mid-century hackney coaches were in demand. In 1775, the Saracen's Head, Glasgow's first hotel, was opened at the eastern end of the city; eight years later the Black Bull in Argyle Street began business, and it was in the smoking rooms of these establishments that Glasgow men began to develop club life. By the end of the century, some of the more prosperous families were living in self-contained houses instead of two-roomed flats, though they were still without water, which was laboriously fetched in buckets from the city wells until 1804. In this year, William Harley set up great cisterns in the appropriately named Bath Street and began delivering halfpenny stoups of water by pony-cart. Glasgow's cornfields and orchards were nearly all obliterated by warehouses, factories, streets and terraces, for the city's population numbered well over 70,000.

The expansion of Edinburgh was slow in starting, for even when George Street and Brown Street were constructed in 1765, their fine new houses were regarded as inconveniently far from the centre of things, because the North Loch lay between them and the old city. During the 1770s, work was at last begun on draining it and filling it with earth and shingle, a process which took some fifty years to complete: to link the Old Town with the new streets, the North Bridge was built across the famous old gully.

When people with capital and social position realized how easy of access the New Town had become, they moved out of their cramped quarters in the Canongate, the Lawnmarket and the High Street, with the sad result that the network of buildings round St. Giles, the heart of the old capital, was allowed to fall into dilapidation. High society set up much more expensive homes in George Street, Queen Street and Charlotte Square. 'There, when the great exodus was made across the valley, and the New Town began to spread abroad its draughty parallelograms, and rear its long frontage on the opposing hill, there was such a flitting, such a change of domicile and dweller as was never excelled in the history of cities: the cobbler succeeded the earl; the beggar ensconced himself by the judge's chimney; what had been a palace was used as a pauper refuge.' So wrote R. L. Stevenson in his rather lugubrious little book on Edinburgh. The New Town bears to this day the dignity and graciousness bestowed upon it by its principal designer and architect, Robert Adam, cynical though R.L.S. chose to be about it. And Charlotte Square is no more draughty than the old High Street.

During the years which followed the Second Jacobite Rebellion, there developed a gradual awakening of interest in literature and the arts. The origins of this development belong to the early years of the 18th century, when the stimulus came from certain family groups.

One famous centre of literary interest was in a most unlikely place—a wigmaker's shop, on the High Street of Edinburgh. Its owner was Allan Ramsay, a man with an insatiable appetite for books, especially books on poetry. His background was a remote, windswept village called Leadhills, on the uplands of Lanarkshire, where his father had been superintendent of the gold and lead mines belonging to the Earl of Hopetoun, and where he had received very little education. Until he was fifteen, Ramsay's acquaintances were the children of miners, men who lived as semi-slaves, bonded to their masters, deprived of legal rights, and often ill from the effects of lead-poisoning. In 1700, he went to Edinburgh, to be a wigmaker's apprentice: there he later married and became, in the course of about a dozen years, the father of ten children. Only three survived infancy, the eldest of whom was named Allan, after his father.

The family lived at first on High Street, where Ramsay dealt with his customers and made his wigs, but he enjoyed far more the trade in satires and verses which became the absorbing interest of his life. During these years he wrote poetry himself, and finally he moved his books to a shop in the Luckenbooths, where in 1725 he opened the first circulating library in Edinburgh. The squat, stout, merry little barber-poet became a well-known and popular figure, who attracted to his premises citizens and visitors of all kinds, delighting them both with his wares and with his wit. One of these visitors was the poet John Gay, who came to Edinburgh in 1725 and became a personal friend.

About this time, Ramsay decided to found a theatre, and he financed and designed a building for this purpose in Carubber's Close, but the project could not survive the disapproval of the church. Ministerial strictures however failed to prevent him from providing his customers with French romances, London publications, Dryden's comedies and many classical works as well, nor could it stem the flow of his own writing, which included not only poems but also the charming pastoral opera called *The Gentle Shepherd*. In 1740 Ramsay retired from his bookshop, to devote his leisure to reading, and moved into an oddly constructed house, known as 'Guse-pie', which became something of a jest in the city, and which was the scene of a considerable skirmish in the Forty-Five.

Allan Ramsay the younger grew up in an atmosphere of books: from his earliest days he was interested in literature, particularly in Horace, and he also learned Italian, French and German. His gift for painting must have surprised his father and he himself wanted to achieve literary rather than artistic distinction. In the summer of 1736 he set forth on the Grand Tour, and in Italy he began to study painting seriously. He settled in London for a while on his return, but during the 1740s he worked often in Edinburgh, making use of a studio in his father's home. He did not stay at Guse-pie long, for he spent much of his time abroad and in London, and until 1765 or 1766 an astonishing number of the aristocracy sat to him for portraits. Although he employed assistants to carry out much of the routine work, very many pictures of his own may still be seen today. Ramsay liked to paint people in splendid dress, but he achieved simplicity in design and serenity in pose, and he had a gift for revealing personality. The graciousness and dignity of the 18th century at its best may be understood if one studies such portraits as those of his wife, Margaret Lindsay, of Mrs. John Sargent and of Lady Susan Fox-Strangways. His royal portraits are more magnificent but less intimate and not so satisfying, perhaps because he turned out so many in quick succession.

All his life, the younger Ramsay longed to make his name as a writer and a patron of literature. In 1754 he founded the Select Society for Encouraging Art, Science and Industry, an enterprise typical of the age when people set themselves seriously and unself-consciously to create a culture. Adam Smith and David Hume both gave Ramsay's society their support and for a while it brought a number of distinguished men together, Lord Kames for example, John and James Adam the architects, William Robertson, George Dempster, John Home, and later Boswell, all men who contributed to the brilliant life of Edinburgh. In his latter years, Ramsay gave up painting, with the curious result that his obituary notice in the *Gentleman's Magazine* made no mention of his portraits. After 1784, when he died, his work was forgotten and it was not until the 20th century that the true value of his painting was re-discovered. Exhibitions of Scottish Art in Glasgow and in London during the late 1930s made him known once more, and to a much larger public than he ever reached during his lifetime.

The Luckenbooths library was not the only unlikely quarter of the capital which produced artists. Allan Ramsay discovered a gifted young man working as a coachbuilder's apprentice on heraldic decorations for the carriages of the gentry. This was Alexander Nasmyth, whom Ramsay took to London to do background work on his portraits. Nasmyth was a person with independent views and in 1778, at the age of twenty, he returned to Edinburgh, where he was successful as a painter of portraits and landscapes, a designer of formal parks and gardens, and also as an architect. Nasmyth's two sons and six daughters all became artists too and regularly exhibited their works in the capital.

Among many other Scottish painters, but outclassing them all, was Henry Raeburn, whose portraits rank with those of Reynolds. He spent almost all his life in the city of his birth, working with enviable happiness and prosperity, and giving his sitters personal, undivided attention, for, unlike Ramsay, he did not believe in employing assistants. On the occasion of the royal visit to Edinburgh in 1822, organized by Sir Walter Scott, George IV knighted Raeburn, whom he sincerely admired.

Meantime in Glasgow, Andrew and Robert Foulis, both graduates of Glasgow University, developed a skill hitherto lacking north of the Border. This was the art of printing, in which Scottish standards had so far been deplorable, for even the Bible was produced in miserable type with numerous misprints. These brothers set up the famous Foulis press, which gave Scotland a series of exquisitely printed classical texts, whose accuracy far exceeded anything known before. Probably their most valuable production was a four-volume folio Homer, still considered one of the finest pieces of Greek printing to be seen; they also published good texts from the works of Sophocles, Aristotle, Horace, Cicero and many more. Andrew and Robert were Printers to the University of Glasgow, and they established a bookshop and a printing press in the quadrangle of the University itself. Just as the elder Allan Ramsay's place of business became a focal point for booklovers and writers, so the Foulis press attracted scholars and thinkers from many places.

These brothers, like the elder Ramsay, had a castle in the air. In 1753, when the theatre in Carubber's Close had already proved a lost cause, Andrew and Robert launched in Glasgow an Academy of Arts, upon which they lavished care and money. In this enterprise they failed as completely as Ramsay, for Scottish people were not yet sufficiently interested in painting and sculpture to support the Academy, nor was the scholarship of the two founders so sound in the selection and purchase of pictures as in the publication of classical texts.

It is rather sad that men who gave so much to the literary world were embittered in their latter years by the collapse of such idealistic schemes as the Carubber's Close theatre and the Glasgow Academy of Arts. Nonetheless, the Academy gave a number of young men their chance, some of whom stood by the Foulis brothers when financial troubles engulfed them. Such was David Allen, the son of quite humble folk in Alloa. His gift for painting found expression when he reached the height of his powers in humorous character studies, but he also became a popular portrait painter in an age that had no photography and when people loved sitting to artists. His designs for Allan Ramsay's *Gentle Shepherd* made him renowned in literary and musical circles too.

Much, perhaps too much, has been made of the 18th century Englishman's distaste for Scotland and the Scots. The English aristocracy of the period were delighted to have their portraits done by Ramsay and Raeburn, English scholars to study their classical texts in the Foulis editions: at the same time it became common for English congregations to worship in the buildings of one famous Scot and for English noblemen to live in the mansions of another. James Gibbs and Robert Adam were both distinguished architects and no account of the period can be made without taking both men into consideration.

James Gibbs, the son of an Aberdeenshire Roman Catholic, was born in 1682, and brought up at a time when people of his persuasion were hemmed in by every legal stricture that could be devised. When he was twenty he went to Holland as a student of architecture and there he met the 11th Earl of Mar, soon to become known as Bobbing John. In Gibbs the Earl recognized a man of great gifts, and he gave him money to go to Rome. Here he worked for a time under Pope Clement XI's surveyor-general; altogether he spent ten years in Italy, after which he settled in London.

Gibbs was fortunate. He enjoyed the patronage both of Mar and of Argyll; he also arrived in London when an ambitious church-expansion scheme was afoot and he at once secured commissions. He designed St. Mary-le-Strand, completed the adjacent St. Clement Danes, where Samuel Johnson later worshipped, and built the present St. Martin-in-the-Fields, perhaps his most distinguished work. Gibbs also built the Radcliffe Library in Oxford, in Cambridge the Senate House and the beautiful block of buildings in King's College, which stands at right angles to the 15th century chapel. His buildings were in keeping with the traditions of his day and yet they were designed with originality. 18th century architecture in Britain represents some of the finest work achieved since the Rennaissance and Gibbs was one of those Scots who contributed much to its development.

Robert Adam was a member of another Scottish family which attained international distinction at this time. His father, William Adam, made a name for himself as an architect in the classical style for which Gibbs did so much. He brought four able sons into his profession, John, Robert, James and William, of whom Robert was by far the most gifted. Robert left Scotland in 1754, to travel as Allan Ramsay had done in France and Italy, and in 1758 he set up a home for himself and his brothers and sisters in London.

From 1758 onwards, Robert Adam was in constant demand among owners of country houses, which he rebuilt or enlarged, combining dignity in proportion with delicacy in detail and ornament. Kedleston in Derbyshire, Compton Verney in Warwickshire and Syon House in Middlesex are three famous works of this sort, though there are many others, and he was responsible too for a number of new mansions which he designed and carried out from the foundations. In every case, Robert devoted his artistry and scholarship as much to interior as to exterior design: his ceilings, staircases, fireplaces and doorways are still to be seen in houses whose structure has often been mutilated in later years by much less gifted architects. Culzean Castle in Ayrshire is a fine example of his work and one of the few such houses he designed north of the Border.

Robert Adam's influence on city architecture was almost more permanent in its effects. The Admiralty Screen, Whitehall, is one of his best-known works, but he was prolific in his designs for town houses, large and small, as well as for whole streets and squares and boldly massed blocks. Many of his structures are now spoiled by subsequent alterations and by neglect, but you can still see some in St. James's Square and Grosvenor Square and in other London streets.

In Edinburgh, Robert was commissioned to build the beautiful Register House and to design much of the New Town. Some of the houses in Queen Street and Castle Street are his, and Charlotte Square would have been one of his most splendid achievements had it been completed according to his plans, but unfortunately only the north and south blocks were built as he meant them to be. He was also asked to rebuild Edinburgh University, but he died in 1792 before his plans were fulfilled. The influence of Robert Adam and his brothers was perhaps greater than that of any other Scottish family; architects all over the country took up their ideas and for at least a century the basic structure, the interior decoration and the outer façade of many buildings were modelled on Adam designs.

During their earlier years when they lived in Edinburgh, William Adam's sons made many friends, who also became well known. One was a cousin, William Robertson, a man of massive intellectual ability, much personal charm and astonishing industry. He was a popular man, at the very centre of Edinburgh society and on intimate terms with Allan Ramsay, Robert Adam, Lord Kames, Adam Smith, David Hume and many another.

The next two chapters refer in more detail to Robertson, but here it is worth quoting Horace Walpole's comments upon him when they met in London, after the publication of Robertson's *History of Scotland*. 'How could I suspect that a man under forty,

whose dialect I scarce understood, and who came to me with all
the diffidence and modesty of a very middling author, and who I
was told had passed his life in a small living in Edinburgh—how
could I suspect that he had not only written what all the world
now allows to be the best modern history, but that he had written
it in the purest English and with as much seeming knowledge of
men and courts as if he had passed all his life in important
embassies?' The first edition of this History sold out in a month,
and nobody was more surprised by his success than Robertson
himself. Lord Cockburn as a boy used to play with Robertson's
grandson and he affectionately recalled the old scholar directing
the children's attention to the best fruit on his favourite cherry-
tree—'a pleasant-looking old man, with an eye of great vivacity
and intelligence, a large projecting chin, a small hearing-trumpet
fastened by a black ribbon to the lapel of his coat, and a rather
large wig, powdered and curled'.

David Hume the philosopher was a close friend of the Ramsays,
of Robertson and also of the Adam brothers, whose mother, however, had her doubts about him, because he was a sceptic. Hume
was the greatest of the sceptics. He carried much further than
Descartes had been able to do the philosopher's task of calling in
question accepted beliefs. The perennial philosophy of Christendom had been profoundly inspired by Plato's teaching that the
truest knowledge is derived, like mathematics, from insight into
the logical implications of self-evident propositions. It was
believed that logic can give us knowledge of the existence of God.
Hume's criticism showed that this system breaks down, that pure
logic gives rules of thought, but not knowledge of existing reality.
He developed a system of his own which claimed to show that all
our knowledge is derived from reflection upon the experience that
comes to us through the senses and through feeling. This system
is itself open to criticism, but Hume's empirical method introduced a fresh line of enquiry and he remains today a dominant
influence in philosophical speculation.

Hume was mortified by the reception accorded to his great
philosophical works, his *Treatise of Human Nature*, which, as he
said himself 'fell dead-born from the press' in 1739, and the
Enquiry Concerning the Principles of Morals, published in 1752.

But he continued to write, always with distinction, over a range of interests so wide and so novel that his influence can be seen in the works of Kant, Adam Smith, Bentham and Comte. Hume never failed to please as a man, and he enjoyed exuberant popularity in France, where he held diplomatic appointments for some years. On his return to Edinburgh, he became a prominent leader in the splendid group of writers living there, 'the Socrates of Edinburgh' as George Dempster called him in one of his letters to Adam Fergusson.

David Hume had a young cousin, whom he befriended and from whom he received much kindness. This was John Home, who insisted to Hume's disgust in spelling his name with an 'o'. He was an ordained minister with a charge at Athelstaneford, but he devoted his leisure to writing plays. In 1754, to the immense delight of secular opinion, but to the horror of the General Assembly, Home's tragedy *Douglas* was produced at the Canon-gate Theatre in Edinburgh.

This was a succulent piece of news for George Dempster to send to Adam Fergusson. 'Nothing', he wrote, 'ever afforded more entertainment to this country than the "Douglass", Mr. Home's tragedy. The novelty of a play being writ by a member of the Church, by a Scotsman, and first represented in Scotland, has given rise to a vast deal of fun. And paper bullets have been flying with great vehemence ever since.' Solemn censure was passed on all the ministers who disgraced themselves by going to see this performance, and William Robertson, then at the beginning of his ministry, was one of only eleven members in the General Assembly who thought this condemnation absurd. Home had to give up his church, but this proved no great financial sacrifice, as Lord Bute negotiated a royal pension for him. His cousin, David Hume, praised *Douglas* to the skies, like other contemporaries, including, most curiously, John Wesley, who read it in 1757 and thought it well written. Posterity's judgment has not upheld the views of Hume and Wesley in this matter.

In 1773 Samuel Johnson came to stay in Edinburgh at the Boswell's flat in St. James' Court, High Street. Mrs. Boswell made him innumerable cups of tea and showed off her baby Veronica, who flattered him by appearing to listen to his conversation, although she was only four months old. Dr. William Robertson was invited to breakfast—a meal Johnson always specially enjoyed in Scotland—and to dinner came all the other celebrities whom Boswell could collect. While Johnson complained of the smells in the High Street, he appreciated the conversation in St. James' Court, to his host's naïve delight. The two set off for their Hebridean tour on August 18th and travelled north to Inverness by St. Andrews and Aberdeen, then west to the islands, in conditions which would daunt most holiday-makers today, but Johnson in his sixties seemed to thrive on the experience. They recorded their impressions, each in his own characteristic prose, and as the 20th century has an insatiable appetite for everything Boswell wrote, the Highland tour is now a classic.

Edinburgh citizens were accustomed to the visits of celebrities, but an unparalleled sensation was created on November 28th 1786, when Robert Burns wearily rode into the Grassmarket, on a borrowed pony. His *Poems, Chiefly in the Scottish Dialect* had been published at Kilmarnock in the spring of the year. The small volume of poems and songs won immediate recognition, as Robert Heron, Burns' first biographer, recorded: 'Old and young, high and low, grave and gay, learned and ignorant, all were delighted, agitated, transported. I was at that time resident in Galloway, contiguous to Ayrshire, and I well remember how that even plough-boys and maid-servants would have gladly parted with the wages they earned the most hardly and which they wanted to purchase necessary clothing, if they might but procure the works of Burns.'

In London and in Edinburgh, the Kilmarnock edition aroused as much enthusiasm as in Ayrshire and Galloway. The poems captured the spirit of the Scottish countryside and its people in a dialect whose fresh and musical rhythm was enhanced by vivid and rather earthy turns of phrase. Burns delighted people too with his shrewd and witty analysis of character, his strong sympathy for common folk, his sense of the ridiculous and, above all, with his gift of crystallizing beauty in lines which were at once terse and exquisite. When people learned that this poet had been born in an Ayrshire cottage which his father had built himself, that by city standards he had hardly been educated at all, that his life had been spent in working on a farm, they were more 'agitated and transported' than ever, and his arrival in Edinburgh in 1786 led to a period of lionizing such as Burns could hardly have anticipated in his wildest dreams.

A new edition of the poems was necessary and for this Burns chose as his literary agent William Creech. The premises used by Creech for bookshop and publishing house were situated in the Luckenbooths, below those formerly held by Allan Ramsay, senior, and like his predecessor, Creech made his shop the centre of literary and intellectual society. Here Burns met as many distinguished people as in the drawing-rooms of the capital and in more congenial circumstances, for he soon wearied of the social engagements which people pressed upon him. Early in 1787, he set out for a tour of the Borders, and though he returned to Edinburgh for some months during the following winter, he never settled there. He died in Dumfries in 1796, only ten years after the publication of his first volume, the victim of an agonizing heart disease which contemporary medicine could not relieve. By the time of his death, fellow-countrymen all over the world were singing his songs and reciting his verses, so that Tam o' Shanter, Holy Willie and many more of his characters were loved and quoted, and the Lowland Scots in which he wrote had won a sure place in the nation's literature. Nobody else painted Scottish folk and their ways in such vivid Scottish language, with one exception—Walter Scott.

Walter Scott was born in 1771, one of a family of nine, of whom only four survived infancy. He had poliomyelitis as a baby, which left him with a limp and made his childhood rather miserable. Because of his poor health, he was sent to stay for long periods on a farm in the Borders. In this environment his physical constitution was built up so that in manhood he could ride and walk longer distances than most of his friends, and here too he discovered folk-lore. The ballads and stories of the district excited him greatly and he spent more time than his father would have approved in collecting and memorizing them, an activity which brought him into contact with many strange characters whom he afterwards described.

Scott's love of Border traditions found expression first in *The Minstrelsy of the Scottish Border*, published in 1802, a collection of ballads which he edited with scholarly devotion. His introduction was packed with fascinating information and, as at least forty-three of the poems had never been printed before, the volume created a great stir in Edinburgh. In January 1805, *The Lay of the Last Minstrel* appeared, the first of his longer poems, and it went through edition after edition. People were ready for a fresh conception of poetry and in Scott's work they found it, for he could combine incisive narrative with lyrical passages of haunting, delicate beauty, and while he seemed to be a genius in the art of lament, he could also write with a headlong, rhythmic speed which can still make the reader catch his breath. *Marmion* and the *Lady of the Lake* followed soon after from the pen of this 'rattle-skulled half-lawyer, half-sportsman', as Scott described himself, and it is hardly possible to exaggerate the effect these works had in reviving people's enjoyment of poetry.

On July 7th, 1814, an anonymous novel in three volumes was published in Edinburgh, priced at a guinea. This was *Waverley*. Three weeks later Walter Scott embarked on the Lighthouse yacht with R. L. Stevenson's grandfather for one of the happiest holidays he ever enjoyed, and he had reason to be in high spirits. Edinburgh was consumed with curiosity as to the authorship of this romance, so rich in eccentricity and whimsical reminiscence; and Scott had amused himself by starting some false trails before he set off.

Cockburn wrote of Edinburgh's reaction to the book: 'The unexpected newness of the thing, the profusion of the original characters, the Scotch language, Scotch scenery, Scotch men and women, the simplicity of the writing and the graphic force of the descriptions—all struck us with a shock of delight'. The author could not maintain his secret for long and the mystery became one of Edinburgh's jokes as one after another the novels in the series captivated the reading public. Hitherto novels had not been written in a style likely to command much respect or popularity, while social history and antiquarian research had hardly been begun. Scott's writing let a flood of light upon a new field of interest, and while he gave the 19th century fresh literary forms, he also showed people that historical scholarship can uncover romantic pictures of life in the past.

Scott was incapable of malicious or narrow-minded judgment and he was the best of companions. After his death, Cockburn's affection for him found expression in words which still give one a most vivid impression of his personality. 'Dear Scott! . . . It is a pleasure, which the next generation may envy, that I can still hear his voice and see his form. I see him in the Court, and on the street, in company, and by the Tweed. The plain dress, the guttural, blurred voice, the lame walk, the thoughtful heavy face with its mantling smile, the honest, hearty manner, the joyous laugh, the sing-song feeling recitation, the graphic story—they are all before me a hundred times a day.'

One of Scott's many friends was Sydney Smith, the English clergyman, who came to Edinburgh as the tutor of young Michael Hicks Beach. This lad's father had wanted him to make the Grand Tour, but Napoleon's activities prevented it and so he sent him to Edinburgh. The fact was that, although barely half a century earlier Englishmen had been wont to express contempt for Scotland, they were now eagerly coming to Edinburgh to find the culture hitherto sought on the continent. Lord Palmerston, the third Marquis of Lansdowne and many other young men from the south had their early training there and carried home with them friendships and memories which drew nostalgic reminiscence from them ever afterwards.

None of them however could compete with Sydney Smith's radiant genius for enjoyment, which made him immensely popular. It was largely owing to Smith's irresistible enthusiasm that the Friday Club was founded, a society which met weekly at Fortune's Tavern for dinner, price £2 a head. Among the original members was Lord Cockburn. Cockburn was a bit of an eccentric, with independent views on gardens, politics and everything else. His dogged upholding of democratic ideas delayed his promotion, until he was made Solicitor-General in the Whig ministry of 1830. Cockburn had a relish for observing and describing human beings and their institutions, so that his *Memorials* are a mine of racy, astringent, charitable comment upon Edinburgh in its heyday. As well as Cockburn, Sydney

Smith rounded up Walter Scott, Henry Brougham, Dugald Stewart and old James Watt, along with other renowned personalities, and riotous evenings at the Friday Club were spent in gales of laughter at Smith's outrageous jests. Francis Jeffrey and Francis Horner were two with whom he became specially intimate and in 1802 these three launched the *Edinburgh Review*.

Journalism at the time was considered an inferior profession because newspaper men were not free to publish unbiassed views, and even the recording of contemporary events was restricted by the reactionary attitude of the Government. The French Revolution intensified this. After 1789 even the mildest of reforms was dreaded by people whose social position afforded them security, lest with a little relaxation of traditional laws a whole spate of revolutionary changes might follow. Nobody who wanted a successful career dared express sympathy for any kind of underdog. Prisoners being tried for their lives were allowed no counsel, the Slave Trade flourished, savage game laws were condoned, lunatics were chained and beaten, chimney-sweeps were allowed to endanger the lives of small boys in the interests of property-owners, suffrage was strictly limited, Roman Catholics suffered many restrictions. To found a periodical which would challenge such scandals and put forward liberal views was a risky venture. Only writers of exceptional quality could successfully have carried the enterprise through. From the beginning Francis Jeffrey and Sydney Smith attracted such writers and paid them much larger fees for articles than was usual in those days.

Too many people remember the Review chiefly for its savage attacks upon the Lake Poets and upon certain religious movements, and there is no doubt that Smith and his friends did publish scathing criticisms. On the other hand, the Review gave scope to some first-class writers and it brought its readers into sympathy with new points of view. The need for political and social reform was made clear to many people who previously had been satisfied with the existing situation because they knew nothing about the way in which less fortunate human beings were living. A liberal-minded Englishwoman called Mrs. Fletcher recorded in her autobiography: 'I, who knew Edinburgh both before and after the appearance of the Review, can bear witness to the electrical effect of its publication on the public mind and to the large and good results, in a political sense, that followed its circulation.'

One result of Smith's initiative in launching the *Edinburgh Review* was that other periodicals shortly followed, such as the *Quarterly* in 1808 and *Blackwood's* in 1817, both in the Tory interest. Also in 1817 there appeared for the first time *The Scotsman*, a weekly paper sold at 10d, which reached a much wider public than the quarterly journals and which exercised an influence of incalculable importance during this troubled period of the 1820s and 1830s.

During the 19th century, the writings of J. G. Lockhart, Scott's son-in-law and biographer, of Thomas Carlyle and of R. L. Stevenson made a permanent contribution to literature and enhanced Scottish prestige in the world of letters. There is no doubt however that the great days of Edinburgh made the period 1760 to 1830 remain unique in the country's literary and cultural history. G. S. Pryde, in a recent history of Scotland, suggests that 'the brilliance of Edinburgh's Athenian age was fatally dimmed by the death of Scott in 1832', and certainly the loss of this great figure deprived society of one unrivalled influence. But this was not the whole story. From time to time in history one particular generation becomes renowned because more than the usual proportion of people are endowed with noble gifts of mind and heart, and through this brought to new-found enjoyment of each other. This was what happened in the latter part of the 18th century, when for several decades the Scottish capital was a focal point of thought and letters and art, and when Scottish authors and thinkers exercised an influence far beyond their own country. But no society seems to be able to live at this level for an unlimited span. Perhaps inevitably the magical energy spent itself, and from about 1830 onwards, though Scotland produced many men and women of distinction, the former brilliance and zest gradually became diluted. Cockburn felt this, but he explained the change simply by the re-opening of Europe after the Napoleonic wars, an event which drew people away from Edinburgh to Paris and to other continental cities. 'A new race of peace-formed youths came on the stage but with little literature

The Heart of Midlothian: W. & A. K. Johnston, 1852.

By courtesy of the City Librarian, Edinburgh.

and a comfortless intensity of political zeal; so that by the year 1820, the old thing was much worn and there was no new thing of the same piece to continue or replace it.' He admitted that much remained to make Edinburgh unique, but he reiterated nostalgically 'The exact old thing was not.'

CHAPTER 24

Religion

In Scotland, during the 18th century, people had more regard
for religion than their English neighbours. Rational detach-
ment and cynical indifference were not yet making it difficult
for Scotsmen to accept the Christian faith. Presbyterians indeed
were immensely proud of their traditions and of the fight their
forbears had made to establish them. Except in districts where
ministers could not penetrate because of long distances or
impossible geographical conditions, Scotsmen enjoyed grappling
with doctrinal problems and discussing spiritual principles. It
was partly a matter of temperament, but partly too it was
because life in Scotland was harder, conditions more rigorous,
personal suffering more constant, so that for many people the
hereafter seemed to be worth more attention than the here and
now. In London and the south-east of England, there were more
amenities, more amusements, more physical comforts, more dis-
tractions, so that there people tended to become more readily
sophisticated and to create for themselves artificial pleasures. All
this militated against the influence of the Church. But this tide
of sophistication reached Scotland later and slowly.

Because people attached such importance to religion, Scottish
ministers exercised great influence. People looked to them for
guidance in matters of principle, for advice in dilemmas, and for
an example in standards of daily living. The reverence accorded
to ministers did not exempt them however from much acid
criticism, especially from the elders, who took themselves
seriously and relished their duty of seeing that the minister
behaved as he should.

The minister's first task each week was of course to prepare
the Sunday sermon. Listening to this gave many people their one
weekly diversion and it was always closely followed and much

commented upon. The congregation sat on uncushioned benches in draughty, unheated buildings for two hours each Sunday morning, and if the minister preached more briefly, the elders lost no time in reprimanding him. Preaching, like praying, was supposed to be done without reference to written notes, and to be guided by spiritual light at the moment of delivery. Sermons and prayers were charged with strong emotion, for the Scots are emotional people, and in the 18th century ministers and congregations found an outlet in corporate worship.

The Church of Scotland observed neither Christmas nor Easter, but special efforts were made to keep the Communion season, which was celebrated in country parishes only once a year. Often several parishes would organize a series of Communion Services in one church after another and to these gatherings, sometimes three or four in succession, people from all over the countryside would flock, camping out for the night in barns, or wherever they could, if their journey had been too long for them to get home the same day. Even in wet weather, such Services were conducted out of doors because no church building could hold the large numbers of people.

The ministers worked hard. Apart from preparing sermons and conducting services, they were responsible for Poor Relief and religious discipline in their parishes, and they had to supervise the local school. The laborious deliberations of the Kirk Session took up much of their time too.

And they had to visit their people. It is easy to overlook the strain involved by this. In October 1955, the minister of Kilfinnan and Kilbryde reported to the Dunoon Presbytery that in twelve months he had journeyed 1,290 miles in Sunday travel and 8,200 miles in weekday travel, an arduous way of life indeed, conditioned by a large and scattered country charge. How did his predecessors manage, with neither car nor bicycle? What of the 18th century ministers in Urquhart? This Inverness-shire parish was thirty miles long, ten to twelve wide, and diagonally intersected by a great boney mountain ridge. Ardnamurchan was another mountain parish of great size, Kilmorack a third, and there were of course many more like them. Long exhausting journeys on horseback in dirty weather and across rough country formed a regular part of the Scottish minister's life.

Many ministers received slender emoluments. Often they were paid partly in kind, with bolls, pecks, firlots, even lippies of meal and bere. They all had a manse and most of them a few acres of glebe. In cash, some received as little as £5 to £10 a year, hardly more than farm labourers: Collace in Perthshire was one of these very poorly paid charges. The average stipend was about £40, as in Sorn, Ayrshire, Abercorn near Edinburgh and many others. Doune was exceptional in paying £100 to £150.

Ministers were glad to get to the General Assembly in Edinburgh. Here they could meet people other than their own parishioners, listen to matters of national importance being discussed, renew friendships and replenish their bookshelves at Allan Ramsay's bookshop in the Luckenbooths. Above all, they could worship in one or other of the city churches and hear somebody else preach, a rare inspiration for an 18th century minister.

During this period, everything Anglican and most things English were under suspicion. The Church of Scotland's services were consequently impoverished because public opinion demanded the omission of the Creed, the Doxology, even the Lord's Prayer, all of which were regarded as Episcopalian devices, though all had been included in the Book of Common Order and Knox would never have dreamed of doing without them.

Singing in church was led by the 'up-taker of the psalm', an official later known as the Precentor, who was often the schoolmaster. 'Up-taking' meant singing the Psalm line by line, the congregation following line by line alternately with the leader, a custom which made the musical part of worship a dreary discipline, especially as for many years there were only twelve accepted tunes. Hymns as we know them did not appear until the early 19th century and they were a development from the Paraphrases, which began to be used in 1781.

In the middle of the 18th century, a change in church music was initiated by Sir Archibald Grant, the agricultural reformer, He instructed the local schoolmaster to select a choir of children with good voices, to train them in choral singing and on no account to let them drone. Practices were held in Sir Archibald's

library, where he had an organ—and he must have been unique
in possessing such an instrument and putting it to such a use.
In 1753, Grant heard of an English soldier called Thomas
Channon, stationed at Aberdeen. Channon had a gift for choral
work and for getting people to sing. The Synod of Aberdeen
arranged his discharge from the army, and Grant secured and
financed his services. This Englishman started a movement which
spread throughout Aberdeenshire, thence to Edinburgh, and
gradually transformed church music. In 1761, John Wesley
visited Sir Archibald and recorded in his diary: 'About six, we
went to church. It was pretty well filled with such persons as we
did not look for so near the Highlands. But if we were surprised
at their appearance, we were more so at their singing. Thirty or
forty sang an anthem after the sermon, with such voices as well
as judgment, that I doubt whether they could have been excelled
at any cathedral in England.'

No cathedral in England could have rivalled the choir practices
of Sir Archibald's church. It was thought irreverent to sing the
words of Scripture except at services, so practice verses were
composed for use in rehearsal. One paid tribute in happy vein
to Sir Archibald himself:

> '*How lovely is thy dwelling-place,*
> *Sir Archie Grant, to me;*
> *The Home-park and the policies,*
> *How pleasant, Sir, they be.*'

The sincerity of the ministers and their congregations was
genuine, and their faith deep-rooted. Their strong religious
convictions gave them spiritual resources which they all sorely
needed. One sad feature of the 18th century, however, was that
the Kirk Sessions used their authority with censorious intolerance and little compassion. The man or woman convicted of
Sabbath-breaking, 'horrid swearing' or immorality was subjected to humiliating cross-examination by the Session and
afterwards made to stand out before the whole congregation
for solemn rebuke by the minister. Sometimes this punishment
was continued for several Sundays running, and the culprit was
further abased by being made to wear sackcloth garments. These
acts of penance were enjoyed by the righteous who witnessed them.

The democratic nature of congregational government led to a good many disagreements and to some major controversies. There was bitterness of feeling about Lay Patronage, the legal right of landowners to appoint the ministers to churches on their own properties, which was restored by Act of Parliament in 1712. While it would be too much to say that this Patronage Act caused most of the ecclesiastical trouble in Scotland during the following decades, it certainly was an important contributory factor. During the 18th century, a number of groups withdrew from the National Church, and these seceding bodies could not maintain their own unity, so they in turn also became divided. They were popularly known by such quaint names as Burghers and Anti-Burghers, Auld Lichts and New Lichts. Scotsmen are by nature intolerant, and they have generally valued truth above unity. These smaller churches provided an orthodoxy of preaching and a warmth of fellowship which were often lacking in the Established Church, and their numbers were swollen by the General Assembly's high-handed enforcement of patronage against the will of dissatisfied congregations. They did not escape the rigid outlook and the intolerance characteristic of struggling minorities, but as time went on most of them did develop political and ecclesiastical principles which were fundamentally liberal.

Some parts of Scotland had hardly been reached by the Reformation, and there were areas in the north-west where Roman Catholicism was still the religion of the majority, and where the priests enjoyed some immunity from the Penal Laws. Poverty-stricken and ill-educated as these men were, they found it impossible to reach, let alone to teach many of their people. After the Forty-Five, efforts were made to carry out Protestant missions in these distant corners of Scotland, by such organizations as the Scottish Society for Propagating Christian Knowledge. This Society published the first Gaelic New Testament in 1767, a measure which was frowned upon by Hanoverians, for Gaelic was the language of Jacobitism and as such, they said, should be suppressed. Samuel Johnson expressed scorn for this point of view, and declared that the Scriptures should be denied to nobody on such grounds.

Elsewhere than in the Highlands, Roman Catholics had to worship in secret, deprived even of the common rights of citizenship, because of their political associations with the Stewarts. In 1779, measures of emancipation were proposed, but these produced such fanatical outbursts in London, Edinburgh and Glasgow that another half-century had to elapse before toleration was extended to Roman Catholics. Their influence counted for little in the country as a whole, though a courageous nucleus braved all difficulties to maintain their faith. The mid-19th century saw a considerable increase in their numbers, because the Act of 1829 abolished the Penal Laws, but also because there developed an enormous labour market in the industrial south, to which flocked crowds of workers from Ireland, driven from their homes by the Potato Famine of 1846.

The Church of Scotland and the minority sects were almost as hostile to Episcopalians as to Roman Catholics. The Revolution Settlement of 1689 stimulated violence against Episcopalian priests and some two hundred parsons were driven out of their benefices, and numbers of chapels destroyed. Only in the north and north-east were the Episcopalians comparatively unmolested. for here there was a traditional support for this way of worship.

In the south, and particularly in the capital, popular prejudice against the Episcopalian Church was strongest. Priests were driven to all sorts of expedients in the effort to conduct their services, as Covenanters and Nonconformists had been in the 17th century. James Greenshields led his small congregation in an Edinburgh flat, with one inside wall removed to join up two rooms, and it was here that he was discovered using the Book of Common Prayer. In consequence he was confined in the Tolbooth during some twelve months, until in 1711 the House of Lords ordered his release. The Toleration Act of 1712 legalized the Episcopal form of worship, so long as it was conducted by parsons who had abjured the Pretender, but this many refused to do, and their Jacobite sympathies brought them into constant trouble.

While some of the Episcopalian priests struggled on in the effort to maintain their congregations by holding frequent celebrations of the Sacraments for tiny groups of worshippers, others found a living by becoming chaplains or tutors to families among the gentry; in the south their numbers steadily declined, although their hold on Aberdeenshire and other northern counties was fairly well maintained. The Forty-Five produced a fresh set of Penal Laws designed still further to restrict their activities. Even those priests who abjured the Pretender were under relentless suspicion. Bishops, clergy and laymen of the Episcopal Church in Scotland lived in chronic poverty, disliked by Presbyterians of all ranks, and excluded from the Universities. Not until Charles Edward died in 1788 did their position improve and only in 1792 were the Penal Laws against them repealed.

Interesting comments on the religious life of Scotland during the second half of the 18th century are recorded in the journals of John Wesley. Between 1751 and 1789 this tireless evangelist made twenty-two preaching tours north of the Border. Book in hand, for he was a peripatetic reader, he travelled on horseback with 'a loose rein', generally in the months of April and May and often in execrable weather. Wesley almost always found a ready hearing, and sometimes, especially 'by the riverside' in Glasgow, he preached to many thousands. People were prepared to endure exposure to harsh rainstorms and biting winds rather than relinquish the quest for the spiritual enrichment which Wesley strove to give them. He was impressed by the Scottish appetite for solid doctrine and plain speaking, nonplussed by the apparent lack of response to evangelistic appeal. Though Wesley made a number of friends in Scotland and became attached to some of the Methodist societies he founded there, he never felt quite at ease with Scottish people. 'I admire this people,' he wrote. 'So decent! So serious! And so perfectly unconcerned!'

Until about the middle of the century, the General Assembly frowned upon organized amusement, especially the theatre, as John Home discovered in 1754. Only thirty years later Alexander Carlyle described quite another state of affairs. 'It is remarkable that in 1784, when the great actress, Mrs. Siddons, appeared in Edinburgh during the sitting of the General Assembly, that court was obliged to fix all its important business for the alternate days when she did not act, as all the younger members, clergy as

well as laity, took their stations in the theatre by three in the
afternoon.'

This relaxation of traditional disapproval for the theatre was
due partly to the impact of economic and social developments,
but partly to the influence of the Moderate group in the Church
which became dominant during the second half of the century.

The leader of the Moderates was Dr. William Robertson, the
historian, who in his young days had protested against the
Assembly's reaction to Home's theatrical ambitions. In riper
years Robertson's scholarship came to be respected all over
Europe and in 1762 he became Principal of Edinburgh University,
and the following year Moderator of the General Assembly, of
which he was the most influential member. Among Robertson's
many friends were the economist Adam Smith, the novelist
Tobias Smollett, and the sceptic David Hume.

Despite the draining away of evangelical fervour into the
smaller groups, the Anti-Moderate or Evangelical party in the
Church of Scotland persisted, and it was ready to take advantage
of the change in atmosphere brought about by the French
Revolution. The excesses of the period seemed to be due in part
to the free thought which was the logical outcome of Moderate
ideas. In some circles, therefore, there developed a reaction from
the cult of reason towards the traditional, the romantic and the
mystical. In others, the revolutionary idea of the rights of man
produced a democratic fervour, secular rather than religious in
nature.

Once again, patronage became a burning question, but only as
part of a larger programme. The Evangelicals realized that the
changes in agriculture and industry, which were making for the
increase of population and its concentration in towns and cities,
had brought about a situation in which a new policy was required
by the Church. Parishes in industrial areas now needed to be
sub-divided, and many new churches clearly were needed too,
as well as new schools. If people were to be drawn into these new
churches, they must be made to feel that they had at least some
say in the choice of ministers.

By 1834, the Evangelical party was dominant in the General
Assembly, and succeeded in putting through the famous Veto

Act. This said that if a majority of the male heads of families in a parish disapproved of the patron's nominee, that should be sufficient ground for his rejection. Thomas Chalmers, the leader of the Evangelicals, considered this Act conservative in tone. His idea was to make the call of the people important in the appointment of ministers, but not to encourage popular agitations for well-liked ministers.

The Veto Act of 1834 brought about a crisis. It was challenged in the case of Auchterarder and some other parishes, and the law courts declared that it could not constitutionally be upheld. To the Evangelicals, this was an invasion of the church's spiritual jurisdiction by the civil courts, and so the question of patronage became merged in the deeper question of spiritual independence.

Would Parliament provide a way out of the deadlock by legalizing the Assembly's Veto Act? More than one political leader framed a measure designed to satisfy both Church and State: but the government in London took the typically English view that an Established Church must pay for its privileges by being definitely subject to the Crown in Parliament. When it appeared that their claims were not going to be met, the majority of the Evangelicals prepared for a break with the State connection. This event, known as the Disruption, took place in May 1843, when some 474 ministers, more than a third of the total number, followed by about the same proportion of the people, formed the Free Church of Scotland. They gave up their former churches, manses and stipends.

The congregations who supported them had to find buildings, and financial resources, also to establish colleges for the training of their clergy. They met with unexpected sympathy from powerful quarters and subscriptions were forthcoming in such quantity that within a few months they were able to set about practical organization. Thomas Chalmers became Moderator of the new Assembly, a fact which gave the Free Church much prestige and strength.

This Disruption revealed a wonderful quality of faith and self-sacrifice in its supporters, but it was a tragedy, for it took most of the ensuing century to heal the breach, and even now the scars are hardly out of sight. The Tory Government of 1843 did something to make amends, though it was done too late. The Benefices Act was passed, and this provided that objections to the nominees of patrons were to be taken into consideration, also the character and number of the objectors. By another Act, the establishment of new parishes in crowded industrial districts was made much easier. Not until Disraeli's time, in 1874, was Lay Patronage completely abolished.

During the rest of the 19th century, the Scottish Presbyterians fell into three main groups—the Church of Scotland, the new Free Church and the United Presbyterian Church. This last was formed in 1847, as the result of a series of re-unions between groups which had seceded in the 18th century. Although these three dominant organizations were not separated by any differences in doctrine, much sectarian bitterness between them led to waste of energy and initiative, which should have been devoted to Christian work, but which in fact found expression in competitive church-building and denominational controversy.

Religion influenced considerable sections of Scottish society until the very end of the 19th century. It was fashionable amongst respectable circles to go to church, and as physical comfort was now more in evidence in people's homes, it began to be expected at worship, so churches were re-constructed: curiously enough, while roofs became rain-resistant, walls draught-proof and pews cushioned, services, and especially sermons, became shorter. On the whole the large middle class maintained the habit of supporting the churches and so did some of the more prosperous artisans and skilled workers, but many thousands of the really destitute never took part in organized religion.

One cannot read the story of the Church in the 19th century without regret. Religious partisanship absorbed high-principled and devout Scotsmen at a time when a different attitude was desperately needed. G. M. Trevelyan says that this period in England was one when the Bible had 'a rival in the ledger' and certainly the same might be said of Scotland. Highland landowners, factory proprietors, business men, iron magnates, industrial leaders and property-owners were engrossed in money making. Many of them were enjoying wealth. The artisans in trades exposed to periodic depressions, the unskilled labourers and those who for a variety of reasons had fallen out of the labour market altogether were suffering destitution of a kind Scotland had never yet seen. The disease-ridden slums were inhabited by hordes of families who earned wages which could not buy them sufficient food to maintain health, and by a submerged population which maintained a precarious existence through devices such as begging, theft and prostitution.

Individual ministers and church members worked here and there with magnificent self-dedication in the interests of slum-ridden parishes; the General Assembly of the Free Church sponsored enquiries into such problems as the housing of working people, the bothy system, the excessive facilities for drunkenness; Temperance Societies were organized both by the Roman Catholic and by the Protestant Churches; Sunday Schools, Ragged Schools and some orphanages were founded. Yet the Church as a whole was timid about being involved in political controversy, its members reluctant to face the terrible problem of wealth and its proper use by Christians. So religious people were inclined to indulge in generalities, while ministers offered too little leadership and guidance to their congregations on subjects like the administration of house property, responsibility for employees and the fair distribution of material riches. The evil effects of the all too frequent divorce in the life of prominent Christians between individual piety and economic and political action have still a baneful influence on the religious situation in Scotland.

CHAPTER 25

Education

One of the ideals envisaged by John Knox was that the Church should assume responsibility for education. Believing like Calvin that unlettered people could hardly sustain an enlightened Christian faith, he set great store by his plans for the foundation of grammar schools and arts colleges in all the towns, together with village schools for even the smallest parishes. Unhappily for Scotland, Knox's plans were not fully carried out, although efforts were made by the Scottish Parliaments during the 17th century to meet the country's need for more schools. The last of these, a statute passed in 1696, required heritors in each parish to find a commodious school building and to settle a salary of £10 on the schoolmaster; but the arrangements were not completed and so, during the difficult opening years of the 18th century, there were parishes which possessed no school at all.

In the more fortunate areas where parish schools did exist, boys, and sometimes also girls, from the age of about six or seven were taught to read. Methods used were simple enough and changed little during the years. The training of Scottish children, both at home and at school, was carried out with the help of frequent and faithfully administered thrashings, which most Scots regarded as essential to moral and intellectual progress.

The abler boys at the age of nine or ten could go on from the parish school to a grammar school in the nearest burgh, which would often be under the care of only one man; in the larger establishments, where there were two or more masters, one would take charge of a class of three or four consecutive years, handing it over at the top of the school to the Rector.

The geologist Hugh Miller, who was born in 1803, wrote an autobiography called *My Schools and Schoolmasters*. It is a most readable and entertaining account of rural life in a fishing community on Cromarty Firth, and it describes the author's education in a single-teacher school, which sent a steady stream of boys to Scottish Universities. To prepare their best pupils for this, schoolmasters, even at the cost of neglecting the less able, would spare neither time nor trouble. Boys went up to the Universities at the age of thirteen or sometimes even twelve, there to live as boarders or in lodgings. Thomas Carlyle was fourteen when he walked the hundred miles from Ecclefechan to Edinburgh in 1809, in order to read for his degree. Because Latin was necessary for students, schoolmasters grounded their bright boys in this subject day in and day out, indeed some of the schools included little else in the curriculum—though it was on a matter of English spelling that Hugh Miller literally came to blows with his teacher.

Lord Cockburn went to Edinburgh High School in 1787, when he was about eight years old, and there he remained for six years. During the first four years he was beaten almost daily, although being afraid of his master he always had his work well prepared; things improved somewhat in the last two sessions when he moved into the Headmaster's class, but he never voluntarily read even fifty pages of a book until he left school, and throughout the whole period he was taught nothing but Latin. It should be added that he became later a voracious reader of classical literature and an advocate of Latin as a valuable school subject if properly taught.

Scottish people have always attached great importance to education and even in the early 18th century many who were not professional educationists were realistic in their thinking about it. They were proud of the tradition which sent even the poorest boys to Universities, if they were of the right intellectual calibre, but it was common knowledge that schools were insufficient in number, uneven in quality and as a rule inexpressibly dull, except for the small number of really gifted boys. In the country, as soon as the spring days began to lengthen, the children disappeared from school, because they were needed in the fields and lessons therefore seemed irrelevant.

It was characteristic of the nation that laymen and ministers, business men and town councillors, merchants and manufacturers, all gave serious thought, and also a good deal of money, to widen the scope of education during the very years when the results of the Jacobite troubles and of the economic revolution might well have blinded people to such concerns as the training of children. In the year of the Union, Glasgow appointed James Muir, at a salary of £100, to teach mathematics and navigation, subjects which were adopted in the Writing or Commercial Schools, and in the Academies founded in many other cities during the 18th century. Book-keeping, surveying and natural philosophy were also introduced into these new foundations which were designed to educate boys for business, seafaring, commerce and engineering.

This departure from the traditional emphasis on Latin was specially noticeable in burghs like Ayr, Dundee, Perth and Dumfries where new industrial developments were taking place, but Elgin and Inverness also experimented on similar lines: technical training and qualifications for a practical career obviously began to influence thought as soon as the effects of economic change became apparent, and the success of Scotsmen at this time in seafaring, engineering and surveying made its mark on school-planning remarkably early.

While burgh councillors were developing these new Academies, wealthy merchants who had amassed large fortunes in the tobacco trade and in other business enterprises made generous endowments for charitable purposes, especially for the support of the aged and the very young. In a number of cases, both age groups were catered for in the same establishment and so there developed the famous Hospitals and Hospital schools which were designed in part as almshouses 'for the aliment and maintenance of old men and women', in part as schools for city orphans. George Watson's in Edinburgh was founded in this way, so was James Gillespie's at the very end of the 18th century. Like the similar foundation of the Hutcheson brothers, set up in Glasgow as early as 1640, these schools survive to this day, though the almshouses they supported have long since been closed.

No such leadership was available to deal with the much more difficult problems of the country districts and especially of the Highlands. Here it was the Church that took the initiative, when the attention of the General Assembly was called to the state of affairs in the north and west. The Assembly carried out some enquiries and was so shocked by what it discovered that sanction was willingly given to the foundation of a new organization. This was the Society for Propagating Christian Knowledge, launched in Scotland in 1709, and not to be confused with the society of similar name founded in England in 1698.

It set up schools in the more remote parishes where the ministers had the most difficulty in covering their work. The first was established on the island of St. Kilda where 'nothing had been taught for many a dark and dreary generation but the art of catching fish and solan geese for the wretched support of mere animal life'. Here Alexander Buchan worked for eighteen years, until he died in an epidemic which swept the island. Buchan was exceptional, as most of the schools were designed to be of a temporary nature and the masters were supposed to move on after only two or three years. The rules of the Society required them to be regularly inspected by at least two ministers of the local presbytery, to ensure that reasonable standards were maintained. Boys and girls of all ages up to twenty-one attended these schools, mainly in the winter months, and they learnt to read and sometimes to write, though the latter accomplishment was rather unusual; their teachers also conducted services for them and instructed them in religion.

Between 1715 and 1795, over 300 such schools were founded. Although the salaries paid were meagre—about £6 sterling a year—and the buildings and equipment pitiful, this achievement was a remarkable one for a voluntary society dependent upon private subscriptions. The work was recognized as more essential than ever after the Forty-Five, yet in 1758 as many as 175 Highland parishes possessed neither school nor teacher. The General Assembly put the facts bluntly enough by referring to 'the many Thousands in this Church and Nation, especially in the Highlands and Islands, who live in Barbarity and Ignorance'.

The parish ministers themselves were well aware of the facts and plainly stated them in their contributions to Sinclair's Statistical Account, published in the 1790s. Entries from all over the country emphasized how inadequate were schoolmasters' salaries, which varied from £10 to £25, and amounted to much less than sums earned by mechanics in industry; they also commented on the miserable school buildings, and on the number of children out of reach of any educational amenities at all. To quote only two of many such records, the minister of Dowally, Dunkeld, wrote: 'There is no salary for a parish schoolmaster here, by consequence there is no parish school.' From the minister of Fossaway and Tulliebole came the comment: 'Parochial schoolmasters commonly receive a good education, are a body of men of great importance to the country and certainly deserve much better encouragement from the landed proprietors than at present they receive.' The concern of the Church continued after the Napoleonic wars, when the movement of population was already causing unmanageable new social problems, and in 1824 the General Assembly appointed a permanent Education Committee which opened 200 schools in the course of a few years.

When the Disruption took place in 1843, an extraordinary situation developed almost overnight. Evangelical influence was strong among schoolmasters, and nearly 400 joined the United Free Church. For this imposing corps of teachers the Evangelicals set up new schools in astonishingly quick time, while in the older schools their places had to be filled by other people. Thus a notable expansion of education came about in the 1840s and 1850s. Scotland's one Government Inspector of Education joined the Free Church too.

So did Scotland's pioneer in the training of teachers. This was David Stow. By 1843, his indefatigable efforts to bring about an improvement in the moral standards of the poor had already given the Church of Scotland a Sunday School Movement and a Teachers Training College. After 1843 Stow was the driving force behind the new Assembly's educational policy and under his guidance two more Training Colleges were opened.

In spite of all these developments, the country's educational system was quite unable to cover the field by the mid-19th century. In rural districts, but still more in the great areas of newly opened mine, mill and factory, literally thousands of children were growing up without any education at all.

Boys and girls were employed in the factories and mills from the age of five and six, a fact upon which the press not infrequently commented; journalists were vociferous in their statements that there was nothing in the factory system which could be considered prejudicial to people's health—even the *Edinburgh Review* of the 1840s published articles to this effect.

As they worked thirteen or fourteen hours daily, the children could not go to the parish schools even where these existed. A pamphlet published by George Lewis in 1835 was entitled *Scotland a half-educated Nation*, but really this caption suggests an over-optimistic attitude. In 1839, St. David's Parish, Dundee, with an industrial population of 9,000, had one public school staffed by one unsalaried teacher, dependent for his living upon the fees brought by his pupils—fees which would amount to a few pence per week per child. There were a few small private schools as well, and between them all, one-third of the children aged 5 to 14 in this parish were having reasonably regular tuition. In 1846, 54 per cent. of Glasgow's children were at school, but in the Gorbals parish, a district of incurable poverty, 93 per cent. of the children were attending no school whatever. After 1833, efforts were made to arrange two hours of 'education' for children each day after the work in the factories had been completed, but on all sides the evidence was that the pupils arrived in the evening so exhausted by the hours spent on their feet in the bad atmosphere of their workrooms that they could give no attention; and parents loudly proclaimed that these children would have been far better in their beds than yawning over books.

Children in the industrial cities were therefore illiterate, over-worked and deprived of healthy recreation. As their homes were tiny slum dwellings, such leisure as they had was spent roaming round the streets in gangs. Juvenile crime was common, and society dealt with it pitilessly. Children were sent to prison on charges which nowadays would qualify them for a period of supervision under a Probation Officer, and they were even transported to Botany Bay. In autumn 1837, the *Glasgow Courier* reported that Joan Alexander, aged 13, stole twenty-nine yards of cotton print and a green apron. She was transported for seven years. The same paper told a few weeks later of four boys who each stole a silk handkerchief by pickpocketing, and they too were sentenced to seven years' transportation. Entered as 'a little boy' was John McColgan, who was transported for house breaking in Dobbies Loan, Glasgow—he had removed a shutter from a window in order to steal blankets—and Robert Kirkwood of Beith had a similar sentence for stealing two shovels and two spades. Respectable people seemed unaware of the iniquitous treatment given to such children, victims of a society which could neither educate nor care for them.

Until the middle of the 19th century, the development of education in Scotland was largely due to the efforts of the Church, but thereafter the State gradually began to take over responsibility in this sphere. In 1856, an Education Department was set up by the Government and a number of Commissions appointed to investigate conditions in Scottish schools. One such Commission, appointed in 1864 under the Duke of Argyll, estimated that of the total child population in Scotland, that is 92,000 children, some two-thirds were enrolled in no school of any kind. This bombshell led to the Education Act of 1872, which brought about a completely changed situation. Every parish and burgh was now to appoint a School Board and education became compulsory for children up to the age of thirteen. In 1885, the Scottish Education Department became a department of the Scottish Office and from that time onwards the Secretary for Scotland handled educational policy. Except in the comparatively small number of independent schools, the State thus became responsible for carrying out the idea entertained so long before by John Knox, and gradually Scotland became a literate country. How horrified he would have been had he realized that his ideal of a school in every parish would take 300 years to achieve, and how much more horrified by the notion of State-run secular education!

In the period following the Union, Scotland still maintained her five universities—one each in St. Andrews, Glasgow and Edinburgh, two small rival institutions in Aberdeen. Their expansion was hindered by political restlessness, by poverty, by the loss of life caused in the rebellions, and later by the emigration of Scotland's more enterprising families. In spite of all this, there was considerable re-organization in the universities during the 18th century, of which one early example was the abolition of the regenting system. This arrangement, to which Andrew Melville had long ago objected, meant that the Regents, that is the university teachers, moved with their classes through the full range of the seven subjects for four consecutive years. By 1727, regenting had been abolished both in Edinburgh and in Glasgow, though it lasted longer in the other Universities, and from the time of the Union onwards a series of Chairs was founded, which enabled men of distinction to concentrate wholly on their own special subjects.

Outstanding among these early Professors was Francis Hutcheson, who held the Chair of Moral Philosophy at Glasgow from 1729 to 1746, a period when the influence of the 17th century Thomas Hobbes was still strong. Hobbes, who was a materialist and a very powerful thinker, believed that people are dominated by fear and self-interest and will only act for the public weal under pressure of these very instincts. Accordingly, he adopted the view that the State should be so organized that from selfish motives men will wish to obey the laws, a doctrine which tended to create a sceptical and disillusioned attitude. Religious thinkers, on the other hand, were under the spell of Calvinism and therefore they frowned on all worldly activities, even those associated with intellectual and aesthetic pursuits. Hutcheson rejected both these views: unlike those who followed Hobbes, he believed that man is endowed with a moral feeling which can enable him to choose the good and reject the evil, that the impulse to do good and to act benevolently is as potent as the impulse to fend for oneself at the expense of others; in contrast to those of the Calvinist school, he held that aesthetic appreciation is as essential to full spiritual growth as intellectual integrity. Unlike his colleagues, Hutcheson delivered his lectures not in Latin but in English. The very many young men who came under his influence were enriched by his enlightened approach, and he did much to prepare the way for the intellectual awakening which took place in the latter half of his century.

Education

Hutcheson's most distinguished successor was Adam Smith, who held first the Chair of Logic, then that of Moral Philosophy, at Glasgow from 1751 to 1763, a period which he afterwards described as the happiest of his life. Adam Smith had few, if any, equals among the thinkers of his day. His *Wealth of Nations*, published in 1776, laid the foundations for the modern study of Political Economy and it is still a sine qua non in the training of economists. With no accurate statistical data upon which to work, Smith set out and interpreted a whole range of basic facts hitherto ignored and he exposed a number of myths which had long been reverenced as truth. Until his day, for example, people had taken it for granted that money and wealth were identical, that free trade and free enterprise would lead to chaotic reduction of profits, that the prosperity of one country must automatically reduce that of its neighbour—the influence of this last notion is well seen in the reluctance of Englishmen to give Scotland any share in commercial activity when the Treaty of Union was being negotiated. The principles which were expounded in the *Wealth of Nations* won almost immediate recognition, in fact the work of Adam Smith led to far-reaching changes in the legislation, the foreign policy and the economic administration of Great Britain. Glasgow University did not lose touch with this brilliant man, for he was made Rector in 1787.

Famous days for Edinburgh University began in 1762, when Professor William Robertson, whose influence on the Moderate party in the Church was so pronounced, entered upon his thirty-one years of service as Principal. He wrote massive historical studies on England, Scotland, Charles V, America and, in his old age, on India. These works earned him a European reputation, partly because of the splendid prose in which they were written, partly because historical scholarship was so rare at the time. Among his most enthusiastic admirers were Edward Gibbon, Samuel Johnson, Horace Walpole and Catherine II of Russia.

Robertson reformed the management of the University Library, and with courageous optimism he launched a huge scheme of re-planning the dilapidated and inadequate College buildings. His cousin Robert Adam was employed to design two stately quadrangles, a hall, a chapel, a set of classrooms, and

295

above all the new Library. The architect's death in 1792, Robertson's death in the following year, shortage of funds and the effects of the Napoleonic wars held up these ambitious schemes, and the work was not completed till the 1820s, when the architect Playfair carried out some of Adam's plans on a modified scale.

Cockburn's unhappy days in Edinburgh High School have already been mentioned. In 1793, when he was fourteen, he went up to Edinburgh University, and there began to attend lectures in Logic delivered by Professor Finlayson. 'Until we heard him, few of us knew that we had minds,' was Cockburn's grateful comment. Even better things were in store, for soon he started going to Dugald Stewart, Edinburgh's most distinguished philosopher, and of him he wrote: 'To me Stewart's lectures were like the opening of the heavens. I felt I had a soul.' These were only two of the brilliant men who were attracted to the capital at this time and there were many more, all inimitably described in Cockburn's *Memorials*—Adam Ferguson, Hugh Blair, John Robison and the rest of them. Robison was perhaps the most picturesque of the lot—'a pigtail so long and thin that it curled far down his back: and a pair of huge blue worsted hose without soles and covering the limbs from the heel to the top of the thigh, in which he walked and lectured, seemed to improve his wise elephantine head and majestic person.' All but Robison were what Cockburn called 'great peripatetics'. Their academic grove lay in the Meadows—'under these trees walked and talked and meditated all our literary and scientific and many of our legal worthies.' These walkers and talkers were responsible to a great degree for Edinburgh's reputation during the Napoleonic wars as a city of scholarship.

Throughout the 18th century, and in fact well on into the 19th, Professors and students all lived on the minimum of material security. In 1708 the Professor of Botany in Glasgow was allotted the salary of £30 a year; the Professor of Anatomy in Edinburgh started with £15. Adam Smith became Professor of Logic in Glasgow with £44 10s. 0d. a year: the Rev. Hugh Blair, Professor of Rhetoric at Edinburgh, with £70. Blair built up an unrivalled reputation as a preacher and his published sermons created such a sensation, in England as well as in Scotland, that they came to be considered as part of the literary revival of the period. George III granted Blair a pension of £200 and he then discovered that he could afford his own carriage. He is believed to have been the first Presbyterian minister in Edinburgh who ever rose to such luxury.

If Professors were expected to live on narrow means, students felt the pinch even more acutely. When Pryse Lockhart Gordon, a son of the manse, went up to Aberdeen at the age of fourteen in 1776, his total expenses for six months' board, tuition fees, travel expenses and incidental extravagances amounted to £17 4s. 3d. This adolescent complained that his grandfather thought him a spendthrift, on the ground that in his day, sixty years earlier, he had never exceeded £12 per session. It is rather touching to find in Gordon's meticulous accounts 13/- to Sweety Nell, an old woman who sold lollipops, 1/4d. for shuttlecocks, 6d. for a fine because he threw a snowball at the sacrist and £1 16s. 0d. for extra food to supplement the college meals, while fees to the Professors of Greek and Latin came to £2 6s. 6d.

It was in such conditions that the Medical Schools of Glasgow and Edinburgh established their reputation. In 1726, Edinburgh instituted four medical Chairs, in addition to that of Anatomy, which already existed; and in 1746 the Royal Infirmary was opened as a teaching hospital. After this, the capital became famous far beyond the boundaries of Scotland for the excellence of its medical training and men came from all over the Empire, and also from Europe, to take their medical degrees there. Until 1834, they all had to present their theses in Latin. Glasgow was expanding its school of Medicine at this time too, although it was still a much smaller city than Edinburgh, since by 1755 its population was less than half that of the capital, and there was no teaching hospital until 1794. Professor William Cullen and Professor Joseph Black each established in Glasgow a reputation as a distinguished teacher of Chemistry, but both were glad to accept appointments in Edinburgh where wider scope was afforded. Incidentally, in Glasgow, men who wanted to study Chemistry had to become medical students, as there was no Professor there for this subject.

The need for vigorous leadership in medical research and surgical skill became greater than in any previous period. In Glasgow's vast industrial growth, factories, mills and shipyards were the scene of many ghastly injuries to workmen handling dangerous tools in dirty surroundings: their wounds were often already infected by the time they reached hospital. Surgery was carried out in such primitive conditions that death from hospital gangrene was a most likely risk, even if the operation to be performed were comparatively simple and no previous infection had complicated matters.

In 1860, an Englishman was appointed to the chair of surgery in Glasgow. This was Lord Lister, who initiated a new approach to surgery, based on his knowledge of Pasteur's researches, so that antiseptic conditions were made compulsory in his operating theatre, with the result that by the exclusion of bacteria risks of infection were immeasurably reduced. Senseless prejudice among the conventional surgeons of the day delayed Lister's recognition, but ultimately his methods were accepted and untold numbers of lives were thereby saved. One of Lister's critics, ironically enough, was James Young Simpson, Professor of Midwifery at Edinburgh, who had himself met with ferocious hostility. He had introduced the use of anaesthesia, a measure which orthodox people regarded as contrary to the laws of God and of nature because, by reducing pain in childbirth, chloroform would eliminate an essential feature of human experience.

From the early years of the 19th century onwards it became increasingly evident that the Scottish University system was in urgent need of reform. There had been constant friction ever since the 16th century over the administration of Edinburgh University, by the terms of its foundation under the jurisdiction of the Town Council. This municipal control limited the freedom needed by research specialists and academic experts, whose attitude was not understood by the bailies and magistrates. The co-existence of two rival establishments in Aberdeen became more and more absurd, for neither could really flourish, yet this was a centre where a vigorous university life was greatly needed. The Disruption of 1843 complicated everything, because a number of professors and other officials followed the lead of

Dr. Chalmers, who held one of the Edinburgh chairs in theology, and the loss of their services was difficult to cover. An Act of 1690, still in force, required every Professor to sign the Westminster Confession of Faith and in so doing to promise loyalty to the Established Church. From the mid-19th century onwards, it would have become much more difficult to find properly qualified men willing to do this.

From the point of view of the students' attitude to university opportunities, much also needed to be done. As there was no entrance qualification and no encouragement to complete degree courses, many young men openly idled their time and, after spending several years at a university, went down with no qualifications, with little advantage derived from the frittered years, but in many cases with some irresponsible habits.

During the 1850s, the constitution of Scottish Universities was reformed by a series of Acts of Parliament. The two institutions at Aberdeen were amalgamated, Edinburgh was released from municipal control, the religious test was abolished except for Principals and theological professors, the status of all professors raised by increases in salary. Scottish students were given several incentives to work harder, including a new Honours degree course, which carried considerable importance as a qualification in professional careers. All these reforms helped to make the Universities a more valuable influence in the nation's life, and although a man could still take several years to amass enough examination passes for his degree, far more students now began to come up with the ambition to make a success of scholarly study.

The expansion of the Universities after these reforms was perhaps most noticeable to the general public in the sphere of Science, in which Glasgow now began to take a much more prominent part than in earlier days. Lord Kelvin was appointed to the Chair of Natural Philosophy at Glasgow in 1846 when he was twenty-two, and he held it until 1899. During this long period of service, he worked on new fields of research and he combined encyclopaedic knowledge with inventive skill, so that his scientific knowledge was applied to practical life. Submarine telegraphy and the provision of heat and light by electricity are only two examples of work in which he made an international reputation.

Little mention has been made so far in this chapter of the education of girls, for the excellent reason that, until the second half of the 19th century, little effort was made by Scotsmen to educate their daughters. In 1695, the Merchant Maidens' Hospital was opened as an orphanage for girls in Edinburgh, and in 1704 a similar institution called the Trade Maidens' was established. The spinning schools set up by the Board of Trustees for Manufactures in the middle years of the 18th century gave some technical instruction to a small proportion of girls, and some were also taken into the schools of the S.P.C.K. Co-educational too were many of the burgh schools, so that sisters sat under the dominies along with their brothers, at least until their parents decided that their daughters' time would be more usefully spent in the house, the dairy or the fields. Well-to-do families employed governesses and there were a few small seminaries for ladies in some of the towns. Not until the Education Acts of the 1870s, however, were girls considered on an equal basis with boys in the nation's educational scheme. From that time until now, there has been much more co-education in Scotland than in England, even at the secondary level, and the number of girls' schools is still relatively much smaller north of the Border than south of it. During the last three decades of the 19th century, some girls' schools were founded, such as St. Leonard's; and some of the older merchant company foundations started separate establishments for girls, Hutchesons' for example in Glasgow, George Watson's in Edinburgh.

The struggle for the entry of women into the Universities began also in the 1870s. An association for the Higher Education of Women was founded in Edinburgh and a number of women began attending courses of lectures in the Universities. They presented themselves for examination, but there were no powers whereby they could be granted degrees. As long as they confined their interests to the Arts Faculties, these seekers after learning met with reasonable sympathy, but the attempts of Miss Jex-Blake and some of her friends to qualify in Medicine caused a minor crisis and shocked reaction was registered by public opinion. This brave lady finally qualified herself in Ireland and in 1886 founded a School of Medicine for Women in Edinburgh, where the authorities held out against the admission of women to the University Medical School until 1916. St. Andrews offered a diploma called the L.L.A. (Lady Literate in Arts) from 1876 and many women took advantage of this during the thirty-four years of its existence. In 1893, however, an ordinance was passed giving women the right to attend the same classes as men in all the Scottish Universities and to graduate in the same way.

The many changes and reforms which were introduced into Scottish schools and Universities during these two centuries sometimes came to maturity long after they were badly needed, so that the problems which were solved only by slow stages always gave place to fresh and more complex difficulties. Looking back over the story, however, one can see certain consistent principles at work, of which the most impressive has been the conviction that in a democratic country as many individuals as possible, no matter what their family circumstances, should have the opportunity to enjoy the widest scope in education. That this education should be based on an academic foundation was assumed until the 20th century, for Scottish people long retained their desire for the knowledge to be derived from books and their respect for the value of an intellectual point of view.

CHAPTER 26

Parliament and Politics

Stalwart in character, forthright in speech, happy in controversy, Scots of all people should have found much to attract them in politics. Yet the 18th century has been described by Dr. G. S. Pryde as 'one of deepest political apathy'.

Why did Scottish M.P.s play so small a part in Parliamentary affairs? Why were people in the constituencies so ill-informed and so indifferent to elections and electoral issues? Why did the nation have to wait till the Napoleonic wars for a full contribution of Scottish energy and intelligence in affairs of state? The Union certainly gave Scotland a disproportionately small number of representatives, 45 in the House of Commons, 16 in the House of Lords: and in the 18th century Scottish business never had its rightful place in the agenda at Westminster. Neither of these facts however explains the 'deepest political apathy' which continued for nearly a hundred years.

The trouble was caused by the marriage of a medieval electoral system to the newly matured parliamentary régime of the United Kingdom.

The Commissioners for the Union assumed, reasonably enough, that the traditional Scottish methods of election should be continued; indeed, had these been interfered with, Scottish opinion would have been outraged. It occurred to nobody that Scottish parliamentary traditions dated in the main from the 15th century; or that they had been devised to suit a population of rather less than a million people, among whom few were qualified to hold political responsibility, fewer still desirous of doing so.

What were these electoral arrangements? And why was reform so long delayed?

Thirty of Scotland's forty-five members were allocated by the Treaty of Union to the shires, of which there were thirty-three. Twenty-seven therefore were given a member each, six shared the remaining three shire members between them. The right to vote for these thirty representatives was confined to landholders whose property was held directly from the Crown—royal tenants-in-chief in fact. This was in keeping with 15th century tradition. As only a small number of landholders held their properties in this way, many lairds of good standing exercised no political rights at all. In 1788, the number of voters in Bute was 12, in Ayrshire—a large county—214. By 1821, when the population was just under two million, barely 3,000 enjoyed the county franchise. It was easy for the Government to secure the shire votes, by offering their supporters posts in the East India Company and in other branches of public service, even by giving such appointments to friends and relatives of the voters. Scottish landowners were glad to take advantage of this, the Government built up its majority in the House of Commons, and not until the 1780s or the 1790s did any appreciable number of Scots see anything wrong in the system.

While thirty seats in the House of Commons were reserved for Scottish shires, fifteen were allocated to the burghs. Again by feudal tradition, only royal burghs were represented, towns which had received their charters from the Crown. There were 66 of these, some large and influential, others small and diminishing. To divide 66 by 15 is a tiresome exercise in mental arithmetic, an impossible one in political organization. A cumbrous solution was worked out. While Edinburgh was honoured with one burgh representative all her own, the other 65 towns were divided into 14 districts or groups, each containing several civic centres, but represented by one member, whose election was perforce carried out by delegates.

Excluded altogether from the burgh franchise were large industrial towns, like Paisley and Greenock, because they had no royal charter. Among the royal burghs, no difference was recognized between, for example, Glasgow whose population in 1821 was 150,000 and Rutherglen with 10,000. So the developing business and industrial interests would have been ill represented in any case. But the situation was made much worse by the ruling that only Town Councillors could vote. There were on average only about twenty of these in any burgh, and vacancies had been filled since the 15th century by co-option. The Councils were therefore self-elected bodies, sometimes consisting of one family's members and friends. While bribery by means of hard cash probably occurred rarely in shire elections, it was common in the burghs, where the councillors were often indebted to some powerful noble.

Even if Scotland had been given double her number of members in the new British Parliament of the 18th century, with such an electoral system she would still have been ill represented. On the other hand, if her 45 M.P.s had been elected in a manner less tied up with feudal usage, they could have made a powerful bloc in the House and therefore influenced legislation. In fact the contribution of Scotsmen to the business at Westminster consisted only in the provision of a solid supply of pro-Government votes on all controversial issues—a result not to be foreseen by the Commissioners in 1707, but eagerly put to advantageous use by the Crown's most powerful ministers later in the century. The 'management' of Scotland—an odious term which significantly seemed to cause little comment—had been reduced to a fine art by the 1780s.

These facts alone would explain a condition of 'deepest political apathy'. There were other circumstances however which contributed to it. Members from Scotland did not feel at home in Westminster, where they were looked upon as odd and indeed rather comical figures, and where they had difficulty in making themselves understood. It took them fully ten days to reach London, where they had to maintain expensive establishments at their own charges.

George Dempster, Member for the Perth group of burghs, managed quite well as long as he was single, because he held some good shares in the East India Company, and though he resented party discipline when the House divided, he was faithfully present as a general rule. In 1775 however he married, and wrote as follows to his friend Adam Fergusson: 'I have great doubts if I shall be in town this winter, and although perhaps at bottom my only reason for not coming is an unwillingness to leave my dear wife on a bleake Scotch hill by herself and my inability to bear the expence of a London jaunt and residence en famille, yet I have more solid and manly ones without which the first would not have operated. I have long thought . . . that unless one preserves a little freedom and independency in Parliament to act in every question and to vote agreeably to the suggestions of one's own mind, a seat in Parliament is a seat on thorns and rusty nails.'

Few of Dempster's constituents would be any the wiser about his decision not to attend Parliament that winter. As newspapers were scanty and ill informed, especially in Scotland, ordinary people did not know what was being said in Parliament or by whom.

Between 1707 and 1789 only three Scotsmen reached Cabinet rank, and their total service amounted to less than ten years. The first Scot to attain high office and to hold it for a long time was one who perfected the art of managing Scottish elections to a degree attained by no previous individual. His services to the Government were therefore so important that he was worth promotion. That he was also an exceedingly able man made him the more successful. He was Henry Dundas, who became later in life the first Lord Melville.

Dundas was very gifted. He was also kindly in disposition, impenitently Scots in diction, phenomenally ambitious and capable of more sustained hard work than one could believe possible. He was not an original thinker and he did not believe that any change in the political set-up could do good. In 1766, when he was twenty-four, Dundas became Solicitor-General for Scotland, eight years later Lord Advocate. In 1782, he was made a Privy Councillor and Treasurer of the Navy, a post which he held for many years, and which ultimately proved his undoing.

The position of Dundas became even stronger in 1783, when Pitt became Prime Minister, for these two were close friends. In 1784, Dundas introduced Pitt's India Bill: under its terms, he became the most powerful member, and subsequently President of the Board of Control for India, a responsibility which he shouldered with infinite personal care until 1801. In spite of this, Dundas accepted the post of Home Secretary in 1791, just when the unrest caused by the impact of the French Revolution was at its height. Indefatigable and supremely confident, he undertook in addition to his other work the War Office and the direction of operations against Napoleon, for some six or seven years. From 1782 onwards therefore, he wielded immeasurable authority, and among all his other commitments he found time to organize Scottish elections with scrupulous care and success.

Lord Cockburn, a consistent Whig during the long period of Tory ascendancy, said of Dundas, 'his business consisted in laying forty-five Scotch members at the feet of the Government.' Dundas would probably have found little objection to this statement, except that to his regret he only once achieved more than 39. He was certain that Pitt could not manage the nation's affairs without his support and he entertained no criticism of the unreformed constitution. The control he established over Scottish elections was based on his friendships with all the great land-owners—to many of whom he was related—and also with the leading business men, lawyers and Town Councillors. He relied too on the literally innumerable offices and posts which were in his gift. Lord Cockburn listed 'the pulpit, the bench, the bar, the colleges, the parliamentary electors, the press, the magistracy, the local institutions' as being under the control of this 'absolute dictator of Scotland', who now became known as Harry the Ninth. Cockburn could have added an equally comprehensive list of appointments in India, where the 'Scotticization' practised by Dundas caused much criticism.

It was the American War of Independence which first stirred Scotland into awareness of politics. Criticism of its conduct led to debate upon the merits of the Government responsible, and thence to enquiry about the electoral system which had thrown up such a Government. A movement was launched to check the abuse of fictitious votes in the shire elections. Efforts had indeed been made before with no result, but in 1782 twenty-three counties sent delegates to a meeting in Edinburgh to draft a bill dealing with the scandal.

At the same time the Whig advocate, Archibald Fletcher, organized a drive to reform municipal government. Throughout the 1780s, committees met, reports were published, petitions lodged: the corrupt state of the burghs was revealed. Some towns were deeply in debt, others almost bankrupt, all were ill-provided

with public works, there was no legal authority competent to
audit burgh accounts, the self-elective councils had fallen into
the hands of dishonest family cabals. That these councillors were
the only persons entitled to vote inflamed public opinion,
especially amongst the Whigs, who were now aware of the grave
social evils caused by the Industrial Revolution and who therefore
wanted fundamental reform.

Dundas headed off all these various pressures by procrastination. He was largely responsible for the repression during the
1780s of all attempts at reform. Had Scottish democracy reached
a more mature state, had their elections been even a little less
shackled, Scotsmen might have succeeded in improving municipal
government before the cataclysm of the French Revolution. Their
success would have been infectious and other reforms might have
followed.

The French Revolution set off the dynamite. Poets and artists,
advocates and professors, ministers and business men in Scotland
hailed it with delight, Scottish working-men took it up as the
beginning of a new age. Everybody wanted news, and there was
a sudden demand for newspapers. It was in English journals that
Scotsmen first read long extracts from Burke's *Reflections on the
French Revolution*, a work which stimulated an outburst of
talking, writing and debating in Scotland.

In 1791 and 1792 there followed the two parts of Tom Paine's
inflammatory gospel, *The Rights of Man*, available at 2d. each.
Again, no part of Britain welcomed this heady mixture with
more enthusiasm than Scotland, indeed it was claimed that
Bunyan's *Pilgrim's Progress* was now forever superseded as the
cottagers' favourite. The equality of man and his natural rights
were discussed in almost every household, nor did the philosophy
lack its poet. Burns delighted the democratically minded by
such verses as the following, from 'Man was Made to Mourn':

> *If I'm design'd yon lordling's slave,*
> *By Nature's law design'd,*
> *Why was an independent wish*
> *E'er planted in my mind?*
> *If not, why am I subject to*
> *His cruelty or scorn?*

Even better known was 'Is there, for honest Povetry', which included:

> Ye see yon birkie ca'd a lord,
> Wha struts and stares and a' that,
> Tho' hundreds worship at his word,
> He's but a coof for a' that,
> For a' that and a' that,
> His riband, star and a' that,
> The man of independent mind
> He looks an' laughs at a' that.

During the 1790s, Harry the Ninth found Scottish affairs more difficult than any previous 'manager'. People were on fire with excitement over the new ideas. Even religious circles were affected by an unprecedented outburst of zeal for lay preaching and foreign missions; and hot denunciations of the slave trade flowed forth in support of Wilberforce. Agitation was exacerbated by the Tory policy on agriculture, for this condoned the enclosures for sheep-farming, and it also upheld the Corn Bills, which virtually excluded foreign wheat and caused home produce to soar in price.

In 1793 the war against France broke out and was denounced by certain factions in Scotland, where popular disturbances made conditions in all the big cities unpredictable, and where contacts with Jacobins were being fostered. The Government was also alarmed by the rapidly growing political organizations of the day, the Corresponding Societies and the Association of the Friends of the People. Their aims were to reform the British constitution, to extend the franchise, to shorten Parliaments, to increase the hold of the public over its chosen leaders.

Dundas and his underlings mistakenly supposed that all these political associations identified reform with revolution. The Society of the Friends of the People was supported by serious-minded Whigs like Archibald Fletcher, who would have nothing to do with violence and whose methods were quite alien to those of the more extreme reformers. One of the tragedies of the time was that during the 1780s, when necessary political reform could have been peaceably introduced, it was stifled, and that during the 1790s its prophets were identified by Tories with leaders of street fights and shouters of unpatriotic slogans.

The Reel o' Tullochgorum: Walter Geikie, (1795–1837).

Parliament and Politics

In 1793, the Government announced that it was seditious to possess or disseminate any of Paine's publications, and a series of notorious State trials began, which continued intermittently for nearly thirty years of repression. Most scandalous of all were the trials of Muir, Margarot, Gerrald and Skirving. They were leaders in the Scottish Corresponding Societies and suspected of Jacobinism, the ogre of the age and equivalent in official eyes to bare faced treason. In 1793 these four men were convicted and sent to Botany Bay for fourteen years each, a vicious sentence unprecedented in judicial annals and in any case of doubtful legal validity. The proceedings were conducted in Edinburgh by Lord Braxfield, who made use of packed juries, Government spies, subsidized press agents and vitriolic declamation. His name now ranks in history with that of Judge Jeffreys.

In the result, Paine's works became much more popular in Scotland, but the political organizations were driven underground, the electoral abuses continued, and deep, dangerous hatred of the Government festered everywhere, nourished by acute economic distress. Dundas remained unshaken in his satisfaction as to the Government's policy. His grip on the Scottish electorate was probably at its height in 1796, for in spite of the problems of the war, and of India, his tireless industry achieved in that year's General Election the return of at least thirty-nine Government 'yes-men' out of the forty-five Scottish M.P.s.

Pitt's administration was interrupted in 1801 by the brief and inglorious service of Addington, whose fall in 1804 ushered in another spell of the old régime, with Dundas again in high office as First Lord of the Admiralty. In 1805, however, the Commissioners of Naval Inquiry published their shattering tenth report. This revealed that while Dundas had been Treasurer of the Navy the Paymaster had speculated on a huge scale, and to his own large profit, with Navy funds. His financial transactions included loans to his chief, Dundas. Dundas was therefore impeached, that is to say, tried before the House of Lords, on the charge of improper handling of public funds. Naturally such a development cost him all his public offices and unleashed a pack of noisy denigrators who voiced the country's pent-up resentment.

Dundas was acquitted on all charges, a decision which some people considered a gross miscarriage of justice. In Scotland it was greeted by general and sincere rejoicing, for one of the strangest facts about Dundas was his popularity in his own country, in both the main political camps. Whigs as well as Tories north of the Border were convinced that if irregularities had taken place Dundas had allowed them inadvertently, since he was never personally greedy for cash, he was far too busy to examine the Paymaster's proceedings, and had he been minded to filch public moneys he could have done so on a much vaster scale. His acquittal therefore was acclaimed with neighbourly celebrations, and during the remaining five years of his life Dundas recovered a good deal of the respect he had formerly enjoyed. Nonetheless, his fall was a portentous affair, and heralded a new era, for never again did any one man achieve such an asphyxiating grasp on the political machine.

After Napoleon's defeat, Britain entered upon one of the most agitated post-war periods of national malaise recorded in her history. The troubles were economic, caused by the strain of twenty-three years of war, and by the Industrial Revolution. Great hopes were set on electoral reform, and every effort was now renewed to achieve this.

When at last the long-needed Reform Bill of 1832 did become law, it introduced some effective changes for Scotland. Eight new burghs were created, so that after this there were 53 Scottish Members. In the re-allocation of seats, Edinburgh and Glasgow were given two members each; some non-royal burghs were recognized, among them Paisley and Greenock; Dundee, Aberdeen and Perth were given one member each. In these ways, some recognition was made of industrial expansion and so the business element now had a voice at Westminster. The franchise was at the same time widened to include in the burghs all householders who paid £10 in rates; while in the shires, owners of property valued at £10, with occupiers of land worth £50, and leased for not less than nineteen years, were also given the vote.

Scorn has been poured on these changes by some historians, on the grounds that they benefited only the middle classes and excluded all the workers in mine, mill, factory and field. This criticism is at once valid and unrealistic. The middle classes were indeed given the right to vote, while the working people in Scotland had to wait for it, like those in England, till 1867 and 1884, when they got it by stages. The delay was unfortunate in many ways, but understandable. It is unrealistic to blame people for moving at the contemporary pace. Not until the mid-19th century did Britain divorce electoral responsibility from property qualifications, and indeed it was not until much later that the country's educational system was sufficiently advanced to carry anything like universal suffrage for men. Until the schools and the social services were developed, and secret ballot introduced, the vast majority of working people on both sides of the Border could have been cruelly exploited in the exercise of votes, by employers and others who already had too much power over them. Had the right to vote been given to all and sundry in 1832, it is open to question whether the 19th century problems caused by social and economic tension would have been more equitably handled.

Complete re-organization of municipal government followed the reform of Parliament. That this was necessary has already been shown: it now became urgent because of the eight new burghs formed in 1832, for which no traditional constitution existed, and because if all the £10 householders were to assist in electing M.P.s, burgh elections could obviously no longer be confined to a charmed circle. By the Act of 1833 therefore, councillors were also to be chosen by £10 householders, at annual municipal elections, and each year one-third of each burgh council was to resign. This marked a real advance in the popular conception of local government, and gone forever were the days when self-elected bodies of councillors could neglect municipal well-being, filch the public funds, and rest assured that no legal authority could audit their accounts.

Because of the reforms in parliamentary and local government, Scottish people became much more interested in politics. There was some purpose in it all now that their representatives could exercise real influence. In reaction against the years of Tory mismanagement, the burghs voted almost solidly Liberal, and so did some of the shires, for something like fifty years. In the

1880s, the Irish Home Rule controversy altered things, but till then the Liberal Party's ascendancy at Westminster was rarely interrupted: its strength derived to a great degree from the consistent backing of the Scottish constituencies.

Scottish people quickly took the Liberal principal of Free Trade to their hearts. North of the Border, Duncan McLaren was the inspiration of the campaign to abolish the Corn Laws, and Cobden and Bright had no more effective colleague on this project anywhere in the United Kingdom. They wanted to do away with the protective taxes on foreign grain, so that bread could become cheaper, in the interests of the working people in the cities. It was ironical that this reform, so ardently desired by the Liberals, was achieved in 1847 when the Conservatives were in power for a short time under Sir Robert Peel. His own party was hotly indignant with Peel for this daring change of policy, but he never regretted it because the dreadful Potato Famine of 1846 made it urgently necessary to provide cheap food quickly. After this, the Liberals' faith in Free Trade was stronger than ever.

Duncan McLaren's status was still further enhanced by his fight for a second Parliamentary Reform Bill. He wanted working men to be given votes, and he was determined too that Scotland should have more representatives. He worked up enormous enthusiasm for these ideas in Scotland and he made some most telling speeches in the House. But again it was a Conservative Government, this time under Disraeli, which brought in the new Electoral Reform Bill in 1868. By this, votes were given to burgh householders, and Scottish members were increased in number from 53 to 60.

Included among new voters both in Scotland and in England, there were now thousands of industrial employees, many of whom were illiterate. For this reason, important educational reforms were set going, so that there could be a larger number of schools, and school attendance was made free and compulsory up to the age of twelve. A revolution in the nation's ideas and habits was represented by this ruling, which aroused grave criticism, but even the sceptics thought that men who were entitled to vote should be able to read. The schools which were opened in the 1870s and 1880s were grim establishments and the teaching administered in them was often very poor in quality. But until their thirteenth birthdays children were now kept out of the mills and shops and factories; though nobody could claim that they were being educated towards political responsibility, small boys were at least spared some physical strains.

To give the vote to thousands of industrial wage-earners was no democratic measure while elections were conducted in public by counting hands, because people could be so readily intimidated by their employers. Gladstone's Secret Ballot Act of 1872 was therefore a most necessary sequel to the Reform Act of 1868. It remained now to give agricultural workers the same rights as their relatives in the cities, and this was done by the Liberal Government of 1884, which introduced manhood suffrage. So far the idea of votes for women was confined to a few visionaries, deemed by society at all levels to be unstable and worth no serious consideration. The 1884 Act again increased Scotland's representation at Westminster, from 60 to 72. Thus, in G. S. Pryde's phrase, Scotland was at last accorded 'her proper share by population'.

The great changes in the political scene stimulated some important developments in journalism, which was also affected by speedier transport.

In the early years of the 19th century, Scottish newspapers provided dull reading, at least by modern standards. This was partly because they were always late with their information, a fact which could not be helped until the railway and the telegraph improved communications. Scottish editors relied for all but local news on excerpts from the English press, sent north with the mails, and the news they published was almost unadorned by any comment. *The Newspaper in Scotland*, by R. M. W. Cowan, a book full of interest, shows that until the franchise was widened journalism was necessarily a disappointing business—'to harangue a voteless public with leading articles would have been merely beating the air.' Uninspiring as they seem to us, the newspapers were however eagerly read. While the circulation was limited— the *Glasgow Herald* in 1815 was bought by about 1,100 people— copies were borrowed and handed on from house to house, until they must have been almost thumbed to pieces.

The Eighteenth and Nineteenth Centuries

When *The Scotsman* was founded in 1817, it was a weekly paper, costing 10d. a copy, a sum equivalent to almost the whole of a working man's daily wage. It made an immediate impression, because it carried a front-page leader and because it adopted a bold and fresh approach, supporting unorthodox ideas about Church and State, and attacking vested interest in both. It was the first newspaper which showed the privileged classes how unpopular they were and for what reasons, though even this progressive organ was complacent about industrial conditions.

Not until the days of railway mania could Scotland support a daily newspaper. The first in the field, founded in 1847, was the *North British Daily Mail.* The main interest was political, though public executions were popular items and always described in lurid detail. Then as now, the reading public liked murders, atrocities and abnormalities to be well documented. J. Y. Simpson's discovery, in 1847, that chloroform could be successfully used as an anaesthetic, passed by contrast almost unnoticed.

The repeal of stamp duties and taxes on advertisements and on paper, all carried through in the 1850s, led to an immediate expansion in journalistic enterprise. In 1852, Scotland had 75 newspapers, in 1856, 105. Many of the newly founded ones were dailies, some published at a penny each, some running to as many as eight pages. Some were local, some national. Every kind of political opinion was now reflected in the press, which could provide ample information and comment upon parliamentary affairs, especially after 1861, when Scottish agents for the first time were allowed independent access to the Press Gallery in the House of Commons.

Had George Dempster lived to see these things happen, he might have found fresh reasons for declaring that a seat in Parliament was one on 'thorns and rusty nails', but the days of political apathy were over, so far as Scotland was concerned. The reform of the electoral system and the development of journalism meant that men of all occupations and every rank could take an active share in the political controversies of their day.

CHAPTER 27

Poverty

The new resources made available during the Industrial Revolution were not so manipulated as to increase the well-being of society as a whole, indeed misery seemed to develop in proportion to man's power over natural forces. As the pace of industry accelerated and population grew, horrifying epidemics swept across the whole United Kingdom, some of a familiar nature, some hitherto uncommon.

Scotland's share in the troubles of the age was complicated by the traditional architecture of her towns, which invited rather than checked epidemic infection; the mass migrations of Highlanders and Irishmen contributed to the congestion in the cities; inflexible systems of law and local government made public control of abuses and relief of destitution doubly difficult. Poverty seems to have been worse in Scottish towns than anywhere else at this time. Many decades elapsed before even well-intentioned and compassionate thinkers fully diagnosed the causes of the trouble or understood its implications.

Scottish urban architecture was influenced by continental designs and also conditioned by the intractable nature of local weather and geography. For reasons of defence and because of steep hillsides, towns were too compact, and tall stone tenements were crammed together in narrow streets. Water for all purposes had to be fetched from public wells or bought in stoups from vendors, then carried up precipitous lanes and stairways. Garbage could only be disposed of by its owners throwing it out of their windows or dumping it in their backyards, around which were clutters of pigsties, stables and dairies. As the population increased, slaughter-houses and tanneries multiplied in ground-floor premises, adding to the traditional accumulations of filth and smells. The farmers who lived nearby knew how valuable much of this heterogeneous sewage and dung could be to them as manure for their fields and they came and bought it by the cartload. People therefore literally treasured their filth in steaming, sodden middens which they piled at their doors with ash and other rubbish, precious capital upon which to rely for the rent.

Burgh councils made repeated attempts to keep the main thoroughfares reasonably clean, but no effort was spent on the networks of vennels and wynds or on the staircases. The tall, solid tenements proved a deadly legacy to the 19th century, becoming more and more impregnated with dirt and vermin: to introduce water-pipes and water-closets to buildings of such height involved far greater expense and skill than was needed for houses or cottages. That people were able to make money from their dunghills meant that there was obstinate opposition to housing reform.

In periods of rapid industrial development, the population of towns always tends to increase at a sharpened pace. This was so in Scotland, as elsewhere in Britain. New building however was not undertaken to anything like the necessary extent, and so people began the disastrous habit of sub-letting and sharing their dwellings, landlords allowed mean hovels and sheds to be thrown up in the backyards, while cellars and basements were rented for all kinds of unsuitable purposes.

The upward trend of the population in the cities was accelerated by the Highland evictions, which sent thousands of destitute families to add to the congestion. These were Gaelic speakers, who had difficulty in making themselves understood and were accustomed to rural ways. Cut off from their traditions, reduced already by privation to poor health, perplexed and disillusioned, they had everything against them in the competitive scramble for house-room and employment.

Along with the Highlanders, came the Irish, in even worse case. Shipping companies brought them at specially reduced rates and disembarked them in hordes every week, especially during the early 19th century. By 1831, there were 35,554 Irish people in Glasgow alone, and they came in even larger numbers after the Potato Famine of 1846. These people were Roman

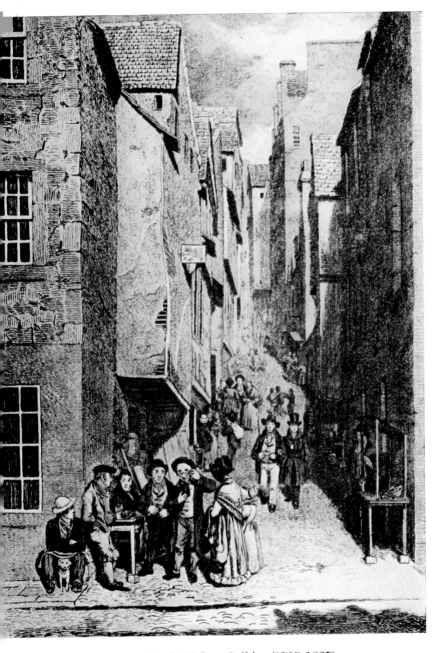

Libberton Wynd: Walter Geikie, (1795-1837).
By courtesy of the Mitchell Library, Glasgow.

Catholics, and like the Highlanders quite unprepared for the particular miseries of city life, though they were well accustomed to desperate poverty.

In 1740, just over 17,000 people were living in Glasgow: by 1791 the number had grown, through industrial progress, to 66,000—a figure well below that of Edinburgh, where there were between 80,000 and 90,000 people. After the turn of the century, Glasgow's industrial expansion was speeded up because of the heavy industries, and during the same years the influx from the Highlands and from Ireland became unceasing: by 1831 therefore, there were nearly 203,000 people in Glasgow, which was now the most highly populated city in Scotland, and thirty years later the figure, almost doubled, had reached 395,503. Other cities in the industrial belt had the same kind of experience, though the scale and speed of the increase naturally varied. Common to them all however was the insoluble problem of poverty and distress.

The early 19th century was a transition period, when processes were rapidly changing, and artisans were liable to find themselves on the street without notice and with no chance of finding another job of their own type. The early stages of automation made many skills redundant and when new inventions deprived people of their accustomed work there was no question of compensation or assistance. The unemployed were offered no guidance by the authorities, and their numbers were swollen by those crowds of unskilled labourers who were thrown out of work by the unpredictable rhythm of over- and under-production. Even when the poorer people were in regular work they were paid on such miserable scales that they recruited all possible members of their families to the task of earning, although this damaged the health of all but the most robust.

The invention of lighter machines meant that women and children could be used in processes formerly reserved for men. The introduction of gas lighting early in the 19th century lengthened the working day in the factories. As the mills became more fully mechanized, much larger numbers of workers were employed, so that relationships between employers and operatives became steadily less personal, factory discipline more rigid and inhumane.

In the 1830s, children from six and seven upwards were employed in the cotton mills at 1/6d. to 2/- a week. A Select Committee of the House of Commons heard evidence in 1832 about the conditions in which children were working. Before this Committee, Peter Smart, overseer of a Dundee flax mill, described children rising from bed at 4 a.m., walking to work, which began at 4.55, and continuing all day till 7.30 p.m. A millowner at Duntruin admitted that the children in his mill had to be beaten with straps to keep them at their tasks. Those whom he employed were orphans from Edinburgh, housed in a bothy which was locked and barred all night, to prevent their running away, and no clock was allowed on the premises lest the older ones should notice when they were doing overtime. These are not isolated incidents: evidence shows that it was quite as common to find such things happening in Scottish as in English factories. Children were also used in coal-mines, where they worked fourteen hours daily in the East, eleven to thirteen in the West, often in the dark and often standing in water. Examples of this were quoted in Parliament during the debates preceding the passage of the Mines Act in 1842.

Women were employed in the coal-mines as hauliers, to drag trucks on all fours along the narrow passageways from the coal face to the cages: these dark passages were often deep in slush and their gradients sometimes reached 1 in 6 or 7. Hugh Miller, the Cromarty geologist, quoted cases of women weeping bitterly with the effort of dragging coal in this way, and other writers in the early 19th century expressed their horror at seeing girls and women crying under their loads. The Mines Act of 1842 put a stop to the employment of women and children underground.

Women were employed much more than men in the textile industries, but they also worked in mills and factories of many kinds. The normal day's work lasted 13 or 14 hours, and 17 was not unknown. Women's wages in the early 19th century generally varied from 4/- to 8/- a week, but in periods of slump they would drop. In 1851 a factory inspector reported that many women were earning as little as 3/-. The fact that female labour was so regularly used helps to account for the heavy incidence of sickness among small children, as infants who were too young to go to work had to be cared for by the very old or by nobody at all. In 1861 the Registrar-General stated that 25 per cent. of children under one year died in the families of cotton operatives: the equivalent figure for agricultural workers, whose women had more chance to look after their babies, was 12 per cent.

Men's wages varied from one industry to another and reacted also to the swing between over- and under-production. In 1825 an Aberdeenshire weaver earned 13/- a week, with which he fed and clothed a family of six, paying school fees for three and 10/- a year for pew rent in church. By 1836 the same work brought him in 8/- and the price of meal had risen. During the 1830s and 1840s weavers' wages dropped to 4/- and 5/-, while mechanics could earn anything up to 18/-. Railway navvies in 1838 were paid 10/-, in 1853 12/-. The purchasing power of money was much greater in the 19th century than now, but men's wages were not related to any subsistence level; indeed the idea that a subsistence level existed, that wages which fell below it would make for malnutrition, was unknown until the 20th century.

The factory buildings had no lavatories, wash-rooms, first-aid centres or feeding arrangements; ventilation was not understood, heating not provided, except in textile mills where it was necessary for the texture of woven goods. Modern knowledge of time and motion in relation to industrial fatigue had yet to be born. With inadequately fenced machinery and ill-planned scaffolding, men working 60-70 hours a week were liable to accidents, but no compensation for injury was given nor could casualties be treated on the spot.

During the first two decades of the 19th century, a unique effort to reform factory conditions was made at New Lanark by Robert Owen, David Dale's Welsh son-in-law. Owen encouraged his employees to form friendly societies for the assistance of the sick and bereaved, and he organized a store where goods of reasonable quality could be bought at 75 per cent. of the normal price. He also undertook strenuous efforts to make houses, streets, lanes and workshops in New Lanark much cleaner. His campaign was remarkably successful and refuse and filth no longer collected at every corner and doorway; lime-washing of buildings was introduced, water made available for personal hygiene. Somehow this remarkable man won the confidence of his people and he contrived to induce in them a certain pride in their community and craft. Owen's reforms reduced drunkenness and improved general health. In the face of indignant expostulation from other industrialists, he reduced the working hours in his mills to 10¾ per day and he refused to engage children below the age of ten. For these youngsters, he started a huge school which was run on principles quite new to Scots people. Corporal punishment and angry reproof were not allowed, music, dancing and drill were taught, history, geography and botany included in the curriculum, visual aids largely employed. The expenses involved were met from the profits of the factory store.

Much of Owen's work was far in advance of his times. His views on labour management and factory organization aroused angry criticism among the leaders of industry at home and he was discredited because he wanted legislation to prevent more than ten hours being worked per day in the mills; also because his religious views were unorthodox.

In spite of his humanitarian methods he made himself wealthy and had he remained in Scotland he might have convinced people that it pays to consider the welfare of factory hands. Unfortunately, obsessed with the desire to found an ideal society, he departed to America, where he started a community at New Harmony, Pittsburg.

The general conditions in Scottish industry went from bad to worse, and working people turned to the form of escape most easily available. Drunkenness among adults and teenagers became so common that revolting scenes were everyday occurrences in the city streets and also in the barracks and bothies of rural workers. Hugh Miller began his working life as a stonemason's apprentice, when he was about fourteen, just after the Napoleonic wars. The heavy labour exhausted him. In his book, *My Schools and Schoolmasters*, he later described how he and his companions sought and found relief in the 'ardent spirits of the dram-shop', which 'gave lightness and energy to both body and mind and substituted for a state of dullness and gloom one of exhilaration and enjoyment. Usquebaugh (whisky) was simply happiness doled out by the glass and sold by the gill'. This kind of happiness brought its own reaction and caused much harm; and it was sought more in Scotland than anywhere else in the United Kingdom. In 1840 seven pints of spirits were consumed per head per annum in England, 13 in Ireland and 23 in Scotland. The *Scotsman* published in 1853 a set of figures cynically termed the 'drunken statistics' which suggested that Glasgow was three times more drunken than Edinburgh and five times more so than London.

Why should Scottish working people have been more given to excessive drinking than their English neighbours? It was partly because Scottish housing was worse than English and a higher percentage of people were thankful to find anywhere to go after work other than their overcrowded, smelly little homes. By tradition too, it has always been harder to remain sober after an hour or so in a Scots pub than in an English one. In the Scottish licensed house, the bar was the most important piece of furniture, the sale and rapid consumption of liquor the prime activity: there was much less sitting about, chatting, playing skittles and general passing of time than in similar English establishments. The rigid administration of Poor Relief, much more stringent in Scotland than in England, offered no adequate help to the destitute: during the Napoleonic wars and the epidemics, breadwinners in vast numbers of families were lost. Drink seemed the only alleviation available, and it was recklessly used.

It is understandable that health could not be maintained among working-class families and that illness was chronic and virulent among them. They suffered from deficiency diseases through lack of nourishment, because their diet consisted almost entirely of farinaceous foods, particularly porridge and potatoes. Pregnant women remained at work till the last possible moment, even when they were hauling heavy weights. Their babies were born in their own filthy dwellings because there was not enough provision for midwifery in the hospitals; and by reason of rickets —which can be caused by malnutrition—these women often suffered from deformities of the pelvis, which made delivery very difficult. As soon as they possibly could, the mothers would struggle back to work, so that the children really had no chance.

Crippling bone diseases and unsightly skin eruptions were every-day matters in the city slums, where children and young people died regularly of illnesses nowadays no longer considered deadly. In certain industries, notably mining and cotton-spinning, the prime killers of young adults were lung complaints, though tuberculosis was everybody's enemy and a lethal agent even among the well-to-do.

The health problem which probably frightened people most was the curse of epidemics. Smallpox was the most familiar of these from the 17th century onwards, and it broke out over and over again in the 18th, sweeping the Highlands and raging in the slums. It killed more young children than any other disease and was brutally termed 'the poor man's friend', so effectively did it reduce the families of the destitute. Inoculation was used fairly extensively from the 1730s onwards, but this was dangerous in itself as it often brought on full-scale attacks of the disease, and it certainly proved no check. Between 1744 and 1763, 10 per cent. of all deaths in Edinburgh, one death in every six in Kilmarnock, were caused by this loathsome 'poor man's friend'. Only when the great physician, Edward Jenner, hit on the technique of vaccination was the disease brought under control. Between 1801 and 1806, 10,000 people in Glasgow were vac-cinated free of charge, and there was a dramatic drop in the scale of smallpox mortality. People soon became casual and careless about vaccination however and then fresh outbreaks would occur, as in 1817 and 1818.

The illness termed 'fever' was dreaded as much as smallpox. This generic term covered typhus and typhoid and other allied infections. It was always active in the overcrowded city districts, but from time to time, in cycles which became ominously shorter, mass epidemics of it would break out, with death rates far surpassing anything else except cholera. This additional scourge originated in the Far East, infected Europe and reached England early in 1831. Like the Black Death of medieval times, cholera pursued its path northwards, and in October 1831 it began its work in Glasgow. During 1832 its effects were such that cholera news in Britain that year superseded all other and even dis-tracted attention from the public excitement over the Reform

Bill. Cholera re-appeared at intervals, particularly in 1848 and 1849 and again, with savage results, in 1853; by 1866 it was still busy in Glasgow. In 1867, a Public Health Act was framed with special reference to Scotland in order to improve sewage control and sanitation in general—a measure brought about because the cholera scourge was so serious.

Even though life was considered a cheap commodity, people gradually became aware that the mortality rates were worth study. In 1755, a minister called Dr. Webster distributed questionnaires on vital statistics to colleagues in Highland parishes. In the result he estimated that half the people born in these parishes died before reaching the age of eleven, and a quarter of the remainder died before their forty-third birthdays. Child mortality remained as a national problem for long after Webster's day. In 1790, 63 per cent. of all the deaths in Scotland were among children; after vaccination was introduced there was some improvement, but by 1838 child mortality still accounted for over 50 per cent. of the whole figure for Scotland. In 1842 the average length of life in Britain was 46 years, in British cities as a whole, 38 years : in Glasgow it was 30.6 years.

While the picture was black enough as a general rule, there were special places and dates for which the vital statistics were really frightening. Between 1833 and 1839—a bad period as regards public health—the mortality rate for England and Wales was 1 in 48, for Scotland 1 in 45, for problem parishes such as St. David's, Dundee, 1 in 32. During the cholera year, 1832, it reached 1 in 21 in Glasgow, where 1 in 24 or 26 was common enough throughout the 1830s. The evidence of the fever years began to frighten the public, for it became evident that the death-dealing diseases had no proper respect for persons. Begin as they might and usually did in poverty-stricken tenements, the epidemics had no difficulty in penetrating the adjacent stairs and closes leading to the houses of the rich and the influential.

The city doctors of the 19th century spared no pains to publish the truth as they saw it. One cannot but admire the medical men who tended the very poor during those terrible decades. Many of them committed their findings to paper and the anger in which they wrote flares up at the reader who looks through the reports with any sensitivity. Medical opinion was emphatic that epidemics were caused by housing structurally unfit even for animals; that infectious illness multiplied in the slum areas because of the lack of drains and sewers; that the fields irrigated with city filth, such as those adjacent to Holyrood House, were poison dépots for infected air; that people who were herded together like beasts and at the same time undernourished and overworked were bound to fall ill once any virulent germ was at work. The doctors also emphasized that the years of fever epidemic often coincided with those of economic slump when unemployment became common and malnutrition bordered on starvation.

Among business men and employers there was strong prejudice against interference with conditions in the factories and the city slums. They were afraid that efforts at reform would deprive them of financial profit by reducing production, but they were also very much influenced by Adam Smith's successors. 'Laissez faire' was the basis both of the Liberal Party's free trade principles and also of its distaste for regulating the interaction of supply and demand in business. This meant that statutory reform was long in coming, which suited the industrialists very well. Not until the end of the 19th century did ordinary people of middle-class upbringing begin to realize how terrible were the abuses needing reform: and even then far too many were apt to adopt the attitude that 'such things must be' in a modern community. As the great Whig Solicitor-General Lord Cockburn asked himself in the 1830s: 'Are not millions of starving people the necessary sloughs of a very manufacturing nation?'

Meanwhile there was no machinery of local government to set going the wholesale campaigns needed in the cities. Until 1833, burgh councils were not empowered to undertake local administration of health and hygiene, and it was not for some decades after that date that people became courageous or experienced enough to tackle it. Even then the rigidities of the law held up much progress, property-owners defended themselves by every traditional and legal means, and only when a building was in such a state that collapse was imminent could it be termed, according to Scottish usage, a 'nuisance' within the technical meaning of the word.

When fever epidemics, and finally cholera scares, at last shocked the authorities into action, there was hopeless confusion. The Government issued orders for the streets to be cleansed, dwellings lime-washed, patients admitted to hospital, contacts isolated, vagrancy prohibited. Instructions flowed, and were often, as is their way, contradictory; often too, there existed in the towns no official body legally competent to carry them through; nor were there enough hospital beds, or proper means by which to enforce quarantine. The end of the story was always that, once the particular crisis in question passed over, all the preventive measures were dropped and the situation was restored to the status quo till the next outbreak. But the evidence of the medical profession accumulated and was endorsed from other sources. In 1840, Captain Miller, Chief Constable of Glasgow, reported to the British Association, then meeting in the city, that they could see there 'an accumulated mass of squalid wretchedness which is probably unequalled in any town of the British Dominions'. Not long after, the great British sanitarian, Edwin Chadwick, stated that he had never seen misery equal to Glasgow's in any other British city, and reckoned it worse than anything to be found in Europe: second to Glasgow, he ranked Edinburgh.

Poor Relief was meanly administered in Scotland. The principles on which it was organized had been set out in 1579, in an Act designed both to stamp out vagrancy and begging and to assist 'pure, impotent and aged persones'. Kirk sessions had charge of such relief as was given and their funds came from church collections. Voluntary giving for the poor was emphasized as the duty of Christians and there was an almost fanatical hostility to any kind of centrally organized or assessed tax for the purpose. The genuine poor were sharply distinguished in the public mind from able-bodied idlers, who were disqualified from assistance and supposed to be packed off to the parishes of their birth. The people who were considered needy were divided into two categories: the 'ordinary' poor, namely the old and disabled, and the 'occasional' poor, those normally able-bodied who were temporarily impeded by sickness. It never occurred to the authorities that anybody actually in work could be classed as 'poor', even though wages were so low. This was one of the reasons why destitution among unskilled labourers and their families was for so long unalleviated. Money grants were allotted by the Kirk Sessions to the 'ordinary' poor, on a scale designed to cover only rent, or part of it. Other necessities were supposed to be met by private charity, though for this nobody was supposed to beg. In no case was assistance given unless the poor concerned had been three years resident in the parish, a qualification often difficult to prove. In 1839, St. David's parish, Dundee, had 161 persons receiving relief, out of an industrial and impoverished population of 9,000, in which almost every sixth family was fatherless and therefore supported by a widow. Grants were given at the rate of 1/- or 1/6d. per head per week to persons who would have qualified in England for 4/- to 7/6d. The 'occasional' poor were given nothing, on the grounds that they should draw on reserves accumulated during periods of employment!

There was no tradition of institutional assistance in Scotland, where by 1839 there were only four poorhouses, three in Edinburgh and one in Paisley, though there were some 'hospitals' designed for the support of the aged. The only practical relief measures adopted by the authorities took the form of soup-kitchens which were set up in the cities during years of acute famine, such as 1783. In these periods Parliament sent thousands of pounds to northern and western parishes for the purchase and distribution of meal, while the soup-kitchens were busy in the cities. Towards the end of the 18th century there were times when over 10,000 people in Edinburgh were being fed at the public cost. These efforts were always regarded as temporary measures and discontinued at the earliest possible moment. Nobody thought that any permanent plans were called for to prevent the chronic want which was accepted as a normal feature of Scottish life in ordinary times.

Ingrained in the public mind was the idea that a man only became destitute or unemployed if he was lazy or immoral. Politicians did not understand the nature of the new industrial society, in which workers were at the mercy of economic forces that they could not control: unemployment was a national affliction, set going often enough by international trends, with results which no individual could avert by personal effort.

The religious leaders of the day did not understand either. The best ministers were deeply shocked by the conditions in the city parishes, but in the main they restricted their efforts to one field—that of Temperance. In this connection, clergymen of all denominations did achieve notable successes. There were 30,000 Irishmen connected with Temperance Societies run by Roman Catholic priests in Glasgow during the early 1840s. Sabbath School and Ragged School Movements were founded too, but the clergy fell far short of the medical practitioners in their general grasp and understanding of the social problems in their parishes.

Dr. Chalmers, the Moderator of the first United Free Church Assembly in 1843, exercised an influence over other Scottish ministers which must have retarded progress for many years. He diagnosed the nation's ills as flowing from 'deep inner dereliction of duty' and his remedies included the subdivision of larger parishes, a drive to improve day schools and Sabbath schools and the encouragement of 'saving' amongst the poor—'saving' when one earned 8/- or 10/- a week he evidently considered quite feasible. He thought that the abolition of the Corn Laws and the reduction of taxes on necessities would help, but the main part of the business, as he saw it, consisted in the building up of respectable habits. He declared each parish should maintain its own poor, that relief should be based on voluntary gifts locally collected by the charitable, that only those paupers who asked for help should be given it, after careful investigation. He had no understanding at all of the social interdependence now obtaining in industrial nations, nor of the great economic and social metamorphosis through which he was living; with an idealized picture of the old country parish in his mind, he set his face against the organization of properly planned relief by secular central authorities.

As early as 1817, Dr. Chalmers expressed his views, which no later experience caused him to modify. 'Which is nobler, to struggle with the difficulties of your situation, or to lay open your house and your circumstances to the scowl of the official inquisitor?' The *Glasgow Chronicle* took up this question in the following terms: 'This means in plain English: Is it nobler to suffer your wife and children to die of hunger in a world which God has stocked for your support, or to abate your pride so far as to solicit relief from the charity which religion inculcates and law has confirmed?' Chalmers' answer to this was that to take away a man's independence by giving him state-administered assistance would do his personality far more harm than physical wretchedness could inflict. He was also deeply impressed by the natural charity of the poor towards the poor. He was in charge of St. John's Parish, Glasgow, for many years, and in this huge slum district he did personal visiting assiduously, along with many voluntary assistants. They all paid tribute to the way in which the destitute tried to help each other and they all believed that this neighbourliness would be destroyed by state welfare schemes. Chalmers greatly influenced the founders of the Charity Organization Society in England, and he was supported in his hostility to officially organized welfare by a paper as avowedly liberal and progressive in its politics as *The Scotsman*.

At last, in January 1840, a different point of view was expressed, by a man well qualified to state it. This was Dr. W. P. Alison, who had had long and valuable experience of medical work in Edinburgh's slums. His pamphlet was called *Observations on the Management of the Poor in Scotland and its Effect on the Health of the Great Towns*. He exposed the evils so well-known to him and to his colleagues. He declared that expert, central administration of the Poor Law was needed, together with the provision of workhouses, improved hygiene, compulsory poor rates and—most significant and most distasteful to contemporary opinion—regular relief for the able-bodied unemployed.

All this was startling enough for thinkers of Chalmers' school. It was followed by a Commission of enquiry in 1843 and 1844, which examined the conditions described by Alison, and which led to a Poor Law Amendment Act for Scotland in 1845. This did *not* introduce relief for the able-bodied unemployed. It did however create a central Board of Supervision in Edinburgh charged with the general administration of poor relief in Scotland. Parish Boards were set up, each to appoint an Inspector of the

Poor, and to work in collaboration with the Central Board. It was also arranged that poorhouses should be built in all the big cities for the care of the destitute—and greatly did those poorhouses come to be hated, so rigorously were they run.

At last, too, Scotland was obliged to accept the principle of a legal poor rate, which was to be used for the assistance of those who were desperate, but who did not qualify for entry to a poorhouse. The sums paid were so niggardly that, by comparison, even the small pittances allowed in England seem generous, but they were an improvement on previous forms of assistance. Sometimes help was given in kind, as in the case of widow Ann Christie of South Uist. She was paralysed and she had four young children. Between November 18th, 1846, and February 19th, 1847, when she died, she received 10 pecks of meal. Her horse and her weaving-loom were sold after her death for £2 15s. 0d. to meet funeral expenses—she had no other saleable possessions as she had parted with everything else to find food for the children, who most illegally helped her by begging. The problem of poverty in Scotland was not solved by the Act of 1845 because it still had not dawned upon people that poverty could only be dealt with by wholesale raising of wages. Reformers were beginning to think in terms of relieving distress, but not of preventing it.

The Scottish Poor Law Amendment Act was passed at the time when the Chartist Movement was at its height. This had been founded in England by people who were disgusted both by the 1832 Reform Bill, which left the working classes without the vote, and by the English Poor Law of 1834, which put a stop to the supplementing of low wages with payments from the rates. The Chartists believed that only by radical reform of Parliament could social justice be achieved for the workers, because not until workers themselves were elected to the House of Commons would legislation to relieve poverty be countenanced. Their programme demanded votes for all adult males, secret ballot—to prevent employers and landowners from exploiting those under their power—equal electoral districts, payments of salaries to M.P.s, the abolition of property qualifications of M.P.s, and annual Parliaments. All these principles except the last have long since been adopted as rational bases of democratic government, but when they were first set out in the People's Charter conservative opinion was profoundly shocked.

Scottish Chartists took the proposals seriously and many recruits were drawn into the movement. Its story was very different from the parallel one in England. The Scottish middle classes were much attracted to the proposed reforms and Chartism drew them into closer sympathy with the working people, of whom however only the more prosperous and reflective were interested. Meetings, lectures and mass demonstrations were organized and supported all over the country, and two Chartist newspapers flourished for a number of years. One of these, the *True Scotsman*, actually had a wider circulation for a while than the original Edinburgh *Scotsman*. Chartist churches were founded, and these tried to link religion and politics: they even started schools, organized adult education, and launched a rather successful Temperance drive.

Throughout the short life of this movement, the Scottish branches insisted that peaceful propaganda and moral persuasion only must be used, and there was very much less extremism and violence associated with Chartism north of the Border than south. The reason for this difference was that in Scotland the explosive ingredients for a violent movement were missing. The really miserable were too miserable, too far down the abyss of suffering, to have the energy for such an affair as Chartism. This was why it was taken up by the middle classes and the more prosperous artisans rather than by the genuine poor. In England, the Poor Law of 1834 was considered so reactionary that industrial workers were stung into a fury of hostility which only needed the publication of the Charter in 1838 to become red-hot. Nobody was accustomed to public assistance in Scotland, indeed the grimly inadequate terms of the 1845 Act brought alleviation rather than disappointment, so that there was one factor the less for revolution.

Chartism collapsed in 1848, in the fiasco of the great Petition lodged at the House of Commons and instantly discredited because so many signatures appended to it were found to be faked. The movement left its mark in Scotland because it awakened people to new ideas and introduced them to fresh experience, but it did not touch the problem of poverty. The Factory Acts of 1833, 1844 and 1847, however, did something for young people and children. Hours of labour were modified a little, some educational facilities were made statutory, factory inspectors were appointed. These reforms were restricted to certain branches of industry only, inspection and penal action were grossly insufficient, and employers quickly found out how to evade them. The Mines Act of 1842 was a much more important advance because it put an end to the dreadful use of women and children in the pits.

The squalid city slums increased in extent and misery, and became breeding-grounds for sickness and crime, all through the 1840s and 1850s. In 1861, the census revealed that 35 per cent. of Scottish families lived in one room, whose average measurements would be 9 or 10 feet square, 7 or 8 feet high: 37 per cent. lived in two such rooms: 7,964 families lived in single rooms containing no window, but depending for ventilation and light upon the chimney and the door. An account was published in 1862 of the Middle Meal Market Stairs in Edinburgh, where 'there are 59 rooms, almost all separate dwelling houses, entered by a steep, dark, stone stair common to the whole. In these dwell 248 individuals (adults 197, children under five, 51) divided into 56 families and in this huge congress of dens there is no water, no water-closet, no sink.'

It was in 1862 that the first Medical Officer of Health in Scotland was appointed, fifteen years after the first such officer in England. Both were Scotsmen—Dr. William Duncan began his service in Liverpool in 1847, Dr. Henry Littlejohn in Edinburgh in 1862. Dr. Littlejohn had already published stringent criticisms of the treatment meted out to the poor. 'The pittances that are given to paupers, through the proverbial economy of the Boards representing the ratepayers of our City, are only intended to allow of life being maintained at a legal flicker and by no means at a steady flame.' His words could have been equally well applied to the treatment of the poorhouse inmates. In 1860, the average weekly cost per head of providing all necessaries for these people, including fuel, light, clothing and food, was 4/5½d. *The Scotsman* estimated that expenditure on food amounted to 3½d. per head per day and commented: 'We express a grave doubt whether aged, sick and broken-down paupers can be sufficiently fed on 3½d. a day.'

During these years, Scottish prisons and lunatic asylums were crammed with people whom no Court of Law to-day would relegate to any such institution. Many of the asylums were very small and were run for personal profit under private management. Solitary confinement, corporal punishment, even chains, were in regular use, and the 'patients' were left in indescribable neglect, short of food and clothes and bedding, in rooms and cells which were always filthy. In the prisons a larger food allowance was permitted than in the poorhouses, but prisoners of all ages and both sexes were herded together in overcrowded quarters and the degrading conditions were such that men and women who had served sentences came out more vicious and more skilled in crime than when they went in.

Although the main body of public opinion tolerated these scandals with equanimity or indifference, the working-men themselves made immense efforts to fight for better conditions. During the first three decades of the 19th century, Trade Unions began to develop in the industries which had been longest mechanized, namely various branches of the textile group. The Unions were formed by working-class initiative and management with two aims in view: one was to contribute funds, by weekly subscriptions, for the assistance of sick and injured members and for widows and children; the other to organize joint pressure on the employers for higher wages. Following on the Unions of spinners, weavers and other textile workers came similar organizations among colliers, metal workers, builders and railwaymen. Always their efforts were directed to securing higher wages, and to this end they tried to stage strikes which would paralyse the mills and force the employers to agree on better wage-scales. Led by men inexperienced in such affairs, these strikes were often ill-timed and badly co-ordinated. They sometimes lasted for weeks on end. They very rarely succeeded. Ultimately the workers had to go back to their jobs, if they were still available, at the old or even at worsened wage-scales.

The employers were afraid of the Unions and afraid of the strikes, although until the very end of the 19th century their position was relatively impregnable. They had capital behind them, and the strikers had not; they had the law and its corps of magistrates and justices on their side, and the strikers had not; they could break the strikes by importing yet more Irish labour, and the strikers had no similar weapon. The Unions therefore fought a losing battle till nearly the end of the century, and a deadly tradition of hatred grew up. Public opinion was against the Unions not only because industrialists dreaded any rising costs of production, but also because any kind of collective bargaining smelt of radicalism. By the end of the century, suspicion and hostility had long roots so that, when the balance of power shifted and the Unions became strong enough to insist on what they wanted, their attitude towards employers and consumers was as unrelenting as that of the industrialists had been in their heyday. The technique of arbitration and the art of personnel management developed too late, and while in the early decades of the Industrial Revolution moderate concessions would have eased everything and made for a much better spirit on every side, the abuse of power by the employers in fact led to the bitter feuds and the Red Clydeside of the 20th century.

CHAPTER 28

The Scot Abroad

Sir Walter Scott once spoke of 'the national disposition to wandering and adventure'. From early medieval times the Scot was well known all over Europe. In the 18th century all who could afford it sent their sons on the Grand Tour, through France into Italy and back through Germany. Sir Archibald Grant explained to his son the purpose of this. 'To goe too early abroad before qualified for conversation, observation and comparissons, I apprehend to be lost time and expense, at least in great degree, whereas reall improvement and usefull friendships may and probably will be the fruits if previously qualifyed. Setting out with proper stock will probably yield more of both in one year than several years would doe without it.' The stock which Sir Archibald wanted his son to acquire before setting out included the study of British History and Geography, and some mastery of French, Latin and Greek. The letters of George Dempster to his friend Adam Fergusson in the 1750s give a vivid impression of the impact of these journeys on the fortunate young men who made them. George Dempster's letters are always good reading.

After the Union, the contribution of the Scots to Britain's influence abroad, and in particular to the development of the Empire, was altogether out of proportion to the size of their own country. They travelled and talked and worked and wrote their way from one continent to another, and everywhere they were to be found in positions of high responsibility. In this book, the story can only be illustrated from typical careers of Scots in diplomacy and administration, in the armed forces, in emigration and exploration and in missionary enterprise. Time would fail to tell of the Scot as engineer, gold prospector, man of business, doctor, novelist.

During the early 18th century, it was difficult for Scots to obtain diplomatic employment abroad, because Sir Robert Walpole disliked them and filled all possible posts with Englishmen. After 1760 there came a marked change however. Between 1760 and 1789, one-seventh of all diplomatic appointments went to Scotsmen, a high proportion at a time when Scottish population was still less than one-seventh of that in England. From 1763 onwards there was nearly always a Scot in charge of the embassies in Austria, Prussia, Poland, Russia and Sweden, also at Constantinople and Naples, while many Scots served in west European cities and in far distant islands. The English press published some sour comment on this infiltration of northerners, for it was at its height during years when Scotsmen were still unpopular in London's political circles.

Scots were well-suited for foreign diplomatic service, because they readily adjusted themselves to strange conditions and unfamiliar company and they were willing to live for years on end in remote middle eastern capitals and semi-barbarous islands. Their philosophical attitude to difficult climates and unhygienic conditions may have been due to the discomfort in which many of them spent their boyhood at home. Their professional success was helped by their flair for foreign languages, in which Englishmen did not distinguish themselves; indeed it was rare to find an English diplomat fluent in any language other than French, while Scotsmen abroad could frequently speak Dutch and German as well. Scottish schools and Universities emphasized Latin and used the continental pronunciation, so that when necessary a Scot could fall back on this and make himself understood without employing an interpreter. A good many interested themselves also in oriental tongues, like Alexander Burnes, the descendant of Robert Burns the poet, and this enabled them to carry out useful negotiations in Persia, China and India.

Many families built up a tradition in the diplomatic corps. The 9th Baron Cathcart and his son were both ambassadors in St. Petersburg for quite long periods. The 7th Earl of Elgin, who transported the famous Parthenon marbles to London, served at the court of the Emperor Leopold in 1790 and afterwards in

Brussels and Berlin; both his sons were distinguished diplomats, indeed the elder became Governor-General first of Canada and afterwards of India. Sir Robert Keith was ambassador in Vienna and St. Petersburg during the 1760s, and he was followed in Vienna by his son, a brilliant linguist fluent in at least seven languages. The 1st Earl of Minto, his son, his brother, and his nephew all held posts of the highest importance in many parts of the world.

While Scotsmen were making their mark in the embassies, they were also to be found in administrative posts, as soldiers and as civilians. Some of them showed initiative and originality which shocked the authorities at home. One of these was Lachlan Macquarie.

Lachlan Macquarie arrived in New South Wales late in 1809, with a long record of distinguished military service behind him. His biographer, M. H. Ellis, describes him as 'yellowed with fever, blotched with curative aids, racked with long courses of mercury, saddened under the strain of grief and marked in every way with the evidences of twenty years in the tropics'. His instructions were to clean up the situation caused by the mismanagement of Governor Bligh, the man whose name will always be remembered in connection with the mutiny on the *Bounty*, but who had probably done more harm than anywhere else in the convict settlement at Botany Bay.

Macquarie's was the first rational administration of this miserable corner of the Empire. His powers seemed rejuvenated by the challenge of his new responsibilities and he set about creating a more normal society. Roads and public works were built on a lavish scale, agricultural improvements encouraged, pioneering and exploration stimulated. Convicts who had served their time were admitted to high positions in society and treated as equals, though delicately nurtured officials bitterly complained about having to receive communion in Church, kneeling beside such riff-raff. Corporal punishments were reduced, drinking habits attacked, a great hospital erected, courts of justice re-organized, land settlement in small lots offered to emancipated convicts, a bank, schools and a printing press established.

The expenses caused by these projects stimulated furious criticism from the Government; Britain was still struggling to pay its way through a war of survival, and the authorities at home could see no excuse for spending so much. In an effort to meet his expenses, Macquarie became involved in financial transactions which brought him to disgrace, and his great services were not recognized till much later. He ended his days in bitterness and poverty. Macquarie's work however did bring permanent and good results to New South Wales. Many thousands of Scots were among those who explored and surveyed and farmed there and elsewhere in Australia, and their names may be seen in plenty on the maps, as indeed is the case in New Zealand and in Canada.

The East India Company at this time was employing great numbers of Scotsmen. In the 18th and 19th centuries, this Company undertook not only vast commercial projects, but also the administration of enormous areas, where conquest and political control had followed on mercantile enterprise. After the terrible Mutiny of 1857, the Company was wound up: the responsibility of government became the direct concern of the British Parliament, and administration on the spot was carried out through the Indian Civil Service, staffed in the main by British officials, till the end of the 19th century.

The British conquest of India is an achievement not to be justified in terms of the modern ethic of self-determination, which even yet is not fully realized. No such ethical notions troubled the heads of Scots or Englishmen or Indians till comparatively recent years: the continent had long been accustomed to wars of conquest by the time the British became involved in them.

The British administration of India attracted some of the best manhood this country had to give, though of course there were rogues and swindlers too, upon whom it is fashionable in some circles nowadays to concentrate at the expense of the better ones. Many were animated by high ideals: these wanted to establish justice, incorruptibility, a better material standard of living for the peasant, and to eliminate such gross cruelties as the burning of widows and infanticide. They were interested in trade and in

religious toleration for Hindu and Moslem alike: in general they
were less interested, until the 1860s, in education and in the
great civilization of India. Very few of them shared the Brahmins'
intense preoccupation with philosophy. As the 19th century
wore on they became concerned with public health and gradually
in the possibility of self-government for India. They found it
easy to be compassionate about the peasant, much harder to
respect the banya (the small-scale man of business). It has
always been difficult for the Briton to appreciate the qualities
of people cleverer than himself and the Hindu is often very clever.
The merit of British administration has been the consistent
efforts to establish peace, order, general justice and a rising scale
of prosperity. Its outstanding defect has been the lack of interest
in the thoughts and feelings, the dignity and aspirations of the
people administered.

Within the limits of temperament and training, the British
went far towards the realization of the ideals they set themselves
in India. To this achievement, the Scot, with his colossal capacity
for work and his strong intellectual endowment, made a contribution described by Professor Dewar Gibb as 'massive and
continuous'.

There was a Dumfriesshire stonemason called Allan Cunning-
ham, born in 1784, who became a minor poet. Of his four sons,
three made their names in India. Joseph entered the Bengal
Engineers and wrote a history of the Sikhs; Alexander became a
major-general, also in the Bengal Engineers, later Director-
General of the Indian Archaeological Survey (from 1870 till 1885)
and he published works on Indian Geography and Numismatics;
Francis joined the Indian Army and produced editions of Ben
Jonson and Marlowe.

Many Scottish families could produce similar records. The
Indian Civil Service was staffed at every level by Scots. They took
an impressive part in the work on the great canals, railways and
telegraph installations which so greatly mitigated famine, and
they shared too in medical and agricultural research. There were
many Scottish Governors of provinces, and of the Viceroys, three
were Scots—two Earls of Elgin and Lord Minto—and Dalhousie
was a half-Scot.

During the 18th and 19th centuries, military and naval service took Scotsmen abroad as much as diplomacy and administration. From 1707 onwards, Lowland regiments served in Europe and in America under many well-known generals, but Highland names were missing till the 1760s. This of course was because the authorities were afraid to give martial training and equipment to people suspected of Jacobite sympathies. Duncan Forbes of Culloden was one of those who deeply regretted this attitude. He was sure that the Forty-Five could have been much curtailed or even prevented had regiments been formed from the loyal Highlands clans. In this view he was fortified by the record of the Black Watch, the one exception to the general rule. Formed in George I's reign from some independent companies of Campbells, Grants, Munros and others of Hanoverian interest, this regiment fought in Europe during the 1740s and won immediate recognition for steadiness and courage.

The Seven Years' War strained Britain's resources to the utmost and the elder Pitt decided at last to enlist Highlanders. In 1766 he made his well-remembered statement on the subject in the House of Commons. 'I sought for merit wherever it was to be found. It is my boast that I was the first Minister who looked for it and found it in the mountains of the north. I called it forth and drew into your service a hardy and intrepid race of men . . . They served with fidelity as they fought with valour and conquered for you in every part of the world.' During the American war, more Highland regiments were brought into being. One of the best-known was the 73rd, raised in 1777 by Lord Macleod, a former Jacobite, who had seen military service in Sweden. The 73rd made its name in India and in the Peninsula.

In 20th century circumstances, it seems fantastic that a man should spend seven to ten thousands of pounds from private resources in order to raise and equip a battalion for national service, while simultaneously exhausting himself on unpaid administrative work in its organization. This was how the British Army was expanded to meet the crisis precipitated in 1793 by Napoleon, and many Scotsmen hastened along with others thus to impoverish themselves in the nation's interests. During the latter part of the 18th century some fifty new Scottish regiments were raised, by private initiative, including the Gordons, Camerons, and Argylls. They fought in the West Indies, in European and Eastern theatres of war, most of them have proud records of their share in the campaigns of Egypt, the Peninsula and Waterloo, and some of their officers attained international reputation.

The naval side of the story is equally interesting. No Scot lives very far from the sea, so indented is the long, crumpled coast-line, and in days when life on dry land presented intolerable disadvantages, life at sea attracted young men in plenty, especially from the islands of the north and west. Long accustomed by the Hudson's Bay men and by traditional deep-sea fishing sagas to the notion of seafaring, these islanders joined the Navy in great numbers, especially during the Napoleonic wars. In 1809 it was believed that from the Shetlands and the Orkneys, upwards of 5,000 men were serving at sea and there were innumerable others as well, from both coastal and inland shires. Ill-fed, battened down in filthy sleeping-quarters, coarsely treated and mercilessly punished by old-style public floggings, these sailors were also irregularly paid, until reforms were belatedly introduced in the early 19th century. But Scottish seamen were found in every kind of vessel all over the world, they took part in all the naval actions fought against Napoleon, and later they shared in some bizarre adventures whose repercussions were far-reaching.

Some of the best-known Scottish sailors came of military families: these included Sir Patrick Campbell, brother of General Sir Colin Campbell, Sir Graham Moore, brother of Sir John of Corunna, and Sir Basil Keith, brother of the great soldier and diplomat. Others came of seafaring families which gave many famous names to the fleet, such as Admiral Duncan of Camperdown, Sir Richard Strachan and Sir Thomas Cochrane. The career of Cochrane was extraordinary and took him into strange spheres. Few individuals can have had a hand in so many different kinds of success, few overcame such dreadful reversals of fortune.

Public service in the diplomatic corps or the armed forces generally led to retirement at home in Scotland. Emigration was quite another matter: it involved permanent settlement in a new country. All through the 18th century this was going on, but it was much more in evidence after the Seven Years' War, which came to an end in 1763. Some Scottish regiments never returned: Fraser's Highlanders, for example, remained in America, sure that there they would have a better chance of making a living than in Scotland. They were more fortunate than later settlers, because they made their homes in places where thriving communities were already established. Their letters dwelt upon the best features of the new life and encouraged others to join them, while propaganda by Scottish landowners and their agents, and later also by shipping companies, intensified the campaign to send the crofters away.

The ship-owners took advantage of the situation. Vessels therefore left which were neither seaworthy nor properly equipped and grossly overloaded. Loss of life was caused when cholera made its way among the overcrowded travellers, and also by shipwreck. In February 1848, Labouchere reported in the House of Commons that of the 106,000 Irish and Scots who had emigrated in the previous year, 12,200 had died at sea or immediately after arrival, while a further 7,100 had failed to survive their journey for more than a few weeks.

Those who did survive tended to settle as far as possible in family groups. Round Quebec were large contingents from Arran; in the Cape Breton district people from Skye: in Nova Scotia families from Ross-shire. In 1815 a settler in New Caledonia wrote to his nephew: 'I suppose there is two hundred Scotch families in this township of respectable people. Your mother will meet with more of her relations here than in Breadalbane.' By the time this letter was written, Gaelic had become a prevailing language in parts of Upper Canada and the Red River Valley, as well as in Cape Breton, Prince Edward Island and a number of other areas.

Some of these emigrants fared much better than others. Those who had the worst experiences were the ones who made their way into country hitherto undeveloped, where they had to build up a new life without the help of any established services.

A typical story was published in 1823 by a John McDonald who went to New Lanark in Upper Canada. It is tempting to quote at length from his short book, which ran through five editions in less than a year, for he describes so much that one wants to know, although there is an undertone of complaint in his writing which is not characteristic of his countrymen.

The crossing from Greenock took six and a half weeks, in atrocious weather, and by the time the ship made Quebec most of the passengers were ill with various infections, though none developed cholera. Then began the laborious journey up the St. Lawrence, first by steamer, afterwards in the flat-bottomed boats used on the upper reaches of the river. Everybody lacked equipment and suitable clothing, so that camping in the open at nights, after days spent largely in hauling boats and baggage over the rapids, caused much illness and many deaths. The last 74 miles were covered overland, across ground rough enough to overturn the waggons.

McDonald wrote of the excessive humidity, the 'noisome exhalations of immense woods', the torrents of rain, the mosquitoes, the snakes, but above all of the continual exposure. When at last, in the month of August, the survivors reached New Lanark, they had to prepare for a winter of five to six months' continuous frost and snow; the nearest town was sixty miles away; draught animals were hard to come by; there were shortages of food, warm clothing and necessaries of all descriptions. McDonald admitted that the prospect of ultimate prosperity was high, but he said that the initial hardships exceeded anything he had ever imagined, and he was continually depressed by the frightening death-roll and, not less, by the irreligious materialism of his fellow settlers. He wrote with disgust of the flattering accounts 'so industriously published' of Upper Canada and stated that all the truth which had been written about it 'would not cover one half of the lies which had been told'.

While he was preparing his book for the press, 'industrious propaganda' continued, and many more Scots were persuaded to set forth on journeys as hazardous and as inadequately planned as McDonald's, some into the wilds of Canada, others to various parts of the United States. Their contribution to the development of the New World was most significant. Driven from their own country by want, they devoted to the new communities, of which they became foundation members, all the drive and initiative which at home had been crushed but which now were stimulated to the full.

Many Scotsmen were attracted to the Hudson's Bay Company, and by about 1800 three-quarters of its servants were Orcadians and so were most of its officials. They operated from a base called York Factory, which was situated on Hudson's Bay, and their purpose was to trade with the Indians, from whom they bought furs for export to Europe. The life was hard and rough, but it brought out the fine qualities of the Orkneymen. As boatmen, fishermen, hunters and carpenters these island folk were unrivalled: they could face privations without complaint and they learned to handle the nomad Indians with confidence and justice. In Stromness, at the northern end of the little street that runs along the shore side of the town, you can see an old well, now sealed up, from which the Hudson's Bay vessels took in their last supplies of water before heading across the Atlantic. They watered there each summer for over two centuries and carried with them untold numbers of men from all the islands.

The North West Company was a rival fur-trading firm, founded in 1783, to work the same area as the Hudson's Bay men. The two organizations hated each other and fighting broke out between them before they were finally amalgamated.

Sir Alexander Mackenzie is probably the most famous of the North West Company's officials. His boyhood home was at Stromness and like so many islanders he went to Canada as a young man. He spent a number of years at Fort Chipewyan, in Hudson's Bay territory, and later carried out two tremendous ventures in exploration. The first one took him in 1789 to the Arctic Ocean, the second in 1792 to the Pacific by way of the Rocky Mountains. Mackenzie's fortitude and success as an explorer were matched by his skill in personal relationships with the men in his crew and with the many unfamiliar Indian tribes through whose land he passed. The negotiations he had to conduct with these Indians demanded of him endless patience and skill and he always avoided arousing hostility. Mackenzie wrote up his journeys himself, most beautifully. Professor Dewar Gibb describes his journals as 'the most unpretentious record of dangerous exploration ever written'.

While the stream of emigration to Canada continued throughout the 19th century, Scotsmen were simultaneously making their way in huge numbers to the United States. Some were seasonal workers, who spent seven or eight months each year working as stone cutters or builders and then returned to Scotland until the following season, but far more were genuine emigrants. Agricultural labourers, carpet workers, weavers, jute and linen operatives poured into New England during the first half of the 19th century, to be followed in the second by as many engineers, iron and steel workers, coal-miners and shipbuilders.

The most famous of them all was Andrew Carnegie, whose parents struggled against the inevitable in Dunfermline for years after it had become clear that weaving as they had known it was finished. Carnegie's enormous success in iron and steel gave him control over a vast network of business firms, newspapers and railroads, and it also made him a household name throughout the Western World. His generous use of wealth added to his prestige, for there was magic in the story of the telegraph boy who worked his way up from the poorest beginnings and ultimately gave away hundreds of thousands of dollars, both in Scotland and in the country of his adoption. The libraries and research centres, the endowments, loans and scholarships which he financed on both sides of the Atlantic make an almost fantastic climax to his story and have enabled great numbers of his fellow countrymen to start life better equipped than he did himself.

Meanwhile Africa was laying its spell upon British explorers. Among the Scotsmen who went there, the name of Mungo Park will always be honoured because of his explorations in Nigeria. Although this gifted and most unusual man ended his life in terrible circumstances—he was killed in Timbuctoo in 1810—many of his countrymen followed him to West Africa and became associated with the British developments on the Lower Niger.

The French Revolution stimulated among religious people an unexpected reaction to Africa and the Far East. Hitherto, little or no missionary work had been done by the British, but in 1792 the Baptist Missionary Society was founded in England and three years later the London Missionary Society.

The Scot Abroad

The notion that every man has an equal right to the Gospel of Christ caught on in Scotland, and Missionary Societies were founded in Glasgow and Edinburgh, enterprises which were frowned upon in powerful quarters. In May 1796, the General Assembly of the Church of Scotland drew up the following resolution: 'To spread abroad among barbarians and heathen natives the knowledge of the Gospel seems to be highly preposterous, in so far as it anticipates, nay, reverses the order of Nature.' This statement illustrates the fear of liberal ideals engendered by the French Revolution, and the difference in attitude between men bred in the 18th century and in the 19th.

Despite the opposition of highly influential religious leaders, many Scottish workers went abroad under the London Missionary Society, which was undenominational, and therefore attracted people of varying persuasions. The Society's first field of operations was in Tahiti and it attracted a high proportion of Scots, but its work expanded very rapidly into Africa, India and the Far East.

The great period of Scottish missionary work came after 1843, when the Disruption brought about a revival of religious zeal throughout the country. By this time the Church of Scotland itself was active in the mission field, for the reactionary dictum of the General Assembly in 1796 was soon abandoned. There is no doubt however that in the mid-19th century the Free Church and the United Presbyterian Church gave the greatest support to missionary and educational enterprise, and they sent their members all over the world.

John Philip, a Congregational minister from Aberdeen, started his missionary career in 1819, when he was well over forty; it was a series of explosions. He has been described as the Elijah of South Africa, the 'outspoken and indefatigable champion of the blacks', a man who horrified Britain by the revelations he publicized about the slave trade, and who was loathed by the Boers for those revelations. During his thirty stormy years abroad, Philip spent himself in the cause of the Hottentots and the Bushmen, thundered against the sale of liquor to native peoples, and revolutionized the organization of the London Missionary Society.

Contemporary with Philip was Robert Moffat, who reached
Africa in 1816. Moffat gave fifty-four years to Africa, living for
most of the time at Kuruman in Bechuanaland, and like Philip
he became a devoted friend to the Hottentots. He reduced the
Bechuana tongue to writing and translated the Bible and other
religious literature into it, a prodigious work for one who never
ceased making extensive and incredibly arduous journeys.

Of Robert Moffat's son-in-law it is difficult to write, for so
much has already been written in many different languages, and
he has attracted the admiration and indeed reverence of Christian
thinkers throughout the world. No account of Scottish history
however would be defensible if it lacked some reference to this
intellectual and spiritual giant, in whose background one can
see many threads of Scotland's story woven together. David
Livingstone's family passed through at least three of the
vicissitudes which afflicted his nation. His great-grandfather
died at Culloden, a Jacobite; his grandfather had to leave his
holding on the island of Ulva, because of the economic drive
which sent so many country folk to the cities; David himself was
caught up in a third national upheaval, the Industrial Revolution, and from the age of ten he worked at the jennies in the
Blantyre cotton mills. Like many Scotsmen, he was brought up
in a home that was short of money but sensitive to religion, and
he shared with his countrymen the traditional reverence for the
classics. With his early savings he bought a Latin primer, which
he propped up in front of him on his machine. As a boy, he
caught the idealism of the age and determined to become a
doctor and go to China, under the London Missionary Society
which attracted him because of its non-sectarian principles.

Livingstone was directed however to Africa, a decision to
which he was somewhat reconciled after his first meeting with
Robert Moffat, whose daughter he subsequently married. Moffat
advised Livingstone to avoid the well-established missionary
centres and go further north, to places described by the historian
Latourette as 'vast reaches' as yet 'untouched by the faith and
where on any clear morning there could be seen the smoke of a
thousand villages in which the name of Christ had not been
heard'.

Moffat did not expect Livingstone to follow this advice quite so enthusiastically as he did. Like Mungo Park, Livingstone had a passionate desire to explore. His travels included journeys across the Kalahari desert, up the unknown Zambesi River, across to the western coast; his discoveries included Lake Nyasa, Lake Mweru, Lake Bangweolu and the Victoria Falls. He wanted to make possible a vast extension of knowledge, and of mission work; all his travelling days were pre-occupied with his urge to put on record scientific information and at the same time to preach the gospel of Christ. By his journeys, he hoped too to open up new channels of commerce which could give traders a profitable substitute for the slave traffic, and it was this hope which drove him from the heart of Africa to the western coast. This ideal fired the imagination of many other Scotsmen, in particular of John Kirk, who was able to go far towards achieving it.

Perhaps the Scot whose spirit was most akin to Livingstone's was Mary Slessor. Like him she passed much of her childhood working in a factory, and during the long hours spent in the Dundee weaving-shed she too kept a book propped up beside her. As an eleven-year-old she worked from 6 a.m. till 6 p.m. at the weaving and also carried out many household chores at home, helping to support her sisters and brother, and to conceal from the neighbours the fact that their father was a habitual drunkard. From early childhood she was deeply religious and she soon became devoted to the missionary ideal.

In 1876, three years after Livingstone's death, Mary Slessor went to Old Calabar in Nigeria, where she developed some surprising qualities of character. Drunken natives, infuriated chieftains, rioting strangers, degraded women, she faced with forthright courage and spontaneous affection. They called her 'Ma' and allowed her to box their ears, confiscate their firearms, fight their insect pests and criticize their primitive habits. Under the influence of her terse yet fluent scoldings, these people found themselves obliged to give up murdering twins and flogging women. Even such practices as human sacrifice, the torture of slaves and trial by poison were gradually abandoned as a result of her astonishing vitality. Her life was constantly endangered by her determination to save life, and most especially she did battle for women, in a society which deemed them to be inferior animals. Her success may be measured by the demand which arose in so many of her villages for a 'White Ma to teach our women book and washing and machine'. Her versatility may be gauged from her recipe for cement-making: 'I just stir it like porridge, turn it out smooth with a stick, and all the time keep praying, "Lord, here's the cement, if to Thy glory, set it" and it has never once gone wrong'. Her courage seemed to grow from year to year, as she endured repeated illness, solitude, hostility, in surroundings which teemed not only with people made grossly cruel by ignorance and superstition, but also with snakes, ants, leopards, hippopotamuses and crocodiles.

During all these years when Scottish initiative was so evident in Africa, there were important developments in the Far East, in India and in the Pacific Islands. Men and women went abroad from the 1840s onwards in such strength that Christian work in all these areas was permeated by Scottish and Presbyterian ideals. In the *History of Church Missionary Societies*, Eugene Stock states that 'Scotland has given a far larger proportion of its ablest and most cultured men to Foreign Missions than any other country in the world'.

A 'national disposition to wandering and adventure' is compatible with fierce and loving pride in one's own country. By their lavish expenditure of ability outside Scotland, the explorers, and administrators, missionaries and many others made generous and substantial contributions to the welfare of many peoples. But they never lost their sense of nationality, or their nostalgic love of their own countryside. One may ask why they did not find an outlet for their tremendous ability and energy at home, but how can a man satisfy his urge to wander, his craving for adventure, in the streets and banks and factories of the city where he was born? It has been to the lasting benefit of many countries that the Scots could not do so and it has given their nation an international prestige that could have been achieved in no other way.

PART FOUR

Scotland since 1870

CHAPTER 29

Economic Developments

The purpose of this chapter, and of the two which follow, is to set out some of the facts which explain the present social and economic state of affairs in Scotland, and to put forward reasons for some of the thoughts and feelings of Scottish people today. The wars which broke upon the world during the years between 1870 and 1945 are not described, nor is the Scottish contribution to the British war efforts, substantial and important though it was. In so short a book, it is impossible to deal with this enormous subject, though the effect of the great conflicts on life and thought in Scotland is suggested.

It seems best to begin by describing some of the economic developments, then to show how changes in social life came about and after that to touch upon public opinion. Throughout the whole discussion Scotland must be considered in relation to Britain and indeed to the world in general, because in modern conditions no country can be understood if it is studied as an isolated unit.

A long and terrible depression in farming destroyed the prosperity of agriculturalists in Britain during the years following 1870. This was the heyday of Free Trade. Housewives could buy relatively inexpensive meat, cereals, butter and cheese imported from the New World, Denmark, Australia and New Zealand. All these countries could produce food of good quality more cheaply than Britain because they had more favourable conditions of climate and soil, and the shipping of such goods was revolutionized by steam and refrigeration. City workers and town-dwellers badly needed cheap food, but the fierce competition from abroad was too much for British farmers. The only ones who could continue successfully were those who had both particularly productive soil and also capital to invest in the new heavy machinery, ploughs, binders, threshing-machines and the like.

South of the Border, the total area of land under farming hardly decreased, but many English agriculturalists turned to pasture. There was much more stock-breeding, especially in cattle, because this involved less outlay in wages and in general upkeep than grain. In the United Kingdom as a whole, some 4½ million acres formerly used for crops other than grass were withdrawn from arable cultivation between 1875 and 1916.

Scottish economy was now so bound up with that of Britain as a whole, that the general depression in agriculture could not fail to affect it. Some farms in the Borders and in central and eastern Scotland still made a success of grain production; and cattle-breeding, both for beef and for dairy products, flourished in Ayrshire and Galloway. On the whole, however, Scotsmen found the most economical thing to do was to rear sheep, so the acres devoted to sheep-farming increased steadily every decade. Land so used is close-cropped and the herbage in a difficult climate can therefore suffer. In any case, the proper balance between arable and pasture was destroyed, quantities of fodder and fertilisers had to be imported, land that could have been ploughed with good results went out of cultivation. Whereas in 1800 there had been about half a million Scotsmen employed on farms and crofts, by 1900, when the total population had trebled, land workers had decreased in number by half. South of the Border the flight from the land was not nearly so marked as this.

The general movement to the cities and the outward flow of emigrants continued throughout the forty years following 1870. Both were fed especially from the Highlands and Islands, where a contributory factor was the fashion for deerstalking. Landowners found it most profitable to preserve their properties for this purpose and about two million acres were therefore enclosed for game, of which fully a third could have been farmed successfully. This land was engulfed by bracken, pests thrived on it, the deer multiplied and wandered on to adjacent farm properties in search of food, especially during winter.

The crofters had the worst of it. They were smallholders in the Highlands and Islands, who lived on tiny stretches of rough country, many of them on the shores of estuaries and sea lochs far removed from the centres of administration. Their rents in some cases amounted to only a few pounds annually, but by tradition they had no security of tenure, no written leases, and in consequence no incentive to improve their holdings. The roads leading to their crofts were bad, their amenities poor, their miserable little plots were mismanaged and they had to eke out a subsistence by fishing and weaving. Most of them abandoned the effort to grow oats or turnips; they concentrated instead on potatoes and kept a few sheep and a cow or two. Many utterly lost heart and gave up the struggle to find even the minimal rents they owed; their young people left for the cities and embarked on the emigrant ships. Lethargic as these crofters were, beaten by poverty and climate and circumstance, they did not go under without protest. The bitterness of feeling among them caused some ugly outbreaks of violence in the 1880s, when, for example in Skye and Lewis, there were organized riots, because crofters who were behind with their rent were being evicted.

The Government appointed a Commission to enquire and report about the crofters' distress, under Lord Napier and the Duke of Argyll, and the result of this was the Crofters' Holdings Act, passed in 1886. It gave these smallholders legal security of tenure, subject to very reasonable conditions, so that they should no longer live under fear of eviction, and it entitled them to compensation for any permanent improvements they made if they did themselves decide to leave their holdings. Rents were revised and in many cases much reduced, and arrears for some of them were cancelled.

The Act would have been more beneficial had all the recommendations of the Commission been fully carried through, but it did bring good results. The crofters now began to take the initiative in improving their houses, steadings and dykes, and even in planning some crop rotation. But it came too late, and conditions were too hard. The crofting districts needed piped water supplies, electricity and a wholesale scheme of improved roads, all of which were gradually introduced, but not until the 20th century was well advanced.

The most noticeable and rapid improvements date from 1943, when the North of Scotland Hydro-Electric Board was set up. Its work has unquestionably brought new amenities of the greatest importance to the crofters. In the interval, men and women continued to book single tickets by rail and sea. Nearly a quarter of Scotland's population lived in the Highland counties in 1881: fifty years later, less than one-tenth. The Commissioners who investigated the situation in 1883 were impressed by the character of the people they met: they wrote of the 'decency, courtesy, virtue and even mental refinement' of crofters inhabiting the squalid black houses. Scotland lost citizens she could ill spare in the depopulation of those areas.

In the cities, the half-century from 1870 onwards proved a most crucial time. There was such rapid and impressive change that to cross from the rural areas into the industrial belt was like entering a different country.

All over the world, capital goods, the raw materials and machines that make the articles we buy over the counters, were becoming the basis of industrial organization. In Scotland, too, heavy industry took possession, especially in the land between the Forth and the Clyde. From the engineering works of this industrial belt, quantities of machines, machine tools, boilers, locomotives, metal equipment of all kinds were sent to customers in all parts of the world. With these exports there went abroad specialists skilled in their use, to demonstrate how they were made and how they should be handled and repaired. There were to be long-term results of British success in this direction: as R. C. K. Ensor puts it, 'we were equipping our customers to cease buying from us.'

It was in marine engineering and in shipbuilding that Scotland specially succeeded. This meant that Glasgow dominated the economic scene, because of the concentration of shipyards and machine-shops on the Clyde. John Brown & Co. in particular became famous because of the battleships, cruisers, merchant vessels and luxury liners the firm built, but there were many other Clydeside builders too, whose ships became familiar on all the oceans—for example Stephen of Linthouse, and the Fairfield Shipbuilding & Engineering Company.

The Crofting Village of Keills, Isle of Jura.

Photo. Douglas Scott 1956.

Ships, like machines and locomotives, were now being made very largely of steel. The processes involved in the production of finished steel were worked up to a high standard of efficiency in Scotland during the 1880s and 1890s. Steel production combined with shipbuilding brought wealth into the country to an extent never experienced before and at the turn of the century the promoters and senior officials of the successful plants must have thought that prosperity had come to stay. On the other hand, the resources of iron ore, still needed for so many processes, were becoming exhausted and by 1900 considerably more iron ore was imported from abroad than could be produced at home, a marked change from the early 1860s.

Oil was available for processing in the black shale fields of the Lothians and Fife. It was refined into paraffin and other products and the oil works employed many thousands of workers until the last thirty years of the 19th century when American, Burmese and other foreign companies were able to send better and cheaper oils into Europe. The Scottish industry survived this competition by concentrating on other substances in the shale, such as ammonia and tar. In 1913 about £165,000 net profits were made in this way.

As yet neither oil nor electricity could compete with coal. All branches of industry and transport were dependent on it, and domestic consumption was very high. In 1854, the year's output in Scotland was $7\frac{1}{2}$ million tons, in 1908 it reached 39 millions, of which more than a third was exported. The coalfields were concentrated in Lanarkshire, Ayrshire and Fife. Many of them had been in use for a long time and were therefore old-fashioned in design and equipment, and it was almost impossible to modernize the working of such mines, because the old cuttings, shafts and passages determined the nature of later developments. Nonetheless, mechanical improvements had been made since the bad early days. Coal-cutting machinery, electrical equipment for lighting, signalling and ventilation, small underground railways and steam haulage were among these.

As soon as the World War broke out in 1914, an artificial boom stimulated industry all over the United Kingdom. There was a sharply accelerated demand for textiles, because uniforms, blankets and cotton products for webbing and the basis of tyres were needed in enormous quantity for the armed forces. The munitions drive meant that in iron and steel works there was almost unlimited scope for expansion. The crisis imposed terrific strain on the Scottish industrial belt which contributed enormously to the war effort. This was true in textiles, in chemicals, in coal, but it was specially evident in engineering and most of all shipping. Clydeside and other yards were under hectic pressure to make good the losses of the fleet in battle and from submarines.

The emergency strained the farming areas to an almost comparable degree. By 1914, Britain was importing something like two-thirds of her food supplies. This obviously meant disaster, because of the naval blockade and the attacks of submarines on the merchant fleet. Emergency plans were drafted to increase the production of all kinds of food, but especially cereals, at home. County Agricultural Executive Committees were formed and the Ministry of Food set up. By the end of 1917, over 280,000 extra acres had been ploughed in England and Wales. This was a tremendous feat. Men were being called up into the forces all the time and the fields had to be tilled by about one-third of the normal number of labourers, though women did their turn and prisoners-of-war were employed on the work as well. There was heavy anxiety in the whole business for farmers, who dreaded a sudden drop in prices once the war was over, which might leave them committed to long-term capital investments in the land, with a new and much higher wage scale for labourers.

Scotland made a very big contribution to this food production drive. Much of her land could never be put under cereals because it is so mountainous and poor, and much had deteriorated to a dangerously low level in recent decades, but 51,000 extra acres were ploughed up for the production of wheat, oats and root crops. The harvests were good and somehow they were taken in, though such a high proportion of Scots joined up that the labour problem was acute. Transport difficulties prevented full use being made of the fish, eggs and dairy produce of the more remote parts of the country which were isolated by roads of severe gradient

and unreliable surface. The prices commanded by the grain
however were high and there was a brief appearance of prosperity
on some of the farms which could produce cereal crops. This was
to prove short-lived.

When peace came, the economic life of the world was completely disrupted: and the financial arrangements set in motion
by the Treaty of Versailles did nothing to help matters. Britain
was by now so bound up with Europe and America that, when
trade cycles or sudden disaster brought boom or slump elsewhere,
the British were bound to suffer with everybody else. And in the
early 1920s there began a long trade depression. There were
periods of alleviation when the full seriousness of the situation
was somewhat masked, but the downward trend of business and
commerce continued till 1929, when America's Wall Street
collapse shook the security of her customers throughout the world.
For some three or four years after that there was the most
appalling stagnation in trade and everywhere people suffered.
From about 1933, improvement slowly began. By 1939, that slow
drive towards greater prosperity had not had time to take full
effect—but re-armament cured unemployment.

Very soon after the First War, it became obvious that people
could no longer afford to buy British manufactures, and that we
were not going to recover markets lost during the war. On the
contrary, our own shops began to sell cheap foreign products—
textiles, bicycles, household gear, equipment of many kinds—
with which our producers could not compete.

Scotland suffered with the rest of the country. There was a
brief revival in the shipyards immediately after the war, because
the merchant fleet needed repair and replacement. This did not
last and, before long, recently launched merchant ships appeared
in the Gareloch and elsewhere, lying up unused, because there
was no business for them to do. The depression hit the engineering
trade equally hard. Shipbuilding and steel production are so
enormously costly that they respond more violently than most
other industries to international slump, because when people
sense that bad times are coming they at once cancel orders for
new heavy equipment. Had Scottish industry been geared to the
making of small articles, and the consumer goods used and

constantly replaced in daily life, the disaster would not have been so acute.

By 1931, the output of pig-iron in Scotland dropped to less than a quarter of what it had been in 1920; so did the production of steel ingots and castings. In 1913, the Clyde shipyards had completed in twelve months very nearly 760,000 tons of shipping: in 1933, the figure was 56,368, a drop of over 700,000 tons. Coal production by the 1930s was about a third of what it had been before the war.

Fully three-quarters of the Scottish people were living in the confined region of the industrial belt where the heavy industries had absorbed the major part of capital and labour. It was almost impossible to rescue the economy of such a district, but the problem was aggravated by the agricultural depression too. Scottish farmers suffered, just as they had dreaded doing, from the falling prices of the 1920s, and many of them went bankrupt.

Most of the industrial belt was officially classified as a De pressed Area. In 1934, the Government Commission, appointed to enquire into the Depressed Areas, issued a report on the West Lothian Coal and Shalefield, the Ayrshire Coalfield, Cowdenbeath and Lochgelly in Fife, districts round Falkirk, Port Glasgow and Alexandria and the whole of Lanarkshire, excluding Glasgow, which was treated as a separate problem. In this highly industrialized and over-populated area, there were whole districts which had lost their one and only industry, so that the inhabitants had literally no alternative employment, and up to 60 per cent. of them were out of work. Almost two-thirds of Scotland's unemployed were concentrated in this terrible region, but there was unemployment in many other places too, especially in the fishing towns round the North Coast, where competition from Norway and elsewhere was complicating the issue.

Many thousands of the unemployed remained without work for several years. Children left school at fourteen and could not find jobs, so that young people in the Depressed Areas grew up without the discipline and incentive of work, frustrated, embittered, and often crushed in spirit. The Carnegie United Kingdom Trust published in 1937 a short survey called *Disinherited Youth* in which are summarized the main facts about unemployment between the ages of 18 and 25 in Glasgow, Liverpool and Cardiff. It is a most sensitively written document, full of understanding, at once compassionate and realistic. It shows with terrible lucidity how deeply the experiences of the 1930s embittered a whole generation of young men and women. Educated people suffered with uneducated, skilled with unskilled, and it cost them their confidence in themselves, in society, in the future, in religion.

For the first few months of unemployment, people drew Insurance Benefit, after that they were put onto Unemployment Assistance, for which they had to report twice weekly at the local Labour Exchange. In 1920, a man drew 15/- a week, a woman 12/-, boys 7/6d., girls 6/6d.; children at school, up to the age of sixteen, were allowed 1/- a week. Thus a man, his wife and one child had to live on 28/- a week, finding rent, fuel, clothing and food for all three.

These figures did not improve as the years went by, because the Government wanted to reduce the expense caused by the 'dole'. It was because of this that the Means Test was introduced as a condition of Unemployment Assistance. The Means Test was a worse indignity than reporting at Labour Exchanges, for people with any spirit or independence. If families joined together and shared a home to reduce overhead costs, the Means Test led to their Unemployment Assistance being reduced to the point when a grown man would draw so little as 3/- or 4/- a week. It led to subterfuges of many kinds, to the break-up of family life and to deep resentments which moulded the character of children in their early years. It was one of the most unhappy features of the long-drawn-out disaster.

One cannot escape the fact that much of the suffering and still more of the frustration and embitterment caused by the Depression could have been mitigated if a better tradition had grown up among the owners and managers during the decades between 1870 and 1920. Materialists on the make were responsible for much social injustice and for gross misuse of resources. Callous and careless mistakes were made, sincere and well-intentioned errors of judgement accepted, bold measures of relief obstructed.

And yet the policy of having Unemployment Assistance at all marked an important change. In earlier periods of depression, nothing of this kind had been done. Older wage-earners regarded it as something to be thankful for. The Means Test itself would not have borne so hardly on people but for the fact that it was applied by untrained Labour Exchange officials who had little skill in such work.

The magnitude of the disaster was due to the fact that people had not yet understood how to manipulate the economic laws of a world-wide community. In 1936, J. M. Keynes published his *General Theory of Employment, Interest and Money*, just when F. D. Roosevelt was launching the New Deal in America, and these two men did more than anybody else to show how government finance, capital investment and public works can be used to tide a country over a period of slump. The collapse of the 1930s was irretrievable, but Keynes in Britain and Roosevelt in America helped to ensure that future crises would be differently handled.

CHAPTER 30

Political and Social Change

The curse of Britain at the end of last century was poverty. It was worse in Scotland than almost anywhere else. Unless one has envisaged what it was like, the political and social changes of the last eighty years cannot be understood. It can best be seen by considering first the houses in which the poor had to live and then the food they could afford to buy.

In cities, towns, villages and clachans, Scottish wage-earners had been expected over a period of many decades to rear their families in one-roomed dwellings.

The Highland crofter inhabited what was known as a 'black house', built of stone, without lime, roofed with heather thatch, provided with one door, no chimney and no window. A beginning was made in the 1860s to replace these hovels by something better, but by 1914 there were still some in use. In well-appointed farms, unmarried labourers were put to live in bothies, tiny single-roomed apartments built alongside the byres in the farm-yard, to be shared by several men for eating and sleeping.

In the cities, tall stone tenements housed great numbers of families in 'single-ends', one-roomed flats, with outside sanitation shared by the whole building, and no piped water for anybody. In 1888, one person in every four of Glasgow's population lived in a 'single-end'.

All the cities of the industrial belt expanded, swallowing up nearby villages and making them into slums. By 1911, nearly 9 per cent. of all Scots people lived in one-roomed houses; in Glasgow and Dundee, 50 per cent. were officially termed 'over-crowded', which meant there were more than two people per room, so that at least seven would inhabit a two-room and kitchen flat. Even in 1951, about 30 per cent. were still in one or two-roomed dwellings and in Glasgow nearly a tenth of the people lived in

Scotland since 1870

'single-ends'. It was a continual and heart-breaking struggle to keep up a decent standard of family life in one room where not only cooking, sleeping and washing had to be done, for also in this one room sickness, childbirth and death had to be witnessed even by small children. Small wonder that there was so much chronic disease. People in such conditions could not even stack kitchen utensils or store food properly, so that they could certainly never nourish their families adequately. Small wonder too that illegitimacy was an everyday matter and that there was more drunkenness in Scottish cities than elsewhere in Britain.

Thomas Ferguson, in his book *Scottish Social Welfare* 1860-1914, shows that standards of living improved in the better farming districts after 1870. He also describes investigations in Dundee and Glasgow in the early 1900s which revealed how miserably poor was the normal diet of working people in cities. Families living on less than 20/- a week simply could not feed their children well enough, and there were many such families. Similar facts are recorded in *Food, Health and Income*, a short work published in 1936 by John Boyd Orr. He set out statistics which show that, in the early 1930s, 50 per cent. of the British nation were living on less than 20/- per head per week, and that in these families less than 8/- was spent on food for each member each week. One person in ten had a total income of less than 10/- a week, of which less than 4/- was spent on food, and there were people spending as little as 2/-.

Boyd Orr showed that in the higher income groups much more milk, eggs, fruit, vegetables, meat and fish were eaten; people spending less than 10/- a week each lived on potatoes and bread, cheap jam, margarine and tea, to which Scottish workers added a good deal of porridge. Nutrition in childhood affects growth. In 1933, children of well-to-do families reached a height as much as $5\frac{1}{2}$ inches more than that of children in poor families, and with this obvious physical difference went less easily detected variations in health and stamina.

'In animal husbandry', wrote Boyd Orr, 'an optimum standard, far from being utopian, is regarded as good practice. Every intelligent stock farmer in rearing animals tries to get a minimum diet for maximum health and fitness. A suggestion that he should

362

use a lower standard would be regarded as absurd. If the children of the three lower income groups (from 10/- to 20/- a week) were reared for profit like young farm stock, giving them a diet below the requirements for health would be financially unsound. Unfortunately, the health and physical fitness of the rising generation are not marketable commodities which can be assessed in terms of money.'

The food rationing of the Second World War represented a much higher standard of nourishment for working people in Boyd Orr's three lowest income groups—half the British population—than they had ever experienced before. In Scotland, the working people of the industrial belt had been consistently under-nourished throughout the period following 1870. Medical Officers of Health and doctors working in slum districts had been saying so for years and years.

Today it is an accepted principle in Britain that people cannot be allowed to go without the basic necessities of life. The poverty accepted by earlier generations shocks us. Why was it tolerated by a wealthy and supposedly Christian community? How did it come about that changes were at last made?

Part of the trouble was that well-to-do people in the 19th century did not know what poverty meant. Till the end of the century, little was done to investigate the facts about it or to bring them home to people in authority. If you read the Parliamentary Debates recorded in Hansard, you will find that the view of many members could be summed up in the words—'Depend upon it, the sufferings of the poor are greatly exaggerated.'

While many people were ignorant about the problem, or indifferent to it, those who could have done something about it were influenced by theories which militated against reform. One of these was derived from the writings of Adam Smith and Ricardo, reinforced by the Utilitarians and the Manchester School. This taught that the prices of everything, including labour, are determined by demand, by the fluctuations of the market; and that if you interfere with this process of price-fixing, you make things worse. Therefore if wages were raised beyond the minimum at which you could hire labour, the price of the product would rise, the expansion of demand would be arrested and this would bring neither you nor your workers any advantage. Poor Law orthodoxy was another influence against reform. According to this, the relief of poverty by donations of money, whether through public or private channels, increases the supposed inclination of the poor to live by begging rather than by work.

This ignorance and these theories were gradually broken down. Well-to-do women of high intelligence were still excluded from professional life, but they were permitted to go into social work and what they saw for themselves, at close quarters in the homes of the very poor, they freely disclosed. Beatrice Webb was the most famous of these women, but there were many others in her generation. The Charity Organization Society made a study of poverty which helped to change public opinion. The Settlement movement, notably at Toynbee Hall in East London, brought into the poorest districts of the great cities highly educated young men, destined for positions of authority in the Church, the Civil Service, politics and the professions. They went to live in the settlements and got to know the slum-dwellers as friends. The experiences of all these individuals, their publications in journals, their pressure on public opinion, led to the great social surveys of Charles Booth in London and Seebohm Rowntree in York. Among these young men were some still prominent in public affairs, like William Beveridge and Clement Attlee.

The press contributed to this process of enlightenment, especially the *News Chronicle*, which ran a campaign against sweating. The Royal Commission on this subject revealed conditions which shocked people very deeply in the early 1890s. In the Rutherglen Chemical Works near Glasgow for example, a twelve-hour day and a seven-day week were worked, day and night shifts alternating. This state of affairs inflamed people who by now had become much more aware of the scandal of poverty.

During these years, the nature of the electorate became very different. In 1884, all adult men were allowed to vote, both for Members of Parliament and for Town Councillors. After 1889, County Councils were established to administer county districts, and soon Parish Councils were also set up, all popularly elected. So people who had never before been able to exercise influence could now share in the choice of responsible representatives both in local and in national government.

And this was the period too when the Trade Unions were gathering power and extending their influence from skilled to unskilled trades. Though Trade Unionism did not become so strong among Scottish working men as among English in the last decades of the 19th century, they did make progress and their influence began to count for something. The Scottish Union leaders were men of great ability and strength. They worked not only in Scotland and for Scottish Unions but also in England where Keir Hardie and Alexander Macdonald, for example, did a great deal for the coal-miners' organization, in the belief that a nation-wide mobilization of workers' resources was needed.

The Union leaders were determined to get the hours of work reduced and to secure a rise in wages, both reforms which were long overdue, and they realized that only by fighting for their rights could they secure success; in the late 19th and early 20th centuries therefore there occurred many tragic strikes, a few of which were followed by slight improvements in working conditions. Employers of labour made a bad showing in these years. Most of them were careless about the lives and safety of their workers, especially in the mines. They resisted, with all their might, the very just wage claims put forward by the Unions. Their behaviour fostered the idea that class warfare between employer and employed was natural and inevitable.

The leaders of labour were led by their chequered story of success and failure to the conclusion that only by entering politics could they make any real progress, and because of the recent electoral reform they discovered that they could organize the working-class vote. They wanted to secure by legislation such reforms as the eight-hour day, a national minimum wage, arbitration courts for the settlement of wage disputes, state insurances against accident and sickness. They also believed that the means of production—the mines, heavy industries, railways and so on—must be nationalized, because only so did they think the community could be safeguarded against vested interest and private gain.

Scotland since 1870

In Scotland these ideas were eagerly fastened upon. One of the first Labour M.P.s was Keir Hardie, a fine man, who won everybody's respect and who knew from personal experience what the extremes of poverty could do to a family. The Labour Party, like the Trade Union Movement, owed much in these years to Keir Hardie and a number of other Scottish leaders, Alexander Macdonald and Alexander Campbell in particular. It was in no small measure due to the co-operation of these Scottish leaders that the Labour Party gained in power more quickly then might have been expected. By 1905, it had won twenty-nine seats in the House of Commons, and as the years went by it succeeded in exercising a formidable influence in Parliament. Its success was built up by a Scot, whose leadership counted enormously in his earlier years, though later he lost the confidence of many Labour members—Ramsay Macdonald.

An epoch-making attack, the first of its kind, was made upon poverty by the Liberal Government of 1905. It was led until 1908 by the Glasgow-born Scot, Sir Henry Campbell Bannerman, and after his death in that year by H. H. Asquith. R. C. K. Ensor describes Campbell Bannerman as a man whose nature was 'to move persistently to the left', and also as one who had qualities of the first order—'shrewdness, steadfast will, directness of purpose and unselfish devotion to his party's cause'. His name became 'the watch word of the radicals and of the young'. His rare statesmanship was shown in his handling of the South African situation. Field Marshal Smuts, years later, said that Campbell Bannerman's negotiations in 1906 led to the evolution of the Commonwealth, a piece of work unequalled in imperial records for nobility and originality. But his government made history too by its programme of social reform, which itself brought in a new era. Campbell Bannerman enlisted the services of some extraordinarily able colleagues, and after his death Asquith was no less successful in his appointments. Among these men were Winston Churchill and Lloyd George.

The Liberals produced legislation to improve the position of smallholders, to safeguard merchant seamen, to extend workers' compensation. They started Old Age Pensions, free school meals for necessitous children and regular medical examination of all

children in State Schools. Winston Churchill was responsible for
the Trade Boards Act of 1909, which initiated a system of
consultation between employers and employed about wage rates,
in an attempt to put an end to sweating. Though it was started
in a very limited way, its success led to much more widespread
use of the system later on. Also in 1909, Labour Exchanges were
set up. W. H. Beveridge was appointed to organize them. He
probably knew more than anybody at that time about unemployment, because he had made a scientific and authoritative study
of it. He had in fact already formed some of the conclusions to
which he held all his life and in which he continually educated
public opinion. He designed the Labour Exchange to assist
unemployed and casually employed men in their search for work.
They were not used at first so much as Beveridge had hoped,
because employers were obstructive in the early stages, but they
became much more effective in later years. So the medieval
method of hawking labour from door to door began to die out.

More important than any other measure was Lloyd George's
National Insurance Act of 1911. This made regular contributions
by employers and employed in certain trades compulsory, so
that men who fell out of work or became ill might receive insurance
benefits. It was the beginning of a completely new approach to
the handling of poverty in Britain.

Today when the welfare point of view is so widely accepted, it
is difficult to realize what a revolution took place between 1905
and 1911. One can estimate the extent of the change by reading
such reminiscences as those of Hugh Miller. His young manhood
was spent in the middle years of last century: thoughtful, compassionate, intellectual as he was, he took for granted conditions
which seem to the modern reader barbarous. Osgood Mackenzie's
A Hundred Years in the Highlands shows the same sort of thing.
Still more revealing are the terrible records of accident and
disaster in the mining and engineering industries.

When the First World War broke out, the shortage of munition
workers became so acute that wages rose suddenly and dramati-
cally, indeed these people had never handled so much money
before. They became much more conscious of their rights and of
their power to enforce those rights. At the same time, many

well-to-do British boys aged eighteen and nineteen went into
trench warfare as subalterns. A high proportion were killed, but
the survivors came back filled with respect for the private soldiers
beside whom they had fought. These young men believed that
class feeling in industry could and must be overcome. Though
they were not at first in positions of authority, their point of
view made an impression and these were the men of influence
during the 1930s and 1940s.

And then the great Depression came and poverty was once
again the nation's scourge. But by this time people had outgrown
the classical economic theory that you cannot effectively interfere
with economic process by means of Government action. So the
unemployed who had used up their insurance benefits were given
the assistance described in the last chapter. Minimal as these
payments were and insufficient for the maintenance of health,
they were nevertheless paid out on the principle that the community is responsible for its members when calamity comes to
them.

The climax of half a century's work towards comprehensive
welfare came during the Second World War. William Beveridge
was asked to be Chairman of an inter-departmental Committee,
to clear up inconsistencies and gaps in what Churchill described
as 'our incomparable system of social insurance'. A better choice
of chairman could not have been made. All his life Beveridge had
worked at the problems of poverty, want and unemployment; he
had already published original views on these subjects; he had
adopted without reserve the principles set out in Eleanor Rath-
bone's book on Family Allowances. Instead of patiently working
at the detailed administration of Workmen's Compensation,
Health and Unemployment Insurance, Old Age and Widows'
Pensions, Beveridge suddenly came out in 1942 with an entirely
new scheme. He produced the plan for a complete system of
social security, the blue-print of the Welfare State.

The Beveridge Report captured the imagination of the
electorate in this country and in the Forces overseas. The General
Election of 1945 returned a Labour Government, supported by
an overwhelming majority. There is no doubt that one reason
for this was that men and women, hitherto right of the centre in

political outlook, now wanted Beveridge's plan to be implemented. So at last, in 1948, a National Health Service and a complete system of National Insurance were put on the Statute Book.

In a history of Scotland, one is justified in expecting to find some record of how events worked out in Scotland. This chapter has been largely concerned with a movement of public opinion and with legislation which affected Britain as a whole. Scottish people were involved for the most part because they were British rather than because they were Scottish. This trend in affairs had weighed on the minds of prominent Scotsmen for a long time.

During the 20th century, the machinery of government became vastly more complicated. The improvement in Social Welfare was won and maintained by prolonged legislative work in Parliament: it was administered by whole new phalanxes of officials employed in the enlarged offices of local Government organizations. The nationalization of industry was carried through after the Second World War by the Labour Cabinet and the necessary legislation was so cumbersome that it was found to override traditions of importance in many parts of the country. Democracy which undertakes the duties of a Socialist State must be served by a bureaucracy and a top-heavy bureaucracy at that.

Scottish people had long been exasperated by matters of urgency to them being held up by the congestion at Westminster. It seemed that it was impossible even to erect in a Glasgow side-street a notice saying 'No Thoroughfare' without applying to London and being kept waiting for months on end.

There was good reason for the angry frustration which grew up in Scotland. People felt that Scottish concerns were shelved, that Parliamentary debating time on Scottish matters was much too brief, that evidence submitted by Scottish representatives was neglected, that Government grants for projects north of the Border were niggardly, that congestion at Westminster was unduly holding up the administration of Scottish business.

Some of the difficulties so far as Scotland was concerned had been understood at quite an early stage and efforts were made to meet them. In 1885, the Earl of Rosebery was given the post of Under-Secretary at the Home Office with Scotland as his special charge. This was because people felt that nobody was really responsible for Scottish affairs and that it was now necessary to revive the old idea, long since in abeyance, of a special Parliamentary Secretary for Scotland.

Rosebery found his new appointment anything but satisfactory because he had neither time nor opportunity to handle Scottish affairs adequately. Within less than a year he succeeded in getting a further change made, and he was supported on both sides of the House in doing so. A Scottish Office entirely distinct and separate from the Home Office was formed, under the direction of a special Minister, who was given Cabinet rank (in 1892), and who was assisted by a whole staff of officials, themselves Scots. Further, in 1894, all Scottish members of the House of Commons were formed into a Scottish Grand Committee whose business was to discuss Bills concerning Scottish affairs.

These changes were well intended, but they proved disappointing. The Scottish Office was in London, four hundred miles distant from the country whose affairs it was supposed to run, its senior members were inaccessible and overworked, and the Grand Committee—which became a Standing Committee permanently established—was not empowered to debate the Scottish Bills in principle, but only in practical application.

The removal of the Scottish Office to Edinburgh in 1939 was therefore very literally a step in the right direction. At St. Andrew's House in their own capital city, citizens of Scotland could now meet the Senior Civil Servants who were administering their affairs and thrash things out with them in discussion.

But Scottish thinkers were still indignant about the way in which their country was being run. Delays at Westminster constantly obstructed proper consideration of Scotland's particular problems, which were indeed very different from many of those affecting England and Wales, and which involved special knowledge of background and current development. It irked people very much too to realize that, even if the wheels of Government moved without any obstruction at all, there was no constitutional way in which Scotsmen could influence legislation in principle at a formative stage, even when it concerned principally or only their own institutions. Scottish Members numbered 70 in a House of over 500. They therefore could not exercise real

Political and Social Change

influence. So an unprecedented measure of devolution was worked out, a most interesting political experiment. In 1948 the Scottish Standing Committee was given authority to examine all Bills affecting Scotland at the second reading and to make recommendations; it was also empowered fully to discuss financial estimates in connection with projects proposed for Scotland. The Committee was to include all the 70 Scottish M.P.s with ten to fifteen others, appointed to ensure that its political composition was approximately in line with that of the House of Commons as a whole.

These changes in Scottish administration are so recent that it is not easy to say how far they will solve the problem. There are some who think they hardly touch it. The views of these critics are discussed in the next chapter.

CHAPTER 31

The Background to Contemporary Thought

It is a bold thing to try to understand the mood of a people at any particular period in history, most of all a contemporary period. Nonetheless it is sometimes of value to consider the influences which have contributed to it and in this chapter the cultural, political and religious movements of the last eighty years are discussed. It is impossible for these movements to be completely or comprehensively described, and much of what has to be said is more a matter of opinion or of interpretation than of history, because it is all so recent and because one is personally involved.

Lord Cockburn complained in the early 19th century of a falling-away in the cultural life, and declared that he found the new race of politically minded young men excruciatingly dull. Perhaps he was indulging himself a little in the prerogative of the older generation which always thinks young men are not what they were; perhaps, as was his habit, he had diagnosed the mind of the times with exactness and understanding.

The 19th century proved to be a time when British writers produced prose that will always live, and poetry of the highest and near-highest quality. On the other hand, the artists and architects could not touch the standard set by their predecessors. Ugliness was tolerated, indeed admired, both indoors and out, even ladies' fashions became over-decorative and unbecoming and everywhere people seemed satisfied with material rather than aesthetic values. As Cockburn said: 'The exact old thing was not.'

In Scotland, the spirit of the times was as apparent as in England. Critics of Scottish history have tried to explain it by saying that the Presbyterian Church discouraged the arts, or that Scotland was overshadowed by England, but the trouble lay elsewhere. You cannot read the records of Queen Victoria's time in Scotland without seeing where Scottish energies were being concentrated. In his book *Economic Developments in Victorian Scotland*, W. H. Marwick describes industrialization as 'an influence more hostile to culture than Calvinistic Puritanism or English domination'.

Regrettably, Scotsmen who employed architects had apparently unlimited resources, except when they were planning working-class houses. Their sham Gothic and sham baronial structures are with us still and there is little comfort either in looking at them or living in them. The lovely work of Robert Adam and his generation was despised and the careful restoration of ancient buildings, especially churches, by people with insufficient knowledge often spoiled them. Mid-19th century artists painted, as their public wished them to do, innumerable Highland Cattle, Stags at Bay and Sheep in Twilight. In Thomas Carlyle and R. L. Stevenson, Scotland had two authors who won recognition, but from about 1870 onwards novelists became obsessed with misdirected romanticism. So there emerged what has been rudely but justifiably called the 'Ben and Glen' or 'Kailyard' style of writing. People's power of appreciation seemed to be blunted. They sought no new forms of expression and they mishandled the old ones.

Towards the end of the century however a fresh inspiration came into Scottish painting, especially through the work of Robert Scott Lauder, who as painter and teacher gave a whole generation of artists a new directions and a new standard. Some of his pupils went to London, where their work was at once influential, Orchardson, for example, and McWhirter. The most important of them all was William McTaggart who grew up speaking Gaelic near the village of Machrihanish, and who spent most of his life in Scotland. His chief interest was in the effect of light and atmosphere, especially on the surface of the sea and on clouds. He was in fact an Impressionist, though he was an original one, who formed his style before the French school became well-known.

In the last twenty years of the century, a group of artists, centred on Glasgow and known as the Glasgow School, began to produce pictures of quite a new kind. Among them were W. T. MacGregor and E. A. Hornel.

These artists abandoned the convention of narrative pictures. They were interested in rich colour, bold composition, decorative pattern, and they handled paint in daring original ways. There was no defect of craftsmanship in their work however as there was with some of their would-be successors. D. Y. Cameron, Muirhead Bone and James Guthrie were all artists of this school who survived both wars, but whose influence was important well before 1914. The fine work done by these three contributed very much to the revival in art. Another aspect was represented by Pittendrigh Macgillivray, the sculptor, and yet another by Charles Rennie Mackintosh and Robert Lorimer, both architects.

Mackintosh was perhaps the most successful of them all. The bold and massive lines of his buildings combined strength with proportion, they were in keeping with the best traditions of earlier Scottish architects and yet the designs were original and stimulating. Admirers of Scottish baronial styles were not pleased, but Mackintosh's work is refreshing to see because it has dignity and there is nothing insincere or bogus about it. He was greatly admired on the continent, where his influence can be detected in much modern work.

The Glasgow School was not the only sign of a reviving culture. From the turn of the century onwards, Scotsmen began to influence the literary forms of the day in many directions. In 1901, George Douglas Brown brought admirers of the Kailyard style down to earth with his tragic story of Scottish village life, *The House with Green Shutters*, a book which made an immense impression. A. J. Cronin and George Blake in the 1930s wrote powerful novels about the city and the river in industrial Scotland. J. M. Barrie, Neil Munro, Compton Mackenzie, Eric Linklater were all prose writers who covered a wide range and produced work of lasting value. Edwin Muir's poetry was of a higher order than any Scot had written for a long time. As novelist, historian, biographer, John Buchan won himself a place in the affections of a very large public, both in Scotland and far afield. These are only some of the well-known names associated with the literary side of this new Scottish Renaissance.

During the forty years preceding the First World War, a ferment of new ideas was also at work among politicians and economists. Until the 1880s the Scottish electorate had been almost consistently Liberal, except of course in some of the shires, where landowners and farmers always voted Conservative. The Radical groups in the cities worked against the tide of public opinion, in their support of the ideals the Chartists had tried to achieve, and it was difficult for them to make headway, so entrenched was the Liberal establishment. In the 1880s, the balance between Liberals and Conservatives was suddenly disturbed. The upheaval, which shocked the complacency of old-style politicians, was partly due to the Irish Home Rule crisis, partly to the appearance of the new Labour Party.

Scottish people had no love for the Irish. They had seen too much of them in the slums of the industrial areas for one thing, and they dreaded their religious influence for another. To grant Home Rule to a predominantly Roman Catholic Ireland would mean that the Ulster Presbyterians, who were largely of Scottish origin, would be submerged. So Gladstone's Irish schemes met with a very critical reception in Scotland, where many former Liberals broke away during the 1880s and 1890s, to become either out-and-out Conservatives, or Liberal-Unionists who were willing to vote with Conservatives. Although the Liberals survived the shock of this long controversy, and returned to power in full force in 1906, they never recovered their old supremacy in Scotland.

While some Liberals were turning to Conservative leadership, others were attracted to Socialism in general and to the rising Labour Party in particular. Working people supported Keir Hardie and Cunninghame Graham and the rest of them, for reasons suggested in the last chapter, but the new movement received much impetus too from an increasing number of professional and middle-class men and women. There was much more awareness of the need for social reforms towards the end of the 19th century and the seriousness and thoroughness with which the Fabians set out their doctrines made a deep impression in Scotland as well as in England. Sidney and Beatrice Webb and Graham Wallas brought in a totally new way of thinking about society and politics.

Socialism was one new dynamic force which undermined the hold of orthodox politicians north of the Border. The uproar over

Irish Home Rule contributed to the rise of another. People began to say that, if Home Rule were being seriously considered for Ireland, there were good reasons why it should be seriously considered for Scotland too. The proposition did not arouse emotions or passions comparable with the outbursts over the Irish question, but Scottish M.P.s and their constituents were becoming more and more indignant about the congestion of business at Westminster. The bottleneck was doing Scotland harm and people felt that this should not be tolerated. In 1889, G. P. Clark, the Member for Caithness, moved a resolution in the House of Commons that Scotland should have a National Parliament for 'the management and control of Scottish affairs'. Similar resolutions were raised each year till 1895 and always voted down. General irritation began to grow more pronounced and it was not allayed by the creation of the Scottish Secretary-ship and the Scottish Standing Committee. But as yet there was no widespread or nationalist fervour about the matter and business leaders in Scotland, especially those of the industrial belt, were against anything that might weaken the Union.

When the Liberal Government of 1905 came in, support for Home Rule in Scotland became much stronger. There was no suggestion that the sovereignty of the Imperial Parliament should be impaired, but far more people now wanted a scheme of devolution, by which a Scottish Parliament should handle Scottish business. Bills framed to implement such a scheme were introduced several times between 1908 and 1914 when, because of the outbreak of war, the matter was dropped.

During the great Depression of the 1920s, feeling about Scottish Home Rule suddenly became much more pronounced. People trying to live on Unemployment Assistance, those subjected to the Means Test, and others who were moved to angry compassion by the terrible destitution in Scotland were inclined to think that the suffering was due in part to Westminster's habit of shelving Scottish business, although conditions on Tyneside and in South Wales were in fact even more acute. Furious comment was published about the negative attitude of the Government towards the Scottish Fisheries, which were suffering from foreign competition: about the refusal of a subsidy to farmers producing oats, while wheat-growers, of whom there were relatively few in Scotland, were generously assisted: about the limitation laid upon Scottish sugar-beet development. The Scottish railway system was amalgamated with England's in 1921 and this led to the closing down of railway workshops at Kilmarnock and Inverness. There was resentment too over such events as the closing of works at Lennoxtown by the Calico Printers' Association, which was interpreted as an effort to rescue some of Lancashire's lost prosperity, also over the removal of textile machinery from the Clyde Spinning Company of Glasgow to Oldham. People felt that English business interests always had better treatment than Scottish.

All these grievances added up to something more than pre-war dissatisfaction had fastened upon, and during the 1920s there was a fresh spate of Home Rule Bills for Scotland. In 1934, two organizations interested in the problem merged and the Scottish Nationalist party was thus formed. No longer was the concern limited to releasing Scottish administration from the congestion at Westminster. Responsible thinkers now wanted a system which would give Scotsmen authority and control to initiate and draft legislation and to order the financial requirements of it. Extremists were enthusiastic for the Union to be ended. Moderate Nationalists saw no need for this, but were emphatic that fundamental re-adjustment was needed.

There was more to it, however, than legal or financial reform would meet. There was strong feeling now that Scotland was becoming anglicized. Education, the radio, the press, the English chain-stores which were buying up Scottish family firms, the influence of the Civil Service, even of the Trade Unions with their London-based head offices—all these things were undermining the traditions of Scotland, overriding Scottish interests, moulding the ideas and changing the speech of the rising generation north of the Border. In the work of the artists and architects of the Glasgow School, whose standing was now very high, Nationalist sympathizers saw plain evidence of a new Renaissance in culture. In poets such as Hugh McDiarmid and novelists such as George Blake the country was finding a new literary stimulus. The Saltire Society, founded in 1936, was one result of this revival and its success was very significant. This Society sought to foster Scottish literature, music and art, to encourage the study of Gaelic, also of Scottish history and archaeology. The out-and-out Nationalists had as yet limited support, but in their desire to preserve Scottish culture and to gain more control over Scottish administration, they had a great deal of sympathy both in their own country and beyond it.

When the Second World War began, the Scottish Nationalist Movement made little headway, because again such interests seemed of smaller moment to most people than the world's crisis. As soon as peace was made, the tide of Nationalist feeling began to flow once more, with new strength. There were fresh reasons now for Scotsmen to criticize the constitutional status quo. The Welfare State was designed to abolish poverty, to safeguard the health and to ensure the education of everybody's children. It vastly enlarged the bureaucratic controls which all stemmed from Westminster. Less than ever did it appear that Scotsmen would make or implement the decisions which would condition the lives of Scotsmen.

There was great indignation when the naval dockyard at Rosyth was closed and the services at Prestwick Airport curtailed. Britain had been glad enough to use these places in wartime, because of their good geographical situation. Why should they be cut off from the movement of capital and business to the great impoverishment of Scotland as soon as peace came? And Scottish people were exasperated by the long delay of the Government in voting money to build a Forth Bridge for road traffic. To southerners, it seemed a wild extravagance. Those whose business took them northwards up the east side of Scotland found powerful arguments in the expense and frustration of the extra miles they had to drive inland, and in the inadequacy of the car ferry service. There had been support for a Mersey Tunnel, to assist road traffic, why not for a Forth Bridge? Scottish opinion was exasperated by the bland way in which an overwhelmingly English legislature seemed prepared to obstruct measures for which politicians hundreds of miles away could not see any urgency, but which were in fact necessary. And it irritated the Nationalist sympathizers when statutes framed in the interests of

England were embellished with complicated codicils which were supposed to make them applicable also to Scotland.

It became obvious that many people who had hitherto been indifferent were now urgently anxious to see a change made in the administrative if not in the legislative set-up. It was in deference to this feeling that the Government enlarged the scope of the Scottish Standing Committee in 1948. That this did not satisfy Scottish Nationalists was made plain the following year when they produced their significantly named 'Scottish Covenant'. This pledged its signatories—of whom some thousands were enrolled in a few weeks—'in loyalty to the Crown and within the framework of the United Kingdom to do everything in our power to secure for Scotland a Parliament with adequate legislative authority in Scottish affairs'.

The extreme Nationalists draw criticism and censure upon themselves because the Press cannot resist making copy out of their sillier gestures. This should not mask the fact that very many people of proved wisdom and undoubted patriotism are now sympathetic with the more moderate Nationalists. British institutions have never been static, over-organized, bonded to fixed theories, in fact they have erred in the opposite direction. Their great merit has been their capacity for development as circumstances have changed. There is unquestionably room for further change now. It is beyond the capacity of neither Scots nor English to work out a fresh system of government and social organization that would bring fresh satisfaction to both, and such re-thinking need not involve a separation which would undoubtedly impoverish each side.

No assessment of Scottish thought in the last eighty years or so could be attempted unless religious opinion in the country were taken into account. Until the First World War, the hold of organized religion continued to be stronger north of the Border than south of it. Church-going, family prayers, and Sunday School for the children formed part of normal routine for a high proportion of people. This did not include the very poor, the lowest paid navvies and labourers in mine, mill and shipyard— Hugh Miller had noticed in the 1840s and 1850s that these people had no religious connections, and their children and grandchildren as a rule did not form any. This was because cities had expanded rapidly, already existing churches could offer no pew accommodation to incomers, and new churches were not built soon enough in sufficient numbers. The working-class districts in the overcrowded industrial areas often had little mission-halls, run by Church members from 'west-end' congregations; but these could not meet the need and so, in Scottish as in English cities, the very poor were not able to form a tradition of church-going.

Scottish theologians and ministers have made a very great contribution to the Biblical Scholarship which in the last eighty years or so has counted for so much. A fresh understanding of the meaning of Christianity has been the result. In the strength of this, the challenge of Darwinism has been understood. The re-thinking of Christian doctrine which has been stimulated has enabled many leaders in intellectual life, especially in the Universities, to find that their desire to follow Christ was not incompatible with intellectual integrity: and among these a number of prominent scientists have been included. Scottish thinkers have taken a most constructive part in this re-interpretation.

But this fresh approach to religion was not passed on effectively to the general run of laymen, in the first two decades of this century. Sermons rarely touched upon Bible Scholarship, exciting and enlightening as it was. Too many people therefore tacitly assumed that to be a Christian meant tolerating in religion modes of thought no longer respected in science and literature, while others accepted orthodox and traditional teaching without thinking about it independently at all.

On their very doorsteps, Scottish Church people could see misery and destitution, disease and distress. They must have known that in Europe and the East the sum of human pain exceeded anything they themselves could really understand. Somehow these things were accepted. But when the 1914 War broke forth, many Christians in Scotland, as in England, found their faith suddenly assaulted. It seemed impossible to them that a loving God could contenance such tragedy.

The War made a profound and terrible impression on all kinds and classes of people. From every city, village, clachan and glen,

Scotsmen served in all the great battle fronts, they served in thousands in the Army, the Royal Navy, the Merchant Navy, the Royal Flying Corps. The casualties suffered by Britain and the Commonwealth during those four years cost a whole generation a great proportion of its finest people, many of them hardly adult, and Scotland's share in this was terribly high. The oldest regiment of the line in the British Army, the Royal Scots, suffered over 11,000 deaths. This was no exception to the general rule. Earl Haig himself was a Scot and his countrymen served and died in every rank of all the services. The deprivation caused by such loss of life and health in so small a nation made it infinitely difficult for those who survived to reconstruct their country's way of life.

The war years caused a complete break with formerly unquestioned traditions. People were suddenly pitchforked out of familiar surroundings and well-loved homes into circumstances of acute danger, and terrible daily strain. Those who remained at home were subjected also to quite new distresses and soul-destroying pressures. Families were divided, children neglected, home life disrupted. In the upheaval, people reacted with resentful and embittered distaste against the society which had precipitated the disasters. Many of them also turned against the Church and its teachings, about which they were disillusioned. Some of the younger generation blamed the Church for having failed in its mission, others dismissed it as obsolete, irrelevant.

The confusion of mind amongst these young people was one symptom of the nation's trouble. They thought they wanted to think independently, but they lacked both the training and the concentration this demands. They thought they wanted freedom from authority, so that they could make their own decisions, emancipated from old restrictions of principle and tradition, but really they were longing for authoritative direction they could respect. They thought they were done with idealism, that the war had proved the hollowness and the sham of all idealisms, but they discovered in themselves a hunger for new ideals. The one obvious fact from which nobody could escape was that security of any sort, emotional, material or political, was apparently beyond the grasp of everybody. Amongst young people so disillusioned and so lacking in stability, Communist enthusiasts were able to make rapid headway. Communism offered an ideal, a gospel, a crusade, an all-embracing purpose, companionship, authority, discipline. Its weaknesses in logic and in historical interpretation, its duplicity, its cruelty, its usefulness to dictators bent on exploitation—none of this was easily apparent to people brought up in the conditions of spiritual confusion and industrial disaster which followed the war.

By this time, many older people had lost confidence in themselves and in their beliefs. They did not trust themselves to give their children guidance even about basic moralities. In homes and schools, teaching about truth and generosity, integrity and courage was often neglected. Religious instruction in particular reached a new low level, and many children whose parents and grandparents had been God-fearing grew up quite ignorant even of the simplest facts about Christianity. Organized religion seemed for a while to have little chance of survival, church attendance decreased steadily and Sundays were devoted by most people to pleasure or to chores about the house.

The pace of life militated against recovery from this sickness of the spirit. By motor coach, car, train and plane people were on the move, both at work and in leisure-time. Even during the depression, when hunger marches, Labour Exchange queues, destitution up and down every street seemed to be breaking people's hearts, commerce laid hold upon the universal craving for distraction. Dance-halls, public-houses, night clubs and the like exploited the need for time-killing and escape. The radio and the film poured a whole new cacophony of noise into the ears of young and old. And there was loneliness too. The old neighbourliness of village and town was replaced by the impersonal character of huge cities, where people travel great distances to work and lose interest in local community life.

In these very years of apparent failure there became evident some signs of a renaissance in religion. The work of the Student Christian Movement had led, especially in Scotland, to a renewal of interest in Foreign Missions. Young, intelligent missionaries coming out from Universities where they had experienced a sense of union with Christians of other denominations, found the divisions of Christendom in the mission fields intolerable. A returning tide of vitality from these mission fields reinforced the desire at home for Church reunion.

As early as 1900, the Free Church and the United Presbyterian Church had joined together under the name of the United Free Church. Again, in 1929, the Church of Scotland and the United Free Church made a successful union, and in doing so they greatly strengthened their position. Unfortunately, in both cases there was a minority which continued as a separate organization.

This union between Presbyterians has been symptomatic of a new desire among Christians to stand together and face together the challenge of the new paganism, the materialism, the ideologies which are threatening civilization. The World Council of Churches has held a number of conferences in recent years, notably one at Amsterdam in 1948, to which representatives from many nations and many branches of the Christian Church came. The work of the World Council aroused much interest in Scotland, as it did in England. In view of this development it was natural that the two leading branches of the Protestant Church in Britain should wish to draw together. And so, in spite of some important differences in doctrine and tradition, the Church of Scotland and the Church of England have been holding discussions together. The result has been the publication of a preliminary report by a joint body of representatives from both sides in 1957. There is a long way to go before a solution can be worked out which will satisfy the rank and file in these two great national churches, but it is a sign of the times that they are seeking to emphasize the principles they hold in common.

The abandonment of conventional church-going has not really been a loss to the church. There is more sincerity and vitality among its members and adherents today and this is apparent in their activities. In Scotland, as in England and France, Industrial Chaplains have been appointed to work in the factories and this seems to meet a real need, and to elicit a real welcome. The Iona Community has contributed to a recovery among ministers and laymen of the sense of Christian fellowship transcending class: it has afforded a fresh experience of the strength gained in corporate devotions and a new conviction of the mission of the Church. The same hunger for religious guidance is met with on the Housing Estates, especially among young people whose parents have no religious teaching to offer them. One fact which should not be overlooked is that the Roman Catholic Church claims to be growing steadily in numbers, and is probably justified in this claim, though exact statistics are difficult to establish.

The renewed interest in religion has been much fostered by the Religious Department of the BBC. And it has also been stimulated by the Scottish theologians. During the years of the Second World War and since, Christian scholarship has reached the lay public of Scotland in terms which can be more readily understood than in any previous period. This is much needed. The advances in scientific research have given mankind a far greater control over the forces of nature, but they have not given anybody renewed confidence in man himself or in his destiny. The materialism of the age is beginning to produce its own reaction and some people are now more willing to turn to spiritual resources.

And what of the future? Poverty, the ancient and continuous enemy of Scotland, has been very greatly reduced in the short period since the Welfare State was inaugurated in 1948. Even in unemployment, no Scottish worker, or his family, suffers now as men did formerly when they were drawing regular wages.

New anxieties are pressing upon many who hold Scotland in high regard. As in England, there has developed with increasing material prosperity an ominous irresponsibility. Everywhere people seem to be more conscious of their rights, their physical comfort, their immediate securities and pleasures than of their due share in the nation's work, their contribution to its wellbeing. The Trade Unions of to-day are fighting, not for the basic welfare of their members, nor for the status of working people in the world as a whole, but for a steadily steepening rise in wage scales, designed to secure monetary advantage in the immediate situation. In pressing for this, the Trade Unions are showing no more understanding of economics or social justice than did the employers of the bad old days; they are trying to substitute one privileged class for another, without regard to the economic laws which affect the nation as a whole, or to the economic condition of the masses in under-developed territories of Asia and Africa.

The enormous and impersonal organizations which to a great extent have ousted family firms and suppressed private enterprise seem to be in a fair way towards eliminating individual initiative and submerging in a mass of colourless mediocrity the brains and courage of younger generations. On matters of principle, individuals are far too ready to remain silent, to go with the crowd, to take the path of least resistance, and in this way to condone policies and behaviour patterns of which they really disapprove. This has often been the case in the strikes which have done such damage to the Scottish firms upon whose stability the country's future must in great measure depend.

Is it not the case too that Scotland has become infected with the notion, which has done much harm elsewhere in recent years, that people should be treated as if one and all were alike in ability, in common sense, in intellectual stamina? This is plainly not true. But Trade Unionists, politicians, educationists, journalists are all endeavouring so hard to give equal opportunity to everybody—a justifiable purpose within limits—that they are in danger of trying to give the *same* opportunity to everybody. It has become almost an indecency to suggest that those who are specially gifted, those who carry heavy or important responsibility, those who can do what others cannot attempt, should be given any advantage or status other than what is accorded to the rest. Carried much further, such an approach will iron out individuality, frustrate initiative and quench the very qualities which in research and enterprise are vital even for economic progress, let alone for fulness of life.

Scottish people claim to be proud of their history. One wonders whether they are proud of the right things. There is an unreal flavour, a fantasy element, in the fashion for idealizing, indeed almost idolizing, a handful of popular characters—Mary, Queen of Scots, for example, Charles Edward and Robert Burns. These people have been made into symbols of something for which they never really stood, and Scotsmen will talk with abandoned romanticism about them, often without any real knowledge of what they were like. Such idolizing of figures of the past may be interpreted as the sentimental escape of men who are subconsciously aware that they have lost control of their own country in the present, and are reacting in opportunist fashion to forces directed upon them from without. Even in the serious study of the past, a sphere where Scotsmen themselves ought primarily to be concerned, not nearly enough original research has yet gone into certain topics of absorbing interest—for example the origins of Scottish Trade Unionism, the Parliamentary and judicial institutions of Scotland, the local traditions of parishes up and down the country.

The habit of going away from Scotland still exercises its traditional hold upon her citizens. Sir Walter Scott said in his day that they went in search of adventure. It seems that many nowadays go for no such reason. They go in search of security. And those who go, or who live in hopes of going, include some who cry out most loudly that Scotland does not have a fair deal in the Union. Many English people are puzzled by this attitude. To them it is plainly apparent that Scotland is a country of surpassing beauty with many natural advantages all its own, that Scottish people inherit qualities and traditions of the highest value, that the Scot's courage and humour and regard for principle make him a first-rate colleague. One asks oneself the question—loving their country as they so justly do, why do they not devote their many gifts to its service instead of seeking their personal fortunes elsewhere?

There is great comfort in knowing that you belong to a splendid nation, and this is one comfort that no Scot can lack. On the other hand, it is not sufficiently realized, on either side of the Border, that Scotsmen and Englishmen have much in common. In principle and belief, in love of freedom and respect for individuals, in traditions of democracy and culture, in zest for adventurous living and for creative thinking, Scotland and England share a great heritage. With such resources of mind and spirit, these two peoples, given that they develop more awareness and realism in their attitude to each other as well as to themselves, could together offer the world of to-day and to-morrow a leadership needed at this moment in history more than ever before. One may well finish a history of Scotland by asking, 'What of the future?'

A Selected list of Books

ALAN O. ANDERSON: *Scottish annals from English Chroniclers*, A.D. 500–1286. London, 1908.

ALAN O. ANDERSON: *Early sources of Scottish History*, A.D. 500–1286. Edinburgh, 1922.

CECIL ASPINALL-OGLANDER: *Freshly Remembered, The Story of Thomas Graham, Lord Lynedoch*. London, 1956.

JOSEPH BAIN: *The Edwards in Scotland, 1296–1377*. Edinburgh, 1901.

E. W. M. BALFOUR-MELVILLE: *James I, King of Scots, 1406–37*. London, 1936.

E. M. BARRON: *The Scottish War of Independence*. (2nd edition). Inverness, 1934.

J. W. BAXTER: *William Dunbar, a biographical study*. Edinburgh, 1952.

R. T. BERTHOFF: *British Immigrants in Industrial America, 1790–1950*. Cambridge (Mass.), 1953.

G. F. BLACK: *The Surnames of Scotland: their origin, meaning and history*. New York, 1946.

JAMES BOSWELL: *Journal of a Tour to the Hebrides with Samuel Johnson*. London, 1928.

P. HUME BROWN: *George Buchanan, humanist and reformer*. Edinburgh, 1890.

P. HUME BROWN: *Early travellers in Scotland*. Edinburgh, 1891.

P. HUME BROWN: *Scotland before 1700 from contemporary documents*. Edinburgh, 1893.

P. HUME BROWN: *History of Scotland*. Cambridge, 1899.

GEORGE BRYCE: *Mackenzie, Selkirk, Simpson*. (Makers of Canada. Anniv. ed., 9). London, Toronto, 1926.

JAMES BULLOCH: *Adam of Dryburgh*. London, 1958.

ROBERT BUTCHART: *Prints & Drawings of Edinburgh. A descriptive account of the collection in the Edinburgh Room of the Central Public Library*. Edinburgh, 1955.

RONALD G. CANT: *The University of St. Andrews: a short history*. Edinburgh, 1946.

ANDREW J. CAMPBELL: *Fifteen centuries of the Church in Orkney*. Kirkwall, 1938.

H. M. CHADWICK: *Early Scotland: the Picts, the Scots and the Welsh of Southern Scotland*. Cambridge, 1949.

V. G. CHILDE: *The Pre-History of Scotland*. London, 1935.

V. G. CHILDE: *Scotland before the Scots*. London, 1946.

V. G. CHILDE: *Skara Brae, a Pictish village in Orkney; with chapters by T. H. Bryce and D. M. S. Watson*. London, 1931.

A Selected List of Books

V. G. CHILDE and W. D. SIMPSON: *Illustrated guide to ancient monuments in the ownership and guardianship of the Ministry of Works. Vol. VI. Scotland.*

J. STORER CLOUSTON: *A history of Orkney.* Kirkwall, 1932.

HENRY, LORD COCKBURN: *Memorials of his time.* Abridged and edited with notes by W. F. Gray. (Scottish Classics, 1). Edinburgh, 1946.

JOHN D. COMRIE: *History of Scottish Medicine.* London, 1932.

LORD COOPER: *Select Scottish cases of the thirteenth century.* 1944.

REGINALD COUPLAND: *Welsh & Scottish nationalism.* London, 1954.

JAMES COUTTS: *History of the University of Glasgow, 1451–1909.* Glasgow, 1909.

R. M. W. COWAN: *The newspaper in Scotland: a study of its first expansion 1815–1860.* Glasgow, 1946.

ALAN D. CUTHBERT: *Clyde Shipping Company Limited.* Glasgow, 1956.

DANIEL DEFOE: *A tour thro' that part of Great Britain called Scotland. (Vol. 4 of A tour thro' the whole island of Great Britain).* Dublin, 1746.

GEORGE DEMPSTER: *Letters of George Dempster to Sir Adam Fergusson 1756–1813.* Edited by James Fergusson. London, 1934.

A. V. DICEY and R. S. RAIT: *Thoughts on the Union.* London, 1920.

WILLIAM C. DICKINSON: *John Knox's History of the Reformation in Scotland.* London, 1949.

JOHN DOWDEN: *The Celtic Church in Scotland.* London, 1894.

JOHN DOWDEN: *The Medieval Church in Scotland.* Glasgow, 1910.

JOHN DOWDEN: *The Bishops of Scotland.* Glasgow, 1912.

JOHN A. DUKE: *The Columban Church.* Edinburgh, 1957.

JOHN A. DUKE: *History of the Church of Scotland to the Reformation.* Edinburgh, 1957.

A. H. DUNBAR: *Scottish Kings, 1005–1625.* Edinburgh, 1899.

ANNIE I. DUNLOP: *The life and times of James Kennedy, Bishop of St. Andrews.* Edinburgh, 1950.

ANNIE I. DUNLOP: *The Royal Burgh of Ayr; seven hundred and fifty years of history.* Edinburgh, 1953.

DAVID E. EASSON: *Gavin Dunbar, Chancellor of Scotland, Archbishop of Glasgow.* Edinburgh, 1947.

MALCOLM H. ELLIS: *Lachlan Macquarie, his life, adventures and times.* Sydney, 1952.

HENRY G. FARMER: *A history of music in Scotland.* London, 1947.

CHARLES R. FAY: *Adam Smith & the Scotland of his day.* Cambridge, 1956.

THOMAS FERGUSON: *The dawn of Scottish social welfare.* London, 1948.

THOMAS FERGUSON: *Scottish social welfare, 1864–1914.* Edinburgh, 1958.

THOMAS FERGUSON: *The young delinquent in his social setting, a Glasgow study.* London, 1952.

THOMAS FERGUSON & J. CUNISON: *In their early twenties, a study of Glasgow youth.* London, 1956.

JAMES FERGUSSON: *Alexander III, King of Scotland.* London, 1937.

JAMES FERGUSSON: *Argyll in the Forty-Five.* London, 1951.

JAMES FERGUSSON: *Lowland Lairds.* London, 1949.

W. IAN R. FINLAY: *Art in Scotland.* London, 1948.

W. IAN R. FINLAY: *Scotland.* London, 1957.

A Selected List of Books

CHARLES H. FIRTH: *Scotland and the Commonwealth*. (Scottish Hist. Soc.) Edinburgh, 1895.

CHARLES H. FIRTH: *Scotland and the Protectorate*. (Scottish Hist. Soc.) Edinburgh, 1899.

DAVID HAY FLEMING: *The Reformation in Scotland: causes, characteristics, consequences*. London, 1910.

J. R. FLEMING: *A History of the Church in Scotland*, 1843–1929. Edinburgh, 1927.

FORFEITED ESTATES PAPERS 1715–1745. Scottish History Society, 1st. Series, Vol. 57.

FORTUNA DOMUS: *A series of lectures delivered in The University of Glasgow in Commemoration of the Fifth Centenary of its Foundation*. Glasgow, 1952.

T. B. FRANKLIN: *A History of Scottish farming*. London, 1952.

HOLDEN FURBER: *Henry Dundas, first Viscount Melville*, 1742–1811. London, 1931.

J. G. FYFE: *Scottish Diaries & Memoirs* 1550–1746 *and* 1746–1843. Stirling, 1942.

WALTER GEIKIE: *Etchings, Scottish Character and Scenery*. Edinburgh, 1885.

A. DEWAR GIBB: *Scottish Empire*. London, 1937.

ROBERT GIBBINGS: *John Graham, Convict, 1824; an historical narrative*. London, 1937.

FREDERICK GOLDIE: *Short History of the Episcopal Church in Scotland, from the Reformation to the present time*. London, 1951.

S. GORDON and T. G. B. COCKS: *A People's conscience. Six typical enquiries (1729–1837) by Select Committees of the House of Commons*. London, 1952.

H. G. GRAHAM: *The Social Life of Scotland in the Eighteenth Century*. London, 1937.

ALEXANDER GRANT: *The Story of the University of Edinburgh, during its first three hundred years*. London, 1884.

MRS. ANNE GRANT of Laggan. *Letters from the Mountains, being the real correspondence of a lady (A. Grant) between the years* 1773 *and* 1807. London, 1807.

ISABEL F. GRANT: *Everyday life on an old Highland farm* 1769–1782. London, 1924.

ISABEL F. GRANT: *The Social and economic development of Scotland Before* 1603. Edinburgh, 1930.

ISABEL F. GRANT: *The economic history of Scotland*. 1934.

MALCOLM GRAY: *The Highland economy*, 1750–1850. Edinburgh, 1957.

A. R. B. HALDANE: *The drove roads of Scotland*. London, 1952.

HENRY HAMILTON: *The Industrial Revolution in Scotland*. Oxford, 1932.

HENRY HAMILTON: *Selections from the Monymusk Papers*, 1713–55. (Scottish Hist. Soc.) Edinburgh, 1945.

JAMES E. HANDLEY: *The Irish in Scotland* 1798–1845. Cork, 1943.

JAMES E. HANDLEY: *The Irish in Modern Scotland*. Cork, 1947.

JAMES E. HANDLEY: *Scottish farming in the Eighteenth Century*. London, 1953.

A Selected List of Books

R. K. HANNAY: *The College of Justice; essays on the institution and development of the Court of Session.* Edinburgh, 1933.

G. D. HENDERSON: *Religious life in seventeenth century Scotland.* Cambridge, 1937.

G. D. HENDERSON: *Presbyterianism.* Aberdeen, 1954.

ROBERT HERON: *Observations made in a journey through the western counties of Scotland in autumn of 1792.* Perth, 1793.

JOHN HIGHET: *The Churches in Scotland to-day, a survey of their principles, strength, work and statements.* Glasgow, 1950.

HUDSON'S BAY RECORD SOCIETY. Vol. XIV.

COSMO INNES: *Sketches of Early Scottish history and social progress.* Edinburgh, 1861.

COSMO INNES: *Scotland in the Middle Ages.* Edinburgh, 1860.

GEORGE PRATT INSH: *The Company of Scotland, trading to Africa and the Indies.* London, 1932.

GEORGE PRATT INSH: *The Scottish Jacobite Movement; a study in economic and social forces.* Edinburgh, 1952.

SAMUEL JOHNSON: *Journey to the Western Islands.* London, 1775.

T. JOHNSTON: *History of the working classes in Scotland.* Glasgow, 1923.

JAMES KEITH: *Fifty years of farming.* London, 1954.

JAMES KINSLEY: *Scottish Poetry, a critical survey.* London, 1955.

G. A. F. KNIGHT: *Archeological light on the early Christianizing of Scotland.* London, 1933.

H. M. KNOX: *Two hundred and fifty years of Scottish education.* Edinburgh, 1953.

J. G. KYD: *Scottish population statistics.* (Scottish Hist. Soc.) Edinburgh, 1952.

A. C. LAWRIE: *Early Scottish charters.* Glasgow, 1905.

J. LEES-MILNE: *The age of Adam.* London, 1947.

T. C. LETHBRIDGE: *Herdsmen and hermits: Celtic seafarers in the northern seas.* Cambridge, 1950.

WILLIAM McCOMBIE: *Cattle & cattle breeders.* Edinburgh, 1886.

D. F. MACDONALD: *Scotland's shifting population, 1770–1850.* Glasgow, 1937.

JOHN McDONALD: *Voyage to Quebec and journey from thence to New Lanark in Upper Canada.* First Edition 1823.

A. M. MACEWEN: *The Thistle and the Rose; Scotland's problem to-day.* Edinburgh, 1932.

DAVID MACGIBBON and THOMAS ROSS: *The ecclesiastical architecture of Scotland.* Edinburgh, 1896.

AGNES MURE MACKENZIE: *History of Scotland* (6 vols.) new edition. Edinburgh, 1957–58.

OSGOOD MACKENZIE: *A hundred years in the Highlands.* New edition. London, 1949.

W. C. MACKENZIE: *Andrew Fletcher of Saltoun, his life and times.* Edinburgh, 1935.

W. M. MACKENZIE: *The medieval castle in Scotland.* London, 1927.

W. M. MACKENZIE: *The Scottish burghs.* Edinburgh, 1949.

J. B. MACKIE: *The life and work of Duncan Maclaren.* Edinburgh, 1888.

A Selected List of Books

JOHN DUNCAN MACKIE: *The University of Glasgow*, 1451–1951, *a short history*. Glasgow, 1954.

ROBERT L. MACKIE: *A short history of Scotland*. London, 1931.

ROBERT L. MACKIE: *King James IV of Scotland, a brief survey of his life and times*. Edinburgh, 1958.

MARTIN MARTIN: *Description of the Western Isles of Scotland circa* 1695. London, 1703.

HUGH MARWICK: *Orkney*. (County Book Series.) London, 1951.

W. H. MARWICK: *Economic developments in Victorian Scotland*. London, 1936.

CYRIL MATHESON: *Henry Dundas, first Viscount Melville*, 1742–1811. London, 1933.

DAVID J. MATHEW: *Scotland under Charles I*. London, 1955.

WILLIAM L. MATHIESON: *Church and reform in Scotland* 1797–1843. Glasgow, 1916.

W. D. MAXWELL: *A history of worship in the Church of Scotland*. London, 1955.

H. W. MEIKLE: *Scotland and the French Revolution*. Glasgow, 1912.

H. W. MEIKLE: *Scotland, A description of Scotland and Scottish life*. London, 1947.

GEORGE MENARY: *The life and letters of Duncan Forbes of Culloden, Lord President of the Court of Session*, 1685–1747. London, 1936.

HUGH MILLER: *My schools and schoolmasters*. Edinburgh, 1905.

DAVID MILNE: *The Scottish Office, and other Scottish government departments*. London, 1957.

E. C. MOSSNER: *The Life of David Hume*. New York, 1943.

DAVID MURRAY: *Early burgh organization in Scotland*. Glasgow, 1924.

WALLACE NOTESTEIN: *The Scot in history*. London (printed U.S.A.), 1946.

C. A. OAKLEY: *The second city*. London, 1946.

J. W. OLIVER & J. C. SMITH: *A Scots anthology from the Thirteenth to the Twentieth Century*. Edinburgh, 1949.

THEODORA PAGAN: *The Convention of the Royal Burghs of Scotland*. Glasgow, 1926.

MILLAR PATRICK: *Four centuries of Scottish Psalmody*. London, 1949.

HESKETH PEARSON: *The Smith of Smiths*. London, 1934.

THOMAS PENNANT: *A tour in Scotland*. Chester, 1771.

LORD EUSTACE PERCY: *John Knox*. 1937.

CHARLES A. PETRIE: *The Jacobite Movement*. London, 1948.

STUART PIGGOTT: *Scotland before history*. London, 1958.

DAPHNE D. C. POCHIN MOULD: *Scotland of the Saints*. London, 1952.

F. M. POWICKE: *Ailred of Rievaulx and his biographer Walter Daniel*. London, 1950.

GEORGE S. PRYDE: *The Treaty of Union*. London, 1950.

ROBERT S. RAIT: *The Parliaments of Scotland*. Glasgow, 1924.

ROBERT S. RAIT: *The Universities of Aberdeen*. Aberdeen, 1895.

ROBERT S. RAIT & G. S. PRYDE: *Scotland*. (Second Edition). London, 1954.

REPORTS OF THE ROYAL COMMISSION ON THE ANCIENT MONUMENTS OF SCOTLAND.

R. L. G. RITCHIE: *The Normans in Scotland*. Edinburgh, 1954.

A Selected List of Books

GEORGE ROBERTSON: *Rural recollections*. Irvine, 1829.

ROYAL MUSICAL ASSOCIATION: *Music of Scotland*, 1500–1700. London, 1957.

R. N. SALAMAN: *The history and social influence of the Potato*. Cambridge, 1949.

L. J. SAUNDERS: *Scottish Democracy* 1815–1840, *the social and intellectual Background*. Edinburgh, 1950.

W. D. SIMPSON: *The historical Saint Columba*. Aberdeen, 1927.

W. D. SIMPSON: *The Celtic Church in Scotland*. Aberdeen, 1935.

JOHN SLEZER: *Theatricum Scotiae*. London, 1693. Reprinted, with the life of the author and large additional illustrations by John Jamieson. Edinburgh, 1874.

ALISTAIR SMART: *The life and art of Allan Ramsay*. 1952.

MRS. ELIZABETH SMITH OF BALTIBOYS: *Memoirs of a Highland Lady*, 1797–1827. Revised and edited by A Davidson. London, 1950.

SAMUEL SMILES: *Lives of the Engineers*. London, 1904.

THOMAS SOMERVILLE: *My own life and times*, 1741–1814. Edinburgh, 1861.

The (Old) Statistical Account of Scotland (1791–99).

The New Statistical Account of Scotland (1845).

The Third Statistical Account of Scotland (1951–   ).

MARGARET STUART: *Scottish family history*. Edinburgh, 1930.

M. W. STUART: *The Scot who was a Frenchman (The Regent Albany)*. London, 1940.

ANDREW SYMSON: *A description of Galloway*.

CHARLES S. TERRY: *The Scottish Parliament*, 1603–1707. Glasgow, 1905.

HUGH THOMSON: *Highways & Byways in Galloway and Carrick*. 1916.

ARTHUR C. TURNER: *Scottish Home Rule*. Oxford, 1952.

JOHN WARRACK: *Domestic life in Scotland*, 1488–1688. London, 1920.

WILLIAM J. WATSON: *History of the Celtic place-names of Scotland*. Stirling, 1922.

C. V. WEDGWOOD: *Montrose*. London, 1952.

C. V. WEDGWOOD: *The King's Peace*, 1637–1641. London, 1955.

C. V. WEDGWOOD: *The King's War*, 1641–1647. London, 1958.

DAVID H. WILLSON: *King James VI & I*. London, 1956.

J. A. WILSON: *A contribution to the History of Lanarkshire*. Glasgow, 1936.

A. P. WOOLLACOTT: *Mackenzie and his voyageurs*. London, 1927.

DOROTHY WORDSWORTH: *Recollections of a Tour in Scotland* A.D. 1803. London, 1874.

LESLIE C. WRIGHT: *Chartism in Scotland*. Edinburgh, 1953.

Index

Index

Index

Henry V, King of England, 98
Henry VI, King of England, 98
Henry VIII, King of England, 119, 128 et seq., 150
Henry, son of David I of Scotland, 55, 68
Henryson, Robert, poet, 110, 111
Hepburn, James, Bishop of Moray, 124
Hepburn, James, Earl of Bothwell, 144
Home, the Rev. John, *Douglas* 262, 268, 282
Honourable Society of Improvers in the Knowledge of Agriculture, 216
Horner, Francis, *Edinburgh Review*, 273
Hudson's Bay Company, 343
Hume, David, philosopher, 262, 266, 267, 268, 283
Hutcheson, Francis, Professor in Glasgow University, 294

Indian Civil Service, 337, 338
Industrial Chaplains, 383
Ingibjorg, wife of Malcolm III of Scotland, 48, 50, 52
Iona, 38, 39, 40, see map 4, facing 35
Iona Community, The, 383
Irish Home Rule, 312, 375, 376
Iron industry, 252, 254, 355, 356, 358
Isabella, wife of Edward II of England, 85

James II, King of England, 184, 188
James I, King of Scotland, 92, 96, 97 et seq., 119
James II, King of Scotland, 97, 119
James III, King of Scotland, 97, 104, 106, 108, 119
James IV, King of Scotland, 97, 107, et seq., 119, 120, 124, 125
James V, King of Scotland, 119, 126, 127, et seq.
James VI and I, King of Scotland and King of England, 120, 145, 147 et seq., 162
James Edward, son of James II, 193, 200 et seq.
Jeffrey, Francis, *Edinburgh Review*, 273
Jenner, Edward, discover of vaccination, 322
Jex-Blake, Dr. Sophia, 300
Joanna, wife of David II of Scotland, 85, 88, 90
Johnson, Samuel, 210, 268, 269, 280, 295
Johnston, Archibald, Lord Warriston, 163, 167, 168
Justiciars, 58

Kames, Henry Home, Lord, 266
Keith, Sir Robert, 336, 340
Keith, Sir Basil, 340
Kelvin, William Thomson, Lord, 299
Kennedy, James, Bishop of St. Andrews and founder of St. Salvator's College, 105, 106
Kenneth McAlpin, King of Dalriada, 46, 47
Keynes, J. M., later Lord Keynes, 360
Killiecrankie Pass, 185
Killing Times, 183, 187
King's College, Aberdeen, 113
Knox, John, 131, et seq., 137 et seq., 188, 287, 293

Labour Exchanges, 359, 367
Labour Party, 366, 375
Largs, Battle of, 1263, 71
Laud, William, Archbishop of Canterbury, 164, 173
Lauder, Robert Scott, artist, 373
Lauderdale, Earl of, see Maitland, John
Leith, Treaty of, 139
Leslie, Alexander, Earl of Leven, 171
Letters of Indulgence, 183
Lewis, George, *Scotland a half-educated Nation* 292
Liberal Party, 312, 375, 376
Liberal Reforms, 1908–1911, 367
Linen industry, 245, 246, 247
Lismore, isle of, 40, 125, see map 4, facing 35
Lister, Joseph, surgeon, later Lord Lister, 298
Littlejohn, Dr. Henry, 331
Livingstone, David, 346, 347
Lochiel, Donald Cameron of, 206
Lockhart, J. G., biographer of Scott, 274
Lollius Urbicus, 27
Lords of the Articles, 101, 154, 184
Lorne, Lord, see Campbell, Archibald
Loudoun Hill, Battle of, 1307, 81, see map 6, facing 85
Loyola, Ignatius, 123
Luther, Martin, 113, 123

Macadam, John, road builder, 241
Macbeth, 47
Macdonald, Alexander, Trade Unionist, 365, 366
Macdonald, Flora, 210
Macdonald, J. Ramsay, 366
McDonald, John, emigrant to Upper Canada, 341, 342
Macgillivray, Pittendrigh, sculptor, 374
Macintosh, Charles Rennie, architect, 374
Mackenzie, Sir Alexander, explorer, 343

Index

Mackenzie, Osgood, *A Hundred Years in the Highlands*, 367
Mackie, R. L., *James IV of Scotland*, 110, 111, 112
McLaren, Duncan, politician, 312
Macquarie, Lachlan, Governor of New South Wales, 336
McTaggart, William, artist, 373
Maes Howe, 19, 63, see map 2, facing 25
Magnus Barelegs, King of Norway, 52, 53
Maid of Norway, 74, 75, 119
Maitland, John, Earl of Lauderdale, 176, 181, 182
Major, John, *History of Greater Britain*, 114, 148
Malcolm II, King of the Picts and Scots, 47
Malcolm III, King of Scotland, 47 et seq., 119
Malcolm IV, King of Scotland, 68, 119
Malt Tax, 1713, 201
Mar, Earl of, see Erskine, John
Margaret, wife of James IV of Scotland, 108, 109, 110
Margaret, wife of Malcolm III of Scotland 48–51, 62
Marston Moor, Battle of, 1644, 175, 176
Marwick, W. H., *Economic Developments in Victorian Scotland*, 373
Mary of Guise, wife of James V of Scotland, 128, 129, 131, 132, 134, 138
Mary, Queen of Scots, 119, 120, 129, 131, 133, 137, 138, 142, 143, et seq., 149, 150, 385
Matilda, daughter of Henry I of England, 65
Maud, daughter of Malcolm III of Scotland, wife of Henry I of England, 53, 65, 119
Maxwell, W. D., *A History of the Church in Scotland*, 136
Medical Schools, 297
Megalithic settlers, 19
Meikle, Andrew, inventor, 221
Melancthon, Philip, 113, 114
Melville, Andrew, reformer, 152, 157, 163, 294
Merchant Gilds, 103
Metrical Psalms, 174
Miller, Hugh, *My Schools and Schoolmasters*, 287, 288, 318, 320, 367, 379
Mines Act, 1842, 318, 331
Missionary enterprise, 344 et seq.
Moffat, Robert, missionary, 346, 347
Monck, George, 1st Duke of Albemarle, 179

Mons Graupius, 26
Montrose, Earl, later Marquis of, see Graham, James
Mousa, Broch, 23, see map 2, facing 25
Muir, Edwin, poet, 374
Mure, Elizabeth, of Caldwell, 245, 246, 256
Myllar, Andrew, printer, 112, 113
Myln, Walter, died 1558, 137

Napier, Robert, shipbuilder and engineer, 256
Naseby, Battle of, 1645, 175
Nasmyth, Alexander, artist, 263
National Health Service, 369
Neilson, James of Shettleston, 254
Neville's Cross, Battle of, 1346, 89
Newcomen, Thomas, inventor, 251
Niall of the Nine Hostages, 36, 37
Norham-on-Tweed, 76, see map 6, facing 85
North of Scotland Hydro-Electric Board, 354
North West Company, 343
Northampton, Treaty of, 1328, 85

Oban, 17, see map 1, facing 21
Oil, Scottish shale oil industry, 355
Ordericus Vitalis, 51
Orkneyinga Saga, 45
Oswy, King of Northumbria, 43
Otterburn, Battle of, 1388, 90, see map 6, facing 85
Overcrowding, 331, 361
Owen, Robert, New Lanark, 249, 319, 320

Paine, Tom, *The Rights of Man*, 307, 309
Paisley, shawls, 250
Park, Mungo, explorer, 344
Parliaments in Scotland, fourteenth century, 87, 90; fifteenth century, 100, 101, 102, 103; 1560, 139; early seventeenth century, 154; 1661, 181; 1690, 184; early eighteenth century, 193
Paterson, William, Darien scheme promoter, 191, 192
Patronage, Lay, 200, 201, 283, 284, 285
Pennant, Thomas, naturalist, 224
Percy, Lord Eustace, *John Knox*, 134, 391
Philip, the Rev. John, missionary, 345, 346
Philiphaugh, Battle of, 1645, 175
Picts, 21, 22, 26, 27, 28, 33, 36, 38, 39, 46
Piggott, S., *Scotland Before History*, 18
Pinkie Cleugh, Battle of, 130

Index

398

Index

Stewart, Alexander, son of James IV of Scotland, 124

Stewart, James, Earl of Moray, 145

Stewart, Patrick, Earl of the Orkneys, 156

Stirling Bridge, Battle of, 1297, 79, see map 6, facing 85

Stow, David, educationist, 291

Stuart, Esmé, Seigneur d'Aubigny, 148

Student Christian Movement, The, 382

Sutherland clearances, 225, 226. For Sutherland, see map 4, facing 35

Sweated labour, 318, 319, 364

Synod of Whitby, 43

Tacitus, 26

Telford, Thomas, engineer & surveyor, 232, 233, 235, 242

Temperance Societies, 286, 327

Tertullian, 28

Thorfinn the Mighty, 48

Tobacco trade, 244, 245

Trade Unions, 332, 333, 365, 366, 384, 386

Transportation, 293, 309, 336

Treaty of Versailles, 357

Tull, Jethro, *Horse-hoeing Husbandry*, 218

Turgot, biographer of Margaret, Queen of Scotland, 51, 53

Turnbull, William, Bishop of Glasgow and founder of Glasgow University, 105

Turnpike Acts, 232

Tyndale, William, 126

Unemployment, 1930s, 358, 359

Urquhart, Sir Thomas of Cromarty, 178

Veto Act, 1834, 283, 284

Vikings, 41, 44 et seq.

Vitrified Forts, 23, see map 1, facing 21

Wade, Field-marshal George, 231, 232

Wade's Roads, see map 7, facing 231

Wallace, William, 79

Walpole, Horace, 209, 266, 295

Walpole, Sir Robert, 204, 335

Wardlaw, Henry, Bishop of St. Andrews, 98

Warriston, Lord, see Johnston, Archibald

Watt, James, 235, 251, 253, 273

Weaving, 249

Wedderburn, James, John and Robert, *The Gude and Godly Ballatis*, 136

Wedgwood, C. V., *The King's Peace*, 167, 392

Wesley, John, 268, 279, 282

Westminster Assembly, 173, 174

Westminster Confession of Faith, 174, 184

Wheelhouses, 28

William the Lion, King of Scotland, 68, 69, 70

William III, King of England, 184, 185, 188

William of Malmesbury, 63

William of Normandy, King of England, 45, 48, 50, 51, 65

William Rufus, King of England, 51, 52

Wilson, D. H., *James VI and I*, 155

Wishart, George, died 1546, 130

Witchcraft, 153

Wodrow, the Rev. Robert of Eastwood, 201

Wood, Sir Andrew, sea-captain, 118

World Council of Churches, 383